THE FATHERS
OF THE CHURCH

A NEW TRANSLATION

VOLUME 25

THE FATHERS
OF THE CHURCH

A NEW TRANSLATION

Founded by
LUDWIG SCHOPP

SAINT HILARY OF POITIERS

THE TRINITY

Translated by

STEPHEN McKENNA, C.SS.R.

New York

FATHERS OF THE CHURCH, INC.

1954

IMPRIMI POTEST:

VERY REV. JOHN SEPHTON C.SS.R.

Provincial, Baltimore Province

NIHIL OBSTAT:

JOHN M. A. FEARNS, S.T.D.

Censor Librorum

IMPRIMATUR:

✠ FRANCIS CARDINAL SPELLMAN

Archbishop of New York

September 24, 1954

INTRODUCTION

S T. HILARY WAS BORN, probably in the year 315, at
Poitiers in Aquitaine.[1] It is uncertain whether or
not his family was Christian. Though the saint does
not settle the question by an explicit statement, the better
opinion seems to be that he was a pagan and has described
the manner of his conversion in the opening chapters of his
work on the Trinity. Additional confirmation for this view
is that he was not baptized until he was an adult.[2]

His edifying life as a Catholic caused him to be chosen
as Bishop of Poitiers in 353 or 354. He entered the episcopate
at a critical moment. Constant I, Emperor of the Roman
Empire in the West, had been murdered in 350, and his
brother, Constantius II, now became the sole ruler of the
whole Empire. But it was not until 353 that the latter's authority was universally recognized and the rebellion against
him had come to an end. While Constans had been a staunch
supporter of the Catholics, the sympathies of Constantius were
clearly with the Arian party in the Church. He was determined to force his religious opinions upon the bishops of the
West as well as of those in the East. His first step was to
summon the prelates of Western Europe to councils at Arles

---

1 For an account of St. Hilary's life cf. G. Girard, *Saint Hilaire* (Paris
1902; Angers 1905) ; J. Reinkens, *Hilarius von Poitiers* (Schaffhausen
1864) ; X. Le Bachelet, 'Hilaire (Saint) , évêque de Poitiers,' *DACL* VI,
cols. 2388-2462.
2 *De Trinitate* 6.21.

and Milan in 355 and to demand that they repudiate St. Athanasius, who had become the touchstone of orthodoxy, and the living symbol of the Council of Nice and of its definition of the *Verbum* as 'consubstantial with the Father.' With only a few exceptions, the bishops at these councils acceded to the emperor's wishes. St. Hilary, who does not seem to have been present at either Arles or Milan, was summoned to a meeting at Béziers. He refused absolutely to condemn St. Athanasius and was banished to Phrygia in 356.

His exile was not too severe, for he was able to keep in touch with his flock in Poitiers and with the hierarchy of Gaul by means of letters. And in a sense his enforced stay in the East was to be a blessing in disguise. Incredible as it may seem, St. Hilary tells us that up to 355 he had not even heard of the term '*homooúsion*' that the Council of Nice had officially promulgated in 325.[3] But now he obtained first-hand information about the controversies regarding the divinity of Christ that had raged in the Eastern Church since the days of Paul of Samosata a century before. He became well informed about the heresy of Arius and the answers that had been given by the Catholic apologists. He likewise took an active part in encouraging the prelates to resist the Arian tendencies that were so evident among the members of the imperial court and among so many of the bishops. Then, in 360, after a period of four years, the exile of St. Hilary suddenly ended. According to Sulpicius Severus,[4] the reason for this sudden change of policy was that the emperor regarded the saint as 'a sower of discord and a disturber of the Orient.'

The death of Constantius soon afterwards and the short and troubled reign of Julian the Apostate gave the Church a breathing spell. Upon his return home, St. Hilary did not confine his activity to his own diocese, but went about Gaul

---

3 *De synodis* n. 91.
4 *Chronica* 2.45.4.

and Italy trying to heal the wounds caused by the anti-Catholic policy of Constantius. On the whole he was successful, although he failed in one of his principal objectives, to have Auxentius, the Arian bishop of Milan, removed from office. The saint, who had accomplished so much for the Church in so short a time, died either in 367 or 368.

Just as Boethius was later to write his best known work, *De consolatione philosophiae,* while in prison, so St. Hilary composed his masterpiece, *De Trinitate,* during his exile in Phrygia. This is clear from his own words: 'Although in exile we shall speak through these books, and the word of God, which cannot be bound, shall move about in freedom.'[5] The work, therefore, was completed during the years 356-360. It may even be that the first three of the twelve books of *De Trinitate* were finished before his exile even began. At least the saint informs us that there was a comparatively long delay between the writing of them and the beginning of the fourth book.[6] One important reason in favor of this opinion is that he does not mention the word '*homooúsion,*' even though it would have fitted in very appropriately with the subject-matter of the first three books, and, as we have already noted, he did not learn of this term until the year 355.

During the years 356-360, when *De Trinitate* was written, the Anomoeans, as the Arians were now called, attained their greatest influence. Supported by the emperor, they were able to bend the bishops to their will, and to banish those, like St. Athanasius and St. Hilary, who refused to submit. In 359, at the Councils of Seleucia and Rimini, they forced the prelates to declare that the *Verbum* was 'like the Father in all things,' a formula of faith that not only repudiated the Council of Nice, but would inevitably lead to a denial of Christ's divinity. St. Hilary was not exaggerating when he wrote: 'Throughout

---

5 *De Trinitate* 10.4.
6 *Ibid.* 4.1.

almost all the provinces of the Roman Empire many churches
have become infected with this deadly doctrine.'[7]

As far as we know, no one requested St. Hilary to write
De Trinitate. He did so because he was vividly conscious of
the fact that his vocation and office of bishop obliged him to
preach the Gospel.[8] Through these books he would make
known the true teaching of the Church about this most sacred
mystery to his fellow Catholics of Western Europe, and expose the hypocrisy of the heretics in appealing to Scripture
to defend their false doctrine, and in pretending to be only
concerned with maintaining the oneness of God when they
denied the divinity of Christ. It was his hope that the people
who had fallen into heresy through ignorance rather than
through malice would return to the Catholic Church, and,
as he picturesquely described it, 'might soar aloft in freedom
and security from the deadly food by which birds are wont
to be enticed into the trap.'[9]

The main enemies against whom he wrote were the Arians.
But the name of Arius appears only twice in this work, and
there is but one explicit mention of this heresiarch's followers.
He usually designates them as 'the new teachers of Christ,'
'the heretics of the present day,' 'the new apostolate of Anti-
Christ.' His detestation of their false teaching is clearly apparent from the adjectives which he is constantly applying to
it: 'impious,' 'irreverent,' 'blasphemous.' It is true that he also
replies to the objections that Valentinian, Hieracas, Ebion,
and others had brought against the Trinity in the earlier centuries. He takes particular care to refuse Sabellius, who spoke
of the Father, Son, and Holy Spirit, but considered them as
merely three different names for one and the same divine
Person. But St. Hilary refutes these men only in order to

---

7 *Ibid.* 6.1.
8 *Ibid.* 6.2.
9 *Ibid.*

combat the Arians more effectively. One of the favorite accusations of the latter was that the Catholic doctrine about
the divinity of the *Verbum,* as it had been defined by the
Council of Nice, was merely a revival under a different form
of errors that had long since been condemned.

In his *De synodis,* which he also wrote during his exile,
St. Hilary gives an account of the machinations of the Arians
and the Semi-Arians, and the various formulas of faith which
they had drawn up.[10] But he does not discuss the historical
aspects of Arianism in *De Trinitate.* Here, his main concern
is with theological considerations.

The root of Arius' errors was that 'he conceived the eternal,
simple, immutable God as essentially unbegotten, so that all
communication of God's substance by way of generation must
imply a contradiction in terms.'[11] It is only natural, therefore,
that the central idea of all twelve Books of *The Trinity* is the
being or essence of God. His previous training had to a certain extent prepared him for this difficult task. As he tells
us, it was God's eternal self-existence, which He had revealed
to Moses in the words 'I AM WHO AM' that had not only
filled him with admiration, but also marked a turning point
in his life.[12]

God was not, as the Arians described Him, a Person living
alone in solitary grandeur. With Him was the Son. The latter
was not a creature, not a cutting off, an emanation, a separation, or a division of the nature of God. He was the true Son
of God, born of Him by an eternal generation. The Father,
who had all, gave to the Son who received all. It is true that
St. Hilary applies the words of our Saviour, 'The Father is
greater than I,' to the divine nature of Christ.[13] But it would
be wrong to conclude from this that he regarded Christ as

---

10 *PL* 10.471-475.
11 B. Otten, *A Manual of the History of Dogmas* I (St. Louis 1917) 254.
12 *De Trinitate* 1.5.
13 *Ibid.* 9.4.

an inferior God. He meant to indicate that the Father is the principle or source from which the Son derives His eternal origin. There is hardly a chapter of this work where the true equality between the Father and the Son is not emphasized.

From the title of this work we might expect that the Holy Spirit would receive equal treatment with the Father and the Son, as in textbooks of dogmatic theology. But this is not the case. The person and nature of the Holy Spirit are not treated at length for the simple reason that St. Hilary was concerned, as were the Arians, with the relationship between God the Father and God the Son. Hilary has been accused of denying the true divinity of the Holy Spirit because he never states explicitly that the Holy Spirit is God. But, as will be shown in the text, the saint refers in so many other different ways to the true divinity of the third Person of the Trinity that his perfect orthodoxy on this subject cannot be reasonably denied.

Similarly, the saint was more interested in proving that the divine nature of Christ was consubstantial with that of His heavenly Father than in bringing out that His human nature was consubstantial with ours. Since the relationship between the divine and human natures in Christ was to be studied systematically only after his death, we cannot expect to find the same precision of thought in his Christological as in his Trinitarian doctrine. We can say, however, that St. Hilary's writings are an anticipation of the definitions of the Councils of Ephesus and Chalcedon, for he clearly holds the reality of the one divine Person in Christ as well as of His divine and human natures.

He speaks of Christ having a 'heavenly' body,[14] but from the context it is evident that he is referring to the fact that Christ's body was not conceived according to the ordinary laws of human generation, and that it was intimately united with a divine Person. A more serious objection is that St.

---

14 *Ibid.* 5.18.

Hilary seems to believe that Christ did not and could not feel sorrow and pain.[15] To those who would later bring up this objection St. Thomas Aquinas would answer: 'In all these and similar words Hilary does not intend to exclude the pain, but the necessity of it.'[16] But most of the difficulties on this subject will be settled if we remember that the Arians claimed that the Logos did not have a rational soul and therefore did not endure the emotions and sufferings that are attributed to Him in the Passion.[17] In his eagerness to show that pain and suffering were not incompatible with Christ's divine dignity, he teaches that, while He felt organic pain, such as hunger, thirst, bodily sufferings, these did not arouse within Him the interior sentiments that they do in ordinary mortals. It must be conceded that St. Hilary does not take into sufficient account the state of physical weakness to which the Son of God voluntarily submitted when He assumed our human nature.[18]

It is by no means a coincidence that Arianism arose in the school of Antioch where the pagan philosophy of Greece had taken such deep roots. One of the characteristics of this philosophy was that the human mind was the measure of all things, and that which man could not comprehend was to be rejected as unreasonable. That is why St. Hilary wrote: 'A firm faith rejects the captious and useless questions of philosophy,'[19] and why he so often and so vigorously condemns the wisdom of this world as folly in the sight of God. He does not, of course, reject reasoning about the mysteries of God, but he insists that the Trinity is incomprehensible and must be accepted by faith. Book 3, in fact, aims particularly at showing that only when man has become convinced of the limitations of his knowledge does he begin to understand the

---

15 *Ibid.* 10.27.
16 *Summa Theologica* (London 1913) III, Q. 15, art. 5.
17 J. Tixeront, *Histoire des dogmes* 2 (4th ed., Paris 1912) 285.
18 X. Le Bachelet, *op. cit.* 2448.
19 *De Trinitate* 1.13.

things of God. The importance which he ascribed to faith may be one reason why this work was known to some early writers as *De fide*.

The Arians sought to justify their teachings by an appeal to the Word of God. They quoted both the Old and the New Testament to prove that there is only one Person in God and that, therefore, the *Verbum* could not possibly be the true God. St. Hilary took up the challenge and showed how they had distorted the true meaning of the Scriptural passages: 'Heresy does not come from Scripture but from the understanding of it; the fault is in the mind not in the words.'[20] His main proofs are naturally found in the New Testament, where the Son of God Himself clearly enunciated this truth. But we know from the saint's other writings that the teachings of Christ are foreshadowed in the Old Testament, and hence he finds many indications there of the great mystery of the Trinity. It is interesting to note that his text is sometimes a direct translation from the Septuagint and sometimes from a Latin version that is no longer extant in its entirety.[21] Since the very action of the heretics was a repudiation of the magisterium of the Church, the saint only refers to the teaching authority of the Church in passing. But he does assert very emphatically that the Church is indestructible, and that she contains the remedy against all types of heresy, just as certain medicines can cure all kinds of diseases.[22]

At the end of Book 1, when he is about to begin a detailed study of the Trinity, St. Hilary humbly turned to God and begged Him to enlighten his mind so that he might comprehend and express this mysterious teaching correctly. For, as he says, he was about 'to undertake what is unlawful, to scale arduous heights, to speak of the ineffable, and to trespass

---

20 *Ibid.* 2.3.
21 J. P. Brisson, *Traité des mystères* (Sources chrétiennes, ed. H. de Lubac et J. Danielou. Paris 1947) 68-70.
22 *De Trinitate* 2.22.

upon forbidden places.'[23] An added difficulty, as he realized, was that, while this subject had been treated for so many years by the keenest minds in the Eastern Church, no Latin writer had written a scientific and systematic treatise before him, for Tertullian had only a few references to the Trinity in his *Adversus Praxeas*.[24] St. Hilary, therefore, was to be a pioneer and had to coin many new words in order to express his thought accurately. Among the neologisms attributed to him are *abscissio, incarnatio, innascibilitas, ininitiabilis, supercreo,* and *consubsisto.* He also gave new meanings to words already in current use, as *sacramentum, dispensatio,* and *substitutio.*

St. Hilary knew, of course, that finite things can never adequately express those that are infinite. On the other hand, he realized that analogies and illustrations from ordinary life were extremely valuable in the understanding of difficult subjects and he does not hesitate to make use of them in this work. For example, the obvious comparison that suggests itself when we hear of God the Father and God the Son is that of parents and their children. While the Arians drew from this similarity the conclusion that Christ could not be eternal, for He must have come after His Father as children come after their parents, St. Hilary applied it in a different sense. Just as a true human nature is transmitted from parents to their children, so a true divine nature is communicated from God the Father to God the Son. Furthermore, like a good teacher he planned to proceed from the unknown to the known, from the more simple to the more difficult teachings about the Trinity. Finally, he co-ordinated and systematized the subject matter, and in Book 1 drew a brief outline of the contents of each book.

---

23 Ibid. 2.2.
24 F. Cayré, *Patrologie et histoire de theologie* I (4th ed. Paris 1945) 236-237.

St. Augustine declared that St. Hilary went out of the Egypt of his false religion and philosophy, adorned with the gold, silver, and costly raiment of his pagan culture.[25] St. Jerome praised him for his elegance of style.[26] The truth of their words is seen more clearly in *De Trinitate* than in the other writings of St. Hilary. The saint devoted particular care to the composition of this work and had even prayed that he might receive the 'nobility of diction' befitting so exalted a subject. Everywhere he gives evidence of the careful training that he had received in Latin rhetoric. Still, he never strives for mere effect, and in general is much more restrained in the ornaments of speech than the other Christian writers of the fourth and fifth centuries.[27] One of the characteristic features of *De Trinitate* is the saint's frequent apostrophes. He often interrupts the argumentation in order to plead with the heretics to abandon their errors; or he will turn to God in prayer. He did not regard the question of the Trinity as a mere theological dispute, but as a matter of eternal life and death for each individual. It is not sufficient for salvation to believe that God is the Creator and that Christ performed miracles. We must accept God as the Father and Christ as the Son if we are to be saved.

St. Hilary felt that his work on the Trinity resembled a well-graded elevation along which his readers could 'ascend without hardly realizing that they are doing so.'[28] In this he was overoptimistic. Erasmus, one of the early editors of the saint's writings, has called attention to the many needless repetitions of the same thoughts throughout the twelve Books. St. Hilary is also difficult to understand because he uses the same words to convey different meanings and one must often

---

25 *De doctrina christiana* 2.40.
26 *Commentarium in Isaiam* 1.8.
27 Cf. Sister M. Buttel, *The Rhetoric of St. Hilary of Poitiers* (Washington 1933) 166-171.
28 *De Trinitate* 1.20.

puzzle over them for a long time before determining their significance in a particular context. His frequent use of involved periods does not make for easy reading, and in many places he compresses his thought in a few words when a longer explanation would clarify his meaning. Finally, the Migne text, which is that of Dom Coustant, a Benedictine scholar of the seventeenth century, needs to be thoroughly revised. There is scarcely a page in which the editor does not call attention to variant readings in the manuscripts.[29] Undoubtedly, many of the obscurities in this work will disappear when *De Trinitate* has been as critically edited as some of the saint's other writings.

Still, this work of St. Hilary is his masterpiece and upon it rests his fame as a theologian. It is generally regarded as one of the finest writings that the Arian controversy produced. Augustine and Leo the Great are among the early writers who praise it, and St. Thomas Aquinas frequently appeals to it when settling disputes about the Trinity. Besides giving to us his own independent thought, he was also the first to bring to the attention of the scholars of the Roman Empire in the West the vast theological riches of the Orient. St. Hilary, therefore, is one of the foundation stones upon which later writers would erect a magnificent theological edifice to pay some measure of honor to their triune God.

---

29 'Leider gehört Hilarius zu den schwerverständlichen und dunkeln Schriftstellern. Seine Sprache . . . bietet dem Leser so erhebliche Schwierigkeiten dass man am Textverderbnis zu denken geneigt ist' (T. Forster, 'Zur Theologie des Hilarius,' *Theologische Studien und Kritiken* 61 [1888] 649).

SELECT BIBLIOGRAPHY

Editions and Translations:

Hilarius Pictaviensis, *Opera* iuxta edit. monachor. ord. Benedic. et omnes alias inter se collatas, ed. J. P. Migne, *Patrologia Latina* 9-10 (Paris 1844-45).

S. *Hilarii episcopi Pictaviensis Tractatus super Psalmos*. Recensuit et commentario critico instruxit A. Zingerle, *CSEL* 22 (Vienna 1891).

Hilarius Pictaviensis, *Opera IV: Tractatus Mysteriorum, Liber ad Constantium, Hymni, Fragmenta, Spuria*, ed. A. Feder, *CSEL* 65 (Vienna 1916).

Antweiler, A., *Des heiligen Bischofs Hilarius von Poitiers zwölf Bücher über die Dreieinigkeit aus dem Lateinischen übersetzt und mit Einleitung versehen*. Bibliothek der Kirchenväter, Zweite Reihe, Bande V-VI (München 1933-1934).

Brisson, J. P., *Hilaire de Poitiers. Traité des mystères* (Paris 1947).

Watson, E. W., *St. Hilary of Poitiers: Select Works Translated, A Select Library of Nicene and Post-Nicene Fathers of the Christian Church* 9 (New York 1908).

Secondary Works:

Bardenhewer, O., *Geschichte der Altkirchlichen Literatur* 3 (2nd ed., Freiburg in Br. 1923).

Beck, A., *Die Trinitätslehre des heiligen Hilarius* (Mainz 1903).

Brown, Sr. M. Vincentia, *The Syntax of the Prepositions in the Works of St. Hilary*, The Catholic University of America Patristic Studies 41 (Washington 1934).

Buttell, Sr. M. Frances, *The Rhetoric of St. Hilary of Poitiers*, The Catholic University of America Patristic Studies 38 (Washington 1933).

Cayré, F., *Patrologie et historie de la théologie* 1 (4th ed., Paris 1945).

Forster, T., 'Zur Theologie des Hilarius,' *Theologische Studien und Kritiken*, 61 (1888), 645-686.

Gimborn, Br. Thomas, *The Syntax of the Simple Cases in St. Hilary of Poitiers*, The Catholic University of America Patristic Studies 54 (Washington 1939).

Girard, G., *Saint Hilaire* (Angers 1905).

Gummerus, V., *Die Homousianische Partei bis zum Tode des Konstantius* (Leipzig 1900).

Kinnavey, R., *The Vocabulary of St. Hilary of Poitiers as Contained in the Commentarius in Matthaeum, Liber I ad Constantium, and De Trinitate,* The Catholic University of America Patristic Studies 47 (Washington 1935).

Labriolle, P., *Histoire de la littérature latine chrétienne* I (3rd ed., Paris 1947).

Le Bachelet, X., 'Hilaire (Saint) évêque de Poitiers,' *Dictionnaire de la théologie catholique* 6, cols. 2388-2462 (Paris 1920).

Reinkens, J., *Hilarius von Poitiers* (Schaffhausen 1864).

Stix, J., *Zum Sprachgebrauch des hl. Hilarius von Poitiers in seiner Schrift de Trinitate* (Rottwell 1891).

Tixeront, J., *Histoire des dogmes* 2 (2nd ed., Paris 1909).

CONTENTS

SAINT HILARY OF POITIERS

THE TRINITY

Translated by

STEPHEN McKENNA, C.SS.R., PH.D.

Immaculate Conception Church

Bronx, New York

BOOK ONE

WHEN I WAS IN SEARCH of an employment, proper to man and sacred, which by its nature or through the researches of prudent men would result in something worthy of this divine gift, that has been bestowed upon him for knowledge, many things came to my mind which, according to the common opinion seemed to make life useful and desirable, particularly the possession of leisure together with riches, which now as formerly mankind regarded as the most excellent, because the one without the other would be a source of evil rather than an opportunity for good, since leisure without wealth is even looked upon as a kind of exile, while an opulent but restless life may bring greater unhappiness the more undeservedly it lacks what it especially desired and sought to use. Although these things contain, indeed, the highest and most pleasant luxuries of life, they do not seem to differ much from the pleasures of animals, that are free from work and are sated with food, as they roam about in the forests or in the rich pastures. If to rest and to abound be regarded as the best and most perfect occupation of human life, then, in accordance with the capacity of each one's nature, the same kind of existence must be common to us as well as to irrational animals, for all the latter have an abundance for their use without the worry of acquiring, since nature itself provides them with the greatest abundance and security.

3

(2) Many people, it seems to me, have rejected this degrading and bestial manner of living in their own case and despised it in that of others for no other reason than that under the inspiration of nature itself they believed it unbecoming for man to be born only for the sake of his belly and idleness, and that they have not entered this life from any desire of devoting themselves to noble deeds or to a good occupation, or that this very life has been granted to them without any gain for eternity. There certainly would be no doubt that such a life ought not to be valued as a gift of God, when, tormented by so great pains and entangled by so many annoyances from the ignorance of childhood to the follies of old age, it would consume its own self even within itself. Therefore, in their teaching and conduct they applied themselves to some of the virtues—patience, temperance, and meekness—because in their opinion good deeds and thoughts are the foundation of a good life, for it must not be imagined that an immortal God would grant them a life that would end only in death, since He would not be recognized as a kind benefactor who would impart the most delightful sense of living for the sake of dying amid the most distressing fear.

(3) Although I did not judge this teaching of theirs unbecoming or useless, that I should preserve my conscience from every fault, and that I should prudently provide for, or wisely avoid, or patiently endure all the misfortunes of life, the men themselves did not appear to me as fit teachers of a good and happy life in laying down precepts that were merely ordinary and adapted to man's power of comprehension, which, although it would be bestial not to understand, still, to understand them and not to act in accordance with them appeared to exceed the rage of a wild beast's cruelty. My soul, however, hastened not only to do these things, which if I had not done I would have been filled with guilt and remorse, but also to know this God and Author of so

great a gift to whom it was indebted for all that it had, to serve whom it esteemed as a mark of nobility, in whom it placed all the certainty of its hope, and in whose goodness it rested as in a most safe and familiar port amid such great afflictions of the present day. My soul, therefore, was enkindled with the most ardent desire of comprehending and knowing Him.

(4) Many of them introduced numerous families of uncertain deities and, imagining that the male and female sex was present in the divine natures, spoke about the birth and the successions of gods from gods. Others proclaimed that there were greater and lesser gods and gods differing in power. Some asserted that there was no God at all and venerated only that nature which came into existence through accidental movements or collisions. A great many declared in accordance with the popular belief that there was a God, but asserted that this same God had no concern or interest in human affairs. Some, however, worshiped those corporeal and visible forms of created things themselves in the elements of earth and heaven. Lastly, certain individuals placed their gods in the images of man, animals, beasts, and serpents, and confined the God of the universe and the Author of infinity within the narrow limits of metals, stones, and genealogies. And it was no longer fitting that they who cling to such ridiculous, degrading, and irreligious theories should be the teachers of the truth, when these men themselves were not in agreement about the principles of their most idiotic beliefs.

In the midst of all this, my soul in its quest for a useful and unmistakable road to the knowledge of its Lord was perplexed, since it considered it unbecoming for God to be unconcerned about the things which He had created, nor could it believe that an omnipotent and indestructible nature was compatible with the sex of the deities and the succession of parents and offspring. Moreover, it held for certain that the

Divine and Eternal was nothing else than one and identical, since that which gave existence would not leave behind anything more excellent than itself. Thus, omnipotence and eternity are to be found in One alone, because in omnipotence it was not fitting that there should be things weaker and stronger, and in eternity nothing before or after. In God, however, nothing was to be worshiped except what was eternal and omnipotent.

(5) While, therefore, I was giving serious thought to these and many other similar problems, I chanced upon those books which according to Jewish tradition were written by Moses and the Prophets. In them I found the testimony of God the Creator about Himself expressed in the following manner: 'I AM WHO AM,'[1] and again: 'Thus shalt thou say to the children of Israel: He who is, hath sent me to you.' I was filled with admiration at such a clear definition of God, which spoke of the incomprehensible nature in language most suitable to our human understanding. It is known that there is nothing more characteristic of God than to be,[2] because that itself which is does not belong to those things which will one day end or to those which had a beginning. But, that which combines eternity with the power of unending happiness could never not have been, nor is it possible that one day it will not be, because what is divine is not liable to destruction nor does it have a beginning. And since the eternity of God will not be untrue to itself in anything, He has revealed to us in a fitting manner this fact alone, that He is, in order to render testimony to His everlasting eternity.

(6) The words of Him who said: 'I AM WHO AM' seem, indeed, to have fully satisfied the definition of infinity, but we must also learn about the work of His majesty and omni-

---

1 Exod. 3.14.

2 'Hilarius betrachtet die richtige Auffassung des göttlichen Seins tatsächlich als den Angelpunkt der trinitärischen Lehre . . .' (A. Beck, Die Trinitätslehre des heiligen Hilarius [Mainz 1903] 11).

potence. Since being is proper to Him, He who always was would never have had a beginning, and the eternal and ever-lasting God has again let us hear a statement about Himself that is worthy of Him: 'He who holds the heavens in his palm and the earth in his hand,'[3] and again: 'Heaven is my throne and the earth my footstool. What is this house that you will build to me? And what is this place of my rest? Did not my hand make all these things?'[4] The entire heavens is held in the palm of God and the entire earth is confined in His hand. Even if the words of God aid the knowledge of a pious mind, still, when the mind penetrates them, they contain a deeper meaning than when they are heard. The heaven, which is held in His palm, is again the throne of God, and the earth, which is grasped in His hand, is at the same time His footstool. This is in order that we might not imagine that the throne and the footstool are an extension of a bodily form as in the position of one who is seated, since that which is His throne and footstool the omnipotent in-finity itself grasps with its hand and once more embraces, but that in all these beginnings of created things God might be recognized as in them and outside of them, reaching beyond them and being found within them, that is, poured about everything and permeating everything, since what the palm and the hand grasp reveal the power of His external nature, and the throne and the footstool show that external things are subject to Him as the One who is within, since He who is within rests upon the things that are without. Thus, He Himself with His whole being contains all things that are within Him and outside of Him, nor is He, the infinite One, separated from all things nor are all things not present within Him who is infinite.

My mind, intent on the study of truth, took delight in these

---

3 Isa. 40.12.
4 Cf. Isa. 66.1,2.

most pious teachings about God. For it did not consider any other thing worthy of God than that He is so far beyond the power of comprehension that the more the infinite spirit would endeavor to encompass Him to any degree, even though it be by an arbitrary assumption, the more the infinity of a measureless eternity would surpass the entire infinity of the nature that pursues it.[5] Although we understood this teaching in a reverent manner, it was clearly confirmed by these words of the Prophet: 'Whither shall I go from thy spirit? Or whither shall I flee from thy face? If I ascend into heaven thou art there: if I descend into hell thou art present. If I take my wings early in the morning, and dwell in the uttermost parts of the sea even there also shall thy hand lead me and thy right hand shall hold me.'[6] There is no place without God, nor is there any place which is not in God. He is in heaven, in hell, and beyond the seas. He is within all things; He comes forth and is outside all things. While He thus possesses and is possessed, He is not included in anything nor is He not in all things.

(7) Although my soul was filled with joy, therefore, at the contemplation of this excellent and ineffable knowledge, because it worshiped this infinity of a boundless eternity in this Father and Creator, still, by a more intensive study it sought for that form itself of its infinite and eternal Lord, so that it believed that the immeasurable immensity was clothed in some of the splendor of beautiful wisdom. While the religious mind was held captive by the error of its own weakness, the words of the Prophet impart to it this method for apprehending the knowledge of God's supreme beauty: 'For by the greatness of the work and the beauty of the creatures

---

5 Cf. *De Trinitate* 12.25, where the saint declares that the eternity of God is continually drawing away from our infinite perceptions that seek to overtake it.
6 Cf. Ps. 138.7-10.

the creator of the generations is reasonably known.'[7] The creator of the great belongs to the greatest and the maker of beautiful things to the most beautiful. And since the work surpasses even our comprehension, so the worker must far exceed our comprehension. The heavens, the sky, the earth, the sea, and the whole universe are beautiful, wherefore, because of its splendor, as even the Greeks agree, it appears to be called deservedly *kósmos,* that is, the ornament.[8]

If the mind by its natural instinct can thus measure the very beauty of things, as even happens in certain species of birds and animals, so that, while their language is not an expression of thought, their mind, although perceiving the object itself, does not speak of it,[9]—again, since all speech proceeds from thought, the mind that perceives it speaks of it to itself, should not the Lord of this beauty itself be conceived as the most beautiful of all beauty, so that, while the form of His eternal adornment eludes the mind's power of comprehension, the ornament is not withdrawn from the mind's power of comprehension? And we must acknowledge God as the most beautiful of all in this manner, that He is not included within the thoughts that we comprehend nor is He beyond the comprehension of our thoughts.[10]

(8) The soul, therefore, imbued with an eager longing for pious beliefs and doctrines, rested, as it were, in a retreat and watchtower of this most august contemplation. It was aware that nothing else was left to it from its nature, whereby it could render a greater or less service to its Creator than

---

7 Wisd. 13.5 (Septuagint).

8 The same proof and Greek word are used by Tertullian, *Apologeticum* 17.

9 His meaning probably is that some species of birds and animals recognize the beauty of the universe by their instinct and express it by some outward sign, e.g., the singing of birds.

10 If the beauty of the universe that we can perceive fills us with delight, then the nature of Him who created the universe, that we cannot perceive, must be the most beautiful of all things.

that it recognize Him as so great that He cannot be comprehended and can be believed, while the faith takes for granted a knowledge of the indispensable religion, and the infinity of the limitless power surpasses this knowledge.

(9) Amid all these speculations, however, a natural yearning was still hidden, that the profession of piety would be encouraged by some hope of an everlasting happiness, which a devout belief in God and a good moral life would merit as a reward for a victorious warfare. Nor would there be any advantage in thinking correctly about God if death were to destroy all sensation and, as it were, the certain setting of an exhausted nature would bring about its destruction. Moreover, reason itself convinced him that it was unworthy of God to have brought man into this life as a sharer in His council and prudence in order that his life might one day end and his death last for all eternity, that it was unworthy of God to have given existence to him who did not exist in order that when he had come into existence he might not exist. For, this can be regarded as the sole purpose of our creation: that what did not exist began to exist, not that what had begun to exist would cease to exist.

(10) My soul, however, was filled with anxiety partly for itself and partly for the body. While it remained unshaken in its devout belief in God, it was gripped at the same time with fear about itself and its dwelling, which, it thought, was destined for destruction. After becoming familiar with the Law and the Prophets, it learned about the promises of the evangelical and apostolic doctrine. 'In the beginning was the Word, and the Word was with God; and the Word was God. He was in the beginning with God. All things were made through him, and without him was made nothing that has been made. In him is life, and the life was the light of men. And the light shines in the darkness; and the darkness grasped it not. There was a man, one sent from God, whose

name was John. This man came as a witness, to bear witness concerning the light. He was not himself the light, but was to bear witness to the light. It was the true light that enlightens every man who comes into the world. He was in the world, and the world was made through him, and the world knew him not. He came unto his own and his own received him not. But to as many as received him he gave the power of becoming the sons of God, to those who believe in his name: Who were born not of blood, nor of the will of the flesh, nor of the will of man, but of God. And the Word was made flesh and dwelt among us. And we saw his glory—glory as of the only-begotten of the Father—full of grace and of truth.'[11]

My mind advances beyond the knowledge of natural reason and is taught more about God than it suspected. It learns that its Creator is God from God; it hears that the Word is God and is with God from the beginning. It knows the light of the world, that remains in the world and is not comprehended by the world. It recognizes Him who comes unto His own and is not received by them, while those who do receive Him through the merit of faith are made the children of God, not by the embrace of the flesh, nor by the conception of blood, nor by the will of the bodies, but are born from God. Finally, it acknowledges that the Word was made flesh and dwelt among us, that His glory has been seen which, as belonging to the only Son of the Father, is perfect in grace and in truth.

(11) By these words my fearful and anxious soul found greater hope than it had anticipated. First of all, it received the knowledge of God the Father. What it previously believed from natural reason about the eternity, infinity, and form of its Creator it now realizes as proper also to the only-begotten God. It does not believe in many gods, because it

---

11 Cf. John 1.1-14.

hears of God from God, nor does it accept a difference in nature between God and God, because it learns that the God who is from God is full of grace and truth, nor does it imagine that there is an earlier and later God from God because it holds that God was with God in the beginning. It perceives that the belief in the life-bringing doctrine is very rare but merits the greatest reward, for His own did not receive Him, and those who do receive Him are raised to be sons of God not by a birth from the flesh but by faith. To be the sons of God, however, is not a compulsion, but a power, since this divine gift is offered to all. It is not obtained from the nature of our parents, but the will merits the reward. And lest this very fact, that the power has been given to everyone to become a son of God, might scandalize some of weak faith who because of the difficulty in obtaining it would be the least disposed to hope for it—for the more something is desired the less it is believed—the Word God became flesh in order that through God the Word made flesh, the flesh might be elevated to God the Word. And in order that the incarnate Word of God might not be anything else than the God the Word, or anything else than flesh of our flesh, He dwelt among us, so that while He dwells He remains nothing else than God. While He dwells among us, God became nothing else than flesh of our flesh. By humbling Himself to take our flesh He did not lose His own proper nature, because as the only-begotten of the Father He is full of grace and truth; He is perfect in His own and true in ours.[12]

(12) My soul, therefore, gladly accepted this doctrine of the divine revelation: to proceed through the flesh to God, to be called to a new birth by faith, to be permitted by His

---

12 This passage is a refutation of the future errors of Nestorius and Eutyches, and teaches that the *Verbum* still remains God even while having a real human nature.

power to obtain a heavenly regeneration. In all this it sees the solicitude of its Father and Creator, nor does it believe that it would be annihilated by Him through whom it had been brought from nothingness to this very thing that it is. All of this is beyond the range of the human mind because reason, incapable of grasping the ordinary teachings of heavenly wisdom, regards this only as proper to the nature of things—to be either what it perceives within itself or what issues forth from itself. It measured the attributes of God according to the magnificence of the eternal power, not with the mind, but with its unbounded faith, so that it refused to give up its belief in the doctrine that God was in the beginning with God, and that the Word made flesh dwelt among us because it could not understand, but it remembered that it would be able to understand if it believed.

(13) Besides, the Apostle, to prevent any error of human wisdom from proving an obstacle, teaches us to have the most absolute certainty in this pious profession of faith by the divine words: 'See to it that no one robs you by philosophy and vain deceit, according to human traditions, according to the elements of the world and not according to Christ. In him dwells all the fullness of the Godhead bodily, and in him who is the head of every Principality and Power you have received of that fullness. In him, too, you have been circumcised with a circumcision not wrought by hand, but through putting off the body of the flesh, a circumcision which is of Christ. You were buried together with him in baptism and in him also rose again through faith in the working of God who raised him from the dead. And you, when you were dead by reason of your sin and the uncircumcision of your flesh, he brought to life along with him, forgiving all your sins, canceling the decree against us, which was hostile to us. Indeed, he has taken it from our midst, nailing it to the cross; having put off the flesh he made a show of powers

openly triumphing over them with confidence in himself.'[13] A firm faith rejects the captious and useless questions of philosophy, nor does truth become the victim of falsehood by yielding to the fallacies of human absurdities. It does not confine God within the terms of ordinary understanding, nor does it judge of Christ, in whom dwells the fullness of the Godhead bodily, according to the elements of the world, so that, while there is in Him the infinity of the eternal power, the power of eternal infinity surpasses the comprehension of the earthly mind.

He who elevates us to the nature of His Godhead has no longer restricted us to the corporeal observance of the commandments, nor has He obliged us through the shadow of the law to the practices of bodily circumcision, but in order that the spirit, when it had been circumcized from vices, might cleanse every natural necessity of the body by the purification from sin. By His death we would be buried together in baptism that we might return to eternal life, while death after life would be a rebirth to life, and dying to our vices we would be born again to immortality. Renouncing His immortality, He dies for us that we may be raised from death to immortality with Him. For, He received the flesh of sin that by assuming our flesh He might forgive our sin, but, while He takes our flesh, He does not share in our sin. By His death He destroyed the sentence of death in order that by the new creation of our race in His person He might abolish the sentence of the former decree. He allows Himself to be nailed to the cross in order that by the curse of the cross all the maledictions of our earthly condemnation might be nailed to it and obliterated. Finally, He suffers as man in order to shame the Powers. While God, according to the Scriptures, is to die, He would triumph with the confidence in Himself of a conqueror. While He,

---

13 Cf. Col. 2.8-15.

the immortal One, would not be overcome by death, He would die for the eternal life of us mortals.

These deeds of God, therefore, are beyond the understanding of our human nature, and do not fit in with our natural process of thought, because the operation of a limitless eternity demands an infinite comprehension of measuring things, so that it is not a conclusion of reason but a limitation of power when God becomes man, when the Immortal dies, when the Eternal is buried. Again, on the other hand, it does not depend on our manner of thinking but on omnipotence that He appears as God from a man, as immortal from one who is dead, and as eternal from one who is buried. Hence, we are revivified together by God in Christ through His death. But, while there is the fullness of the Godhead in Christ, God the Father is pointed out, who brings us back to life in one who is dead, and also Christ Jesus, whom we are to confess as none other than God with the fullness of the Godhead.

(14) For this reason my soul was at rest, conscious of its own security and full of joy in its aspirations; it feared the coming of death so little as to regard it as the life of eternity. No longer did it look upon the life of this body of his as troublesome or wearisome, but believed it to be what the alphabet is to boys, medicine to the sick, swimming to the shipwrecked, training to the adolescent, warfare to the future commander, namely, as the patient endurance of the present trials of life in order to gain a blissful eternity. Indeed, the soul, entrusted with the ministry of the priesthood, also preached to others what it believed for itself, and thus extended the duties of its office in order to provide for the salvation of all mankind.

(15) In the meantime, men of ungodly rashness appeared, despairing in themselves and merciless toward everyone. They measured the omnipotent nature of God by the

weakness of their own nature, not that they exalted themselves to the heights of infinity in their conjectures about infinite things, but confined infinite things within the boundaries of their own power of comprehension and made themselves the judges of religion, since the practice of religion is an obligation of obedience. They were unmindful of who they were, reckless in divine matters, and reformers of the commandments.

(16) To pass over in silence the other extremely ridiculous beliefs of the heretics—but which we shall discuss when the opportunity presents itself in the course of our treatise—there are certain individuals who so distort the mystery of the evangelical faith that they deny the birth of the only-begotten God, while piously professing that there is only one God, that there is an extension rather than a descent into man, that He who became the Son of Man from the moment He assumed our flesh never existed previously and is not the Son of God, that in Him there is not a birth from God but the same one comes from the same one, in order that this unbroken, unweakened continuity, as they believe, may preserve intact our faith in the one God, while the Father, who has extended Himself even to the Virgin, is born as the Son.[14] There are others, on the contrary (since there is no salvation without Him who as God the Word was with God in the beginning), who, while denying the birth, have acknowledged creation alone, so that the birth does not admit the true nature of God, and creation teaches that He is a false God, and, while this would misrepresent the faith in the nature of the one God, it would not exclude it in the mystery.[15] In place of the true birth they substitute the name

---

14 This is the teaching of Sabellius.
15 According to the heretics, Christ could not be the *true* Son of God, since He was created by God, not born from God, but they claimed that in the 'mystery,' or God's plan of salvation, Christ, although a creature, could be called the adopted Son of God, just as many other creatures are called the sons of God. Such is Coustant's opinion of this difficult passage, where the manuscripts are not in agreement.

and faith of creation, and separate Him from the true nature of the one God in order that a creature may not usurp the perfection of the Godhead, which had not been given by the birth of a true nature.

(17) My soul burned with the desire of replying to the fury of these men, since it remembered that this fact is particularly helpful to salvation not only to believe in God but also in God the Father, not only to hope in Christ but to hope in Christ as the Son of God, and not as a creature but as God the Creator who was born from God. Therefore, relying for the most part on the testimony of the Prophets and the Gospels, we hasten to refute the madness and ignorance of those who, by this teaching of the one God as the only doctrine that is indeed useful and reverential, either deny that Christ was born as God or contend that He is not the true God, so that the creation of a mighty creature does not destroy the mystery of faith in the one God, because the birth of God would lead those astray who profess their belief in the one God. But we, who have been taught by God to proclaim that there are neither two gods nor a solitary one, in professing our faith in God the Father and God the Son shall follow the method of instruction used by the Gospels and the Prophets, namely, that in our creed both are one nature and not one person, nor do we acknowledge that both are one and the same, nor is there something else between the true and false God, because, where God is born from God, the birth does not allow them to be the same, nor something else to be between them.[16]

(18) And you, indeed, who have been inspired to read by your ardent faith and zeal for the truth, that is unknown to the world and to the wise ones of the world, must re-

---

16 This is a fundamental principle of St. Hilary's that he is constantly repeating throughout this work. If Christ is born from God, then He must be a different Person from the Father, and at the same time He cannot have a different divine nature from His Father.

member that the shallow and foolish opinions of men are to be rejected and all the narrow limits of our imperfect knowledge are to be extended by a pious eagerness for knowledge. The regenerated spirit needs new faculties in order that everyone's conscience may be enlightened by the gift that comes from heaven. Therefore, as holy Jeremias warns,[17] he must take up his stand by faith in the nature of God so that, when he shall hear about the nature of God, he may direct his mind to the things that are worthy of God, but he must do so in accordance with no other norm for judging except that of infinity. Since he is conscious of being made a sharer in the divine nature,[18] as blessed Peter declares in his second Epistle, he must measure the nature of God not by the laws of his own nature but evaluate the divine truths in accordance with the magnificence of God's testimony concerning Himself. The best reader is he who looks for the meaning of the words in the words themselves rather than reads his meaning into them, who carries away more than he brought, and who does not insist that the words signify what he presupposed before reading them. Therefore, since our treatise will be about the things of God, let us concede to God the knowledge about Himself, and let us humbly submit to His words with reverent awe. For He is a competent witness for Himself who is not known except by Himself.

(19) If in our study of the nature and birth of God we shall cite some examples for the sake of illustration, let no one imagine that these are in themselves a perfect and complete explanation. There is no comparison between earthly things and God, but the limitations of our knowledge force us to look for certain resemblances in inferior things as if they were manifestations of higher things, in order that, while

---

17 Jer. 23.14. The word *substantia,* which the saint uses, is according to the Septuagint; the Vulgate has *consilio.*
18 2 Peter 1.4.

we are being made aware of familiar and ordinary things, we may be drawn from our conscious manner of reasoning to think in a fashion to which we are not accustomed. Every analogy, therefore, is to be considered as more useful to man than as appropriate to God, because it hints at the meaning rather than explains it fully. And the comparison should not be regarded as presumptuous in placing the natures of the flesh and the spirit, the invisible and the tangible, on an equality, since it declares that it is necessary for the weakness of the human understanding and bears no ill-will because it is only an unsatisfactory illustration. We proceed, therefore, to our task and shall speak of God in the words of God, but at the same time we shall come to the aid of our understanding by analogies drawn from circumstances in our own life.

(20)   First of all, we have planned our work in such a manner that the Books are connected and follow an order that is best adapted for the readers' progress. We have decided not to offer anything that was not well co-ordinated and assimilated, in order that the work might not appear like a tumultuous gathering of peasants who are shouting in confusion. Because precipitous places cannot be scaled except by climbing gradually to the top along the steps placed one upon the other, we have also, so to speak, arranged certain beginnings of our ascent in an orderly fashion and have alleviated the arduous journey of knowledge as if it were to a more pleasant elevation. We have done so not by cutting out steps, but by a gradual slope of the surface, so that the walkers are ascending and hardly realize that they are doing so.

(21)   After the present Book, the first of the treatise, the next explains the mystery of divine faith in such a manner that those who are to be baptized in the Father, Son, and the Holy Spirit may understand the true nature of the names and not confuse the meaning of the words, but con-

ceive each one as He is and as He is named. From the statements that are made they will realize very clearly that the
true nature is appropriate to the name and the name to the
true nature.

(22) Then, after a simple and brief description of the
Trinity, Book 3, although slowly, still continues to make
progress. That which the Lord revealed about Himself as
being beyond the comprehension of the human mind, as
when He says: 'I in the Father and the Father in me,'[19] He
adapts to the understanding of faith by the greatest possible
examples of His omnipotence, so that which man does not
grasp because of his sluggish nature may be now obtained
by the faith of a reasonable knowledge,[20] because we must
believe God when speaking about Himself and must not
imagine that the understanding of His power is beyond the
reasonableness of faith.

(23) Book 4 then begins with the doctrines of the heretics
and is not tainted with those defects by which the faith of the
Church is brought into evil repute. It cites that very explanation of their unbelief, which many of them issued only
recently, and denounces them for defending the one God
from the Law in a sly and therefore in a most godless manner.
From all the evidence in the Law and the Prophets it is
shown to be blasphemy to acknowledge the one God without
Christ as God, and a lack of faith not to proclaim the one
God after asserting that Christ is the only-begotten God.

(24) In Book 5, however, when replying to the heretics,
we have followed the order which they adopted in their
profession of faith. Since they misrepresented the teaching
that there is one God according to the Law, they were also
guilty of self-deception when they concluded from it that

19 John 10.38.
20 Faith is called 'reasonable knowledge' because our reason tells us
that we must believe God, and also that God can do more than our
human mind can conceive.

there is only one true God, so that by isolating the one true God they would deny the birth of Christ our Lord, for where there is a birth the possession of a true nature is understood. But step by step, while we are teaching the doctrine itself which has been denied, we have proclaimed from the Law and the Prophets that there are not two gods or one solitary God, but the true God the Father, so that we have neither perverted the faith in the one God nor denied the birth. Since, according to them, the Lord Jesus Christ has been created rather than born, the name of God should be attributed to Him rather than be inherent in Him. From the prophetical books we have established that He possesses the true nature of the Godhead in such a manner that, after proclaiming the Lord Jesus Christ as the true God, the true nature of His divine birth has strengthened us in the understanding of the one true God.

(25) Book 6 now reveals the complete duplicity of this heretical declaration. In order that their own words might be believed, they condemn the statements and mistakes of the heretics—Valentinian, Sabellius, Mani, and Hieracas—and have stolen the pious beliefs of the Church as a disguise for their own impious teachings, in order that, when they have twisted the words of these godless men into a better meaning and have modified their ambiguous language, they might suppress the pious doctrine under the pretext of disapproving impiety.[21] After explaining the words and statements of these individuals, we have clarified the holy teachings of the Church and we have not tolerated anything in common with these accursed heretics, in order that, while condemning what must be condemned, we might cling to those beliefs which are to be held in veneration. Thus, we conclude that

---

21 The Arians interpreted the doctrines of other heretics in such a manner that they seemed to be in agreement with the doctrines which the Church had defined at the Council of Nice.

the Lord Jesus Christ is the Son of God, which they especially deny, from these facts: the Father bears testimony to Him, He Himself makes such a profession about Himself, the Apostles preach it, devout people believe it, the devils cry out against it, ignorant heathens understand it, so that we are no longer justified in doubting about that which was left to us to become known.

(26)   Book 7 next directs the tone of the discussion which we have undertaken according to the standard of the perfect faith. In the first place, after a sound and frank exposition of the unassailable faith, it joins in the quarrel between Sabellius, Ebion, and those who do not proclaim the true God, and asks why Sabellius denies His existence before the world whom the others confessed that He was created. Sabellius did not know about the existence of the Son, while he did not doubt that the true God worked in a body. But these others rejected the birth and declared that He was only a creature, while they do not recognize His miracles as the miracles of the true God. Their disagreement is our faith. For, while Sabellius repudiates the Son (and therefore errs), he conquers in this, that the true God (as he correctly shows) has worked, and the Church triumphs over those who have denied the true God in Christ. When the others prove against him that Christ who exists before the world has always worked, then we share in their triumph, for, like them, we have condemned Sabellius, who knows the true God but does not know the Son of God. Ebion is conquered by both groups in this manner, that the one [Arius] convincingly demonstrates that He exists before the world, and the other [Sabellius] that He always worked. All, by conquering one another, are mutually conquered, because the Church testifies against Sabellius, against those who recognize Him only as a creature, and against Ebion that the Lord Jesus Christ is

the true God and from the true God, born before the ages
and afterwards begotten as man.

(27)   Since, on the authority of the Law and the Prophets,
we had first proclaimed Him as the Son of God and later
on as also the true God in the mystery of unity, no one
doubts that it is very much in harmony with the doctrine
of godliness for the Gospels to give added confirmation to
the Law and the Prophets and to teach from them, first of
all, that He is the Son of God, and, afterwards, that He is
also the true God. It was therefore most fitting that, after
giving the name of the Son, we should reveal His true nature,
although, according to the common opinion, the title of Son
is a clear indication of the true nature. In order that those
who oppose the true nature of the only-begotten God may not
be provided with any opportunity for deception or mockery,
we have based the faith itself in His true nature on the
truth of His divinity. We teach that He is God, who is
admitted to be the Son of God, in the following ways: by
His name, birth, nature, power, and confession, so that He
is nothing else than what He is called, nor is the name
incompatible with the birth, nor has the birth taken away
the nature, nor has the nature forsaken the power, nor has
even the power remained unknown, since the true nature has
been consciously revealed. We have, therefore, added all the
proofs from the Gospels for these specific attributes, so that
the confession was not silent about the power, the power does
not keep to itself the revelation of the nature, nor does the
nature not belong to His birth, nor does the birth belie His
name. Thus, unbelief has been afforded no pretext for misrepresentation, since Jesus Christ Himself, by making known
the true nature, which is His by birth, has also taught us the
divinity of the true God from the true God according to the
name, birth, nature, and power.

(28) Since the two preceding Books about the Son of God and the true God have enabled the believers to make progress in the faith, Book 8 is entirely concerned with the evidence for the one God. It does not eliminate the birth of the Son; neither does it admit the divine nature in two gods. It has first informed us of the methods whereby the heretics seek to avoid the true nature of God the Father and God the Son by exposing their ridiculous and absurd evasions. To them, therefore, such quotations as the following: 'But the multitude of the believers were of one heart and one soul,'[22] and again: 'Now he who plants and he who waters are one,'[23] and once more: 'Yet not for these only do I pray, but for those also who through their word are to believe in me, that all may be one, even as thou, Father, in me and I in thee; that they also may be one in us,'[24] lead to the conclusion that the true nature is a result of the will and harmony rather than of the Godhead. When we study these statements themselves in accordance with the meaning of the words, we prove that they contain in themselves the faith of the divine birth. While we consider the whole contents of the Lord's words, from the statements of the Apostles and the properties of the Holy Spirit, we have taught the complete and perfect mystery concerning the majesty of the Father and the only-begotten Son, since through the concept of the Son in the Father and the recognition of the Father in the Son there is taught the true birth of the only-begotten God and the true nature of the perfect God in Him.

(29) It is of little help, however, in matters that are most necessary for salvation to meet the requirements of faith by quoting only the evidence that is in agreement with it. As a rule, assertions which are made without proof deceive even

---

22 Cf. Acts 4.32.
23 1 Cor. 3.8.
24 John 17.20,21.

while flattering our understanding, unless the emptiness of
contrary arguments is also shown and the very fact that they
are shown to be absurd strengthens our own faith. The whole
of Book 9, therefore, is devoted to refuting the testimony
which these impious men have used to undermine the birth
of the only-begotten God, unaware as they are of the mysterious plan of salvation that has been hidden since the beginning of the world, and who do not recall that the faith of
the Gospel proclaims Him as God and man. When they
deny that our Lord Jesus Christ is God, that He is like God
and equal to God, as God the Son to God the Father, that He
is born from God, and, according to the true nature of His
birth, that He is in possession of the true nature of the
Spirit, they are wont to appeal to these statements of the
Lord: 'Why dost thou call me good? No one is good but
God only,'[25] so that, since He disapproves of being called
good and testifies that the one God alone is good, He does
not possess the goodness of God who is good, nor the true
nature of God who is one. To these words they also join the
following to corroborate their blasphemous doctrine: 'Now
this is everlasting life, that they may know thee, the only true
God, and him whom thou hast sent, Jesus Christ,'[26] so that,
when He acknowledges the Father as the only true God, He
Himself is not the true God, nor is He God at all, because in
this limitation of the only true God we do not go beyond Him
who possesses the true nature that has been designated.[27]

We must realize that these words were not spoken in an
ambiguous manner, because the same one has declared:
'The Son can do nothing of himself, but only what he sees
the Father doing,'[28] so that, since He can do nothing unless

---

25 Luke 18.19.
26 John 17.3.
27 The meaning is that the attributes of the Father are contained in
   Him in such a manner that they cannot be communicated to anyone
   else, and therefore Christ could not be true God.
28 John 5.19.

there is a pattern of the work before Him, a weakness of nature must be recognized in Him. That which must make use of the work of someone else certainly cannot be likened to omnipotence, and our own power of reasoning convinces us that there is a distinction between being able to do and not being able to do all things. They differ to such an extent that He expressed Himself in this manner concerning God the Father: 'The Father is greater than I.'[29] May this uncompromising statement put an end to the intrigues of our adversaries, because it is indicative of blasphemy and madness to confer the glory and nature of God on one who rejects them! In any case, He is so far removed from the nature of the true God that He even testified: 'But of that day or hour no one knows, neither the angels in heaven, nor the Son, but the Father alone,'[30] so that, since the Son does not know what the Father alone knows, the one who does not know is far different from the one who does know, because a nature which is liable to ignorance does not possess the divinity and power of that which is not subject to the domination of ignorance.

(30)   Therefore, while we pointed out that these texts were interpreted in such a most blasphemous manner because their meaning was misrepresented and distorted, we have adduced all the reasons for these statements from the very nature of the questions, or the circumstances of time, or the plan of salvation. We make the words dependent upon the reasons rather than consider the reasons as mere adjuncts to the words. Thus, since the words, 'The Father is greater than I,'[31] and 'I and the Father are one,'[32] do not agree, and the same thing is not contained in the words, 'No one is good

---

29 John 14.28.
30 Cf. Mark 13.32.
31 John 14.28.
32 John 10.30.

but God only,'[33] as in 'He who sees me sees also the Father,'[34] and there certainly is just as great a difference between 'Father, all things that are mine are thine'[35] and 'That they may know thee, the only true God'[36] as between 'I am in the Father and the Father in me'[37] and 'But of that day or hour no one knows, neither the angels in heaven, nor the Son but the Father alone,'[38] we are to understand in each instance the promulgations of the plans of salvation and the deliberate assertions of a natural power, since the same individual is also the author of both statements. When we have pointed out the properties of each nature, however, it will be seen that what we teach concerning the plan of salvation, whether the cause, the time, the birth, or the name, pertains to the mystery of the evangelical faith and does not lead to any abasement of the true Godhead.

(31) The arrangement in Book 10 is the same as that in the faith itself. Since they have distorted certain things about the nature of the Passion and statements made during it by comprehending them in a foolish manner for the sake of lessening respect for the divine nature and power in the Lord Jesus Christ, so we must bring out that they have placed a most godless construction upon them and that they were mentioned by our Lord as a testimony to the true and perfect glory that is His. For, in order to be blasphemous under the guise of piety, they interpret these words in their favor: 'My soul is sad, even unto death,'[39] so that He is far from enjoying the blessedness and indestructibility of God whose soul allows itself to be dominated by the fear of imminent sorrow, and who was so crushed by the necessity of

---

33 Luke 18.19.
34 John 14.9.
35 John 17.10.
36 John 17.3.
37 John 14.11.
38 Mark 13.31.
39 Matt. 26.38.

having to suffer that He prayed: 'Father, if it is possible, let this cup pass away from me.'[40] And there is no doubt that He seemed to fear to endure that which He prayed that He might not suffer, because the fear of suffering caused Him to pray that it might be taken away. The power of this sorrow oppressed Him so much in His weakness that at the time of the crucifixion He cried out: 'God, my God, why hast thou forsaken me?'[41] He who was afflicted by the bitterness of His suffering so as even to complain of His desolation was also in need of the Father's help, and gave up His spirit when He spoke these words: 'Father, into thy hands I commend my spirit.'[42] The dread of giving up the spirit afflicted Him and He commended it to the protection of God the Father and His own lack of confidence and assurance forced Him to commend Himself to another.

(32) These most irrational and irreverent men do not realize that there is nothing contradictory in the same things which the same individual has uttered, and by adhering only to the words they have lost sight of the reasons for which they were said. Since there is a great difference between 'My soul is sad, even unto death'[43] and 'Hereafter you shall see the Son of man sitting at the right hand of the Power,'[44] and 'Father, if it is possible, let this cup pass away from me'[45] is not the same as 'Shall I not drink the cup that my Father has given me?'[46] and the words 'God, my God, why hast thou forsaken me?'[47] do not agree with 'Amen I say to thee, this day thou shalt be with me in Paradise,'[48] and the sen-

40 Matt. 26.39.
41 Cf. Matt. 27.46.
42 Luke 23.46.
43 Matt. 26.38.
44 Cf. Matt. 26.64.
45 Matt. 26.39.
46 John 18.11.
47 Matt. 27.46.
48 Luke 23.43.

tence 'Father, into thy hands I commend my spirit'[49] is at
variance with 'Father, forgive them for they do not know
what they are doing,'[50] they have fallen into ungodliness
and do not understand the words of God.

Since fear cannot be reconciled with courage, willingness
with pleading, complaint with exhortation, lack of confidence
with mediation, these men, unmindful of the divine and
natural confession, have alleged the deeds and words of the
economy of salvation as proofs for their impiety. Therefore,
since we have explained everything in the mysterious doctrine
of the soul and body of the Lord Jesus Christ, there is nothing
that we have not examined, and nothing that we have not
discussed, and we have produced a harmonious reconciliation
of all these words by placing each one in its proper category
so that confidence does become faint-hearted, nor does
willingness seek to escape, nor does peace of mind complain,
and He who recommended Himself in prayer sought pardon
for others. And we strengthen the faith in all these words by
teaching the mystery of the Gospel in its entirety.

(33)   Since, then, not even the glory of the Resurrection
itself has made these most reckless men listen to reason and
remain within the limits of religious knowledge, either they
have forged the weapons of their impiety from the admission
of His abasement, or they have made use of the revealed
mystery in order to offer insult to God, so that, because of
what was said: 'I ascend to my Father and your Father, to
my God and your God,'[51] while we as well as He have the
Father in common as our Father, and His God as our God,
the acknowledgment of something in common precludes Him
from being the true God, and the need of being created has
made Him as well as us subject to God the Creator, and

49 Luke 23.46.
50 Luke 23.34.
51 John 20.17.

adoption elevates Him to be His Son. According to the words of the Apostle, no attribute of the divine nature should be ascribed to Him: 'But when he says all things are subject to him, undoubtedly he is excepted who has subjected all things to him. For when all things are made subject to him then he himself will be subject to him who subjected all things to him, that God may be all in all.'[52] Because subjection testifies to the weakness of the subject and indicates the power of the ruler, Book 11 is also concerned with these questions and discusses them with the most thorough explanation of godliness. It also proves that these very words of the Apostle not only do not lead to any weakness of the divinity but reveal the true nature of the God who is born from God. Therefore, from the fact that His Father is our Father and His God our God, we gain much and nothing is taken away from Him, that is to say, since He was born as man and endured all the sufferings of the flesh, He ascended to our God and Father in order that in our manhood He might be glorified into God.

(34) That which is always observed, according to our recollection, in every branch of learning—that when they have been instructed from the beginning and for a long time in some insignificant exercise and have become familiar over an extended period with the more humble task, then they are permitted to be tested in the subjects to which they have been accustomed, so that when those who plan a military career have been well trained in the art of war they are received into the army, or that when those who have completed the classroom practices in the rhetorical schools are admitted to the disputes in the courts, or that when the sailor has courageously guided the vessel in the inland waters he is then exposed to the storms of the large and strange sea—we have attempted to do in the most important and weighty knowledge of the entire creed.

---

52 Cf. 1 Cor. 15.27,28.

When we had previously instructed the immature faith in the simple rudiments concerning the birth, the name, the divinity, and the true nature, and by moving steadily forward had encouraged the eager readers to avoid all the snares of the heretics, then we led them into the very arena of the great and glorious combat in order that, inasmuch as the human mind, according to the common opinion, fails to grasp the idea of an eternal birth by means of ordinary knowledge, so much the more should they rely upon divine meditations in order to understand matters that are beyond the comprehension of our rational nature. We expose particularly the sophistry that is so prevalent because of the stupidity of worldly wisdom, and which imagines that it is correctly stated about the Lord Jesus: 'There was a time when He was not' and 'He did not exist before He was born,' and 'He was made out of non-existing things,' because birth seems to take for granted that He should receive being who did not possess it, and that He should be born since He did not exist. For this reason they also subject the only-begotten God to the order of time (just as if the faith and the account of the birth themselves prove that at one time He did not exist), and therefore they assert that He was born from the very fact that He did not exist, because birth had given to Him a nature which He did not have.

While we proclaim, in accordance with the testimony of the Apostles and the Gospels, that the Father always was and the Son always was, we shall teach that the God of all was not after some things but before all things. Nor does this rash and godless doctrine apply to Him that He was born from non-existing things and that He was not before He was born, but that He always was in such a manner that we proclaim that He was also born, but born in such a manner that we make known that He always was. It is not the unique privilege of not being born, but of an eternal birth that is proper to

Him, because birth also requires a parent, and divinity is not lacking in eternity.

(35) Because they are ignorant of the words of the Prophets and unskilled in heavenly doctrine, they attempt by a distortion of the sense and meaning to maintain that God was created rather than born because it was said: 'The Lord created me for the beginning of his ways, for his works,'[53] so that He belongs to the common order of created things, although in a higher class of creation, nor does He enjoy the glory of the divine birth, but the power of a mighty creature. Without citing anything new or without presupposing anything extrinsic to the subject, we shall explain the true meaning and intention of this testimony from Wisdom Itself. We cannot apply the words, that He was created for the beginning of His ways for His works, to the concept of the divine and eternal birth, because there is a difference between being created for these things and being created before all things, since, where a birth is meant, there is an avowal only of the birth, but, where the term creation is used, there always exists a prior cause of this creation. Since Wisdom was born before all things, but since it was also created for some things, that which is before all things is not the same as that which began to be after some things.

(36) Therefore, it seemed logical that, after rejecting the name of creation from our faith in the only-begotten God, we should also teach those things which are also suitable and reverential in our profession of faith concerning the Holy Spirit, in order that those who had been already strengthened by the long and careful discussions of the earlier Books might not be wanting in a complete knowledge of our entire creed, since, after the heretical and erroneous teachings concerning the Holy Spirit had been eliminated, the mystery of the Trinity, through which we are reborn, remained unharmed and

---

53 Cf. Prov. 8.22.

undefiled within the saving definition by the authority of the
Apostles and Gospels. Certainly, no one would dare any longer
to follow the views of human reason and place the Holy Spirit
in the ranks of creatures whom we would receive as a pledge
of immortality and for a share in the divine and indestructible
nature.[54]

(37)   O almighty God the Father, I am fully conscious
that I owe this to You as the special duty of my life that all
my words and thoughts should speak of You. This readiness
of speech which You have granted to me can obtain for me
here no greater reward than to serve You by proclaiming
You, and by revealing to the world that does not know You
and to the heretic that denies You what You are, namely,
the Father of the only-begotten God. This is, to be sure, only
the expression of my will. Besides this, I must pray for the
gift of Your help and mercy that You may fill the sails of
our faith and profession which have been extended to You
with the breath of Your Spirit and direct us along the course
of instruction that we have chartered. The Author of this
promise is not unfaithful to us who says: 'Ask, and it shall
be given to you; seek, and you shall find; knock, and it shall
be opened to you.'[55] We, of course, in our helplessness shall
pray for those things that we need, and shall apply ourselves
with tireless zeal to the study of all the words of Your
Prophets and Apostles and shall knock at all the doors of
wisdom that are closed to us, but it is for You to grant
our prayer, to be present when we seek, to open when we
knock. Because of the laziness and dullness of our nature, we
are, as it were, in a trance, and in regard to the understanding
of Your attributes we are restricted within the confines of
ignorance by the weakness of our intellect. Zeal for Your

---

54 In these words St. Hilary expresses his belief in the true divinity of
the Holy Spirit. The latter is not to be classified as a creature and
He will enable us to share in the nature of God Himself.
55 Luke 11.9.

doctrine leads us to grasp the knowledge of divine things and the obedience of faith carries us beyond the natural power of comprehension.

(38) We hope, therefore, that You will set in motion the beginning of our timid venture and will encourage it by a steady progress and will summon us to share in the prophetic and apostolic spirit in order that we may understand their words in no other sense than that in which they spoke them, and that we may explain the proper meaning of the words in accordance with the realities they signify. We shall speak of subjects which they have announced in the mystery: that You are the eternal God, the Father of the eternal only-begotten God, that You alone are without birth, and the one Lord Jesus Christ who is from You by an eternal birth, not to be placed among the number of the deities by a difference in the true nature, nor to be proclaimed as not being born from You, who are the true God, nor to be confessed as anything else than God who has been born from You, the true God the Father.

Bestow upon us, therefore, the meaning of words, the light of understanding, the nobility of diction, and the faith of the true nature. And grant that what we believe we may also speak, namely, that, while we recognize You as the only God the Father and the only Lord Jesus Christ from the Prophets and the Apostles, we may now succeed against the denials of the heretics in honoring you as God in such a manner that You are not alone, and proclaiming Him as God in such a manner that He may not be false.

BOOK TWO

HE WORD OF GOD, together with the very power of its own truth which we received from the testimony of the Evangelist, was sufficient for those who believe, since He says: 'Going now, teach all nations, baptizing them in the name of the Father, and of the Son, and of the Holy Spirit, teaching them to observe all that I have commanded you; and behold, I am with you all days, even unto the consummation of the world.'[1] For, what is there pertaining to the mystery of man's salvation that it does not contain? Or is there anything that is omitted or obscure? Everything is full as from fullness and perfect as from perfection. It includes the meaning of the words, the efficacy of the actions, the order of procedure, and the concept of the nature.

He commanded them to baptize in the name of the Father, the Son, and the Holy Spirit, that is, in the confession of the Origin, the Only-begotten, and the Gift. There is one source of all. God the Father is one from whom are all things; and our Lord Jesus Christ is one through whom are all things; and the Holy Spirit is one, the gift in all things. Everything is arranged, therefore, according to its power and merits. There is one Power from whom are all things, one Offspring through whom are all things, and one Gift of perfect hope. Nor will anything be found wanting to a

---

1 Cf. Matt. 28.19,20.

35

perfection so great within which there is found in the Father, the Son, and the Holy Spirit: infinity in the Eternal, the form in the Image, and the use in the Gift.[2]

(2) The guilt of the heretics and blasphemers compels us to undertake what is unlawful, to scale arduous heights, to speak of the ineffable, and to trespass upon forbidden places. And since by faith alone we should fulfill what is commanded, namely, to adore the Father, to venerate the Son with Him, and to abound in the Holy Spirit, we are forced to raise our lowly words to subjects which cannot be described. By the guilt of another we are forced into guilt, so that what should have been restricted to the pious contemplation of our minds is now exposed to the dangers of human speech.

(3) Many have appeared who understood the simplicity of the heavenly words in an arbitrary manner and not according to the evident meaning of the truth itself, interpreting them in a sense which the force of the words did not warrant. Heresy does not come from Scripture, but from the understanding of it; the fault is in the mind, not in the words. Is it possible to falsify the truth? When the name father is heard, is not the nature of the son contained in the name? Will He not be the Holy Spirit who has been so designated? For, there cannot but be in the Father what a father is, nor can the Son be wanting in what a son is, nor can there not be in the Holy Spirit what is received. Iniquitous men confuse and complicate everything and in their distorted minds even seek to effect a change in the nature so that they deprive the Father of what the Father is and take away from the Son what the Son is. They despoil Him, however,

---

2 St. Augustine, *De Trinitate* 6.10, praises these names, which distinguish the Persons of the Trinity, as does St. Thomas Aquinas, *S. T.* III, Q. 39, art. 8. Later writers would restrict the word *usus* to creatures, and *fruitio* to God the Creator, but St. Hilary applies the word *usus* even to the Son of God.

since according to them He is not a son by nature. He does not possess the nature if the one born and the begetter do not have the same properties in themselves. He is not a son whose being is different from and unlike that of the father. In fact, how will he be a father if he has not begotten in the son the substance and nature that belong to him?

(4) Therefore, although they are unable to make any changes at all in these facts concerning Him, they invent new doctrines and human vagaries so that Sabellius extends the Father into the Son and believes that He must be acknowledged as the Son in name rather than in reality, since the one whom he represents to himself as the Son is also the Father. Thus, Ebion, assuming that the starting point of the Son of God is entirely from Mary, produces not a man from God but a God from man,[3] so that the Virgin did not receive the pre-existing Word of God, that was with God in the beginning, but brought forth flesh through the Word. He says that previously in the Word there was not the nature of the existing only-begotten God, but the utterance of a voice, as some in this present age teach, who cause the form, wisdom, and power of God to arise from nothingness and in time, lest, if the Son is from the Father, God may suffer a loss in the Son, for they are excessively worried that the birth of the Son from Him may weaken the Father. For this reason they wish to help the Father in the creation of the Son by bringing Him forth from non-existing things, in order that the Father may continue within the perfections of His own nature, since nothing has been born from Him.

Is it, then, a cause of wonder that these men think differently about the Holy Spirit, they who have been so reckless in creating, changing, and abolishing His Dispenser? Thus, they destroy the true nature of this perfect mystery by

---

3 Ebion did not believe that Christ was God and then became man, but that He was first a man and then became God.

devising differences of substances in things that are so common,[4] since they deny the Father when they rob the Son of what a son is, and reject the Holy Spirit when they do not know His use or His author. Thus, they lead the ignorant into ruin when they emphasize the reasonableness of their teaching, and deceive their hearers while they divest the nature by means of the names, because names cannot take away the nature. I pass over the remaining names which are a danger to man, the Valentinians, the Manichaeans, and the other corrupt men who seize possession of the souls of the unlearned and infect them by the very contact with their manner of life, so that all are victims of the one plague, while the disease of the teachers is poured into the minds of the listeners.

(5) The unbelief of these men, therefore, forces us into a critical and dangerous position, so that we must violate the heavenly command[5] and speak about such lofty and mysterious subjects. The Lord said that the people were to be baptized 'in the name of the Father, the Son, and the Holy Spirit.' The formula of faith is certain, but, in so far as the heretics are concerned, its meaning is wholly uncertain. Accordingly, we must not add anything to the precepts, but must set a limit to their audacity. And because this malevolence, which has been stimulated by the instigation of diabolical deceit, shuns the true nature of the things by the names of the nature, we emphasize the nature of the names. After we have explained the dignity and office of the Father, the Son, and the Holy Spirit, as we have them in the words, it will be seen that the names do not deceive us about the

---

4 Here again St. Hilary clearly indicates his belief in the divinity of the Holy Spirit, since he condemns the heretics for seeking to divide the nature that the Father, Son, and Holy Spirit have in common.

5 According to 2.1 (above), the Lord commanded His Apostles only to preach the Gospel, but the action of the heretics forces him to go beyond this command and investigate the secrets of the divine nature.

properties of the nature, but the properties are kept within
the meaning of their nature by means of the names.

I do not know what is in the minds of those who think
differently about these things, who falsify the true nature,
prefer darkness to light, sever the indivisible, split up the inseparable, and break asunder the imperishable. If for them
it is only a trivial matter to tear apart what it perfect, to fix
a law for omnipotence, to set limits to the infinite, for me,
on the contrary, who answers them, these problems are a
source of anxiety, my mind is confused, and my understanding in a daze, but by my words I shall acknowledge
not my weakness but my inability to speak.

In truth, the resolution to do this is forced upon me in
order to hold rashness in check, to take action against error,
and to counteract ignorance. I must undertake something that
cannot be limited and venture upon something that cannot
be comprehended, so that I may speak about God who cannot be accurately defined. He fixed the names of the nature— *nature*
the Father, the Son, and the Holy Spirit. Whatever is sought
over and above this transcends the meaning of words, the
limits of perception, and the concepts of the understanding.
It may not be expressed, attained, or grasped. The nature
of this subject exhausts the meaning of words, an impenetrable light darkens the vision of the mind, and whatever is
without limits is beyond the capacity of our power of reasoning. But, owing to the necessity of doing this, we beg pardon
of Him who possesses all these attributes, and we shall dare,
we shall seek, and we shall speak. In the discussion of a
matter so exalted we make only this promise to believe whatever shall be made known.

(6)   It is the Father from whom everything that exists
has been formed. He is in Christ and through Christ the
source of all things. Moreover, His being is in Himself and
He does not derive what He is from anywhere else, but pos-

sesses what He is from Himself and in Himself. He is infinite because He Himself is not in anything and all things are within Him; He is always outside of space because He is not restricted; He is always before time because time comes from Him. Stir up your understanding if you believe that anything is the ultimate limit for Him. You will always find Him, because, while you are always seeking after it, there is always some object present after which you can seek. Thus, it is always characteristic of you to seek after His place as it is for Him to be without any limits. Language will weary itself in speaking about Him, but He will not be encompassed. Again, reflect upon the periods of time; you will find that He always is, and, when the numerals in your statement have finally come to an end, the eternal being of God does not come to an end.

Arouse your understanding and seek to comprehend the totality of God in your mind; you hold on to nothing. This totality of God has always something over and above your power of comprehension, but this something over and above always belongs to the totality of God. Therefore, neither this totality, which lacks something over and above, nor this something, that is over and above, includes everything that the totality of God does. What is over and above your power of comprehension is only a part, but everything means the totality of God. But, God is also present everywhere and is present in His entirety wherever He is. Thus, He transcends the realm of understanding, outside of whom nothing exists and of whom eternal being is always characteristic. This is the true nature of the mystery of God; this is the name of the impenetrable nature in the Father.

God is invisible, ineffable, infinite. In speaking of Him, even speech is silent; the mind becomes weary in trying to fathom Him; the understanding is limited in comprehending Him. He possesses, indeed, as we have said, the name of His

36631

nature in the Father, but He is only the Father. He does
not receive His Fatherhood in a human way from anywhere
else.[6] He Himself is unborn, eternal, and always possesses in
Himself what He is. He is known to the Son alone, because
no one knows the Father except the Son and he to whom
the Son wills to reveal it, nor does anyone know the Son except the Father. Between them there is a mutual knowledge
and again between them there is perfect cognition. And,
because no one knows the Father except the Son, let us keep
before our mind the Father together with the Son who reveals
Him and who alone is a reliable witness.

(7) I would rather think of these things about the
Father than speak of them, for I am not unaware that all
language is powerless to express what must be said. Moreover, in regard to what He is in Himself, that He is invisible,
incomprehensible, and immortal, in these words there is
admittedly an encomium of His majesty, an intimation of
our thoughts, and a sort of definition of our meaning, but
speech will surrender to the nature and words do not portray
the subject as it is. When you hear that He is 'in Himself,'
this statement does not strike human reason as free from
ambiguity, for there is a distinction between possession and
the object of possession, and that which is will be one thing,
and that in which it is will be another thing; similarly if you
learn that He is 'from Himself,' for no one is Himself both
the giver and the gift. If [you learn] that He is immortal,
then there is something which does not come from Him to
which He is not made subject by His nature, nor is that the
only thing that is claimed by this word;[7] if that He is incom-

---

6 God is the Father by His very nature, whereas among men human
  nature and fatherhood are not synonymous terms.
7 The obscurity of this passage arises from the discrepancies in the
  manuscripts to which Coustant calls attention. According to him, it
  means that the Father, being immortal by nature, is not subject to
  death. Now, if death does not pertain to God, then it is outside of God,
  and exists independently of Him.

prehensible, He will be nowhere because He cannot be contacted; if that He is invisible, then He Himself is lacking in that which does not appear before our vision. Consequently, a confession in name is defective. No matter what kind of language is used, it will be unable to speak of God as He is and what He is. The perfection of learning is to know God in such a manner that, although you realize He is not unknown, you perceive that He cannot be described. We must believe in Him, understand Him, adore Him, and by such actions we shall make Him known.

(8) We have been led from the unsheltered places near the stormy ocean out into the high seas, and, although we can neither return nor go forward without danger, the journey that we are to follow offers more difficulty than that which we have already completed. The Father is as He is and must be believed to be what He is. My soul is filled with consternation upon arriving at the Son and all my words tremble at revealing themselves. He is the offspring of the unbegotten, the one from the one, the true from the true, the living from the living, the perfect from the perfect, the power of power, the wisdom of wisdom, the glory of glory, the image of the invisible God, the form of the unbegotten Father.

How shall we represent to ourselves the birth of the only-begotten from the unbegotten? The Father often declares from heaven: 'This is my beloved Son in whom I am well pleased.'[8] This is not a separation or a division, for He who has begotten is immutable and He who is born is the image of the invisible God and testifies: 'Because the Father is in Me and I in the Father.'[9] There is no adoption, for He is the true Son of God and exclaims: 'He who sees me, sees also the Father.'[10] He did not come into being as others do by a

---

8 Matt. 3.17.
9 John 10.38.
10 John 14.9.

command, for the Only-begotten is from one and has life in Himself, as He who begot Him has life in Himself, for He declares: 'As the Father has life in Himself, even so He has given to the Son to have life in Himself.'[11] Neither is there a part of the Father in the Son, for He affirms: 'All things that the Father has are mine,'[12] and again: 'All mine are thine and thine are mine,'[13] and: 'Whatever the Father has He has given to the Son,'[14] and the Apostle also bears witness: 'For in Him dwells all the fullness of the Godhead bodily.'[15] Nor does the fullness of being belong to that which is a part. He is the perfect one from the perfect one, but He who has all has given all. And we must not imagine that He did not give, because He has, or that He does not have, because He has given.

(9) Both possess, therefore, the secret of this birth. And if someone perhaps will blame his own understanding for being unable to grasp the mystery of this birth, since both the Father and the Son are clearly known, he will learn with even greater sorrow that I am ignorant of it. I do not know, I do not seek, and still I am at peace. The Archangels have not fathomed it, the Angels have not heard it, the Generations have not grasped it, the Prophet has not preached it, the Apostle did not ask about it, and the Son did not reveal it. Let the mournful laments cease!

Whoever you are that will inquire into these things, I do not summon you to the heights, I do strive for expansion, I do not lead you into the depths. Will you not bear calmly your ignorance of the birth of the Creator, since you do not know the origin of the creature? This at least I want to know: Do you believe that you are born, and do you understand

---

11 Cf. John 5.26.
12 John 16.15.
13 John 17.10.
14 The nearest approach to these words is the text of John 3.35.
15 Col. 2.9.

what has been begotten from you? I do not inquire whence you drew your consciousness, or where you obtained life, or from what place you received your understanding, or what is the nature of smell, touch, sight, and hearing. Certainly, no one is unaware of what he is doing. I ask how you will pass on these things to those to whom you will give birth? How will you insert the ideas, light up their eyes, and attach their heart? Describe these processes if you can. Hence, you possess what you do not know and bestow what you do not understand. You are unperturbed about your lack of knowledge in matters concerning yourself and are arrogant in the affairs of God.

(10)   For this reason, pay attention to the unbegotten Father, listen to the only-begotten Son: 'The Father is greater than I.'[16] Hear: 'I and the Father are one';[17] hear: 'He who sees me sees also the Father';[18] hear: 'The Father is in me and I in the Father.'[19] Hear: 'I came forth from the Father,'[20] and 'He who is in the bosom of the Father,'[21] and 'All things that the Father has He has delivered to the Son,'[20] and 'The Son has life in Himself, as the Father also has life in Himself.'[21] Hear about the Son, the image, the wisdom, the power, and the glory of God, and understand the Holy Spirit who declares: 'Who shall proclaim his generation?'[22] And criticize the Lord as He testifies: 'No one knows the Son except the Father; nor does anyone know the Father except the Son, and him to whom the Son chooses to reveal him.'[23] Force yourself into this secret, and amid the one unbegotten God and the one only-begotten God immerse yourself in the

16 John 14.28.
17 John 10.30.
18 John 14.9.
19 John 10.38.
20 John 16.28.
21 John 1.18.
22 Isa. 53.8.
23 Matt. 11.27.

mystery of the inconceivable birth. Begin, go forward, persevere. Even though I know that you will never reach your
goal, I will congratulate you for having gone ahead. Whoever
seeks after infinite things with a pious mind, although he
never overtakes them, will still advance by pressing forward.
Your power of comprehension comes to a standstill at this
boundary line of the words.[24]

(11) The Son is from that Father who is, the only-
begotten from the unbegotten, the offspring from the parent,
the living one from the living one. As the Father has life
in Himself, so the Son has been given life in Himself. The
perfect one from the perfect one, because the whole one from
the whole one. There is no division or dissection, because
the fullness of the Godhead is in the Son. The incomprehensible one from the incomprehensible one, for only they themselves know each other mutually. The invisible one from the
invisible one, because He is the image of the invisible God
and because He who sees the Son sees also the Father. One
is from the other because they are the Father and the Son.
The nature of the Godhead is not different in one and in the
other, because both are one. God is from God, the one only-
begotten God is from the one unbegotten God. There are
not two gods, but one from one. There are not two unbegotten gods, because He is born from Him who is unborn.
The one is from the other and is not different in anything,
because the life of the living one is in the living one.

We have touched upon these facts concerning the nature
of the divinity, not in order to assemble in one place the
sum total of our knowledge, but in order to make us realize
that what we are discussing cannot be comprehended. You
declare that faith serves no purpose if there is nothing that

---

24 Our human mind, illumined by faith, can go only so far as the words,
that is, it can know that there is a true Father and a true Son in the
one God, but it cannot comprehend the manner of this divine birth.

can be comprehended. On the contrary, faith proclaims that this is its purpose: to know that it cannot comprehend that for which it is seeking.

(12) Something still remains to be said about this un-utterable birth; in fact, the something that still remains is everything. I am restless, hesitant, listless, at a loss as to where to begin. I do not know when the Son was born, and it is wrong for me to be ignorant of the fact that He was born. To whom shall I appeal? Whom shall I implore? From what books shall I borrow words to explain such difficult mysteries? Shall I consult all the scholars of Greece? But I have read: 'Where is the "wise man?"' . . . Where is the disputant of this world?'[25] In this matter the wise and the prudent are dumb, for they have rejected the wisdom of God. Shall I seek for advice from the scribe of the Law? But he does not know, because the cross of Christ is a scandal to him. Shall I, perhaps, advise you to take no notice of and be silent about all these questions, because we pay suffi-cient reverence to Him when we declare that by Him the lepers were cleansed, the deaf heard, the lame walked, the paralytics stood up, the blind obtained the light, the man blind from the womb received his sight, the devils were put to flight, the sick were restored to health, and the dead rose again? The heretics acknowledge these things, and they are lost.

(13) Hence, do not look for something which would be inferior to the lame walking, the blind seeing, the devils taking to flight, and the dead coming back to life. In solving these difficult questions that I have just mentioned I am aided by the poor fisherman who stands at my side. He is unknown, unlearned, a fishing line in his hands; his clothes are drenched; he is oblivious to the mud beneath his feet; he is in every respect a sailor. Inquire and understand whether

---

25 1 Cor. 1.20.

it was more wonderful to raise up the dead than to instruct
an uneducated man in the knowledge of this doctrine. He
said: 'In the beginning was the Word.'[26] What is the meaning of the phrase 'in the beginning was?' The periods of time
are passed by, the centuries are omitted, and the ages are laid
aside. Think of any beginning that you please, you cannot
contain Him in time for at the beginning of the period of
which you are thinking He already 'was.' Gaze upon the
world; study what has been written about it. 'In the beginning
God made the heavens and the earth.'[27] What is created,
therefore, is made in the beginning and it is contained in
time because it is included in the beginning in order that it
might be made.[28] My illiterate and unlearned fisherman, however, is not subject to time; he is independent of the centuries; he has raised himself above every beginning, for that
which is 'was,' and it is not included in any time so that
it would have to begin, because He was rather than was
made 'in the beginning.'

(14)   Perhaps we shall discover that our fisherman has
deviated from the order of procedure that we have proposed.
He has liberated the Word from time and it belongs to itself
and lives for itself because it is free, solitary, and subject to
no one. Let us listen to the other words. He says: 'And the
Word was with God.'[29] He was already with God without a
beginning who was before a beginning. He who was therefore
is 'with God,' and He for whom a conceivable time is wanting is not wanting in a begetter. Our fisherman has escaped,
but perhaps he will become confused in other matters.

(15)   You will say: 'The Word is an utterance of a voice,
an announcement of what is to be done, a communication

---

26 John 1.1.
27 Cf. Gen. 1.1.
28 What *was made* in the beginning has its origin in time, not what *was*
in the beginning.
29 John 1.1.

of thoughts. This was with God and was in the beginning. The expression of the thought is eternal, since he who thinks is eternal.'[30] For the present I shall answer you in a few words in behalf of my fisherman, until we shall see how he defends his lack of culture. A word by its nature has the possibility of being, but the consequence of being uttered is that it shall not be; in fact, it is only when it is heard. And how was that 'in the beginning' which is not before time nor after time? I do not know whether it can even be in time itself, for the speakers' word is not heard before they speak and it will not be when they have spoken; but, when they conclude the very subject that they are discussing, that with which they began will no longer be.

These things are spoken by me as one of the ordinary people. But the fisherman speaks in his own defence after a different fashion. First of all, he will reprove you for your carelessness in listening to him. For, even if as an uneducated hearer you did not retain the first statement, 'In the beginning was the Word,' why do you complain of what follows: 'And the Word was with God?' Did you hear 'in God' (and not 'with God') in order to conceive it as the utterance of a concealed thought? That which was in the beginning is said to be not in another but with another. But, I make no claims from the preceding statements; let those that follow be their own defence. Bear in mind what the Word is and what it is called: 'And the Word was God.' There is an end to the utterance of a voice and the expression of a thought. This Word is a thing, not a sound; a nature, not a word; God, not a voice.

(16) Still, I tremble at saying it and the unusual language startles me. I to whom the Prophets have announced the one God hear: 'And the Word was God.' But, in order that my agitation may continue no longer, explain to me, my fisherman, the method for reconciling so exalted a mys-

---

30 This was the teaching of Ebion.

tery and lead all things back to the one God without
degrading them, without destroying them, without subjecting
them to time. He says: 'This was in the beginning with
God.' Since 'this was in the beginning,' it is not included in
time; since it is 'God,' it is not associated with a voice; since
it is 'with God,' no insult is offered and nothing is taken
away. Not only is it not annihilated into something else, but
we proclaim it as being with the one unbegotten God from
which it itself is the one only-begotten God.

(17)   O fisherman, we are still awaiting the full explanation of the Word from you. It was, it is true, in the beginning,
but it could possibly be that it was not before the beginning.
Here, also, I offer something to support my fisherman. Regarding that which was, it was impossible for it not to
have been, for that which 'was' is incompatible with a time
when it was not. What does he say in his own defence? 'All
things were made through Him.' If, therefore, there is nothing
without Him through whom all things began, He, also, is
in eternity through whom everything that is has been made.
Time is a fixed measure of extension that exists not in space
but in duration. Since everything is from Him, there is
nothing that is not from Him; therefore, time is from Him.

(18)   But, my fisherman, someone says to you: 'In this
instance you are too superficial and indiscriminate.' 'All things'
were made by Him does not have any limitation. There is
the unbegotten God who was made by no one, and He Himself has been born from the unbegotten. 'All things' admits
of no exception and allows nothing over and above that is
outside of itself. While we do not dare to say anything further,
or perhaps, while we are preparing our reply, you meet
them with: 'And without Him was made nothing that has
been made.' You have indicated the Author while you
acknowledged His companion. Since there is 'nothing without
Him,' I realize that He is not alone. There is one through

whom and another without whom. By these two expressions a distinction is drawn between the one who intervenes and the one who performs.

(19) I was worried about the Author who is the only unbegotten one, lest from the words 'all things' that you used nothing might be excluded. But, you have relieved my fears by declaring: 'And without Him was made nothing.' Still, I am embarrassed and troubled by the fact that 'without Him was made nothing.' Is there something made by someone else, therefore, but which was not made without Him? And if something was made by another, although not without Him, then all things were not made by Him, for it is one thing to have made something, it is another thing to have come to the help of the one making it. My fisherman, I have no opinion of my own that I can offer in this case as I did in the others. I must immediately reply in your own words: 'All things were made through Him.' I understand, for the Apostle has taught: 'Things visible and things invisible, whether Thrones, or Dominations, or Principalities, or Powers. All things through Him and unto Him.'[31]

(20) Since, therefore, 'All things were made through Him,' come to my help and describe what was not made without Him! 'What was made in Him is the life.'[32] Hence, what was made in Him was not made without Him, for that which was made in Him was also made through Him. All things were created through Him and in Him. But, they were created in Him because God the Creator was born. It also follows from this that nothing was made without Him that was made in Him, because the begotten God was the life, and He who was the life was not made the life after He was born, for in Him there is not one thing which was born

31 Cf. Col. 1.16.
32 Cf. John 1.4.

and another thing which He received when He was born. There is no intervening time between birth and growth.

None of those things which were made in Him was made without Him, because He is the life in whom they were made, and the God who was born from God appeared as God in His birth, not after He was born. He who is born is the living from the living, the true from the true, the perfect from the perfect, and He was not born helpless in His birth, that is to say, He did not become aware of His birth only later on, but recognized Himself as God by the very fact that He was born from God. This, the only begotten from the unbegotten; this: 'I and the Father are one';[33] this, the one God in the confession of the Father and the Son; this, the Father in the Son and the Son in the Father. Hence: 'He who sees me sees also the Father.'[34] Hence: 'All things that the Father has he has given to the Son.'[35] Hence: 'As the Father has life in himself, even so has he given to the Son to have life in himself.'[36] Hence: 'No one knows the Son except the Father; nor the Father except the Son.'[37] Hence: 'In him dwells all the fullness of the Godhead bodily.'[38]

(21)   This life is the light of men, this light which illuminates the darkness. And to offer us some consolation because, according to the Prophet, it is impossible to describe this birth, the fisherman adds: 'And the darkness grasped it not.'[39] Language has surrendered to the nature and has no means of escape; still, the fisherman, who rested on the Lord's bosom, acquired this knowledge. This is not the language of the world, because the subject which it discusses

---

33 John 10.30.
34 John 14.9.
35 John 16.15.
36 Cf. John 5.26.
37 Matt. 11.27.
38 Col. 2.9.
39 John 1.4.

is not of this world. If more can be found in the meaning of the words than that which has already been mentioned, let it be displayed; if there are any other names for the nature that we have explained, let them be produced. And if there are none, in truth because there are none, let us admire the doctrine of the fisherman and let us cling to and adore the confession of the Father and the Son, the unbegotten and the only-begotten, that cannot be expressed and that transcends the entire scope of our language and thought. According to the example of John, let us rest on the bosom of the Lord Jesus in order that we may be able to apprehend and to express these truths.

(22)   The authority of the Gospels, the teaching of the Apostles, as well as the useless duplicity of the vociferous heretics on all sides, are a recommendation for the integrity of this faith. This foundation stands firm and immovable against all the winds, rains, and torrents, and will not be overturned by the storms, or penetrated by the drops of rain, or washed away by the floods. And the best thing of all is that which has been attacked by so many can be demolished by no one. But, as certain kinds of medicine are so prepared that they are useful not only for specific ailments but to heal all of them together and are in themselves a powerful help for all of them, so in like manner the Catholic faith provides an efficacious remedy for everything, not only against individual maladies, but against every form of sickness. It is not weakened by their nature, nor overcome by their number, nor deceived by their variety, but it stands erect, one and the same against each one and all of them together. It is truly marvellous that this one contains as many antidotes as there are diseases, and just as many true doctrines as there are false speculations.

Let all the names of the heretics be drawn together, and

let all their followers step forward, and let them hear of the one unbegotten God the Father and the one only-begotten God the Son, the perfect offspring of the perfect Father, that He was not born as the result of a diminution, nor is He a part that has been cut off from the whole, nor brought into being by a derivation or emanation, but born from all things and in all things from Him who does not cease to be in all things in which He is. He is independent of time and not subject to the ages, for He could not be in those ages that He Himself has called into being. This is our Catholic and apostolic profession of faith which is based upon the Gospels.

(23) If he dares, let Sabellius proclaim the Father and the Son as one and the same, and that they who are designated as two are the very same person, so that, according to him, the two are one person and not one nature. He will at once hear from the Gospels, not once or twice, but frequently: 'This is my beloved Son in whom I am well pleased.'[40] He will hear: 'The Father is greater than I.'[41] He will hear: 'I go to the Father.'[42] He will hear: 'Father, I give thee thanks'[43] and 'Father, glorify me'[44] and 'Thou are the Son of the living God.'[45] Let Ebion creep near, who concedes the origin of the Son of God from Mary, and recognizes the Word from the day that He assumed our flesh. Let him read again: 'Father, glorify me with thyself, with the glory that I had with thee before the world existed,'[46] and: 'In the beginning was the Word, and the Word was with God; and the Word was God. . . . All things were made through him,'[47] and: 'He was in the world and the world was made

---

40 Matt. 17.5.
41 John 14.28.
42 John 14.12.
43 John 11.41.
44 John 17.5.
45 Matt. 16.17.
46 John 17.5.
47 John 1.1-3.

through him, and the world knew him not.'[48] Let the preachers of the new apostolate now arise, who come from Anti-Christ and who mock the Son of God by every kind of insult, and let them hear: 'I came forth from the Father,'[49] and 'The Son in the bosom of the Father,'[50] and 'I and the Father are one,'[51] and: 'I in the Father and the Father in me.'[52] Finally, let them in company with the Jews rage against Christ, who made Himself equal to God by declaring that God was His own Father, and together with them they will hear: 'Or believe my works, because the Father in me and I in the Father.'[53] This is, therefore, the one immovable foundation, this is the one blessed rock of faith which confessed through the mouth of Peter: 'Thou art Christ, the Son of the living God.'[54] This contains in itself arguments just as powerful in favor of the truth as those advanced by the sophistries of the heretical doctrines and the false accusations of infidelity.

(24) The will of the Father in the economy of the Redemption is now seen in other occurrences. The Virgin, the birth and the body, and later the cross, death, and hell are our salvation. The Son of God is born of the Virgin and the Holy Spirit[55] for the sake of the human race, and in this work He rendered service to Himself. And by His own power, namely, the overshadowing power of God, He planted the origin of His body and decreed the beginning of His

---

48 John 1.10.
49 John 16.28.
50 Cf. John 1.18.
51 John 10.30.
52 John 14.11.
53 John 14.20,12.
54 Matt. 16.17.
55 Here, as in other places in *De Trinitate* (e.g., 9.15; 10.22), St. Hilary applies the term Holy Spirit to the Second rather than to the Third Person of the Trinity in the work of the Incarnation. But in his *Tractatus mysteriorum* 1.1, the saint seems to refer explicitly to the work of the Holy Spirit, the Third Person of the Trinity, in enabling the Son of God to assume human flesh. Cf. Brisson *op. cit.* 73.

flesh in order that He might receive the nature of our flesh from the Virgin when He became man, and through this commingling and fellowship the body of the entire human race might be sanctified in Him,[56] in order that, as He willed that all should be included in Him through that which was corporeal, so He Himself would again pass over into all through the invisible part of Him. Accordingly, the image of the invisible God did not reject the shame of a human origin, and endured all the humiliations of our nature in His conception, birth, crying, and cradle.

(25) How shall we make a fitting recompense for so great a condescension? The one only-begotten God, born of God in an unutterable manner, is enclosed in the form of a tiny human body in the womb of the Virgin and grows in size. He who contains all things and in whom and through whom all things come into existence is brought forth according to the law of human birth, and He at whose voice the archangels tremble and the heavens, earth, and all the elements of this world dissolve is heard in the cries of infancy. He who is invisible and incomprehensible and is not to be judged according to sight, feeling, and touch is covered up in a cradle. If anyone consider these things unbefitting a God, then he will have to acknowledge that his indebtedness for such generosity is all the greater, the less suitable they are for the majesty of God. It was not necessary for Him through whom man was made to become man, but it was necessary for us that God become flesh and dwell among us, that is, to dwell within all flesh by the assumption of one flesh. His abasement is our glory. What He is, while appearing in the flesh, that we have in turn become: restored unto God from the flesh.

---

56 These words do not mean that the *Verbum* assumed human nature in all of us. From the context it is clear that St. Hilary is referring to the fact that the Son of God has glorified all mankind by selecting a specific human nature as His dwelling place.

(26)   But, lest the faint-hearted perhaps be scandalized at the cradle, the weeping, the birth, and the conception, each of these must be shown as suitable to the dignity of God, so that the display of power precedes the voluntary humiliation, and lowliness is not wanting in majesty. Let us, therefore, glance at the events attendant upon the conception. An angel speaks to Zachary; one who is sterile gives birth; the priest goes forth dumb from the place of incense; John, while still concealed in his mother's womb, begins to speak; the angel blesses Mary and promises that a virgin will be the Mother of the Son of God. She, conscious of her virginity, is puzzled about the manner in which this difficulty can be solved. The angel explains how this divine work will be accomplished, for he declares: 'The Holy Spirit shall come upon thee and the power of the Most High shall overshadow thee.'[57]

The Holy Spirit, coming from above, has sanctified the Virgin's womb and, breathing upon it (for the Spirit breathes where He wills), has become intermingled with our human flesh, and by His power and strength has assumed that which was alien to Him. And, in order that the weakness of the human body might not appear as something contradictory, the power of the Most High overshadowed the Virgin, and strengthened her weakness as if a shadow were cast about her, in order that the overshadowing of the divine power might prepare her bodily substance for the procreative activity of the Spirit who enters into her. This is the dignity of the conception.

(27)   Let us observe the honor that comes after the birth, the crying, and the cradle. The angel tells Joseph that the virgin is about to bring forth a child and that He who is to be born was to be called Emmanuel, that is, God with us. The Spirit proclaims it through the Prophet; the angel

57 Luke 1.35.

is a witness; He who is born is God with us. The new light
of a star in the sky appears to the Magi and a heavenly sign
follows the Lord of heaven. An angel makes known to the
shepherds the birth of Christ the Lord, the Salvation of
mankind. A multitude of the heavenly army comes together
to glorify the birth, and the praise bestowed upon so exalted
a work betrays the joy of the court of heaven. Then there
is announced the glory of God in heaven and peace on earth
to men of good will. The Magi now appear and adore the
child wrapped in swaddling-clothes and after the mysterious
offering of their vain science genuflect before the cradle. Thus
the Magi adore the lowliness of the crib, thus the divine
exultation of the angels pays honor to the weeping, thus
the Spirit through the Prophet foretells the birth, the angels
announce it, and the star with the new light is at its service.
In this manner the Holy Spirit coming from above and the
overshadowing power of the Most High arrange the begin-
ing of the birth. One thing is comprehended; another is seen;
one thing is observed by the eyes; another, by the soul. The
Virgin begets; the birth comes from God. The infant weeps;
the praise of the angel is heard. The swaddling-clothes are
humiliating; God is adored. Thus the majesty of omnipotence
is not lost when the lowliness of the flesh is assumed.

(28)   The remainder of His life follows a similar pattern.
During the whole period that He lived as man He performed
the deeds of God. There is no time to mention the particular
events. In all the miracles and cures of various kinds one
thing only must be kept in mind: in the assumption of His
flesh He appears as man, but in His deeds as God.

(29)   Concerning the Holy Spirit, we should neither be
silent nor should we speak. But we cannot remain silent because of those who do not know Him. It is not necessary,
however, to speak about Him in whom we must believe to-

gether with the Father and the Son who begot Him.[58]
Indeed, in my opinion there should not be any discussion
about whether He is. He is, since as a matter of fact He is
given, accepted, and obtained, and He, whom in our profession we must join with the Father and the Son, cannot be
separated in such a profession from the Father and the Son.

To us, the whole is imperfect if something is missing from
it.[59] If anyone will seek for an understanding of the manner
in which we arrive at this knowledge, the two of us will read
in the Apostle: 'And because you are sons, God has sent
the Spirit of his Son into our hearts, crying, Abba, Father';[60]
and again: 'Do not grieve the Holy Spirit of God in whom
you are sealed';[61] and again: 'Now we have not received
the spirit of the world but the spirit that is from God that
we may know the things that have been given to us by
God';[62] and again: 'You, however, are not carnal but
spiritual, if indeed the Spirit of God dwells in you. But if
anyone does not have the Spirit of Christ, he does not belong
to him';[63] and again: 'But if the Spirit of him who raised
Jesus from the dead dwells in you, then he who raised Christ
from the dead will also bring to life your mortal bodies because of his Spirit who dwells in you.'[64] Therefore, because
He is, He is given and possessed and belongs to God. Let the
words of the calumniators cease! When they say through
whom is He, or what is His purpose, or what kind of a nature
does He have, and our answer displeases them when we say

---

58 St. Thomas Aquinas, *S. T.* III, Q. 36, art. 4, thus explains these
words of St. Hilary: 'we can say that the Father and the Son are two
[Persons] spirating by reason of the plurality of subjects, but not two
spirators by reason of the one spiration.'
59 Since we must join the Holy Spirit to the Father and the Son, and
since the whole is imperfect if something is missing from it, the Holy
Spirit is equally God with the Father and the Son.
60 Gal. 4.6.
61 Eph. 4.30.
62 1 Cor. 2.12.
63 Rom. 8.9.
64 Rom. 8.11.

that He is the one through whom are all things, and from whom are all things, that He is the Spirit of God, the Gift given to the faithful, then the Apostles and the Prophets, who only say of Him that He is, will also offend them, and, moreover, the Father and the Son will also arouse their indignation.

(30) I believe, indeed, that certain people remain in ignorance and doubt because they see this third one, that is, the one called the Holy Spirit, often referred to as the Father and the Son. In this there is nothing contradictory, since, whether we speak of the Father or the Son, each is a spirit and each is holy.

(31) In regard to what we read in the Gospels: 'Because God is Spirit,'[65] we must carefully examine in what manner and for what reason they were uttered. There is a motive for every statement that is made and we shall grasp its meaning when we understand the purpose for which the words were spoken, in order that, because the Lord replied 'God is Spirit,' there may not be a denial of the use and the gift together with the name of the Holy Spirit. The Lord spoke to the Samaritan woman because the redemption of all had come. After a long discourse about the living water, her five husbands and the present one who was not her husband, the woman replied: 'Sir, I see that thou art a prophet. Our fathers worshiped on this mountain, but you say that at Jerusalem is the place where one ought to worship.' The Lord answered: 'Woman, believe me, the hour is coming when neither on this mountain nor in Jerusalem will you worship the Father. You worship what you do not know; we worship what we know, for salvation is from the Jews. But the hour is coming, and is now here, when the true worshipers will worship the Father in spirit and in truth. For the Father also seeks such to worship him. God is Spirit, and

---

65 John 4.24.

they who worship him must worship in spirit and in truth because God is Spirit.'[66]

The woman, therefore, mindful of the traditions of her ancestors, believed that God must be adored as Samaria did on the mountain or as Jerusalem did in the Temple, because Samaria, in violation of the Law, had chosen a mountain to worship God, but the Jews had chosen the Temple built by Solomon as the site for worshiping God. Both in their presumption restricted the God, within whom are all things and outside of whom there is nothing capable of containing Him, to the crest of a hill or to the hollow vault of a building. Accordingly, since God is invisible, incomprehensible, and boundless, the Lord said that the time had come when God should not be adored on the mountain or in the Temple, because 'God is Spirit,' and a spirit is neither circumscribed or held fast that is everywhere by the power of its nature, is not absent from any place, and exists in every place in all its fullness. Hence, they are the true worshipers who will adore in the Spirit and in truth.

For those, however, who will adore God the Spirit in the Spirit, the one is to render assistance, the other is to be worshiped, because a distinction is made in the worship that each one receives.[67] Because it was said 'God is Spirit,' the name and the gift of the Holy Spirit are not taken away. The reply was addressed to the woman who confined God to a temple and a mountain, that all things are in God and God in Himself, and He who is invisible and incomprehensible must be adored in that which is invisible and incomprehensible. Thus, the nature of the gift and the adoration were

---

66 John 4.19-24.
67 These words seem to indicate that the Holy Spirit, who 'is to render assistance' is inferior to God who is to be worshiped, but, since St. Hilary had already indicated the equality of the three divine Persons, this means that the Holy Spirit is inferior to God the Father in the sense that He proceeds from Him.

indicated when He taught that God the Spirit must be adored in the Spirit, while He shows both the liberty and knowledge of the adorers as well as the infinity of the one to be adored, since God the Spirit is adored in the Spirit.

(32) There is also a similarity between this text and those words of the Apostle: 'Because the Lord is the spirit; but where the Spirit of the Lord is, there is freedom.'[68] He drew this distinction in order to emphasize the idea of Him who is, from Him of whom He is. To possess and to be possessed is not the same thing, nor do the words 'who is' and 'of whom He is' have the same meaning. Thus, when he says: 'The Lord is the spirit,' he reveals the nature of His infinity; when he adds: 'where the Spirit of the Lord is, there is freedom,' he indicates Him from whom He is, because the Lord is also the Spirit and where the Spirit of the Lord is there is freedom. We have mentioned these things not because the case requires it, but that there might not be any obscurity about them. There is one Holy Spirit everywhere who enlightens all the Patriarchs, the Prophets, and the entire assembly of the Law, who inspired John even in his mother's womb, and was then given to the Apostles and to the other believers that they might understand the truth that had been bestowed upon them.

(33) But, let us now hear from the Lord's own words the service that He renders to us. He says: 'Many things yet I have to say to you, but you cannot bear them now.'[69] 'It is expedient for you that I depart. If I do go I shall send the Advocate to you.'[70] And again: 'And I will ask the Father and he will send you another Advocate to dwell with you forever, the Spirit of truth.'[71] 'He will direct you in all the truth. He will not speak on his own authority, but what-

---

68 Cf. 2 Cor. 3.17.
69 John 16.12.
70 Cf. John 16.7.
71 Cf. John 14.16,17.

ever he will hear he will speak, and the things that are to come he will declare to you. He will glorify me, because he will receive of what is mine.'[72] These words, which we have borrowed from many places, were spoken to prepare the road for our understanding, and in them are included the will of the donor, as well as the character of and the requisites for the gift, in order that the gift of the Holy Spirit, which is, as it were, the pledge of His assistance, might throw light upon the difficult article of our faith, the Incarnation of God, since our human weakness cannot comprehend the Father and the Son.

(34)   It is logical that we should now hear the Apostle as he also explains the power and function of the gift, for he says: 'For as many as are led by the Spirit of God, they are the sons of God. Now you have not received again a spirit of bondage so as to be again in fear, but you have received a spirit of adoption, by virtue of which we cry, Abba! Father!'[73] And again: 'Because no one speaking in the Spirit of God says "Anathema" to Jesus. And no one can say "Lord Jesus" except in the Holy Spirit.'[74] And again: 'Now there are varieties of gifts, but the same Spirit; and there are varieties of ministries, but the same Lord; and there are varieties of workings, but the same God, who works all things in all. Now the manifestation of the Spirit is given to everyone for profit. To one through the Spirit is given the utterance of wisdom; and to another the utterance of knowledge, according to the same Spirit; to another faith, in the same Spirit; to another the gift of healing in the one Spirit; to another the working of miracles; to another prophecy; to another the distinguishing of spirits; to another various kinds of tongues; to another the interpretation of tongues. All these things are the work of one and the same

---

72 Cf. John 16.13,14.
73 Cf. Rom. 8.14.
74 1 Cor. 12.3.

Spirit.'[75] Hence, we have the cause of this gift, we have its effect, and I do not know why there is any ambiguity about it, since its cause, its manner of acting, and its power are clearly determined.

(35) Let us, therefore, make use of such generous gifts, and, above all, let us strive to exercise this necessary gift. As we have already pointed out, the Apostle declares: 'Now we have received not the spirit of this world but the spirit that is from God, that we may know the things that have been given us by God.'[76] Hence, this is received for the sake of knowledge. Just as a faculty of the human body will be idle when the causes that stir it to activity are not present, as the eyes will not perform their functions except through the light or the brightness of day, as the ears will not comprehend their task when no voice or sound is heard, as the nostrils will not be aware of their office if no odor is detected, not that the faculty will be lost because the cause is absent but the employment of the faculty comes from the cause, even so the soul of man, if it has not breathed in the gift of the Spirit through faith, will, it is true, possess the faculty for understanding, but it will not have the light of knowledge.

The one gift, which is in Christ, is available to everyone in its entirety, and what is present in every place is given in so far as we desire to receive it, and will remain with us in so far as we desire to merit it. This is with us even to the consummation of the world; this is the consolation of our expectation; this, through the efficacy of the gifts, is the pledge of our future hope; this is the light of the mind, the splendor of the soul. For this reason we must pray for this Holy Spirit; we must strive to merit Him and to retain possession of Him by our belief in and observance of the commandments.

---

75 1 Cor. 12.4-11.
76 Cf. 1 Cor. 2.12.

BOOK THREE

ANY PEOPLE FIND THE Lord's words obscure when He says: 'I in the Father and the Father in Me,'[1] and there is nothing blameworthy in this, for man's natural power of reasoning does not grasp the meaning of this statement. It does not seem possible that the very thing which is in another is at the same time outside of it, and, since those things which we are discussing cannot exist apart from themselves, and, if they are to preserve the number and position in which they are, it seems that they cannot mutually contain each other, so that he who contains something else within himself and remains in this position and always remains outside of it can likewise be always present within him whom he contains within himself.

Human knowledge will certainly never grasp these truths and a comparison drawn from human things does not afford any similarity to divine things, but what man cannot conceive is possible to God. In thus expressing myself on this subject I have not meant that, because God has spoken these words, His authority alone suffices to apprehend them. We should examine[2] and seek to realize the significance of this declaration: 'I in the Father and the Father in Me,' provided we

---

1 John 14.11.
2 Throughout *De Trinitate* St. Hilary first expresses his absolute confidence in God, who can neither deceive nor be deceived, and then examines the words of God in the light of human reason.

shall grasp it such as it really is, in order that what is regarded
as incompatible with the nature of things will be obtained by
the wisdom of the divine truth.

(2)   And that we may penetrate more easily into the
knowledge of this most difficult question we must first understand the Father and the Son according to the teaching of the
divine Scriptures, in order that, when we have learned to
know them and have become familiar with them, our words
may become clearer. As we explained in the preceding Book,
the eternity of God transcends places, times, appearances,
and whatever can be conceived by the human mind. He is
outside of all things and within all things; He comprises all
things and is comprised by none; He does not change either
by increase or decrease, but is invisible, incomprehensible,
complete, perfect, and eternal; He does not know anything
from elsewhere, but He Himself is sufficient unto Himself
to remain what He is.

(3)   This unbegotten One, therefore, brought forth the
Son from Himself before all time, not from any pre-existing
matter, because all things are through the Son; nor from
nothing, because the Son is from Him; nor as an ordinary
birth, because there is nothing changeable or empty in God;
nor as a part that is divided, cut off, or extended, because
God is incapable of suffering and is incorporeal and these
things are characteristic of suffering and the flesh, and according to the Apostle: 'In Christ dwells all the fullness of
the Godhead bodily.'[3]

But in an inconceivable and ineffable manner, before all
time and ages, He gave birth to the only-begotten God from
that which in Him was unbegotten, and through His charity
and power He bestowed upon His birth everything that God
is, and thus from the unbegotten, perfect, and eternal Father
there is the only-begotten, perfect, and eternal Son. But

3 Col. 2.9.

that which belongs to Him because of the body that He assumed results from the eagerness of His good will for our salvation. For, since He as one born from God is invisible, incorporeal, and inconceivable, He has taken upon Himself as much matter and abasement as we possessed the power to understand, perceive, and comprehend, adapting Himself to our weakness rather than abandoning those things which belonged to His own nature.

(4) He is, therefore, the perfect Son of the perfect Father, the only-begotten offspring of the unbegotten God, who has received everything from Him who possesses everything. He is God from God, Spirit from Spirit, Light from Light, and He proclaims with assurance: 'I in the Father and the Father in Me.' As the Father is Spirit, so the Son also is Spirit; as the Father is God, so the Son also is God; as the Father is Light so the Son also is Light. From those things, therefore, which are in the Father are also those things which are in the Son, that is, from the whole Father the whole Son is born; He is not from anywhere else, because nothing was before the Son; He is not from nothingness, because the Son is from God; He is not a God in part only, because the fullness of the Godhead is in the Son, not in some things because He is in all things, but as He willed who could, as He knows who begot Him.[4]

Whatever is in the Father is also in the Son; whatever is in the unbegotten is also in the only-begotten, one from the other and both are one substance, not one person, but one is in the other because there is nothing different in either of them. The Father is in the Son because the Son is from Him; the Son in the Father because He is not a Son from anywhere else; the only-begotten is in the unbegotten because the only-begotten is from the unbegotten. Thus, they

---

4 These words mean that the Father was not forced to bring about the Incarnation of the Son, as the Arians claimed.

are mutually in each other, because as all things are perfect in the Father, so all things are perfect in the Son. This is the unity in the Father and the Son, this the power, this the charity, this the hope, this the faith, this the truth, the way, and the life, not to spread false reports about God concerning His attributes, nor to disparage the Son because of the mystery and power of His birth, not to place anything on an equality with the unbegotten Father, nor to separate the only-begotten from Him in time or power, but to acknowledge Him as the Son of God because He is from God.

(5) There are powers in God of such a nature that, even when the manner in which they are done is incomprehensible to the human mind, our faith does not make any objections because of the evidence of what was done. We shall find this to be true not only in spiritual matters but in material matters as well, where something is shown not to give us an example of the birth but to arouse our admiration for a deed that can be perceived.

On the wedding day in Galilee, wine was made from water. Will our language and power of reasoning be able to ascertain how this nature was changed so that the insipidity of water disappeared and the taste of wine originated? This was not a mixture but a creation, and a creation which did not begin from itself but emerged from one thing into another. That which was weaker was not the result of the pouring out of something stronger, but that which was comes to an end, and that which was not comes into being. The bridegroom is sad, the family is embarrassed, the celebration of the wedding banquet is endangered. Jesus is requested to help; He does not rise or come nearer, but while at rest completes the work. Water is poured into the vessels, wine is drawn out from the cups. The knowledge of the one who pours does not agree with that perceived by the one who draws. Those who pour imagine that water is being drawn,

and those who draw believe that wine was poured. The
time which intervenes is not sufficient for a liquid nature to
arise and disappear. The manner in which this came about
baffles the sight and the understanding, but the power of God
is realized in what was done.

(6) In regard to the five loaves, we also admire a
similar deed. By this increase the hunger of 5,000 men and
innumerable women and children is satisfied. The insight
into this miracle eludes the eyes of our mind. Five loaves
were offered and broken, and what I may call created fragments slip from the hands of those who are breaking them.
It does not become smaller when it is broken; nevertheless,
the hand of the one who is breaking it is always filled with
pieces. The movements deceive your sight. While you are
watching one hand filled with pieces of bread, you see an
unbroken portion in the other hand. Meanwhile, the number
of pieces is increasing. Those who break the bread are serv-
ing, while those who eat it are occupied. The hungry are
filled; the remains fill twelve baskets. Neither the mind nor
the sight can follow the progress of so conspicuous an operation. There is what was not; something is seen which is not
understood. It only remains for us to believe that all things
are possible to God.

(7) There is no cajolery, therefore, in divine things,
nor does God make any pretence at pleasing or deceiving us.
These miracles of the Son of God were not performed
from any motive of ostentation, for He whom the countless
thousands and thousands of angels serve has not flattered
man. What possessions of ours does He require through whom
we have received everything that belongs to us? Does He seek
our congratulations, we who are now in a stupor from
sleep, now weary after the night's revelry, now with a guilty
conscience after the quarrels and bloodshed of the day, now
inebriated after the banquets, whom the Archangels, the

Dominations, the Principalities and the Powers of heaven, without sleep, without interruption, without guilt praise in their eternal and untiring voices? They acclaim Him because He, the invisible image of God, has created all of them in Himself, has made the generations, has strengthened the heavens, has formed the abyss, and then, when He Himself was born as man, He conquered death, broke the gates of hell, gained the people as co-heirs with Himself, and brought our flesh from corruption into eternal glory. He was not lacking, therefore, in anything that we could offer so that these ineffable and inconceivable miracles should pay honor to Him in our midst as if He were in need of praise. Since God foresaw the aberrations of human iniquity and folly, and since He knew that infidelity would even go so far as to claim for itself the judgment over divine things, He has triumphed over our rashness by the examples of those things which would not be called into question.

(8) There are many wise people of the world whose wisdom is folly before God, who, when they hear that God was born from God, the true from the true, the perfect from the perfect, the one from the one, contradict us as if we were teaching something that is impossible. They cling to certain conclusions from their own reasoning when they argue thus: 'Nothing could be born from one, because every birth comes from two. Now, if the Son is born from one, He received a a part of Him who begot Him, and, if a part, then neither is perfect, for something is missing from Him from whom He went forth, nor will there be any fullness in Him who is composed of a part. Therefore, neither is perfect, since He who begot loses His fullness and He who is born does not obtain it.'

God, foreseeing this wisdom of the world, thus condemns it through His Prophet, when He declares: 'I will destroy the wisdom of the wise and will reject the understanding of their prudent men.'[5] He says the same thing through His Apostle: 'Where is the "wise man?" Where is the scribe? Where is the disputant of this world? Did not God make foolish the "wisdom" of this world? Since, in God's wisdom, the world did not come to know God by "wisdom," it pleased God, by the foolishness of our preaching, to save those who believe. The Jews ask for signs, and the Greeks look for "wisdom"; but we, for our part, preach a crucified Christ— to the Jews indeed a stumbling-block and to the Gentiles foolishness, but to those who are called, both Jews and Greeks, Christ, the power of God and the wisdom of God. The foolishness of God is wiser than men, and the weakness of God is stronger than men.'[6]

(9) Since the Son of God, therefore, had charge of the human race, He became man first of all in order that He might be believed, in order that as one of ourselves He might be a witness for us concerning the things of God, and in the weakness of our human flesh might proclaim God as His Father to us frail and carnal mortals, while at the same time He fulfills the will of God the Father, as He declares: 'For I have come down from heaven not to do my own will, but the will of him who sent me,'[7] not that He does not also will what He does, but He manifests His obedience in carrying out the will of His Father, while He Himself wills to fulfill the will of His Father. Similarly, it was this will of fulfilling to which He bears testimony in the words: 'Father, the hour has come! Glorify thy Son, that thy Son may glorify thee, even as thou hast given him power over all flesh, in order that to all thou hast given him he may give everlasting life. Now this is everlasting life, that they may know thee, the only true God, and him whom thou hast sent, Jesus Christ.

---

5 Isa. 29.14.
6 Cf. 1 Cor. 1.20-25.
7 John 6.38.

I have glorified thee on earth, since I have accomplished the work that thou hast given me to do. And now do thou, Father, glorify me with thyself, with the glory that I had with thee before the world existed. I have manifested thy name to the men whom thou hast given me.'[8] In these brief and few words He has explained the whole task entrusted to Him and the plan of salvation; nevertheless He has guarded the true nature of the faith against every prompting of diabolical deceit. Let us run hurriedly through the meaning of each phrase in this statement.

(10)   He says: 'Father, the hour has come! Glorify thy Son, that thy Son may glorify thee.' He does not say the day or the time, but the hour has come. An hour is a portion of the day. And what will this hour be? That one, namely, to which He referred when He consoled His disciples at the time of His Passion: 'Behold, the hour has come for the Son of man to be glorified.'[9] Hence, this is the hour wherein He prays that He may be glorified by the Father as He Himself glorifies the Father. What does this mean? Does He await His own glorification who is about to give glory and to render honor, and will He be in need of what He will in turn bestow? Let the sophists of the world and the wise men of Greece come together and inveigle the truth by their syllogisms! Let them ask how, whence, and why this comes about, and while they hesitate let them hear: 'Because the foolish things of the world has God chosen.' Therefore, by our folly we understand these things that are incomprehensible to the wise ones of the world. The Lord has said: 'Father, the hour has come.' He revealed the hour of the Passion, for He was speaking about it at that moment, and then added: 'Glorify thy Son.' But how was the Son to be glorified? For, He was born of the Virgin and has come from the cradle

---

8 John 17.1-6.
9 John 12.23.

and infancy to perfect manhood. He has lived as man by sleep, hunger, thirst, weariness, tears, and even now was to be spit upon, to be scourged, and crucified. And why? These things were to vindicate only the manhood of Christ.

We do not experience the shame of the cross, we are not condemned beforehand by the scourges, we are not defiled by the spittle. The Father glorifies the Son. How? He is finally nailed to the cross. Then what follows? The sun does not set, but hides itself. Why do I say hides itself? It was not taken into a cloud, but failed to complete its ordinary course, and together with the other elements of the world shared in the experience of His death. In order that none of the heavenly works might be present at this crime, they escaped from the necessity of such co-operation by what may be called their self-extinction. What did the earth do? It trembled at the burden of the Lord hanging on a tree, and testified that it would not receive within itself the one who was about to die. Do not the rocks and the stones also refuse to take part? But they break asunder, fall apart, and lose their nature, and acknowledge that the tomb, hewn out of stone, cannot contain the body that is to be buried in it.

(11) What happens after these incidents? The centurion in charge of the cohort and the guardian of the cross cries out: 'Truly he was the Son of God.'[10] The creature is liberated by the mediation of this atonement; the rocks do not retain their firmness and strength. Those who had nailed Him to the cross avow that He is truly the Son of God. The result agrees with His assertion. The Lord had said: 'Glorify thy Son.' He testified that He is the Son not only in name but also in the true meaning of the word, wherefore it is said 'thy.' Many of us are the sons of God, but not such as this Son. He is the true and the proper Son, by origin, not by adoption; in truth, not in name; by birth, not by creation.

10 Matt. 27.54.

Accordingly, after His glorification, the confession of the true nature followed. The centurion acknowledged Him as the Son of God in order that none of the believers might doubt what a man from among the persecutors had not denied.

(12)   Perhaps we believe that the Son requires the glorification for which He prayed, and will be deemed weak while awaiting His glorification from one who is stronger. And who will not admit that the Father is superior as the one unbegotten to the one begotten, as the father to the son, as the one who sends to the one who is sent, as the one who wills to the one who obeys? He Himself is a witness for us: 'The Father is greater than I.'[11] These things are to be understood in the manner that they are, but we must be on our guard lest the honor paid to the Father weaken the glory that it due to the Son. Nor is this glorification itself which He requests compatible with weakness, for the words 'Father, glorify thy Son' are also followed by 'that thy Son may glorify thee.' The Son is certainly not weak who, although He must receive glory, shall in His turn confer glory. If He is not weak, for what reason does he offer such a prayer? No one asks except for something that he needs. Or is the Father also weak? Or has He been so lavish in squandering His possessions that the Son must render glory to Him? But this one was not in want of it, and that one does not have any need of it, yet each will bestow glory upon the other. Therefore, the petition for the glory that is to be mutually given and returned does not take away anything from the Father nor does it weaken the Son, but it reveals the same power of the divinity in both of them since the Son prays that He be

---

11 John 14.28. Modern interpreters refer these words to the superiority of the Father over Christ as the God-Man. But St. Hilary, in common with other early Fathers of the Church, applied them to the superiority of the divine nature of the Father over that of the Son. This superiority proceeds not from any inequality of nature, but from their respective origins. The Father is unborn, while the Son is born from the Father.

glorified by the Father and the Father does not disdain the glorification by the Son. These things show rather the unity of the Godhead in the Father and the Son by the glory which they give and receive in turn.

(13) We must now study the nature of this glorification and whence it comes. I believe that God is unchangeable and that neither defect or improvement nor gain or loss affect His eternity, but what He is He always is, for this is peculiar to God. That which always is will never have anything in its nature that is compatible with non-being. How, therefore, will He be glorified, since His nature has all that it needs and no decline has set in within Him so that He may not receive anything in Himself nor take back anything that He has lost? We are embarrassed and we hesitate. The Evangelist does not leave the weakness of our understanding in a quandary, for he shows the glory that the Son will render to the Father when he says: 'Even as thou hast given him power over all flesh, in order that to all thou hast given him he may give everlasting life. Now this is everlasting life, that they may know thee, the only true God, and him whom thou hast sent, Jesus Christ.'[12]

The glory which the Father receives from the Son consists in this, that He must be perceived by us. The glory was this, that the Son, who had become incarnate, received power from Him over all flesh because He would bestow eternal life upon those who had fallen from grace, who were corporeal, and who were subject to death. Eternal life for us was not the result of an act but of a power, since the glory of eternity is acquired not by a new atonement but by the recognition of God alone. Therefore, the glory of God is not increased, for He has not suffered a loss so that there should be an increase. Through the Son, He is glorified in the midst of us, who are ignorant, fugitives, sinners, hopelessly dead, and sur-

---

12 John 17.2,3.

rounded by lawless darkness. And He is glorified by this, that
the Son has received from Him the power over all flesh to
which He will give everlasting life. Hence, these words of the
Son glorify the Father. As a consequence, when the Son
received everything, He was glorified by the Father; on the
other hand, the Father is glorified when all things are done
through the Son. The glory that has been received is returned
in such a manner that whatever glory the Son possesses belongs completely to the glory of the Father, because He has
received everything from the Father. The honor paid to the
servant tends to the honor of Him who sent him, as the
honor of the begetter redounds to the honor of the begotten.

(14) Finally, he tells us in what eternal life consists:
'that they may know thee, the only true God and him whom
thou hast sent, Jesus Christ.' What difficult questions arise
here and what is the nature of the contradiction in terms?
It is life to know the true God, but this in itself does not
obtain life. What is, therefore, connected with it? 'And him
whom thou hast sent, Jesus Christ.' The Son renders the
honor that is due to the Father when He says: 'thee, the
only true God.' The Son, however, does not disassociate
Himself from the true nature of God, since He adds: 'And
him whom thou hast sent, Jesus Christ.' The faithful in their
profession of faith make no discrimination, since the hope
of obtaining life rests upon both of them, nor is the true God
wanting to Him who is immediately joined to Him. Accordingly, when it is stated: 'that they may know thee, the only
true God and him whom thou hast sent, Jesus Christ,' by
this designation, that is, of the sender and the one sent, the
true nature and divinity of the Father and the Son is not
differentiated by any kind of a distinction, either in name or
in time,[13] but our God-fearing faith is taught to acknowledge the begetter and the begotten.

---

13 The name of the one sent is immediately connected with that of the
one who sent him. Hence, the Father and Son are not separated in
time.

(15)   Therefore, the Son clearly glorifies the Father in that which follows: 'I have glorified thee on earth, since I have accomplished the work that thou hast given me to do.'[14] The praise of the Father comes entirely from the Son, because those things for which the Son will be acclaimed will be a commendation of the Father. He fulfills everything that the Father has willed. The Son of God is born as man, but the power of God is manifested at His birth from the Virgin. The Son of God is seen as man, but appears as God in the works of man. The Son of God is nailed to the cross, but on the cross God overcomes the death of man. Christ, the Son of God, dies, but all flesh is vivified in Christ. The Son of God goes to limbo, and man is brought back to heaven. The more such things are praised in Christ, the greater will be the approbation of Him from whom Christ as God derives His origin. By such means as these, therefore, does the Father glorify the Son on earth, and, again, the Son by the miracles of His power gives glory to Him from whom He comes in the sight of the ignorant pagans and the foolish world. And this interchange of glory is certainly not concerned with an increase in the divine nature, but with the honor that He received from those who did not know Him. Of what did not the Father possess an abundance, He from whom everything comes? Or what was wanting to the Son in whom, as it pleased Him, all the fullness of the Godhead dwelt? Consequently, the Father is glorified on earth because the work which He commanded is accomplished.

(16)   Let us see the glory that the Son expects from the Father and this discussion is concluded. In the sentences that follow it is stated: 'I have glorified thee on earth, since I have accomplished the work that thou hast given me to do. And now do thou, Father, glorify me with thyself, with the glory that I had with thee before the world existed. I have

---

14 Cf. John 17.4.

manifested thy name to the men whom thou hast given me.'[15] Therefore, the Father has been glorified by the miracles of the Son when He is recognized as God, when He is revealed as the Father of the only-begotten, when for our salvation He even willed that His Son be born as man from the Virgin, and in Him all those things, which began with the birth from the Virgin, are accomplished in the Passion. Consequently, because the Son of God, perfect in every part that He possesses, and born before all time with the fullness of the Godhead, and, now become man according to the origin of His flesh, was approaching His consummation in death, He prays that He may be glorified with God as He was glorifying Him on earth, for at that time the powers of God were being glorified in the flesh before a world that did not know Him.

Now, what is the nature of the glory that He expects with the Father? It is that, of course, which He had with Him before the world was made. He had the fullness of the Godhead and still has it, for He is the Son of God. He who was the Son of God also began to be the Son of man, for the Word was made flesh. He did not lose what He was, but began to be what He was not. He did not cease to possess His own nature, but received what was ours. He prays that what He had assumed might derive profit from that glory of His which He had never lost. Therefore, since the Son is the Word and the Word was made flesh, and the Word was God and this was in the beginning with God, and the Word was the Son before the foundation of the world, the Son now made flesh prayed that the flesh might begin to be to the Father what the Word was, in order that what belonged in time might receive the splendor of His glory which is timeless, in order that when the corruption of the flesh was transformed it might be assimilated into the power of God and the incorruptibility of the Spirit. Hence, this is the prayer of

---

15 John 17.5.

God, this the profession of the Son to the Father, this the petition of the flesh in which all will see Him on the day of judgment and which they will recognize from the wounds and the cross, in which He was prefigured on the mount, in which He ascended into heaven, in which He sits at the right hand of God, in which He was seen by Paul, in which He was honored by Stephen.

(17) Accordingly, after the name of the Father has been made known, he asks these questions: But under what name? Was the name of God ignored? Moses heard it from the bush; Genesis proclaimed it at the beginning of the creation of the world; the Law explained this; the Prophets made it known; men perceived it in these works of the world; even the pagans by their lies venerated it. The name of God, therefore, was not unknown. Yet, it was completely unknown. No one knows God unless he confesses the Father as also the Father of the only-begotten Son, and the Son originating not as a part, or an extension, or an emanation, but born from Him in an ineffable and inconceivable manner, as this Son from a Father who possesses the fullness of the Godhead from which and in which He was born, as the true, infinite, and perfect God, for this is the fullness of God. If any of these things is wanting, there will not be the fullness which, according to His pleasure, should dwell in Him. This is proclaimed by the Son, this is revealed to the ignorant. Thus, the Father is glorified by the Son when the Father of the Son is recognized as such.

(18) The Son of God, wishing to strengthen our faith in His birth, placed before us the example of His miracles, in order that by the indescribable manner in which His unutterable deeds were performed we would be taught about the power of the inconceivable birth, when water is made wine, and when five loaves of bread satisfy 5,000 men, not including others of the opposite sex and of a different age

group, and fill twelve baskets with the fragments. The incident is seen and is unknown; it is done and it is not understood; the manner is not apprehended and the result is evident. It is foolish to raise an unwarranted objection in an inquiry when the subject under investigation cannot by its very nature be comprehended. For, as the Father is inexplicable by the fact that He is unborn, so the Son cannot be described because He is the only-begotten, since He who is born is the image of the unborn. When we conceive an image in our mind and words, we must also include in it the one of whom He is the image. But we are pursuing invisible things, and we are venturing upon incomprehensible things, we whose understanding is restricted to visible and material objects. We do not blush at our folly, we do not plead guilty to impiety, when we criticize the mysteries of God and the powers of God. We make inquiries about how He is the Son, whence He is the Son, or whether He has been born with any loss to the Father or from any portion of the Father. The evidence you have had in His works should have caused you to believe that God can do things, although you cannot understand His manner of doing them.

(19)   You seek to know how Christ was born according to the Spirit and I ask you about material things. I do not inquire how He was born of the Virgin, but whether her flesh, begetting a perfect flesh from herself, suffered any loss in herself. Indeed, she did not receive that which she bore and her flesh brought forth flesh without any blemish from the ordinary process of birth, and she brought forth from herself Him who was perfect, although her own integrity was not impaired.[16] And it would doubtless be proper to hold

---

16 The saint here takes for granted the perfect virginity of Mary. He argues from it that, just as she brought forth her son without any loss of her integrity, so Christ was born without any loss to the nature of His Father.

that a thing is not impossible with God that is done by His power in a human creature.

(20)   But I ask you, whoever you are, as an investigator of incomprehensible things and an eminent judge of the divine secrets and power, to give at least an explanation of the following fact to an unlearned person like myself who only believes all the things about God as God has revealed them. I hear the Lord, and because I put my trust in those things that are written, I know that after His resurrection He often allowed Himself to be seen in the body by many who did not believe in Him, to Thomas certainly who would not be convinced except by touching His wounds, as he declares: 'Unless I see in his hands the print of the nails, and put my finger into the place of the nails, and put my hand into his side, I will not believe.'[17]

The Lord adapts Himself to all the weaknesses of our understanding and, to put an end to the doubt of the unbelieving, He performs a mystery of His invisible power. O examiner of heavenly things, whoever you are, describe for me the manner in which this was done. The Apostles were behind closed doors and had secretly come together after the Lord's Passion. The Lord appears before Thomas in order to strengthen his faith by fulfilling the proposed conditions. He granted him permission to feel His flesh and to touch His wounds. Unquestionably, He whose wounds were to be recognized must have offered a body that was pierced. I want to find out, therefore, through what parts of the closed doors did He enter with his bodily form. The Evangelist particularly emphasized this when he said: 'Jesus came, the doors being closed, and stood in their midst.'[18] Did he force himself through the structure of the walls and the solid woodwork and slip through the material which by its nature is impene-

---

17 John 20.25.
18 John 20.26.

trable? He stood before them with a real body, not an apparent one or a deceitful imitation. Let the eyes of your soul follow the admission of Him who passes through, and let your intellectual vision enter the closed room with Him. Everything is locked and bolted, but He stands in their midst, He who by His power can penetrate all things. You find fault with invisible things and I demand an explanation for those that are visible. The solid mass does not give way, nor is it in accordance with the natural quality of wood and stone to admit anything as if it were falling apart in an imperceptible manner. The body of the Lord does not depart from Him that He may assume it again from nothing, and whence does He come into their midst who is present before them? In such questions our reason and language are powerless and the true nature of the fact is beyond human comprehension.

Consequently, if we are guilty of misrepresentation in regard to the birth, we lie likewise about the entrance of the Lord. Let us grant that the deed was not done, because we do not apprehend how it was done, and that, since our understanding of it has reached its limit, the effects resulting from the deed have reached their limit. Our certainty about the deed has triumphed over our untruthfulness. The Lord stood in the closed house before His disciples, and the Son is born from the Father. Do not deny that He stood there because by the weakness of your intelligence you do not grasp the manner in which the one standing there made His entry. Do not remain in ignorance of the fact that from the unbegotten and perfect God the only-begotten and perfect Son was born because the power of the birth transcends the concepts and the language of our human nature.

(21)   And, furthermore, all the works of the world could be cited as witnesses about the unlawfulness of doubting the actions and the power of God. But our infidelity dashes

against the truth itself, and we rush headlong to destroy the power of God. Were it possible, we would lift up our bodies and hands to heaven, we would upset the sun and the other stars in the annual movements within their orbit, we would disturb the ebb and flow of the ocean, we would also forbid the flowing of the fountains, we would reverse the natural course of the rivers, we would shake the foundations of the earth, and we would rage with murderous fury against these works of God. Fortunately, the nature of our bodies restricts us within these necessary limits of moderation. Assuredly, we do not disguise what we would do if it were possible. In the insolence of our sacrilegious will, we desire to distort the nature of truth and we declare war against the works of God, because these are things that lie within our power.

(22) The Son said: 'Father, I have manifested thy name to the men.' Why are we scrupulous about these things? Why are we perplexed? Do you deny the Father? But, this was the greatest achievement of the Son, that we might know the Father. Evidently, you deny Him, since, according to you, the Son was not born from Him. Why should He be called the Son, if He was made like others according to the will? I can admire God, the Creator of Christ, the maker of the world, and it is a deed worthy of God that He has produced the author of the archangels and angels, of things visible and invisible, of heaven and earth and of this whole creation. The Lord does not labor for this purpose, to teach you that God can create all things, but to inform you that God is the Father of the Son who is speaking.

In heaven there are many powers, both mighty and eternal, but there is one only-begotten Son, who does not differ from the others in power alone,[19] because all things were made through Him. Because He is the true and the

---

19 This was one of the assertions of the Arians.

only Son, let Him not be robbed of His origin, so that He is born from nothing. You hear of the Son; believe that He is the Son. You hear of the Father; remember that He is a Father. Why do you break in upon these names with your suspicion, ill-will, and impudence? Names are applied to divine things in accordance with the concept of their nature. Why do you do violence to the true meaning of the words? You hear the words 'Father' and 'Son.' Do not doubt that they are what they are named. The essence of the doctrine revealed by the Son is that you should know the Father. Why do you frustrate the work of the Prophets, the Incarnation of the Word, the birth from the Virgin, the power of His works, the cross of Christ? All these things were bestowed on you, offered for you, in order to make the Father and the Son known to you. You now substitute the will, the creation, and the adoption. Examine the warfare and the campaign of Christ. Truly does He cry out: 'Father, I have manifested thy name to the men.' You do not hear: 'You have created the creator of heavenly things.' You do not hear: 'You have called the maker of earthly things into being.' But you hear: 'Father, I have manifested thy name to the men.' Use the gift of the Saviour. Realize that He is the Father who begot, and that He is the Son who was born, born with a true nature from that Father who is. Remember that it was revealed to you not that the Father is God but that God is the Father.

(23) You hear: 'I and the Father are one.'[20] Why do you separate and divide the Son from the Father? They are one, that is to say, He who is has nothing that will not also be found in Him from whom He is. When you hear the Son declare: 'I and the Father are one,' apply this statement to the persons, and allow to the begetter and the begotten the truth that has been revealed concerning them. They are one

20 John 10.30.

as are he who begets and he who is begotten. Why do you
exclude the nature? Why do you suppress the truth? You
hear: 'The Father in me and I in the Father,'[21] and the
works of the Son bear testimony to this declaration about the
Father and the Son. In our concept, we do not represent Him
as a body in a body, or as the pouring of water into wine,
but we acknowledge the same similarity of power and the
fullness of the divinity in each of them. The Son received
everything from the Father, and He is the form of God and
the image of His substance.

The 'image of His substance' merely distinguishes Him
from the one who is, in order that we may believe in His
existence and not that we may also assume that there is a
dissimilarity of nature. For the Father to be in the Son and
the Son in the Father means that there is a perfect fullness of
the Godhead in each of them. The Son is not a diminution
of the Father nor is He an imperfect Son from the Father.
An image is not alone and the likeness is not to itself. Nothing
can be like God unless it is from Him. That which is similar
in everything does not originate from somewhere else, and
the similarity of the one to the other does not allow them to be
joined together by anything contradictory. Do not change
similar things and do not separate things that are not distinct
from each other! He who said: 'Let us make mankind in our
image and likeness' reveals that mutual similarity between
them from the fact that He uses the phrase 'our likeness.'
Do not touch, do not handle, do not destroy! Hold fast to the
names of the nature, hold fast to the revelation concerning
the Son! It is not my wish that you flatter, that you praise
the Son with your own words. It will be sufficient if you are
content with what is written.

. (24) We must not, however, rely upon human wisdom
to such a degree as to believe that what we understand we

---

21 John 10.38.

understand perfectly, and to imagine that the contents of our knowledge is absolutely perfect when, after examining it ourselves in our own mind, we conclude that in every respect it rests upon a satisfactory concept of the truth. That which is imperfect cannot form an idea of that which is perfect, nor can that which derives its existence from something else have a perfect understanding either of its author or of itself. Indeed, it knows itself only in that which it is, because its concepts do not extend beyond the limits which have been assigned to it by its nature. It is indebted for its activity not to itself but to its maker, and, therefore, that which depends upon something else for its being because it has been created is imperfect, since its existence comes from outside itself. And in those matters, where it believes itself to be perfectly wise, it must be foolish, for, when it disregards the insurmountable barriers of its nature and thinks that everything can be encompassed within the limits of its own helplessness, at that moment it glories in that which is erroneously given the name of wisdom. It cannot be wise beyond the capacity of its own power of comprehension, and just as it lacks the power to subsist by itself, so it is limited in the range of its ideas.

Therefore, the substitution of an imperfect nature,[22] that boasts of possessing the wisdom of a perfect nature, is derided and scorned as a foolish wisdom, for the Apostle says: 'For Christ did not send me to baptize, but to preach the gospel, not with the wisdom of words, lest the cross of Christ be made void. For the doctrine of the cross is foolishness to those who perish, but to those who are saved it is the power of God, for it is written, "I will destroy the wisdom of the wise and the prudence of the prudent I will reject." Where is the "wise man?" Where is the scribe? Where is the disputant

---

22 'The substitution of an imperfect nature' is a metonymy for 'man' and implies his mental limitations. Cf. R. Kinnavey, *The Vocabulary of St. Hilary of Poitiers* 262-3.

of this world? Did not God make foolish the wisdom of this world? Since, in God's wisdom, the world did not come to know God by "wisdom," it pleased God by the foolishness of our preaching to save those who believe. The Jews ask for signs and the Greeks look for "wisdom"; but we, for our part, preach a crucified Christ Jesus—to the Jews indeed a stumbling block and to the Gentiles foolishness, but to those who are called, both Jews and Greeks, Christ, the power of God and the wisdom of God. For the foolishness of God is wiser than men, and the weakness of God is stronger than men.'[23] All unbelief, consequently, is folly because it employs the wisdom of its imperfect understanding and measures everything according to the standard of its impotence, and concludes that nothing can be performed which it does not comprehend. The origin of unbelief proceeds from a verdict of its infirmity, while it does not believe that anything can be done which it decides cannot be done.

(25) Hence, the Apostle, realizing that our defective manner of reasoning regarded only that as true which it understood, declared that he would not preach in the language of wisdom, lest the doctrine that he taught appear as vain. And, in order that he might not be considered as a preacher of folly, he added that the word of the cross is foolishness to those who perish, because the unbelievers regard as prudence only that which they understand. Since they grasped nothing except that which is within the nature of their own infirmity, they consider the only perfect wisdom of God to be folly, and thereby become foolish by this very decision of their own helpless wisdom.

Therefore, what is folly for those who perish is the power of God for those who are saved, because they do not measure anything by the weakness of their natural understanding, but judge the activity of the divine omnipotence according to

23 Cf. 1 Cor. 1.17-25.

the unlimited power of heaven. And for this reason God rejects the wisdom of the wise and the prudence of the learned, because by the recognition of human folly salvation is granted to those who believe, and, while the unbelievers regard as foolish whatever is beyond their comprehension, the faithful submit to God's power and strength in the mysterious doctrines whereby their salvation is to be obtained. What comes from God, therefore, is not foolish and the prudence of human nature is ridiculous which demands miracles or wisdom from their God before it will believe.

For the Jews it is natural to ask for miracles, because, as a consequence of their familiarity with the Law, they are not altogether ignorant of the name of God and irritated by the scandal of the cross. But for the Greeks it is appropriate to seek for wisdom, because with their Gentile absurdity and human prudence they demand an explanation of why God was raised aloft on a cross. Since this is concealed in a mystery, out of consideration for the mental capacity of our weak nature, folly becomes unbelieving, for, what the mind, naturally imperfect, cannot comprehend by natural reason it rejects as outside the realm of wisdom. Because of this foolish wisdom of the world, which formerly did not recognize God in the wisdom of God, that is, in the splendor of the world and the beauty and orderly arrangement of creation, and did not pay homage to the wisdom of its Creator, it pleased God by the preaching of folly to save those who believe, that is, by faith in the cross to procure eternal life for men, so that the judgment of human knowledge might be put to shame and salvation might be found in that which they considered to be an absurdity. Christ, who is folly to the Gentiles and a scandal to the Jews, is the power of God and the wisdom of God, because what is considered weak and foolish in the things of God from a human viewpoint surpasses earthly prudence and might by the genuineness of its wisdom and power.

(26) For this reason, nothing in the actions of God is to be treated in accordance with the reasoning of the human mind, nor may the matter of the work itself that has been created pass judgment upon its Creator. We must clothe ourselves with folly in order to acquire wisdom, not by the comprehension of folly, but by the consciousness of our nature, in order that what the wisdom of earthly thinking may not grasp may, on the other hand, become known to us by the wisdom of the divine power. When we realize the idea of our foolishness and have noted the ignorance of the natural foolishness within us, we are then led by the knowledge of divine wisdom to the wisdom of God, since we place no limitations upon the attributes and the power of God, since we do not restrict the Lord of nature within the laws of nature, and since we perceive that this alone is the orthodox belief concerning God, of which He Himself is for Himself and for us both its witness as well as its author.

BOOK FOUR

LTHOUGH WE BELIEVE that it is clearly evident from our earlier Books, written some time ago, that our faith in and profession of the Father, Son, and Holy Spirit are derived from the teachings of the Gospels and the Apostles, and that we hold nothing in common with the heretics, certain facts must be brought together in the following Books that the knowledge of the truth may become clearer after we have pointed out all their fallacies and blasphemous doctrines. We must realize in the first place the rashness that is associated with their beliefs, and the dangers into which their godlessness leads, then the opinions which they hold in opposition to the apostolic faith to which we subscribe, but which they habitually deny, and, finally, how their method of interpretation distorts the true meaning and significance of the divine words.

(2) We are conscious of the fact, however, that the language of men or human comparisons cannot offer a satisfactory explanation for the things of God. That which is ineffable surpasses the limits and measure of any kind of a description, and that which is spiritual differs from the nature and analogy of human things. Although our treatise is concerned with heavenly natures, we shall have to speak of those things which lie within the realm of spiritual concepts by employing an ordinary manner of speech, not, of course,

because this is suitable to the dignity of God, but because it is necessary in view of the feebleness of our understanding. This is to say, we shall have to speak of what we think and understand in accordance with our own environment and in our own words. As we have already touched upon these matters in Book 1,[1] we are also mentioning them in this place so that no one may believe that we are thinking of God as we do of corporeal natures when we employ human analogies, or that we are placing spiritual matters on the same plane as our bodily sufferings; rather, that we have made use of the outward appearance of visible things in order to throw light upon invisible things.

(3)   The heretics declare that Christ is not from God, that is, the Son is not born from the Father nor is He God by nature, but by a decree. His adoption appears particularly in His name, because, as there are many sons of God, so He also is the Son of God; hence, their liberality in regard to this dignity, because, as there are many gods, so He also is God. They are inspired, however, by a more tender affection toward His adoption and designation, so that He was adopted before all the others and is greater than all the rest of the adopted sons and, since He was created in a more excellent way than all the other creatures, He Himself is superior to all the other creatures. There also are some who confess the omnipotence of God and declare that He was created in the likeness of God and, like all other things, was brought into existence from nothing in order to become the image of that eternal Creator; that is to say, a word commanded Him to exist from non-existing things, since an all-powerful God can form a likeness to Himself from nothing.

(4)   In fact, when they learn that the bishops of former times have taught that the Father and the Son are of one substance, in order to weaken these words under the subtle

---

1 Cf. above, 1.19.

pretext of being an heretical opinion they even add the following explanation. They declare that the meaning of this phrase, that is, of one substance, which in Greek is called *homooúsion,*[2] must be used and expressed in this sense, that He Himself is the Father who is also the Son; in other words, as a consequence of His infinity He has been extended into the Virgin, from whom He assumed flesh and annexed the name Son to Himself in that body which He assumed. This is the first error in regard to *homooúsion.* Their second is to claim that *homooúsion* means that the two of them are in common possession of a pre-existing and different substance, as if this prior substance, or essence of some matter already existing in which both shared and which was consumed by both, offers evidence that both of them belonged to an already existing nature as well as to the one substance. Consequently, they state that we should reject our profession of faith in *homooúsion* because, on the one hand, this expression does not distinguish the Father from the Son, and, on the other hand, it reveals that the Father comes after the matter which He shares in common with the Son. Thirdly, they also allege this reason for their disapproval of *homooúsion,* that, according to their meaning of this phrase, the Son receives His existence from a division of the Father's substance, as if He were cut off from Him so that one thing is divided into two. Therefore, they are said to be of one substance, because the part cut off from the whole possesses that nature in itself from which it has been cut off, yet it is impossible for God to fall into a state of dismemberment, because He would also be changeable if He were subject to a diminution as a result of a division, and He would be made imperfect if the substance of His own perfection went forth from Him into a different portion.

---

2 In *De synodis* 81-92, the saint gives a brief history of the word *homooúsion.* He urges the Semi-Arians to use it as that best suited to safeguard the divinity of Christ.

(5)   They also believe themselves capable of contradicting the teaching of the Prophets, and also of the Gospels and Apostles, in such a skillful manner as to proclaim that the Son was born in time. Since they claim that we are wrong in asserting that the Son always was, then, since they exclude the fact that He always was, they must admit that He was born in time. If His being is not eternal, then there will be a time when He was not. And, if there was a time when He was not, then time will be before Him, because He whose being is not eternal begins to be in time. On the other hand, He who is not subject to time cannot but possess the attribute of eternal existence. But, they allege as a reason for rejecting His eternal being that, if He always was, then we must hold that He was not born, just as if we teach that He cannot be born, because He always was.

(6)   O foolish and irreverent fears and impious anxiety about God! These meanings, which they attach to and find blameworthy in the expression *homoousion,* and in the assertion that the Son always was, are abominated, rejected, and condemned by the Church. She knows the one God from whom are all things, and she also knows our one Lord Jesus Christ, through whom are all things, the one from whom and the one through whom, the source of everything from the one, the creation of everything through the other. In the one from whom she understands the origin without birth, in the one through whom she venerates the power that does not differ in anything from its origin, since there is a common source of authority between the one from whom and the one through whom, in that which was created and in those things which have been created.

She recognizes in the Spirit that God is Spirit, impassible and indivisible, for she has learned from the Lord that a spirit does not have flesh and bones,[3] lest we might possibly believe

---

3 Cf. Luke 24.39.

that He is subject to the laws of bodily suffering. She knows the one unbegotten God, she also knows the one only-begotten Son of God. She asserts that the Father is eternal and not subject to any origin; similarly, she acknowledges the derivation of the Son from the eternal one, not that He Himself has a beginning, but that He is from one who is without a beginning—He does not originate through Himself, but from Him who is from no one and who always is; He is born from one who is eternal; in other words, He receives His birth from the eternity of the Father.

Our Faith, therefore, is free from the deformity of heretical error. We have proclaimed our profession of faith, though as yet we have not cited our proofs for it. But, in order to prevent any doubt from arising about the expression *homoousion,* which the Fathers used, and about our belief that He always was, we have mentioned these things that it may be known that He subsists in the nature in which He was born from the Father, and by the birth of the Son nothing has been taken away from the nature of the Father in which He remained. The saintly men, full of zeal for God's doctrine, have designated the Son as consubstantial with the Father, not because of the errors and reasons that we have already referred to, but in order that no one might believe that the term *usia* did away with the birth of the only-begotten Son because He was said to be consubstantial with the Father.

(7) In order to realize the necessity for using these two expressions,[4] and to grasp their meaning as the best possible defense of the faith against the raging heretics of those days, I think that we should answer the falsehoods of the heretics and refute their absurd and destructive teachings from the testimonies of the Gospels and Apostles. In their own eyes they appear to offer a reasonable explanation for the individual doctrines which they teach, because they have alleged

---

4 *usia* and *homoúsia.*

certain passages from the divine books in favor of each of their assertions, but these are distortions of the true meaning, and, in keeping with the perverted minds of the interpreters, offer nothing but the appearance of the truth.

(8) After they have magnified only the divinity of the Father, they seek to take away from the Son that He is God, because it is written: 'Hear, O Israel, the Lord thy God is one.'[5] The Lord says the same thing to the doctor of the Law who asked Him what was the greatest commandment in the Law: 'Hear, O Israel, the Lord thy God is one.'[6] Again, Paul expresses it in this manner: 'For there is one God, and one mediator between God and men.'[7] Then, because He alone is wise, so that no wisdom may be left to the Son according to the words of the Apostle: 'Now to him who is able to strengthen you in accordance with my gospel, and the preaching of Jesus Christ, according to the revelation of the mystery which has been kept in silence from eternal ages, which is manifested now through the writings of the prophets according to the precept of the eternal God, and made known to all the Gentiles to bring about obedience to faith—to the only wise God, through Jesus Christ, to whom be honor forever and ever. Amen.'[8] Then, because He is without birth and the only true one, since Isaias has said: 'They shall bless thee, the true God,'[9] and because the Lord bore witness to the very same thing in the Gospels when He says: 'Now this is eternal life, that they may know thee, the only true God, and him whom thou hast sent, Jesus Christ.'[10]

Because He alone is good, so that no goodness may be left to the Son, because He has said: 'No one is good but God

5 Cf. Deut. 6.4.
6 Mark 12.29.
7 1 Tim. 2.5.
8 Cf. Rom. 16.25-27.
9 Cf. Isa. 65.16.
10 John 17.3.

only.'[11] Then, because He alone is mighty, since Paul has
declared: 'This coming he in his own time will make manifest,
who is the Blessed and only Sovereign, the King of kings
and Lord of lords.'[12] Then, because they know this one alone
as immutable and unchangeable, because the Prophet has
stated: 'I am the Lord your God and I change not,'[13] and
the Apostle James has proclaimed: 'With whom there is no
change.'[14] He is the just judge, because it is written: 'God,
a just judge, strong and patient.'[15] He is the one who cares
for all things, because the Lord has uttered the words when
He was speaking about the birds: 'And your heavenly father
feeds them,'[16] and again: 'Are not two sparrows sold for a
farthing? And yet not one of them will fall to the ground
without your Father's leave. But even the hairs of your head
are numbered.'[17] He foresees everything, as blessed Susanna
asserts: 'O eternal God, the one who knowest hidden things,
who knowest all things before they come to pass.'[18] He cannot be conceived according to what is written: 'Heaven is my
throne, but the earth my footstool. What is this house that
you will build to me? And what is this place of my rest? My
hands made all these things, and all these are mine.'[19] He
also permeates everything, as Paul testified: 'For in him we
live and move and have our being,'[20] and the Psalmist asks:
'Whither shall I go from thy spirit? Or whither shall I flee
from thy face? If I ascend into heaven, thou art there: if
I descend into hell, thou art present. If I take my wings
before the light, and dwell in the uttermost parts of the sea:

---

11 Mark 10.18.
12 1 Tim. 6.15.
13 Cf. Mal. 3.6.
14 James 1.17.
15 Cf. Ps. 7.12.
16 Cf. Matt. 6.26.
17 Cf. Matt. 10.29.
18 Cf. Dan. 13.42.
19 Cf. Isa. 66.1,2.
20 Acts 17.28.

for there also shall thy hand lead me: and thy right hand shall hold me.'[21]

This one is also incorporeal, because it is said: 'For God is spirit, and they who worship him must worship in spirit and in truth.'[22] He is immortal and invisible, as Paul avows: 'Who alone has immortality and dwells in light inaccessible, whom no man has seen nor can see,'[23] and according to the Evangelist: 'No one has at any time seen God, except the only-begotten Son who is in the bosom of the Father.'[24] He also remains alone and is unborn, because it was stated: 'I AM WHO AM,'[25] and again: 'Thus shalt thou say to the children of Israel: He who is, hath sent me to you,'[26] and by Jeremias: 'Who art the Lord, O Lord.'[27]

(9) Who does not perceive that these interpretations are utterly false and deceptive? Although they are blended and mixed together very ingeniously, they clearly reveal the artificial cunning and absurdity of their malice and stupidity. Among other things, they have added that they recognize the Father alone as unbegotten, as if from this anyone could suppose that He—from whom that one was born through whom are all things—obtained that which He is from someone else. By the very fact that He is called the Father He is shown to be the author of Him whom He begot, because He has a name by which we recognize that He came forth from no one else, and which teaches us that He who was born began to exist from Him who is.

Accordingly, in regard to that which is proper to the Father, let us leave as proper to Him and as a secret, while we profess our belief in the unborn power of His eternal

---

21 Cf. Ps, 138.7-10.
22 John 4.24.
23 Cf. 1 Tim. 6.16.
24 Cf. John 1.18.
25 Exod. 3.14.
26 *Ibid.*
27 Cf. Jer. 1.6.

power. Still, no one doubts, I think, that this is the reason why they declare that certain qualities are personal and exclusive to the Father, when they profess their faith in Him, in order that no one else may be considered as having a share in them. When they say that He alone is true, alone just, alone wise, alone invisible, alone good, alone powerful, alone immortal, then in their opinion the fact that He alone possesses these attributes means that the Son is excluded from any share in them. For, as they say, no one else participates in the attributes that are peculiar to Him. And if these attributes are in the Father alone, then we must believe that God the Son is false, foolish, a corporeal being composed of visible matter, spiteful, weak, and mortal. He is debarred from all these attributes because no one but the Father possesses them.

(10) Since we are about to speak of the most perfect majesty and the most complete divinity of the only-begotten Son of God, we do not believe that anyone will conclude from all these words that we employ that our aim is to dishonor God the Father, as if it would lessen His dignity if any of these are ascribed to the Son, for the glory of the Son redounds rather to the glory of the Father, and the author is exalted from whom has sprung one deserving of such honor. The Son has nothing else than birth,[28] and the tribute of praise which the begotten receives tends to the glory of his begetter. Hence, any supposition of disrespect disappears if our faith teaches that whatever majesty the Son possesses will aid in magnifying the power of Him who begot such a Son.

(11) After discovering what they profess about the Father in their attempts to disparage the Son, our next step

---

28 St. Thomas Aquinas, *S. T.* I Q. 40 a. 3, in approving these words, 'the Son has nothing else than birth,' concludes: 'if filiation be removed, the Son's hypostasis no longer remains, and the same holds as regards the other Persons.'

is to listen to their assertions about the Son. Since we shall reply to all of their propositions and shall expose their ungodly doctrine by proofs drawn from the divine Scriptures, we must connect what we have said about the Father with what we shall later mention about the Son, so that, when we have compared our profession of faith about both of them, we may then follow one and the same order in answering each of the doctrines which they have proposed.

They claim that the Son of God has not been born from any pre-existing matter, because all things were created through Him, nor is He from God, because nothing can be separated from God, but He belongs to those things which were not, that is, He is the perfect creature of God but not like the other creatures. He is, in truth, a creature, for it is written: 'The Lord created me for the beginning of his ways.'[29] He is also the perfect handiwork, but not like other things that were made; He has been made indeed, but in the manner that St. Paul says to the Hebrew: 'Having been made so much superior to the angels as he possesses a more excellent name than they.'[30] And again: 'Therefore, holy brethren, partakers of a heavenly calling, consider the apostle and high priest of our confession, Jesus, who is faithful to him who made him.'[31] But, in order to weaken His might, power, and divinity, they appeal particularly to His own words: 'The Father is greater than I.'[32] But they admit, therefore, that He is not one of the other creatures, for it is written: 'All things were made through him.'[33] For this reason they concentrate all of their godless teachings in that well-known formula of theirs in which they assert.[34]

---

29 Cf. Prov. 8.22.
30 Cf. Heb. 1.4.
31 Heb. 3.1.
32 John 14.28.
33 John 1.3.
34 This formula of faith is contained in a letter, which Arius and his followers wrote to Alexander, Patriarch of Alexandria, before the formal condemnation of their heresy by the Council of Nice.

(12) 'We know the one God, alone unmade, alone ever-lasting, alone without a beginning, alone true, alone possessing immortality, alone the best, alone powerful, the Creator of all, the unchangeable, immutable, just, and best regulator and ordainer of the Law, the Prophets, and the New Testament. This God gave birth to the only-begotten Son before all the ages, through whom He also made the world and all things, born not in appearance but in truth, obedient to His will. He is unchangeable and immutable, the perfect creature of God, but not just as one of His creatures; He was the handiwork, but not as the others things that were made. The Son is not, as Valentinian asserted, an emanation of the Father, nor is the Son, as Manichaeus taught, a portion of the one substance of the Father, nor as Sabellius, who divides the union and calls the same one the Son whom he also called the Father, nor, as Hieracas declares, is He a lamp from a lamp, or a torch divided into two parts.

'Nor is He one who previously was, and then was born or created anew into the Son, but, as even you yourself, O most blessed Father, in the presence of the Church and the council of the brethren have frequently condemned those who introduce such doctrines. But, as we have stated, He was created by the will of God before all times and ages, and has received both His life and His being from the Father, and the Father makes His own glorious qualities exist in Him. For the Father, in conferring the inheritance of all things upon Him, has not deprived Himself of those which have not been made and are still in His possession; He is still the origin of all things.

(13) 'Wherefore, there are three substances, the Father, the Son, and the Holy Spirit. And, truly, God is the cause of all things, completely alone, without a beginning; the Son, however, has been brought forth from the Father without time, and has been created and has been formed before

the world; still, He was not before He was born, but was born without time before everything, and He alone has the same substance as the Father alone. He is not eternal or co-eternal, nor was He uncreated at the same time with the Father, nor, as certain ones say, does He possess His being at the same time with the Father, or according to some, who advance two unborn principles, but as the oneness or principle of all things, in this manner God is also before all things. Therefore, He is likewise before the Son, as we have also learned from you when you taught publicly in the church.

'In so far as God confers upon Him His being, His glory, His life, and everything that has been given to Him, in so far God is His principle. But, He is His principle, that is to say, His God, since He is before Him. For, if the expressions "from Him" and "from the womb" and "I came forth from the Father and have come," are understood as if He were a part of this one substance, and as if He were the extension of an emanation, then, according to them, the Father would be a composite being, divisible and changeable, and a body, and, in so far as it depends on them, the God without a body is subject to the limitations of a body.'

(14) This is their error, this is their fatal teaching! To corroborate it they bring in evidence from the divine words, but with a distorted interpretation of their meaning, and lie about them while they take advantage of human ignorance. No one, it is true, should doubt that we ought to make use of the teachings of God in order to acquire the knowledge of God. By itself, our human weakness will not apprehend heavenly things, nor will the mere knowledge of corporeal things bring with it an understanding of those that are invisible. That which is created or carnal within us, or that which God has given us for the usefulness of human life, cannot by their own perspicacity arrive at the distinction

between the nature of their Creator and His work. Our faculties do not rise to the heavenly science nor does our helplessness grasp the incomprehensible power by any kind of knowledge.

We must believe God when He speaks about Himself and we must not resist those truths which He has revealed to us for our understanding. We must either deny Him after the manner of the heathens if we reject His proofs or, if we believe Him to be God as He is, then we cannot have any other concept of Him than that which He has revealed about Himself. Let there be an end, therefore, to the personal opinions of men, and do not allow our human judgment to trespass upon the order established by God! For this reason we pursue the godless and impious teachings about God by the very same texts of the divine words, and we shall base everything on the testimony of Him who is the subject of our investigation, and we shall not attempt to deceive or to mislead our unlearned listeners by merely citing some quotations from the texts without explaining all the attendant circumstances. The understanding of the words is to be deduced from the reasons why they were spoken, because the words are subordinated to the event, not the event to the words. But we shall examine everything, while at the same time we shall explain the reasons why they were said and the meaning of the words. We shall reconsider each statement, therefore, according to the plan that we have drawn up.

(15) This is their central doctrine: 'We know that there is only one God, for Moses has declared: 'Hear, O Israel, the Lord thy God is one.'[35] Has anyone dared to raise any doubts about this doctrine? Has any one of those who believe in God been heard to teach anything else except that there is one God, from whom are all things, one power without birth, and this one power without a beginning? But, we can-

---

35 Cf. Deut. 6.4.

not deny that the Son of God is God simply because there is only one God. Moses, or, rather, God through Moses, ordered that this first commandment, to believe in the one God, should be given to the people both in Egypt and in the desert who were addicted to idolatry and to the worship of the pretended deities. This decree was right and fitting, for there is one God from whom are all things. Let us see whether the same Moses also acknowledges the divinity of Him through whom are all things. For, since God is one, nothing is taken away from the Father because the Son is also God.

He is God from God, one from one; wherefore, there is one God, because God is from Him. On the other hand, He is not, therefore, less a God because the Father is one God, for He is the only-begotten Son of God; He is not unborn, so that He does not deprive the Father of being the one God, nor is He Himself anything else than God because He was born from God. Although in regard to Him it should not be doubted that He is God by His birth from God, so that, according to our faith there is one God, still, let us see whether Moses who said to Israel: 'The Lord thy God is one' has proclaimed the Son of God as God. In professing our faith in the divinity of our Lord Jesus Christ, we shall have to refer to the testimony of him upon whose authority the heretics, while acknowledging only the one God, believe that we must deny to the Son that which God is.

(16)   Therefore, since according to the Apostle we profess our faith in God completely and perfectly when we speak in this manner: 'One God the Father from whom are all things, and our one Lord Jesus through whom are all things,'[36] let us examine the origin of the world and what Moses says about it. He declares: 'Then God said, "let there be a firmament in the midst of the waters, and let there be a division between the water and the water." And so it was.

---

36 Cf. 1 Cor. 8.6.

God made the firmament, and God divided through the midst of the water.'[37] Hence, you have the God from whom and the God through whom. Or, if you will deny this, then you must explain through whom that was made which was made, or at least you must show how the very nature of the things to be created was obedient to God, for, upon hearing the words: 'Let there be a firmament,' it established itself in accordance with the command of God. But the revelation of the divine Scriptures does not allow this explanation. According to the Prophet, everything has been made from nothing,[38] and no existing matter has been changed into anything else, but that which was not was created and is complete. Through whom? Listen to the Evangelist: 'All things were made through him.'[39] If you ask through whom, you will hear the same Evangelist declaring: 'In the beginning was the Word, and the Word was with God; and the Word was God. He was in the beginning with God. All things were made through him.'[40] And if you wish to deny that the Father has said: 'Let there be a firmament,' you will again hear the same Prophet asserting: 'For he spoke and they were made: he commanded and they were created.'[41] Hence, the words that were said, 'Let there be a firmament,' reveal that it was the Father who spoke, but when it was added: 'And so it was,' and when it is said that God made it, we are to understand by this the person of the agent who made it. For, 'he spoke and they were made.' He alone was certainly not the one who willed it and did it. 'He commanded and they were created.' Certainly, it did not come into existence because it pleased Him, so that the function of a mediator between Himself and what was to be created would have been superfluous. Consequently, the God

37 Cf. Gen. 1.6,7.
38 Cf. 2 Mach. 7.28.
39 John 1.3.
40 John 1.1-3.
41 Ps. 148.5.

from whom are all things says that they are to be made, and
the God through whom are all things makes them, and the
same name is applied equally in the designation of Him who
commands and for the work of Him who carries it out. If
you will dare to claim that the Son is not referred to when
it is stated: 'And God made it,' what will be your attitude
to where it is said: 'All things were made through Him,'
and those words: 'And our one Lord, Jesus Christ, through
whom are all things,' and that statement: 'He spoke and
they were made'?

If these divine words will carry conviction to your rash
mind, nothing will be taken away from the divinity of the
Son of God by the words: 'Hear, O Israel, the Lord thy God
is one,' since the one who spoke them also proclaims the Son
as God at the very creation of the world. Still, let us see
what progress we can make from this distinction between
the God who commands and the God who performs. Even
though it contradicts the concept of our ordinary reasoning
to believe that by the words: 'He commanded, and they
were made,' is meant a being that is solitary and one and the
same person, still, in order that there may not be any ambiguity, we must explain those things that took place after the
creation of the world.

(17)   When, therefore, the world was completed and
its inhabitant was to be made, the following words are used
about him: 'God said: Let us make mankind in our image
and likeness,' and again: 'God made man. To the image
of God he made him.'[42] I now ask whether you believe that

---

42 Gen. 1.26,27. In his other writings (e.g., *Tractatus mysteriorum*) St.
   Hilary regards the persons and events of the Old Testament as fore-
   shadowing the life and the teaching of Christ. Hence, it is only
   natural that he should look for indications of the central mystery
   of the Christian religion, the Trinity, in the Old Testament. The
   passages from the Old Testament upon which he comments in this
   Book and the following are often interpreted by the early Fathers
   of the Eastern and Western Church in a similar manner.

God spoke to Himself alone, or whether you consider these words as being directed not to Himself but to someone else? If you say to Himself alone, you are refuted by the very voice of Him who declares: 'Let us make mankind* in our image and likeness.' God spoke these words through the lawgiver according to our understanding, that is to say, by means of the words which He Himself wished us to use while He would impart to us the knowledge of what He had done. The Son of God, through whom all things were made, was pointed out by the words that were uttered: 'And God said let there be a firmament,' and again because it was thus expressed: 'And God made the firmament.' But, in order that these words might not be regarded as vain or superfluous if He had said to Himself that it should be, and, again, if He had done it (for there is nothing so incongruous than for one who is alone to tell himself to do something, since an act of the will is all that is required to do it), He wished it to be more clearly understood by expressing it in this manner that it did not refer to Him alone.

By declaring: 'Let us make mankind in our image and likeness,' He does away with any idea of isolation, since He reveals this mutual participation. But He Himself who is alone cannot have any kind of companionship for Himself. Again, the words 'let us make' are not compatible with the loneliness of a solitary, nor does anyone address another as 'our' who is a stranger to himself. Both expressions—'let us make' and 'our'—cannot be reconciled with a being that is unique or who is one and the same; likewise, they do not signify one who is different from or alien to Him. I ask whether, when you hear that He is alone, you do not believe that He is one and the same? Or, when you hear that He is not one and the same, whether you do not conceive of Him only as one who is alone? In so far as He is alone, He will be alone; but, in so far as He is not one and the same,

He will not be found as one who is alone. Hence, to one who is alone, the words 'I will make' and 'mine' are appropriate, but to one who is not alone the words 'let us make' and 'our' are appropriate.

(18)   Therefore, when we read the words: 'Let us make mankind in our image and likeness,' because both expressions signify that He does not live only by Himself and that one is not different from the other, we must also profess our belief in the teaching that He does not live by Himself and that one is not different from the other, while we know that both of them possess the property of the one nature, because He says 'our image' and not 'our images.' It is not enough merely to explain the meaning of the words if the understanding of them is not also followed by the performance of the actions. Thus, is it written: 'And God made mankind in his image. In the image of God he made him.' If these words come from one who is alone and addressed by Himself to Himself, then I ask what is your opinion about their meaning in this passage. For I see a threefold meaning here: the one who makes, the thing that is made, and the likeness. Man is the one who is made; God is the one who has made him, and the one whom He has made is made according to the image of God. If Genesis were speaking about a solitary person it would surely have said: 'And he made him in his image.' But, when it announced the mystery of the Gospel, it did not speak of two gods but of God and God, since it declares that God made man to the image of God. Thus, we find God making men in a common image and in the same likeness with God, so that the designation of an agent is not compatible with isolation, and a work that is produced according to the same image and likeness does not permit any distinction in the Godhead.

(19)   Although some may regard it as superfluous to add anything else after these explanations, because in divine mat-

ters the statements alone and not the frequent repetition of them are sufficient, we should become familiar with whatever has been said on this same subject. We shall not have to render an account of the divine words, but of our understanding of them. Among the many commands that He gave to Noe, God spoke thus: 'Whoever sheds the blood of man, his soul shall be shed for his blood, for in the image of God I made man.'[43] Here, a distinction is also made between the likeness, the work, and the agent. God testifies that He made man in the image of God. When man was to be made, because He was speaking of Himself, not to Himself, He declared 'in our image,' but, when man was made, 'God made man in the image of God.' Were He Himself speaking to Himself, He was certainly aware that the appropriate terminology to use was 'I made man in my image.' For, to reveal the unity of nature, He had said: 'Let us make mankind in our image.' And, again, He did not confuse the idea of one who is alone and one who is not alone, since God in making man made him 'in the image of God.'

(20) If you wish to claim that God the Father, as one who is alone, said these words to Himself, even if we grant that a person may speak to himself as he does to another, and we must believe that He wanted the words, 'God made mankind in the image of God,' to be understood as if He meant: 'In my image I made man,' first of all you yourself are refuted by your own testimony. For, you have declared: 'All things from the Father, but all things through the Son.' From that which was said, 'Let us make mankind,' the origin is from Him from whom the discourse also began, but from the fact that 'God made man in the image of God,' He through whom the work is brought to completion is also pointed out.

(21) Furthermore, in order that you may not be able

---

43 Cf. Gen. 9.6.

to practise any deception is this matter, Wisdom, which you yourself acknowledge as Christ, will contradict you by the words: 'When he placed certain fountains under the heavens, when he made the strong foundations of the earth, I was with him forming it. But it was I in whom he rejoiced. But daily I rejoiced in his sight at all times, when he rejoiced after the completion of the world, and he rejoiced in the sons of men.'[44] Every pretext is hemmed in, and every error is restricted to the acknowledgment of the truth. Wisdom, that was born before the ages, is present with God; not only is she present, but she also arranges. Understand the office of arranging and ordering! The Father is the cause of that which He says, and the Son sets it in order by carrying out the command about what must be done. But the distinction between the Persons has been made in such a manner that the work may be refered to either of them. When it is said 'let us make,' the command and the deed are placed on an equal level; but the words that are written, 'I was with him forming it,' mean that He was not alone by Himself in producing the work.

She rejoices before Him who, as she pointed out, shares His joy with her. 'But daily I rejoiced in his sight at all times, when he rejoiced after the completion of the world, and he rejoiced in the sons of men.' Wisdom has taught the cause of her joy. She rejoices because of the joy of the Father, who rejoices over the completion of the world and in the sons of men, for it is written: 'And God saw that it was good.' She rejoices that her works are pleasing to the Father which she has completed in obedience to His command. For she declares that her joy springs from the fact that the Father would be joyful over the completion of the world and in the sons of the men; 'in the sons of men,' therefore, because the whole human race already had its beginning in the one

44 Cf. Prov. 8.28-31.

person of Adam. In the creation of the world, consequently, the Father does not speak to Himself as one who is alone, for Wisdom is with Him, co-operates with Him, and rejoices that by her co-operation the work has been brought to completion.

(22) We realize, it is true, that many problems and very great problems still remain for a more complete explanation of these words, but we are postponing rather than neglecting them, reserving a more comprehensive study to our later treatises.[45] Our only concern now is in preparing a reply to the explanation of their faith, or, rather, of their perfidy, which these blasphemous men give; namely, that Moses taught that there is only one God. And we realize indeed that He taught thus in accordance with the truth, because there is one God from whom are all things; nevertheless, we must not ignore the fact that the Son is God, since the same Moses throughout the entire body of his work acknowledged God and God. For this reason we must see how the election and the law,[46] following a similar order in their confession, proclaim God and God.

(23) After God had spoken many times to Abraham, Sara was moved to anger against Agar, for she was jealous of her handmaid who had conceived, while she, her mistress, was sterile. When Agar had departed from her presence, the Scripture speaks of her in this manner: 'The angel of the Lord said to Agar, "Return to your mistress and humble yourself under her hands." The angel of the Lord said to her, "Multiplying I will multiply your posterity and it shall not be numbered because of the multitude." '[47] And again: 'She called the name of the Lord who spoke to her, "Thou,

---

45 This passage about Wisdom is treated more fully in Book 12.
46 By the terms 'election' and 'law' are meant the New and the Old Testaments. This terminology is undoubtedly based upon the words of St. Paul, Rom. 11.7.
47 Cf. Gen. 16.9,10.

God, who hast seen me." '[48] The angel of God speaks. (But 'an angel of God' has a twofold meaning: he himself who is, and he of whom he is.) And he speaks of matters that are not in keeping with the name of his office, for he says: 'Multiplying I will multiply your posterity and it shall not be numbered because of the multitude.' The power to increase the posterity exceeds the office of an angel. What, then, has Scripture testified about the one who, as an angel of God, spoke about matters that are proper to God alone. 'She called the name of the Lord who spoke to her, "Thou, God, who hast seen me." ' First, the angel of God; secondly, the Lord, for 'she called the name of the Lord who spoke to her'; then, thirdly, God, 'Thou, God, who hast seen me.' The same one who is called the angel of God is the Lord and God. But, according to the Prophet, the Son of God is 'the angel of the great council.'[49] In order that the distinction of persons should be complete, He was called the angel of God, for He who is God from God is also the angel of God. But, that due honor should be rendered to Him, He was also proclaimed as the Lord and God.

(24)   And here, indeed, He appears first as an angel, then the same one is later the Lord and God, but to Abraham He is only God. Since the distinction of persons had already been mentioned in order to do away with the error of regarding Him as one who is alone, His complete and true name could now safely be mentioned. For it is written: 'And God said to Abraham, "Behold, Sara your wife shall bear you a son, and you shall call his name Isaac. I shall establish my covenant with him as a perpetual covenant and for his seed after him. But for Ismael, behold, I have heard you, and I will bless him and will increase him exceedingly. He shall beget twelve tribes, and I will make him a great people." '[50]

---

48 Gen. 16.13.
49 Isa. 9.16 (Septuagint).
50 Cf. Gen. 17.19,20.

Can there be any doubt that He who was called the angel is also the same one who is again given the name of God? Similarly, the words refer to Ismael, and here, as in the previous instance, it is the same one who is to multiply him. And, in order that no one might believe, perhaps, that the one speaking was not the same one who addressed Agar, the divine word testifies that the same person is meant when it affirms: 'I have blessed him and I will multiply him.' The blessing refers to what has passed, for He had already spoken to Agar, but the increase is concerned with the future, for now for the first time God speaks to Abraham about Ismael. And God speaks to Abraham, but an angel of God spoke to Agar. It is God, therefore, who is also the angel, because He who is also the angel of God is God, born of God. He was called the angel of God, therefore, because He is the angel of the great council. The same one, it is true, was afterwards revealed as God in order that no one might believe that He who is God is an angel. Let our discussion follow the sequence of events. The angel of the Lord spoke to Agar, the same one speaks as God to Abraham. It is the same one who speaks to both of them. Ismael is blessed and the promise is given that He will be increased to a great people.

(25)   Scripture also reveals through Abraham that it was God who spoke. A son Isaac is also promised to Abraham. Then, later on, three men appear. After observing the three of them, Abraham adores one and acknowledges him as the Lord. Scripture has informed us that three men were present, but the patriarch knows which of them he must adore and confess. There is no distinction in the appearance of the three men, but through the eyes of faith and the intuition of the soul he recognized his Lord. Then there follows: 'And he said to him, "Returning I will come to you later at this time, and Sara your wife shall have a son." '[51] And after this

---

[51] Cf. Gen. 18.10.

the Lord said to him: 'I shall not conceal from Abraham, my servant, what I am about to do.'[52] And again: 'Then the Lord said, "The outcry against Sodom and Gomorrah has been filled, and their sins are very great." '[53] And again, after another long discourse, which we omit for the sake of brevity, when Abraham was concerned about the just being destroyed with the unjust, he said: 'Far be it from you, who judge the earth, to make this judgment. And the Lord said, "If I find that there are fifty just men in the city of Sodom, I will spare the whole place for their sake." '[54] And, again, Scripture declares after the words to Lot, the brother of Abraham, were finished: 'The Lord poured down on Sodom and Gomorrah sulphur and fire from the Lord out of heaven.'[55] And again: 'The Lord visited Sara as he had said, and the Lord did to Sara, as he had said, and Sara conceived and bore Abraham a son in his old age, and at the time, as the Lord had said to him.'[56] Afterwards, when the servant and her son had been driven from the home of Abraham, and when she was in the desert and was afraid that her child might die because of the lack of water, the same Scripture declares: 'And the Lord God heard the voice of the child where he was, and the angel of God called to Agar from heaven, and said to her, "What is the matter, Agar? Fear not; for God has heard the boy's cry from the place in which he is. Rise up, take the boy, and hold his hand, for I will make him a great people." '[57]

(26)   What treacherous blindness, what obstinacy of the unbelieving mind, what godless rashness it is not to know these things, or not to observe them when they are known. Assuredly, they have been explained and expressed in this

---

52 Cf. Gen. 18.17.
53 Cf. Gen. 18.20.
54 Cf. Gen. 18.25.
55 Cf. Gen. 19.21.
56 Cf. Gen. 21.1,2.
57 Cf. Gen. 21.17,18.

way in order that our understanding of the truth may not be hindered by an error or ambiguity. And, if we teach that they cannot remain unknown, then it must be the sin of ungodliness to deny this. The angel of the Lord began by telling Agar that Ismael would grow into a great people, and an innumberable posterity would be granted to him. She who listens teaches us by her confession that He is the Lord and God. The conversation begins with the angel of God, but ends with the confession of God. So, He Himself, who is the angel of God when fulfilling His function of announcing the great council, is also God by His nature and His name. A name is suited to the nature, not the nature to the name. God also speaks on the same subjects to Abraham. It is revealed that Ismael has already been blessed and will be multiplied into a great people. He declared: 'I have blessed him.'[58] Therefore, He did not change the meaning of His own person, for He makes known that He has already given His blessing. Scripture has indeed adhered to the order of the mystery as well as to the method of teaching the truth, since it begins with the angel of God and afterwards acknowledges the same one as God, who speaks on the same subjects.

(27) The divine word goes on to develop this doctrine more fully. God speaks to Abraham and there assures him that Sara shall give birth. Later, while he is seated, three men appear before him. He adores one and confesses that He is the Lord, and this same one whom he adores and confesses assures him that He will return at the same time, and as God told Abraham that Sara would have a son. The same man, whom he saw later on, speaks to the same one about these very subjects. Only the name has been changed, but nothing has been missing from the confession. Although Abraham saw Him as a man, he adored Him as the Lord, that is, he

---

58 Cf. Gen. 17.20.

recognized the mystery of the future Incarnation. Nor do we lack a testimonial to such great faith, for the Lord declares in the Gospels: 'Abraham your father rejoiced that he was to see my day. He saw it and was glad.'[59] The man who was seen, therefore, promises that He will return at the same time. Watch for the outcome of this promise, but remember that it is a man who makes this promise!

What, therefore, does Scripture say: 'And the Lord visited Sara.' Hence, that man is the Lord who fulfills what He has promised. Then what follows? 'And God did to Sara as he said.' He is called a man when He is speaking, He is designated as the Lord when He is visiting, and He is proclaimed as God by His action. Certainly you are aware that it was a man who was seen by Abraham and conversed with him. How will you not recognize Him as God, since the same Scripture, which had stated that He was a man, also acknowledged Him as God? For, it has said: 'And Sara conceived and bore Abraham a son in his old age, and at the time as the Lord had said to him.'[60] But the man declared that He would come. Consider Him only as a man unless He who comes is also the Lord and God. Compare the accounts! The man indeed will come for this purpose, that Sara may conceive and give birth. Learn about the fulfillment! The Lord and God came, therefore, that Sara might conceive and give birth. The man spoke with the power of God, but it was God who performed the work of God. Thus, by word and action, He indicates that He is God. Then, two of the three men who were seen take their departure, but He who remains is the Lord and God. Not only is He the Lord and God, but He is also the judge. For, standing before the Lord, Abraham said: 'Far be it from you to do this word, to kill the just with the wicked, and the just will be as the unjust.

59 John 8.56.
60 Cf. Gen. 21.1,2.

Far be it from you, who judge all the earth, to make this judgment.'[61] In this whole discourse, therefore, Abraham teaches the faith for which he was justified, and professes his belief in Him whom he sees in the midst of the three men, adores Him alone, and acknowledges Him as the Lord and judge.

(28) In order that you may not perhaps imagine that the acknowledgment of the one included a glorification of the three men who were seen at the same time, consider what Lot said when he saw the two men who had departed: 'And as Lot saw them, he rose to meet them, and with his face to the earth, adored them and said, "Behold, come aside, my lords, in to the house of your servant." '[62] Here, a mere glance at the angels and the plural form is retained; there, the faith of the patriarch renders glory to only one of them; here, the history of sacred Scripture indicates that two of the three men were merely angels; there, it proclaims the Lord and God. For it says: 'And the Lord said to Abraham, "Why did Sara laugh, saying, Shall I therefore bear a child? But I have grown old." Is anything impossible to the word of God? At this time I will return to you, and there will be a son to Sara.'[63] Accordingly, Scripture adheres to the order of the truth, since it does not confuse the plural meaning with Him who was recognized as the Lord and God, nor does it grant the honor that was shown to God alone to the two angels. Lot, it is true, calls them lords, but Scripture calls them angels. There, is the obeisance of a man; here, the avowal of the truth.

(29) After this there is seen the punishment of a just verdict upon Sodom and Gomorrah. And what, finally, is the significance of this event? 'The Lord poured down

61 Cf. Gen. 18.25.
62 Cf. Gen. 19.1,2.
63 Cf. Gen. 18.13,14.

sulphur and fire from the Lord.'[64] As the Lord from the Lord; thus, He did not make any distinction in the name of the nature between those whom He had already kept separate from each other by this designation. We read in the Gospel: 'The Father does not judge anyone, but has given all judgment to the Son.'[65] Hence, the Lord gave what the Lord had received from the Lord.

(30) You, who have become aware that there is the knowledge of a judge in the Lord and God, recognize that there is a common sharing of the same name in God and God. When Jacob, fearing his brother, had taken to flight, he saw in a dream a ladder placed on the earth and reaching to heaven, on which the angels of God were descending and ascending, while the Lord rested upon it and bestowed upon him all the blessings which He had given to Abraham and Isaac. Afterwards, God spoke to him in this manner: 'But God said to Jacob, "Rising, go up to the place, Bethel, and dwell there, and build there an altar to the God, who was seen by you, when you fled from the face of your brother." '[66] God desires glory for God and desires with the designation of a second person, 'who,' He says, 'appeared to you when you fled from the face of your brother,' in order that no confusion might arise about Him being the same person. It is God, therefore, who speaks, and it is God of whom He speaks. The tribute of honor does not separate them in the name of their nature who had been kept distinct by the designation of their existence.

(31) I know, of course, that certain things are necessary for a more complete discussion of this passage, but we must also keep the order of our reply in harmony with the order in which the questions have been proposed. Accordingly, we

---

64 Cf. Gen. 19.24. The same word, 'Lord,' is applied to both, and St. Hilary argues from this that there is no distinction in their nature.
65 Cf. John 5.22.
66 Cf. Gen. 35.1.

shall discuss the problems that still remain at the proper place in the next Book.[67] These points alone now need to be clarified about the God, who asks glory for God: the angel of God who spoke to Agar was both God and the Lord, since He Himself also spoke to Abraham about the same subjects, and the man who was seen by Abraham was both God and Lord; but the two angels who appeared with the Lord and whom He sent to Lot were proclaimed by the Prophet as nothing else than angels. God not only appeared to Abraham as a man, He also came to Jacob as a man. Not only did He come, but it is revealed that He struggled with him; not only did He struggle, but He also became helpless against him with whom He struggled. We neither have the time nor does the subject matter permit any further discussion about the mystery of the struggle. He is certainly God, because Jacob prevailed against God and Israel saw God.

(32) Let us see whether there is any other place, in addition to that of Agar, where this angel of God is identified as God. He was positively identified as such and was discovered to be not only God but the God of Abraham, the God of Isaac, and the God of Jacob. For the angel of the Lord appeared to Moses in the bush, and the Lord speaks from the bush. In your opinion, whose voice is to be understood: that of the one who is seen, or that of someone else? There is no room for deception. Scripture says: 'And the angel of the Lord appeared to him in a flame of fire out of the midst of the bush.' And again: 'The Lord called to him out of the midst of the bush and said: Moses, Moses. And he answered: Here I am. And he said: Come not nigh hither. Put off the shoes from thy feet: for the place whereon thou standest is holy ground. And he said to him: I am the God of thy fathers,

---

67 He discusses the same apparitions in the following Book in order to prove that the Son is not only God but is the *true* God.

the God of Abraham, the God of Isaac, and the God of Jacob.'[68]

The vision and the voice are in the one place, nor is anyone else heard except the one who is seen. He who is an angel of God when He is seen is the same one who is the Lord when He is heard, but He Himself who is the Lord when He is heard is recognized as the God of Abraham, Isaac, and Jacob. When He is called the angel of God, it is revealed that this is not His true nature, and that He is not alone, for He is the angel of God. When He is called the Lord and God, He is proclaimed as possessing the glory and name of His own nature. Accordingly, you have in an angel who appeared in the bush Him who is also the Lord and God.

(33) Run through the testimonies of Moses and see whether he neglects any opportunity to proclaim the Lord and God. Surely, you grasp his words: 'Hear, O Israel, the Lord thy God is one.'[69] Now, grasp the words of that divine canticle of his: 'See, see that I am the Lord, and there is no God besides me.' And, since he has expressed all the words up to the end of the canticle in the person of God, he declares: 'Rejoice together with him, ye heavens, and let all the sons of God adore him. Rejoice, ye people, with his people, and let all the angels of God adore him.'[70]

God is to be honored by the angels of God, for He says: 'Since I am the Lord and there is no God besides me.' He is the only-begotten God, nor does the name 'only-begotten' admit of any companion (just as the unbegotten does not admit of any participator but only in so far as He is unbegotten), for He is the one from the one. Nor is there another unborn God besides the unborn God, nor is there another only-begotten God besides the only-begotten God.

---

68 Cf. Exod. 3.2,4,5.
69 Cf. Deut. 6.4.
70 Cf. Deut. 32.39,43.

Therefore, each of them is unique and alone, namely, as a consequence of the attribute in each of innascibility and birth. Thus, each one is God since, between the one and the one, that is, the one from the one, there is not a second nature of the eternal Godhead. Hence, He is to be adored by the sons of God and glorified by the angels of God. Thus, the sons of God and the angels of God are asked to render honor and worship to God. Grasp the significance of Him who is to be honored and of those by whom He is to be honored, that is, God by the angels and the sons of God! And that you may not believe that the glorification is demanded for one who is not God by nature, and that you may not conclude that this passage referred to the glory that was to be given to God the Father, although the Father is certainly to be glorified in the Son, take note of the blessing which He confers upon Joseph in the same discourse: 'And let the things that were pleasing to him who appeared in the bush come upon the head and the crown of Joseph.'[71]

God, therefore, is to be adored by the sons of God, but the God who is also the Son of God. And God must be honored by the angels of God, but the God who is the angel of God, for God, the angel of God, appeared in the bush, and when Joseph was blessed those things were desired which were pleasing to Him. Neither is He, therefore, not God because He is the angel of God, nor, again, is He, therefore, not the angel of God because He is God, but the meaning of the persons which He pointed out, the distinction which He drew between innascibility and birth, the plan of the heavenly mysteries which He made known, these have taught us that we must not think of God as being alone, since both the angels of God and the sons of God adore the angel of God and the Son of God as God.

(34) These quotations from the books of Moses may

71 Cf. Deut. 33.16.

indeed serve as our reply, or, rather, as the reply of Moses himself, because the heretics, who cite him as an authority, imagine that by his profession of faith in the one God we can be made to believe that the Son of God should not be proclaimed as God. They are irreverent in opposing the testimony of their own witness, since, although he acknowledges the one God, he has not ceased to teach that the Son of God is God. Our next step is to cite the many testimonies of the Prophets concerning this same one.

(35) You grasp the words: 'Hear, O Israel, the Lord thy God is one.' And would you had grasped them correctly! But, in keeping with your interpretation, I want to know the meaning of a prophetic utterance. In the Psalms it is stated: 'God, thy God, hath anointed thee.'[72] In order to make the reader understand, keep the one who anoints separate from the one who is anointed; distinguish between 'thee' and 'thy'; point out to whom these words are addressed and whom they concern. The order which this confession follows is connected with what has preceded. For he had said: 'Thy seat, O God, is forever and ever: the sceptre of thy guidance, the sceptre of thy kingdom. Thou hast loved justice and hated iniquity.'[73] Now, to these words he also added: 'Therefore God, thy God, hath anointed thee.'

Hence, the God of the eternal kingdom was anointed by His God because of the merit which He had acquired by His love for justice and His hatred of iniquity. Are there at least some distinctions between the names that will create confusion in our minds? For, by 'thee' and 'thy' a distinction has been made only in regard to the person, but none whatsoever in the confession of the nature. For, 'thy' has been referred to the author, but 'thee' to point out Him who is from the author. He is God from God, as the Prophet acknowledges in

72 Ps. 44.8.
73 Cf. Ps. 44.7.

the same passage: 'God, thy God, hath anointed thee.' But, there is no other God before the unborn God, as He Himself declares: 'Be witnesses to me and I shall be a witness, saith the Lord God, and my servant whom I have chosen, that you may know, and believe, and understand that I myself am, and there is no other God before me, and there shall be none after me.'[74]

The dignity of Him who is without a beginning has, therefore, been shown, and the glory of Him who is from the unborn one has been preserved, for 'God, thy God, hath anointed thee.' The word 'thy' which he used refers to the birth, but does not destroy the nature. And for this reason He is His God, since He has been born from Him into God. But it does not follow that, because the Father, therefore, is God, the Son also is not God, for 'God, thy God, hath anointed thee.' That is to say, while he indicates both the author and Him who has been born from Him, he has assigned to both the name of the same nature and dignity in one and the same statement.

(36) In order that no possible pretext for the teaching of blasphemy may be derived from what has been said: 'Since I am, and there is no other God before me and there shall be none after me,' just as if the Son, therefore, is not God because He is after God, before whom there is no God and after whom there will be no God, we must on this account explain the meaning of this entire passage. God Himself is a witness for His own words, but His chosen servant also testifies with Him that there is no God before Him nor will there be one after Him. Of course, He Himself is a competent witness for Himself, but He has joined the testimony of His chosen servant to His own testimony about Himself. Hence, the two are one in affirming that there is no God before Him, for from Him are all things, and that

74 Cf. Isa. 43.10.

there will be no God after Him, but by no means that no God has been from Him. The servant had already expressed these teachings when he gave evidence about the Father, the servant of the tribe from which the chosen one was to be born. The same truths are thus revealed in the Gospels: 'Behold my servant, whom I have chosen, my beloved in whom my soul is pleased.'[75] Accordingly, there is no other God before Me, and there will be no other God after Me. That is to say, He makes known the infinity of His eternal and unchangeable power from the fact that before Him and after Him there will be no God besides Him, but after He has given to His servant a share both in His testimony and His name.

(37)   The same truth may be readily learned from His own person. He says to Osee the Prophet: 'I will not add any more to have mercy on the house of Israel, but as their adversary I shall oppose them. But I shall have mercy on the sons of Juda, and I shall save them by the Lord their God.'[76] The Father unmistakably gives the name of God to His Son in whom He chose us before the eternal ages. For this reason He says 'their God,' because the unborn God is from no one, and God the Father has given us as an inheritance to His Son. We read: 'Ask of me, and I will give thee the Gentiles for thy inheritance.'[77] For there is no God to the God from whom are all things, who is eternal and without a beginning. On the other hand, God is the Father to the Son, since He has been born as a God from Him. For us, the Father is God and the Son is God, since the Father acknowledges that His Son is our God, and the Son teaches that His Father is our God. The Son has been called 'God' by the Father, that is, with the very name of His own unborn

75 Cf. Matt. 12.18.
76 Osee 1.6,7.
77 Ps. 2.8.

power.[78] These remarks are a sufficient explanation of Osee.

(38) How explicit is the revelation of God the Father concerning our Lord in the Prophet Isaias. He says: 'Thus says the Lord God, the holy God of Israel, who made all things that are to come. Ask me concerning your sons and your daughters, and concerning the work of my hands give ye charge to me. I made the earth and man upon it, I commanded all the stars, I raised up the king with justice, and all his ways are right. This one shall build my city and shall turn away the captivity of my people not for ransom, nor for presents, saith the Lord of hosts. Egypt will labor and the trade of Ethiopia and Sabaim. Men of stature shall come over to thee, and they shall be thy servants, and they shall walk after thee, bound with manacles, and they shall worship thee and shall make supplication to thee, since God is in thee, and there is no God besides thee. For thou art God and we did not know it. O God of Israel, the Saviour. All those who oppose him shall be confounded and shall be ashamed and they shall go away in confusion.'[79] Is there still any subterfuge for your rashness? Has any excuse for pleading ignorance been left to you, except that it only remains in your power to reveal your godlessness in its true colors? God, from whom are all things, and who made all things by His command, claims the completed work for Himself—for certainly it would not have come into being if He had not said that it should be made. He testifies that He has raised up a just king, who builds a city to Him, His God, and delivers the people from captivity not through a ransom or through gifts, for we are all saved by grace. Then He speaks in this manner, that, after the labor in Egypt, that is, after the calamity of the world, and after the trade of the Ethiopians and the

---

78 The name 'God' properly belongs to the Father as the One who is unbegotten, and He has endowed His Son with this same name.
79 Cf. Isa. 45.11-16.

Sabeans, men of stature shall come over to Him. What, finally, are we to think of the labor in Egypt and the trade of the Ethiopians and the Sabeans?

Let us recall the Magi from the East who adore God and bring gifts, and let us take into consideration the labor involved in making this long journey to Bethlehem in Judaea. In the labor of the princes all the labor in Egypt is represented. For, in the person of the Magi, who falsify the works of God by means of their deceitful trickery, the greatest tribute of a godless religion was offered by the entire world. From their trade with the Egyptians and the Sabeans these same Magi bring gifts of gold, frankincense, and myrrh, and certainly this same incident had also been foretold by another Prophet when he says: 'The Ethiopians shall fall down before his face, and his enemies shall lick the ground. The king of Tharsis and Saba shall bring gifts, and the gold of Arabia shall be given to him.'[80] The labor in Egypt and the trade of the Ethiopians and the Sabeans are revealed, therefore, in the Magi and their gifts, that is, the error of the world in the worship of the Magi, and the gifts of the Gentiles, which had been chosen and offered to the Lord whom they adored.

(39) Finally, there is no mystery about those men of stature who shall come over to Him and follow Him in chains. Look at the Gospels! Peter girds himself in order to follow his Master.[81] Behold, Paul, the servant of Christ, glories in his chains.[82] And let us see whether Christ Jesus, when bound, fulfilled what God had revealed about God His Son. He said: 'They shall make supplication since God is in thee.'[83] Recall, therefore, what the Apostle had said and grasp the meaning of what you recall! 'God was in Christ,

---

80 Cf. Ps. 71.9,10.
81 John 21.7.
82 Philem. 1.1.
83 Isa. 45.14.

reconciling the world to himself.'[84] Then come the words:
'And there is no God besides thee.' And, immediately, the
same Apostle says: 'For there is one Lord, Jesus Christ,
through whom are all things,'[85] and no other one is seen to
be besides Him, because He is one. Thirdly, he also states:
'You are God and we did not know it.' But the former persecutor of the Church has said: 'Whose fathers from whom
is Christ, who is over all things, God.'[86] Consequently, these
men in chains will preach these doctrines, that is, the men
of stature who on the twelve thrones shall judge the tribes of
Israel, and shall follow their Lord as the witnesses of His
doctrine and suffering.

(40) God, therefore, is in God and He is God in whom
God is. And how can it be said: 'There is no God besides
thee,' since God is in the same one? O heretic, you employ
the words, 'There is no God besides me,' for your belief in a
solitary God the Father. How will you interpret the teaching
of God the Father, who declares: 'There is no God besides
thee,'[87] if from the words that were said: 'There is no God
besides me,' you are eager to assert that the Son of God is
not God. Accordingly, to whom, then, did God say: 'There
is no God besides thee'? In this instance, you will be unable
to claim that the person is solitary. For, in the person of the
men of stature, who worship Him and pray to Him, the Lord
said to the king whom He had raised up: 'Since God is in
thee.' Those words are not compatible with one who is alone.
The expression 'in thee' means that someone is, as it were,
present to whom His words are directed. That which follows,
'God is in thee,' reveals not only one who is present, but one
who remains in Him who is present. He separates the one

84 Cf. 2 Cor. 5.19.
85 1 Cor. 8.6.
86 Rom. 9.5.
87 Cf. Deut. 32.39.

who dwells from the one in whom He dwells, but only by a distinction of person, not of nature. God is in Him and He is God in whom God is. God does not take up His abode in a nature that is different from or alien to His own, but abides in His own, and in the one who has been begotten from Him. God is in God because God is from God. 'For thou art God, and we did not know it. O God of Israel, the Saviour.'[88]

(41)   If you deny that God is in God, the following passage will refute you: 'All those who oppose him shall be confounded and ashamed and they shall go away in confusion.' This is the judgment of God against your impiety. You oppose Christ, and the testimony of the Father's voice about Him is a rebuke to you. For, He is God whom you will not acknowledge as God. But you deny it on the pretext of honoring the Father, who says: 'There is no other God besides me.' Be embarrassed and blush for shame! The unborn God does not need the glory that you have brought to Him. He does not ask you to confer this honor of solitude upon Him. He does not desire this idea of Him that comes from your own reasoning, so that you will not acknowledge that He is God, whom He begot from Himself, because of what He said: 'There is no God besides me.'

And, in order that you might not regard this as something personal to Him for the purpose of destroying the divinity of the Son, He completed the glory of His only-begotten with the dignity of the perfect Godhead when He said: 'There is no God besides thee.' Why do you discriminate between those that are equal? Why do you make a distinction between what is placed side by side? It is proper to the Son of God that there is no God besides Him. It is proper to God the Father that no one is God without Him. Use the words of God in reference to God! Express your belief in this manner

---

88 Cf. Isa. 45.15.

and pray to the king: 'Since God is in thee, and there is
no God besides thee. For thou art God and we did not know
it. O God of Israel, the Saviour.'

The tribute of honor does not contain any indignity, nor
does the formula of praise arouse any contradiction, especially
since its denial is burdened with shame and disgrace. Remain
in the words of God! Express your belief in the words of
God and avoid the disgrace that He has proclaimed! When
you deny that the Son of God is God, you will not so much
worship God, as if He were alone in the majesty of glory,
as you will despise the Father by dishonoring the Son. Before
the unbegotten God confess the glorious faith, that there is
no God besides Him; before the only-begotten God, proclaim
that there is no God without Him.

(42) Besides Moses and Isaias, listen in the third place
to Jeremias, who teaches the same doctrine when he declares:
'This is our God, and there shall be no other accounted of
in comparison with him, who has found all the way of
knowledge and gave it to Jacob his servant and to Israel
his beloved. Afterwards, he was seen upon earth and conversed with men.'[89] Previously, he had already declared:
'And he is a man, and who shall know him?' You have,
therefore, a God who was seen on earth and who dwelt with
men. And I want to know how you believe these words are
to be understood: 'No one has at any time seen God, except
the only-begotten Son, who is in the bosom of the Father,'[90]
since Jeremias proclaims a God who was seen on earth and
who dwelt with men. The Father certainly cannot be seen
except by the Son alone. Who is He, therefore, who was seen
and who conversed with men? He is indeed our God and is

---

89 Cf. Bar. 3.36-38. The early Fathers of the Church considered the
   Book of Baruch, the secretary and disciple of Jeremias, as a part of
   the prophecy of Jeremias.
90 Cf. John 1.18.

both visible and tangible in man. And learn from the Prophet, who declares: 'And there shall be no other accounted of in comparison with him.' If you want to know in what manner, then hear what follows, in order that you may not believe that the words, 'Hear, O Israel, the Lord thy God is one,' are not also proper to the Father. For the statements are connected: 'And there shall be no other accounted of in comparison with him, who found all the way of knowledge and gave it to Jacob his servant and to Israel his beloved. Afterwards, he was seen upon earth and conversed with men.' There is one mediator of God and men, God and man, the mediator both in the making of the law and in the assumption of a body. No one else, therefore, is to be compared to Him. Here is one born from God into God, through whom all things in heaven and on earth have been created and through whom the times and the ages have been made. For, everything that is receives its being through His operation. This one, therefore, is the one who draws up the covenant with Abraham, who speaks to Moses, who bears testimony to Israel, who dwells in the Prophets, who is born of the Virgin through the Holy Spirit, who nails the powers opposed and hostile to us to the wood of His Passion, who destroys death in hell, who strengthens the confidence of our hope by His resurrection, and who puts an end to the corruption of human flesh by the glory of His body.

No other one, therefore, shall be compared to this one. For these things are proper to the only-begotten God alone, and this one alone has been born from Him in the peculiar beatitude of His own powers. No other God will be likened to Him, for He does not come from a different substance, but is God from God. Accordingly, in Him there is nothing new, nothing strange, nothing of recent origin. For, when Israel hears that its God is one, and no other God will be made equal to God, the Son of God, so that He is truly God, it is revealed that God the Father and God the Son are clearly one, not by a union of person, but by the unity of nature.[91] The Prophet does not permit God the Son of God to be likened to a second God, because He is God.

---

91 *non unione personae, sed substantiae unitate*: St. Hilary always uses *unio* when referring to the Persons of the Trinity and *unitas* when referring to their nature.

BOOK FIVE

HEN WE WERE REPLYING to the impious and insane doctrines of the heretics in the previous Books, we realized that we were being driven by necessity into such a contradictory position that our answer as well as our silence would be equally dangerous for our hearers. Since their unbelieving statement declared that there was one God in an impious sense, our sound faith could not then deny that there was one God in a religious sense, and it was not possible for us to discuss this subject without becoming conscious of a twofold danger, that it was no less impious to admit it than it was to deny it. And surely, according to human logic, it must be regarded as inconsistent and unreasonable to admit as blasphemous the very same doctrine which it would be blasphemous to deny. The piety of the confession is incompatible with the impiety of the denial, nor is it reasonable to uphold as useful that which it would be useful to destroy.

The human mind, incapable of grasping the wisdom of God and foolish according to the standards of heavenly wisdom, passes judgment in harmony with its helplessness, and is wise in keeping with the weakness of its own nature. It should become foolish in its own estimation in order to be wise unto God, that is to say, by admitting the poverty of its own reasoning and seeking after the wisdom of God, it may become wise, not in conformity with human wisdom, but in those things that lead to God, in order to pass from the knowledge of the folly of the world into the wisdom of God.

The subtlety of the heretics has exploited this folly of human wisdom in order to deceive us, and, by appealing to the authority of the Law and the Gospels, they have asserted that there is one God because it was said: 'Hear, O Israel, the Lord thy God is one.'[1] They realize how much danger is involved either in answering or keeping silence, and in either case seek an opening for their impious doctrine. Thus, our silence would connive at and approve the holiness of these words, which they have employed in a blasphemous sense, and consequently, since there is only one God, the Son of God would not be God, and God would remain one as He really is.[2] On the other hand, if we should contradict this presumptuous and impious profession of faith, our reply, which did not acknowledge the one God, would be untrue to the evangelical faith, since the profession of our faith centers around the one God, or a profession of faith which would confess the Father and the Son as one God would fall into the godlessness of another heresy.

Thus, the wisdom of the world, which is folly before God, would practise its deception under the guise of a flattering and pernicious simplicity, since it would take as the starting point of its faith that which it would be blasphemous either to accept or to deny. As a consequence of this dilemma, they would wring from us the admission that the Son of God is not God, because there is one God, or they would force us into another heresy, so that, if we acknowledge the Father as God and the Son as God, we would be regarded as proclaiming the one God in accordance with the teaching of

1 Cf. Deut. 6.4; Mark 12.29.
2 This is the conclusion which the Arians drew.

Sabellius. Thus, by their manner of teaching about 'the one God' they would exclude another God, or, if there is another God, there would not be one God, or they would be one only in name, because unity does not recognize another God, and another God does not permit a union, and two cannot be one.

(2) We who have acquired the wisdom of God which is folly to the world, and who shall reveal the deception of this poisonous doctrine by the salutary and sincere confession of faith in the Lord, have arranged our reply in such a manner that it will gain admission for the truth that we are to make known, and at the same time will escape the danger of an heretical profession of faith. We have adopted a middle course between these two positions. We do not deny the one God, but teach that there is God and God on the testimony of the very man who proclaimed that there is one God. We do not teach that there is one God as a consequence of a union, and again we do not divide Him into a number of contradictory gods, nor do we, on the contrary, acknowledge only a nominal distinction, but show Him as God and God, while we pass over the question about the union for the time being in order to discuss it more thoroughly later on. On the one hand, the Gospels are right in asserting that Moses has proclaimed the one God; on the other hand, the latter, who reveals the one God, bears witness to the correctness of the Gospel teaching that there is God and God. Thus, our reply is not in opposition to his authority but is drawn from it, so that it would be unlawful to deny that the Son of God is God because for Israel there is one God, since the same one authorizes us to confess the Son of God as God who justifies us in proclaiming the one God.

(3) Accordingly, the order of the subject matter which we have drawn up in this Book adheres to the order of the questions. Since this is the next assertion of their blasphemous

deception: 'We know the one true God,' the entire contents of this second Book[3] centers about the question whether the Son of God is the true God. Without doubt, the craftiness of heretical ingenuity has arranged this plan, while it first speaks of the 'one God' and then confesses 'the one true God' in order to exclude the Son of God from possessing the nature or the divinity of God, since the Godhead which remains in the nature of the one would not go beyond the natural Godhead of the one.

Since, therefore, there is no possibility of doubting that Moses, who proclaimed the one God, is known to have declared that the Son of God is God, let us again examine the testimonies of his words and see whether he also taught that He whom he pointed out as God is the true God. No one doubts, however, that a true nature arises from its nature and power. Thus we say, for example, that wheat is true which has grown to a head, has been covered with awn, has been freed from the chaff, has been ground to flour, has been kneaded into bread, has been taken as food, and has shown in itself both the nature and the effect of bread. Since, therefore, the power of nature is suitable to the true nature, let us see whether He is the true God whom Moses pointed out as God. We shall later discuss the one God, who is at the same time the true God, in order that there may not be any delay in carrying out our promise, and in affirming that the one true God subsists in the persons of the Father and the Son, and thus the wearisome fear of anxious waiting will not be filled with dangerous suspicions.

(4)   Inasmuch as we have received the knowledge of God which indicates that the Son of God is God, I therefore raise the question: In what way does the creation of the world

---

3 Since in Book 4 the saint began a new treatise, i.e., his reply to the errors of the heretics, this present Book 5 may be regarded as the 'second' Book.

deny that He is the true God? There is no doubt that all things are through the Son, since, according to the Apostle: 'All things are through him and in him.'[4] If all things are through Him, and all things are from nothing, and nothing is except through Him, I ask wherein does He lack the true nature of God, since He is not wanting either in the nature or the power of God? For He used the power of His nature that these things should be which were not, and that these things should be which pleased Him. For God has seen that all things are good.

(5) The Law did not indicate any other meaning except that of person when it declared: 'And God said: let there be a firmament,' and added: 'And God made the firmament.'[5] Moreover, it did not make any distinction in the power, nor did it separate the nature, nor did it make any change in the name, for it merely acquainted us with the thought of Him who speaks in order to bring out the meaning of Him who acts. But the designation of one who speaks does not do away with the truth of his nature or power; rather, it gives its approval to this very truth by assigning to Him as great a nature as it possibly can. To accomplish what has been said belongs to a nature in which the agent can carry out what the speaker has declared. In-what, then, will He, who accomplishes, not be the true God, since He is the true God who speaks, when, in fact, the truth of the action follows the truth of the word? He who spoke is God; He who made is God. If there is a true nature in the word, I ask why there is a denial of the true nature in the deed?[6] Unless, perhaps, this one who speaks is true, and that one who executes is not true. Accordingly, we have a true nature in God the Son

4 Col. 1.16.
5 Gen. 1.6,7.
6 If He who speaks is the true God, then He who carries out what has been commanded must also be the true God.

of God. He is God, He is the Creator, He is the Son of God, He can do all things.

It is an insignificant matter that He can do what He wills, because the will always accompanies the power, but He can even do whatever is told to Him. It is characteristic of absolute power that the nature of the agent can do what the speaker can designate. Thus, since the same thing that can be said can likewise be accomplished, that operation, which is placed on an equal level with the word, possesses a true nature. The Son of God, therefore, is not a false God, nor an adopted God, nor a God in name, but a true God. And there is no need to explain anything from the contrary opinion that He is not God, for to me it suffices that there is in Him the name and the nature of God. For, He is God through whom all things have been made. The creation of the world has told me this concerning Him. God is made equal to God by the name; the true nature is made equal to the true nature by means of the work. As the indication of an omnipotent God is contained within the word, so the concept of an omnipotent God is contained in the deed. And, now, in regard to your profession of the Father and the Son, I ask by what authority do you reject the true nature that has been verified by the power of His name and by the name of His power?

(6)   It is necessary to remind the reader that I am not forgetful of or apprehensive about those questions that are generally cited as objections to these subjects that I am now passing over in silence. I am not wanting either in knowledge or understanding about the text that usually is quoted: 'The Father is greater than I,'[7] and others of a similar nature, as if these statements teach that the nature of the true God Himself is not in the Son of God. But, in making our reply, it is fitting that we should adhere to the same order that has

---

7 John 14.28.

been adopted by the opposing doctrine, in order that this step
of the God-fearing doctrine may follow that of the godless
teaching, and destroy the first traces of this deceitful teaching
on its sacrilegious and irreligious journey.

This is the reason why we have postponed and reserved
the utterances of the Gospels and Apostles until the end.[8]
For the present we shall center our entire controversy with
the heretics around the Law and the Prophets, and shall in
the meantime refute their lying and deceitful errors by the
very same texts with which they attempt to mislead others.
For, the truth cannot be understood in any other way than
by pointing out that those things are false which are brought
against the truth. And, certainly, the embarrassment of these
liars will be all the more complete if the lies themselves lead
to the truth. Certainly, according to our human way of thinking, it is commonly agreed that falsehood and truth are not
at all united, and matters of this sort are not brought together
in a mutual agreement. For, when one nature is opposed to
another by reason of a difference of genus, what is contradictory is never brought together, nor do things that are
distinct act together in harmony, nor do things that are
mutually alien to one another have anything in common.

(7)   Granting that such is the case, if there is a distinction
between a true and a false God, then how are we to understand this pronouncement: 'Let us make mankind in our
image and likeness'?[9] These words express the thought, the
thought is the conclusion of a process of reasoning, the truth
sets the process of reasoning in motion. From the words, therefore, let us seek for the thought, from the thought let us
understand the reasoning, and from the reasoning let us
grasp the truth. Concerning the one to whom it was said:
'Let us make mankind in our image and likeness,' I want

---

8 The proofs from the Gospels and the Apostles are given in Books 9-12.
9 Gen. 1.26.

to know wherein He is not true, as is the one who speaks to Him, for, without doubt, these words express the speaker's sentiments and thought. Therefore, He who says 'let us make' indicates that, in regard to the thing that is to be made, there is with Him one who does not oppose Him, one who is not a stranger to Him, one who is not weak but is capable of carrying out what has been said. Accordingly, we must conclude that the speaker certainly had such thoughts in His mind, since He expressed them by His words.

(8) But, in order to inform us more completely about the truth of the nature and activity, He who expressed His thought in words also added that the conclusion of His thought, which arose from the nature, was in agreement with the truth when He says: 'in our image and likeness.' In this case, where is the false God to whom the true God says: 'in our image and likeness'? 'Our' indicates that there is no union, no unlikeness, no distinction. For, according to the true meaning of the word, man was created according to a common image. But, it is not compatible for a true and false God to share things together. The God who speaks speaks to God. Man is fashioned according to the image of the Father and the Son. Their names do not differ, nor is there any distinction in their nature. The image after which man was made has only one form. And how will the true nature be lost, since the two of them have a mutual share in what was made, as well as in the truth of the common image? I do not have time at this moment to discuss this question thoroughly, but we shall point out later the nature of the image of God the Father and God the Son in accordance with which man has been made.[10] In the meantime, we shall now determine whether He is the true God to whom the true God declared: 'Let us make mankind in our image and likeness.'

---

10 This subject is discussed below, 11.25, when it is indicated that the human race will share in the glory of the risen Saviour.

Distinguish, if you can, anything true or false in this sharing together! In your heretical rage, divide what is indivisible! For they are one according to whose image and likeness mankind is the one copy.

(9) Let us follow the order of our reading, so that the truth, which is always consistent with itself, may not be altered by the stumbling block of falsehood. 'And God made man; in the image of God he made him.' There is a common image: God made man to the image of God. To him who denies that the Son of God is God I put the question: According to what image of God does he believe that man has been made by God? Let him always bear in mind that all things are through the Son, lest, perhaps, an heretical interpretation may attribute His work to God the Father. If, therefore, man is made according to the image of God the Father through God the Son, he is likewise made according to the image of the Son, because no one denies that the words 'in our image and likeness' were addressed to the Son. The divine statement, therefore, expressed the idea of the true nature by its words, while the work revealed it by its deeds. God formed man to the image of God, and thus pointed out that He was God and did not deprive Him of the nature of God, since He would also be the true God by the common sharing of the image who was recognized as the Son of God by bringing the work to completion.

(10) Oh, the accursed rage of a despairing soul! Oh, the foolish audacity of godlessness! You hear God and God; you hear 'our image.' Why do you introduce true and not true, or insert natural and false? Why do you attempt to prove by the one God and the one true God that there is not one true God? I shall not as yet crush your raging spirit by the words of the Gospels and the Apostles, according to which the Father and the Son are not one in person but in nature and each of them is God. Meanwhile, let the Law by itself

bring about your destruction! Does it speak of a God that is true and a God that is not true? Has it ever employed any other name except that of nature in regard to each of them? The Law, which gave them the name of the one God, gave them the name of God and God. Why do I say it only gave them this name? By the true nature of the image it proclaimed the true God and the true God. In designating them, it first referred to the name of this nature; then, in giving their origin, it refers to their true nature. For, since he who is made is created according to the image of each one, it is impossible for him to be formed by one that is not true, since each one is the true God.

(11)   Let us now resume the journey of our instruction along which the sacred Law has been teaching us about God. The angel of God speaks to Agar, and the same angel is God. Perhaps for this reason He is not God, because He is an angel of God? For, this name seems to belong to a lower nature, and, where you have the name of a different nature, there, it is believed, the truth of the same nature is not present. The preceding Book has assuredly indicated the futility of this objection. For, by the angel, we understand the office rather than the nature. The Prophet is my witness when he declares: 'Who makest his angels spirits and his ministers a burning fire.'[11] His ministers, therefore, are this burning fire and His angels this coming spirit. For, by these words, there is made known either the nature or the power of these messengers who are called angels or ministers. Hence, this spirit becomes an angel and this burning fire a servant of God, and this nature of theirs assumes the function of a messenger or servant. Since the Law, therefore, or, rather, God through the Law, wished to reveal the person with the name of Father, it spoke of the Son of God as an angel of God, that is, as a messenger of God. By the messenger it

11 Cf. Ps. 103.4.

indicated the meaning of his office; by the name it gave
approval to His true nature, since it called Him God. Here
in the present instance we have the order of salvation, not
of nature.

We do not teach anything else than the Father and the
Son, and thus we place the nature of their names on an
equal plane in order that the birth of the only-begotten Son
from the unbegotten God may preserve the true nature of
God. Here, the designation of the one sent and the sender
acquaints us with nothing else than the Father and the Son;
moreover, it does not take away the true nature, nor does it
destroy the significance of the divinity which the Son received
by His birth, for no one doubts that the nature of the author
is born with the birth of the son, so that it is formed from
one into one, because by the one it is not made distinct from
the one, and thus they are one by the fact that the one is
from the one.

(12) Oh, the impatience of an ardent faith and the
silence that cannot restrain the words that sought for utterance! Even in the preceding Book we went beyond the limits
of the plan of instruction that we had proposed, since, while
we were refuting the impious remarks of the heretics about
the one God, and were proclaiming, according to the teaching
of Moses, that there is God and God, we allowed ourselves
to be swept along by a God-fearing, though injudicious,
haste to express our true and reverent belief in the one God.
Even now we are being delayed by the discussion of another
subject and have deviated from the order that we have drawn
up, and, while speaking about the Son of God as the true
God, in the ardor of our fervent soul we burst forth into the
confession of the true God in the Father and the Son. But
the truth of our faith shall be reserved for its own special
treatise,[12] and what was begun for the sake of our reader's

12 The unity of nature between the Father and the Son is the principal
  subject of Book 8.

peace of mind must still be discussed and developed more
fully in order to reduce our opponents to despair.

(13)   The name of the office, therefore, does not produce
a change in the nature, for He who is the angel of God is
God. But, He may not be the true God in every respect,
if He did not speak of and perform the deeds of God. He
raised Ismael to a great nation and promised that all the
people of the world will be blessed in His name. I ask whether
this is the work of an angel? If it is the work of God, why do
you deprive Him of the truth of His nature from whom you
do not take away the power of His truth? The power of
His nature, therefore, preserves the faith in His true nature,
and He who is the true God, even amid the salutary mysteries
of the Redemption, does not know how to be ever anything
else than the true God.

(14)   First of all, I ask what is the meaning of the true
God and the God that is not true? If it be said to me: 'This
is fire but not true fire, or this is water but not true water,'
I do not grasp what these words signify, and I would like
to know how a true nature of the same kind differs from a
true nature of the same kind? For, that which is fire cannot
be anything else except true fire, and, while its nature remains,
it cannot be lacking in that which true fire is. Take away
from water what water is, and you will be able to destroy it
as true water. Furthermore, if it remains water, it must also
continue to be true water. In fine, a nature can be lost in
such a manner that it does not exist, but it must be a true
nature if it continues to exist. Either the Son of God is true
God in order to be God, or, if He is not true God, then He
cannot even be that which God is. If the nature is wanting,
then the name of the nature is not suitable for Him. If the
nature belongs to Him, then the true nature cannot be wanting to Him.

(15)   Since the angel of God is called God, perhaps this

name has been bestowed upon Him by way of adoption, and He possesses the title rather than the true nature of God. If at the time when He was called an angel of God the nature of God could hardly be recognized in Him, then see whether He revealed the true nature of God in Himself under the name of a nature inferior even to that of the angels. For, a man spoke to Abraham, but Abraham adored God. But, O accursed heretic, Abraham acknowledged Him to be God whom you do not recognize as God. O blasphemer, which of the blessings promised to Abraham do you expect? He is not for you, as He is in reality, the father of the nations, nor will you who have been born again through the blessings of his faith enter into the household of his descendants. You are not raised up from the stones to be a son of Abraham, but, as the enemy of his confession, you have become one of the brood of vipers. You are not the 'Israel of God,' you are not of the race of Abraham, you are not justified by faith, for you have not believed God. For, Abraham was justified by faith and made the father of the nations, and by this faith he worshiped the God in whom he believed. That blessed and faithful patriarch adored God, and learned that He is the true God for whom, as He Himself said of Himself, nothing is impossible.[13] Or is it not to God alone to whom everything is possible? Or, if everything is possible to Him, then I raise the question: What attribute of the true God is wanting to Him?

(16)   And I ask who is this God, the destroyer of Sodom and Gomorrah? For the Lord poured down from the Lord. Is it not the true Lord from the true Lord? Or is it anything else than the Lord from the Lord? What other meaning besides that of person do you find in the Lord and the Lord? Remember that He whom you know as 'the only true God' is the same one whom you have acknowledged as the 'only

---

13 Cf. Gen. 18.14; Luke 1.37.

just judge.' And bear in mind that the Lord who poured down from the Lord, while He does not put the just to death with the unjust, and while He judges the whole earth, is at the same time the Lord and the just judge and poured down from the Lord. Meanwhile, let me ask who He is whom you have called the just judge?

The Lord poured down from the Lord, and you will not deny that He is this just judge who poured down from the Lord. Abraham, the father of the nations but certainly not of the unbelievers, declared: 'Far be it from you to do this word, to kill the just with the wicked, and the just will be as the unjust. Far be it from you, who judge the earth to make this judgment.'[14] This God, the just judge, therefore must also be the true God. O blasphemer, I trap you in your own lie. For the present I do not cite the Gospels in relation to God as the judge; the Law has spoken to me of God as the judge. Debar the Son from being a judge in order to deprive Him of being the true God! For, you have acknowledged Him as the only true God whom you have recognized as the only just judge, and you cannot consistently deny that He is the true God of whom you teach that He is the just judge. He who is the judge is the Lord and He is able to do everything. He is the pledge of eternal blessings; He is the judge of the just and the unjust. He is the God of Abraham and is adored by him. At least invent some lie, in the impudence of your blasphemous and ridiculous statement, from which it will follow that He is not the true God!

(17) The mysteries of heavenly mercy[15] do not destroy the true nature; neither do the forms which He assumed in order to be seen by faith cause saintly persons to be seduced from the faith.[16] The revelations of the Law prefigure the

---

14 Gen. 18.25.
15 This refers to the Incarnation.
16 By this is meant the forms under which the Son of God appeared in the Old Testament.

mystery of the Gospel dispensation in such a manner that what the patriarch sees and believes the Apostle gazes upon and proclaims. Since the Law is the shadow of things to come, the appearance of a symbolic figure has represented the genuineness of the body. And God is seen, believed, and adored in man, who in the fullness of time is to be born as man. For, in the vision, the form of the true nature that was to be forthcoming is assumed. At that time, however, God was only seen in man and not born, but, soon, that which was seen was also born. But familiarity with the external appearance which He adopted for our contemplation aids us in accepting the reality of His birth.

There, God, in accordance with the weakness of our nature, assumed the form of a man who can be seen; here, what was seen is born to help the weakness of our nature. The shadow receives a body, the appearance truth, and the vision a nature. But no change takes place within God when as man He is seen by us or born for us, and the true relationship of the vision and the birth to each other is brought home to us, so that what was born is seen, and what was seen would be born. But, since this is not the place to make a comparison between the Gospels and the Prophets, let us continue in accordance with the plan that we have begun. From the Gospels we shall later prove that the true Son of God was born as man; for the present we shall now show from the patriarchs that the Son of God was the true God under the appearance of man. For, when He appeared as man to Abraham, He was also adored as God and proclaimed as a judge. And when the Lord poured down from the Lord there is no doubt that the Law is speaking of the Father and the Son by the phrase, 'the Lord poured down from the Lord.' On the other hand, we are not to imagine that the patriarch did not know that he was adoring the true God when he adored Him whom he recognized as God.

(18)   Godless infidelity has no little difficulty in grasping the true faith, for the knowledge of a religious doctrine does not gain admission into a mind that has grown narrow through impiety. Thus it comes about that an unbelieving soul does not comprehend the mysterious actions that God performed for the salvation of the human race when He became man, nor does it realize that His work of the Redemption is the power of God. And when they consider the delivery at His birth, the weakness of His infancy, His growth to boyhood, the time of His youth, the pains of His body, the cross of His sufferings, His death on the cross, they do not recognize the true God in such things, since He begot them in Himself as an addition to a nature which formerly He did not possess, so that He did not renounce His true nature, nor by becoming man did He cease to be God, for He who is God began to be man.

Why do they not realize that it is only by the power of the true God that He should be what He was not, without ceasing to be, however, that which He was, since the assumption of a lower nature would not be possible except through the strength of a powerful nature which, while it remained in Him what it was, still could be that which it was not?[17] Ah, the heretical folly and the foolish wisdom of the world that does not perceive that the opprobrium of Christ is the power of God and does not know that the folly of faith is the wisdom of God! For you, therefore, Christ is not God, because He who was is born, because He who is unchangeable grows in age, because He who is impassible suffers, because He who is the living one dies, because He who is dead lives, because everything in Him is against

---

17 To realize the force of this argument we must remember that St. Hilary understood by the Holy Spirit, who overshadowed the Virgin Mary in the conception of Christ, none other than the Word of God Himself, who revealed His power by the formation of His own human body. Cf. above, 2.24.

nature. I ask what else does all this signify except that He is omnipotent because He is God. O holy and venerable Gospels, I do not refer to you as yet in order that you may reveal Christ as God even in the midst of His sufferings! You are derived from the Law, and the latter must point out that He who is God does not cease to be God by taking our weakness upon Himself. By the power of its own mysteries it has given testimony to the mystery of your faith.

(19)   O holy and blessed patriarch, Jacob, be with me, be with me now by the spirit of your faith against the poisonous hissings of infidelity and, while you prevail in the struggle with the man, plead with him as the stronger to bless you.[18] What is this that you are asking from one who is weak? What do you expect from one who is feeble? This one for whose blessing you pray is the one whom you, as the more powerful, weaken by your embrace. The activity of your soul is not in harmony with the deeds of your body, for you think differently from the way you act. By your bodily motions during this struggle you keep this man helpless, but this man is for you the true God, not in name, but in nature. You do not ask to be sanctified by adoptive, but by true, blessings. You struggle with a man, but you behold God face to face. You do not see with your bodily eyes what you perceive with the glance of your faith. In comparison with you He is a feeble man, but your soul has been saved by the vision of God.

During this struggle you are Jacob, but after your faith in the blessing for which you prayed you are Israel.[19] The man is subject to you according to the flesh in anticipation of the sufferings in the flesh. You recognize God in the weakness of His flesh in order to foreshadow the mystery of His

18 Cf. Gen. 32.26-30.
19 According to St. Hilary and other Fathers of the Church, Israel means 'he who saw God.' Actually, it has the idea of 'striving with God.'

blessing in the spirit. His appearance does not prevent you from remaining steadfast in the faith, nor does His weakness deter you from seeking His blessing. Nor does the man bring it about that He is not God who is man, nor is He who is God not the true God, because He who is God cannot but be the true God by the blessing, the transfer, and the name.

(20) The shadow of the Law still adheres to the order of the revelations in the Gospel, and, striving for the truth in its own mysteries, it prefigures the truth of the apostolic doctrine. While asleep, blessed Jacob saw God in a vision; during his sleep there is the revelation of a mystery, not a corporeal manifestation. The angels are represented as descending and ascending to heaven on a ladder, and God is seen resting upon the ladder, and the revelation of the dream has been prophesied by the explanation of the vision. The words of the patriarch, 'the house of God and the gate of heaven,' inform us that this is where the incident took place. Then, after a long account of his actions, he declares: 'But God said to Jacob: Rising, go up to the place, Bethel, and dwell there, and offer there a sacrifice to the God, who was seen by you, when you fled from the face of your brother Esau.'[20]

If the faith of the Gospels has access to God the Father through God the Son, and God cannot be understood except by God,[21] now inform me how the God who asks that glory be given to the God resting upon the ladder is not the true God. And where is there any distinction of nature between the two, when each one possesses one and the same name of the same nature? God is seen and God speaks of the God who is seen. God cannot be known except through God, just as God does not receive worship except through God. We will not realize that He is to be worshiped if He does not teach

20 Cf. Gen. 35.1.
21 Cf. John 14.6; Matt. 11.27.

us that He is to be worshiped, for we will not know of God at all unless this God is known. The revelation of the mysterious doctrines follows its course. God teaches us how to give glory to God. The nature confirms its name; both are nothing else than God. And in the midst of the one name of the one nature of the Father and the Son, how is it possible for God the Son to be deprived of His noble lineage so that He is not the true God?

(21) We must not judge God according to our human sense of values. Our nature cannot lift itself up by its own power to the comprehension of heavenly things. We should learn from God what we are to think about God, because He is the only source of information about Himself. You may be carefully trained in secular learning, you may have led an innocent life, but, while such things assuredly will bring happiness to your conscience, they will not help you to acquire the knowledge of God. Moses was adopted as a son by the queen, he was taught all the lore of the Egyptians. Although his passionate nature, it is true, led him to avenge the injustice shown toward a Hebrew by slaying an Egyptian, he did not know the God who had showered blessings upon his ancestors. For, when he fled from Egypt, fearing the consequences that would follow the discovery of his murder, when he was a shepherd in Madian, when he saw a fire burning the bush without consuming it, he heard God, asked Him His name, and learned about His nature. He would not have become acquainted with these facts about God except through God. Accordingly, we must not speak about God in any other way except that which He Himself has used about Himself so that we may understand Him.

(22) It is an angel of God who appeared in the burning bush, and God speaks from the burning bush. You possess the plan of salvation in the angel because you have an office, not a nature, in the angel. You possess God in the name of the

nature, because the angel of God is God. But, perhaps He is not the true God. Is not the God of Abraham, the God of Isaac, and the God of Jacob the true God? The angel who speaks from the bush is their God forever. And in order that you might not use this opportunity to insinuate that it is only an adoptive name, this God who is speaks to Moses. So it is written: 'But the Lord said to Moses: "I AM WHO AM." and he said: "Thus shalt thou say to the children of Israel: HE WHO IS hath sent me to you." '[22] The angel of God began this discourse in order that he might understand the mystery of our human salvation in the Son. The same one is the God of Abraham, the God of Isaac, and the God of Jacob, in order that he might recognize the name of His nature. The God who is sends him to Israel that he might comprehend that He is in truth that which God is.

(23)   Oh, the useless folly of heretical blasphemy! Why does your insane spirit lie about these matters and, in opposition to the knowledge of such great patriarchs, why does it, like the sower in the night, cast the cockle that is to be burned among the seeds of excellent wheat? But, if you believed Moses, you should also believe that the Son of God is God, unless you will not admit that Moses has spoken about Him. If you wish to deny this, then you will hear the words of God: 'For if you believed Moses you would perhaps believe me also, for he wrote of me.'[23] This one will refute you in unmistakable language; he will refute you with the whole volume of the Law, which he received from the hands of the mediator as it was arranged by the angels. Ascertain whether He who gave the Law is also the true God, since it certainly is the mediator who gave it. Or did not Moses lead the people to the mountain in order to meet God? Or did not God come down from the mountain? Or is this name

22 Exod. 3.14.
23 Cf. John 5.46.

perhaps fictitious and adopted rather than the name of His nature? Notice the sound of the trumpets, the flare of the torches, the clouds of smoke pouring out as if from furnaces on the mountain, the people, realizing their helplessness, trembling at the approach of the Lord, asking Moses to speak to them and admitting that they would die at the voice of the Lord. O heretic, is He not the true God, when Israel feared to die at merely hearing Him, and whose voice human frailty could not endure?

Do you believe, therefore, that He is not the true God because He spoke to you through the weakness of man in order that you might hear and see Him? Moses ascended the mountain and during the period of forty days and nights was instructed in the divine and heavenly mysteries, prepared everything according to the form that had been shown to him on the mountain, acquired the splendor of a dazzling glory because of his intimate conversation with the Lord, and his corruptible countenance could hardly be looked upon, for it was filled with a brightness akin to that of majesty itself. He bears testimony to God, speaks of God, and amid the joy of the people calls upon the angels of God to adore Him, and prays that the desired blessings may come upon the head of Joseph. After these things, will anyone dare to deny that He is the true God and merely concede this name to Him?

(24) We are now of the opinion that the thorough discussion of this subject shows no solid argument that would justify anyone in thinking that there is a true and false God when the Law speaks of God and God and Lord and Lord, and that it has not expressed any distinction either in the names or in the natures, so that we cannot grasp the nature of the names from the names of the nature. The might of God, the power of God, the thing of God,[24] and the name

---

24 *Res Dei*: by this phrase the saint designates the nature of God. Cf. below, 7.13; 9.37.

of God are in Him whom the Lord proclaimed as God. According to the plan that was revealed in the Gospel, it indicated a distinction in person in the God who is obedient to the commands of God in the creation of the world, in God the Creator forming man according to an image that was common both to Him and to God, and the Lord from the Lord as a judge in passing sentence upon the people of Sodom, as God the angel of God in the distribution of blessings, and in the imparting of knowledge about the mysteries of the Lord. While God is always revealed as God the Father and God the Son for our salutary profession of faith, the truth of the nature is taught by the very name of nature, since the Law indicated that each one is God and does not leave us in any doubt about the true nature.

(25)   The moment has now finally arrived when we must call a halt to the theft of heretical folly that proclaims in a godless manner what the Law taught in a pious and reverent manner. When it wishes to deny the Son of God, it begins thus: 'Hear, O Israel, the Lord thy God is one.'[25] And because this blasphemy was imperiled by the name, since the Law spoke about God and God, they added: 'They shall bless thee, the true God,'[26] in order to destroy the nature of the name by the authority of this prophetic utterance, just as if the Law were speaking, therefore, of the one God, and as if God the Son of God were such in name rather than in nature, while we must think of the one God as the only true God.

O foolish one, perhaps you imagine that we are contradicting your words so that we deny the one true God! Of course we do not deny it and acknowledge it just as you do. This is our faith, this is our conviction, this is our preaching. We know that there is one God, and we know that the same one

25 Cf. Deut. 6.4.
26 Cf. Isa. 65.16.

is the one true God. And our profession of faith, which proclaims that the one true God is in the nature of the Son, is
not endangered by the name. Learn the meaning of your
own profession of faith and admit the one true God, so that
you may explain the one true God in a reverent manner.
You seize our pious profession for your own impious purpose,
and you deny what He is while you do not deny what He
is.[27] Thus you deceive the foolish wisdom[28] in order to uproot
the truth under the appearance of truth. You admit the one
true God in order to deny the one true God. Your profession
is regarded as so pious that it is the more blasphemous, as
so true that it is false. You proclaim the one true God in such
a manner that He is no longer such. For you deny that the
Son of God is the true God, although you do not deny that
He is God, but acknowledge Him as God, not in nature, but
in name. If His birth is one in name rather than in truth,
you deny the truth of His name, but, if He was truly born as
God, then, I ask, how is it possible that He is not truly that
which He was born? Either deny Him to be what He is,
or, if He is, how will He not be what He is, since He cannot
be that which He is in such a manner that He is not. We
shall soon speak about the birth. Meanwhile, I shall refute
the blasphemy of your lie about the true nature of God from
the Prophet's own confession, but shall explain the one true
God in such a manner that the heresy of Sabellius may not
dare to claim that the same one is the Father and the Son,
nor may you falsify the truth about the Son of God by
proclaiming that there is only one true God.

(26) In itself, godlessness has no wisdom whatsoever,
and, where the fear of God, which is the beginning of wisdom,
is lacking, it carries away with it the entire foundation of

---

27 This means: you deny that the Son is the true God, while you do not
deny the one true God.
28 The saint here means that the heretics deceive those who trust
more in human reasoning than in the words of God.

wisdom. For, to weaken our faith about the true God in the Son they refer to the prophetic statement wherein it is said: 'And they shall bless thee, the true God.' Here was the first folly of godlessness, either that it misunderstood what the Prophet had previously asserted or, if it did understand, passed over it in silence. Then they applied themselves to deception by the addition of a syllable, which is not found in the Scriptures, thus employing a lie in their folly, just as if we would give so much credibility to their words that we would not think of consulting the prophetic writings at their very source. It was not written thus: 'They shall bless thee, the true God,' but 'they shall bless the true God.' There is no small amount of equivocation between 'thee, the true God' and 'the true God.' Where 'thee' is used, this pronoun seems to indicate another person, but, where this monosyllabic pronoun is not found, there the name also refers to the author of the statement.[29]

(27) So that the explanation of the truth which we must understand may be complete, we shall quote the very words of the Prophet in their entirety: 'Therefore thus saith the Lord: behold, those who serve me shall eat, but you shall be hungry; behold, those who serve me shall drink, but you shall be thirsty. Behold, those who serve me shall rejoice in gladness, but you shall cry for sorrow of your heart and shall howl for grief of spirit. For you shall leave your name in gladness to my elect but the Lord shall slay you. But for my servants a new name shall be called, which shall be blessed upon the earth, and they shall bless the true God, and those who swear upon the earth shall swear by the true God.'[30]

There is always a reason for every departure from the

---

29 According to St. Hilary, Christ spoke these words. Now, if Christ had said: 'They shall bless thee, the true God,' this would mean that Christ was addressing some other person; if 'thee' is omitted in this sentence, then the word 'true God' refers to the one who is speaking, i.e., Christ Himself.
30 Cf. Isa. 65.13-16.

established procedure in teaching, and where there is a motive
for falsification there is a motive for introducing a novelty.
Since there were such wonderful prophecies about God in
former times, and the simple name of God alone was mentioned to show forth the dignity and the nature of God, the
question will be raised as to why the spirit of prophecy now
declared through Isaias that 'the true God' was to be blessed
and men were to swear on earth by 'the true God'? First
of all, we must bear in mind that these words foretell a future
event. And I ask whether He was not the true God who,
in accordance with the teaching of the Jews, was then being
blessed and by whom they were to swear? For, the Jews, not
being acquainted with the revelations of God's mystery, and
therefore ignorant of the Son of God, did not even worship
the Father but only God alone. Certainly, if they worshiped
the Father, they would also worship the Son. These men,
therefore, blessed God and swore by Him. But the Prophet
asserts that 'the true God' was to be blessed. He refers to
Him as 'the true God' because in the mystery of the flesh
which He assumed not everyone would perceive the true
nature of God within Him. And there was the need of em-
phasizing the word 'true' when the word 'false' might suddenly come forth. Let us now review each thought that is
expressed in these same words.

(28) 'Therefore thus saith the Lord: behold, those who
serve me shall eat, but you shall be hungry; behold, those
who serve me shall drink, but you shall be thirsty.' Note that
the same statement indicates two periods, in order that you
may realize the mysterious significance that is associated with
time. 'Those who serve me shall eat'; that is to say, He
rewards the piety of the present generation with future gifts,
so that the punishment of the hunger and thirst that are to
come may afflict the godlessness of the present generation.
Then He added: 'Behold, those who serve me shall rejoice

in gladness, but you shall cry for sorrow of your heart and shall howl for grief of spirit.' In accordance with the above intrepretation we have now another manifestation of the future and the present, so that those who serve shall be glad and those who do not serve shall continue to cry out and howl in their sorrow of heart and affliction of spirit. Next, He declared: 'For you shall leave your name in gladness to my elect, but the Lord shall slay you.' These words are addressed to the carnal Israel of the future, and He reproaches them because He shall leave His name to the elect of God. I ask what kind of a name is this? Naturally, it is Israel to whom these words were directed. Then I ask who is Israel today? And the Apostle testifies without any hesitation that those who walk according to the teaching of Christ, 'in the spirit not in the letter,'[31] are the Israel of God.

(29)   Furthermore, since it was stated above: 'Therefore thus saith the Lord,' we must try to understand why they are followed by 'But the Lord shall slay you,' and, finally, what is the meaning of this sentence, 'But for my servants a new name shall be called, which shall be blessed upon the earth.' Is there any doubt at all that the words 'Therefore thus saith the Lord,' and those that follow, 'But the Lord shall slay you,' make known to us that He who was speaking and He who would slay was anything else than the Lord, who later would also reward those who served Him with a new name, and who would be recognized as having spoken through the Prophets, and as the future judge of the pious and the blasphemers? Hence, these other words have explained the mystery of the revelation contained in the Gospel so that there may not be any doubt that it is the Lord who speaks and the Lord who slays. 'But for my servants a new name shall be called, which shall be blessed upon the earth.' This entire discourse is concerned with the future. And what

31 Rom. 2.29.

is this new name for the religion that shall be blessed upon the earth? If the ages gone by had formerly enjoyed the blessedness of the Christian name, then it is not new. But if this hallowed name of our reverence toward God was unknown, then this new profession of faith assuredly brings us the heavenly blessings which are our reward on earth.

(30) The following words have by now strengthened us in the conviction of all that we believe: 'And they shall bless the true God, and those who swear upon the earth shall swear by the true God.' These to whom a new name has been given in the service of God shall certainly bless the true God; moreover, the God by whom they are to swear is the true God. Or is there any doubt about the one by whom they are to swear, and who is to be blessed, and through whom a new name will be granted to those who serve Him? O heretic, in opposition to your godless doctrine, I am supported by the unmistakable faith of the ecclesiastical pronouncements, by the new name that has been received through you, O Christ, and by the title which shall be blessed upon earth in acknowledgment of the service that has been rendered in swearing that you are the true God. The voice of all those who believe in you, O Christ, speaks of you as God. The entire faith of the believers swears that you are God, acknowledging you as the true God, proclaiming you as the true God, convinced that you are the true God.

(31) Therefore, although these words of the Prophet have cleared up every difficulty, so that we know that they indicate God, that it is He who is being served by a new name, and through whom the newness of the same name will be blessed on earth, that He is the true God who will be blessed, that He is the true God by whom they shall swear, and in the fullness of time the pious faith of the Church will acknowledge all these things in its worship of Christ the Lord (and the statement of the Prophet has joined

the words together in such a manner that he did not cause any innovation by introducing a pronoun in order to point out a second person. If he had added 'thee, the true God,' then the words of the speaker would have referred to another person, but when he says 'the true God' he let it be known that the speaker was meant), and although there is no doubt about the one whom the present words designate, still, it is evident from the connection with what has preceded to whom the sentence refers. He says: 'I appeared openly to those who did not ask for me, and I have been found by those that sought me not. I said: Behold me, to a nation that did not call upon my name. I have spread forth my hands all day to a people that did not believe in me and contradicted me.'[32]

Is godless falsehood still hesitant about its dishonest teaching, and will He not be recognized as the true God who speaks these things? I raise the question: Who appeared to those who did not ask for Him and was found by those who did not seek Him? And who stretched forth His hand all the day long to the people who did not believe in Him and contradicted Him? Compare these words with that sacred and divine canticle of Deuteronomy,[33] wherein God, in His anger at those who are not gods, incited the infidels to zeal against those who are no people and a foolish people, and recognize who it is that is revealed to a people that did not know Him, who is taken away by strangers as their special God, and who stretches forth His hands to a people that mistrusted and opposed Him, and who nails the handwriting of a former decree to the cross. Here, the spirit of the Prophet declares in an orderly and connected discourse: 'For my servants a new name shall be called, which shall be blessed

32 Cf. Isa. 65.1-2.
33 Deut. 34.21.

upon the earth, and they shall bless the true God, and those who swear upon the earth shall swear by the true God.'

(32) If the heretics in their folly and godlessness shall lyingly assert that these words were spoken by the person of God the Father in their efforts to deceive the ignorant and the more simple-minded, so that they may not be ascribed to the Son of God, they shall hear the Apostle and the teacher of the Gentiles charging them with a lie, for he declares that all these things are related to the mysterious events of the Lord's Passion and to the time when the faith of the Gospel was made known, since he reproached the people of Israel for their unbelief in not understanding the coming of the Lord in the flesh. He spoke thus: 'For whoever calls upon the name of the Lord shall be saved. How then are they to call upon him in whom they have not believed? But how are they to believe him whom they have not heard? And how are they to hear, if no one preaches? But how are men to preach unless they be sent? As it is written, "How beautiful are the feet of those who announce peace, of those who announce good things!" But all do not obey the Gospel. For Isaias says, "Lord, who has believed our report?" Faith then depends on hearing, and hearing on the word. But I say: Have they not heard? Yes, indeed, "Their voice has gone forth into all the earth, and their words unto the ends of the world." But I say: Has not Israel known? First of all, Moses says, "I will provoke you against those who are not a nation; I will stir you to anger against a senseless nation." Then Isaias dares to say, "I appeared to those who did not seek me, and I was found by those who did ask me." But to Israel what does he say? "All the day long I stretched out my hands to a people that did not hear me." '[34]

Who are you that you have gone beyond the circles of heaven, uncertain whether in the body or out of the body,

---

34 Cf. Rom. 10.13-21.

and have become a more reliable interpreter of the prophetic words than Paul? Who are you that you have heard the ineffable revelations of the heavenly mystery, have been silent about them, and have taught the knowledge that was made known to you with greater assurance? Who are you that you have been preserved to fill up the Lord's Passion on the cross?[35] And how should you, after leaving Paradise, to which you had previously been transported, have imparted better instructions about the divine Scriptures than the vessel of election, you who do not know that these words and deeds come from the true God, and that His true and chosen Apostle had proclaimed them in order that we might have knowledge of the true God?

(33) It may be, perhaps, that the Apostle was not inspired by the spirit of prophecy in using the words of the Prophet, and hence has become an arbitrary interpreter of another man's statements. The Apostle, it is true, expresses everything according to the revelation of Christ, but he is familiar with the words of Isaias from the words of Isaias himself. At the beginning of his discourse, where, he mentions the true God, who is to be blessed by those who serve Him and by whom they are to swear, we read the following prayer of the Prophet: 'From the beginning of the world we have not heard, nor have our eyes seen any God besides thee, and thy works which thou wilt do for those who await thy mercy.'[36] Isaias declares that he has seen no one except this God. And he had seen the glory of God and foretold the mystery of His incarnation from a virgin. And if you do not realize, O heretic, that he saw the only-begotten God in this glory, then listen to words of John the Evangelist when he says: 'But Isaias said these things when he saw his glory

---

35 These words probably refer to Col. 1.24.
36 Cf. Isa. 64.4.

and spoke of him.'[37] O blasphemous heretic, you are driven back here by the words of the Apostle, there by the words of the Gospels, and elsewhere by the words of the Prophet. Isaias saw God and it is written: 'No one has at any time seen God. The only-begotten Son, who is in the bosom of the Father, he has described him.'[38] The Prophet saw God and beheld His glory to such a degree that he was hated for his prophetical dignity. And it was on this account that the Jews passed the sentence of death upon him.

(34) Therefore, the only-begotten Son, who is in the bosom of the Father, has described the God whom no one has seen. Either reject the account of the Only-begotten, or believe in Him who was seen, who appeared to those who did not know Him, who became the special God of the Gentiles who did not invoke Him, who extends His hands before the people who opposed Him, but in such a manner that a new name is given to His servants, and on earth people bless Him and swear by Him as the true God! The prophecy declares, the Gospel testifies, the Apostle interprets, the Church professes that He who was seen is the true God, since no one asserts that it was God the Father who was seen.

Still, the madness of the heretics has gone so far as to deny Him while pretending to acknowledge Him. It denies by a new and godless kind of confession, and withdraws from the faith while imitating it in a very subtle manner. When they profess that there is only one God and this same one is alone true, alone just, alone wise, alone unchangeable, alone immortal, alone powerful, they make the Son also subject to Him by a distinction in substance, not as one born from God

---

37 Cf. John 12.41. St. Hilary reasons as follows: According to the testimony of St. John, Isaias saw God. But, according to this same Evangelist, no one has seen God the Father except God the Son. Hence, Isaias saw God the Son.

38 Cf. John 1.18.

into God but adopted as the Son by creation. He does not possess His name by nature, but has been allotted this name by His adoption; thus, He must be wanting in all those attributes which they proclaim as belonging exclusively to the solitary majesty of the Father.

(35) Heretical perversity is incapable of knowing and acknowledging the one true God, and the faith and understanding of this revelation are beyond the comprehension of its godlessness. We must first make our profession of faith in the Father and the Son in order to understand the one true God, and, when we have become aware of the mysteries of man's salvation, which are accomplished within us through the power of regeneration into the life of the Father and the Son, then we strive to penetrate the mysteries of the Law and the Prophets.

Godlessness, in its ignorance of the teaching of the Gospels and the Apostles, does not comprehend the one true God. Although from their own writings we shall present the knowledge of this truth until we have attained the most complete profession of true piety, that the only-begotten Son exists by the Father as one undivided and inseparable from Him, not according to person but according to nature, that He is understood as existing from the Father, and for this reason He is God because He is God by the nature of God, still, from the prophetical words the faith of this unity is to be constructed and from them must be laid the foundations of the Gospel structure, so that by the same nature of the one Godhead one God may be understood, and the only-begotten God may not be represented as a second God.

Throughout our entire discussion in this Book we have followed an order so that the proofs whereby we showed in the previous Book that the Son was God, by these self-same proofs we now taught that He is the true God. And, as I hope, the explanation of all these words was such that He was recognized as the true God who is not denied to be God.

The remaining portions of this treatise will aim to prove that He who is understood to be the true God should not be looked upon as a second God, and what does not lead to a second God is to be regarded as pertaining to the one God; this one, however, does not destroy the subsistent nature of the Son, but preserves the nature of the one God in God and God.

(36) Respect for the truth demands that the first account of this knowledge should be taken from him through whom God began to manifest Himself to the world, that is, from Moses through whom the only-begotten God confessed: 'See, see that I am God, and there is no God besides me.'[39] And in order that the godlessness of the heretics may not, perhaps, apply the meaning of these words to the unbegotten God the Father, the sense itself of the words and the authority of the Apostle come to our aid, who, as we have already explained, interprets this whole passage as pertaining to the person of the only-begotten God. He has also pointed out that the words, 'Rejoice, you Gentiles, with his people,'[40] are proper to Him, and to gain credence for these words he adds: 'There shall be the root of Jesse and he who shall arise to rule the Gentiles . . . in him the Gentiles shall hope.'[41] Moses, therefore, has indicated the one who said: 'There is no God besides me,' while he declared: 'Rejoice, you Gentiles, with him,' and the Apostle understands these very words of the Lord Jesus Christ, the only-begotten God, in whom a king shall rise from the root of Jesse, according to the flesh, who is the hope of the Gentiles. We must now consider the significance itself of these words, in order that we may understand the circumstance under which they were uttered, since there is no doubt that they were spoken.

(37) The true, complete, and perfect mystery of our faith is to profess God from God and God in God, not by a

---

39 Cf. Deut. 32.39.
40 Rom. 15.10.
41 Rom. 15.12; cf. Isa. 11.10.

corporeal process but by the divine powers, not by a transfusion of a nature into a nature, but by the mystery and power of nature. God is not from God by a division, an extension,/ or an emanation; He subsists while He is born by the power of nature into the same nature. The following Books, in explaining the words of the Gospels and Apostles, speak about these very questions more plainly; in the meantime, we must teach what we preach and believe from the Law and the Prophets. The birth of God, therefore, must contain that nature from which it has proceeded, for that does not subsist other than God that subsists from no other source than from God. He possesses the same nature in such a manner, not that He who begot is the same as He who is born (for how will He Himself be, since He has been born?), but that He who was born subsists in those very things which He who begot Him possesses in their entirety, because what is born is not from anywhere else. For this reason, what subsists from one into one cannot be referred to anything else, and what lives from the living is not new in itself, and there is not wanting to Him what the living one begot in the living one.

Thus, the incorporeal and unchangeable God preserves His own nature in the generation of the Son, while He begets an incorporeal and unchangeable God, nor does the perfect birth of the incorporeal and unchangeable God from the incorporeal and unchangeable God lead to a loss of nature; as a matter of fact, this is the mystery of the God who subsists from God. The only-begotten Son thus bears testimony to these things through the saintly Moses: 'See, see that I am the Lord and there is no God besides me.' There is no other nature of the Godhead so that there should be any God besides Him. Although He Himself is God, God is also in Him through the power of nature. And by this fact that He Himself is God and God is in Him there is no God besides Him. That which God is does not have its existence from anywhere else, and God is in Him, and He has in Himself both that which He Himself is and that from which He exists.

(38)   One and the same prophetic spirit confirms the true and salutary profession of our faith in very many persons, and amid the changes and intervals of time preserves the God-fearing doctrine in its entirety. In order that the words which the only-begotten God spoke through Moses may encourage us to greater progress in our comprehension, the same prophetic spirit, in the person of the men of stature, repeats the words of God through Isaias: 'For God is in thee, and there is no God besides thee. For thou art God, and we did not know it. O God of Israel, the Saviour.' Let the hopeless frenzy of heretical impiety venture forth against this inseparable profession of the nature and the name, and let the raging mouth of its folly tear apart, if it can, things that are united in words and deeds!

God is in God, and besides Him there is no God. Let it separate Him who dwells within from Him within whom He dwells, and divide the understanding of this mystery by making a distinction in their natures. By the words, 'God is in thee,' he taught that the true nature of God the Father is in God the Son, since God is known to be in Him who is God. But, in the words that he added, 'There is no God besides thee,' he reveals that there is no God besides Him, because God dwells in God Himself. This third part, however, 'Thou art God and we did not know it,' offers testimony to a pious and loyal profession of the human mind which, after it had become aware of the mysteries of the birth, and of the name [Emmanuel] that had been made known to Joseph by the angel, declared: 'Thou art God, and we did not know it. O God of Israel, the Saviour.' They perceive that the nature of God subsists in Him, since God dwells in God, and outside of Him who is God there can be no other God, since

God Himself, and the God with Him, do not allow us to fall into the error of believing in another God. And Isaias, indeed, thus prophesied about these things while he was bearing estimony to the undivided and inseparable Godhead of the Father and the Son.

(39)   Jeremias was endowed with a similar prophetical power, and thus informed us that the nature of the only-begotten God was inseparable from the nature of God the Father, when he declared: 'This is our God, and there shall no other be accounted of in comparison of him, who has found all the way of knowledge and gave it to Jacob his servant and to Israel his beloved. Afterwards, he was seen on earth and conversed with men.'[42] O heretic, why do you suppose that there is another God in God the Son of God? Learn to know and to acknowledge the one true God. No other God is likened to Christ in order to be God. He is God by nature, by birth, and by God. What God is is from God; it is not in addition another God. Another will not be compared to Him, for there is no other nature in Him except that which is the true nature of God. Why do you group together a true and false God, a spurious and genuine God, a like and an unlike God, under the false pretense of worshiping the one God? The Father is God; the Son is also God. God is in God, and besides Him there is no God. No other is made equal to Him to be God. If by these things you will understand that God is one rather than unique, you will profess the God-fearing teaching of the Church which acknowledges the Father in the Son. If in your ignorance of the heavenly mystery you pretend that there is one God, in the sense of a solitary God, then you are outside the knowledge of God, since you do not confess that God is in God.

---

42 Cf. Bar. 3.36-38.

BOOK SIX

REALIZE THAT I have undertaken to write these treatises, at a most trying and unfavorable moment, against the idiotic heresy of the blasphemers who affirm that the Son of God is a creature. Throughout almost the entire Roman Empire, many churches have already become infected with the disease of this fatal teaching, and by long familiarity with its doctrine and its deceptive name of the true worship of God have become attached to this maliciously and unlawfully appropriated belief, as if it belonged to this pious faith. I know that it is difficult to bring about an improvement in the will when it has become rooted in its error, because many have approved of it and the weight of public opinion is in its favor. An error among a large number of people is serious and dangerous, and many of them fall away. Even if they become aware of their predicament, they presume upon their prestige to prevent them from undergoing the shame of rising from their error, and because of their numbers they are impudent enough to wish that their false doctrine be regarded as wisdom, and to assert that an error, which they share in common with others, is the knowledge of the truth, since they assume that a false doctrine is less likely to be found among so many.

(2) In addition to the obligation of my vocation and office, whereby as a bishop of the Church I must indeed

169

devote myself to the ministry of preaching the Gospel, I was the more inclined to assume the burden of writing, the more threatening was the danger to so many who were being held by this false belief. I anticipated a greater measure of happiness from the salvation of many, if, after they had acquired the knowledge of the perfect faith in God, they would renounce the blasphemous teachings of human folly, would repudiate the heretics and return to God, would soar aloft in freedom and security from the deadly food by which birds are often enticed into a trap, would follow Christ as their leader, the Prophets as messengers, the Apostles as guides, and the complete faith and perfect salvation in the profession of the Father and the Son, and, when they recalled the words of the Lord: 'He who does not honor the Son, does not honor the Father who sent him,'[1] would seek to give glory to the Father by glorifying the Son.

(3) A destructive and fatal plague lately appeared among the people, and this frightful contagion spread everywhere and led to the disaster of merciless death. The sudden devastation, with their inhabitants, of cities that were reduced to chaos, or the frequent and mournful loss of life in the time of war, or the widespread epidemics of incurable disease have never wrought as much damage to the human race as this deadly heresy. To God, unto whom all the dead live, only that is destroyed which destroys itself. He Himself will be the judge of all, and in accordance with the mercy of His majesty will moderate the penalty that was deserved in the case of one who went astray through ignorance, but, for those who deny Him, He will not pass judgment upon them at that moment; quite the contrary, He will deny them.[2]

(4) It denies, this raging heresy denies, the mystery of the true faith, and uses the principles of piety to teach its

---

1 John 5.23.
2 Cf. Matt. 10.33.

impious doctrine, when it begins the explanation of its infidelity, as indicated in the preceding Books, in this manner: 'We know the one God, alone unmade, alone everlasting, alone without a beginning, alone true, alone possessing immortality, alone the best, alone powerful.' The beginning of our pious profession of faith aids this one that has been unlawfully appropriated, for it is stated there: 'One God, alone unmade, alone without a beginning,' so that by the ostentatious display of words in a religious sense they might add others in an irreligious sense. After many other assertions of a similar nature in regard to the Son, which they have also brought forward in the confession of their pretended worship of God, they continued: 'the perfect creature of God, but not just as one of His creatures; He was the handiwork, but not as the other things that were made.' Then, after many other things, in which they concealed the design of their heretical blasphemy by inserting confessions of the truth in order to bolster their opinion that He came into existence from non-existing things, by means of a subtle and ingenious explanation they declared: 'And He has been created and has been formed before the world; still, He was not before He was born.'

Finally, as if everything in defence of their godlessness were guarded most securely, in order that He might not be recognized either as the Son or as God, they went on: 'If the expressions "from Him," and "from the womb," and "I came forth from the Father and have come," are understood as if He were a part of this one substance, and as if He were the extension of an emanation, then,' according to them, 'the Father would be a composite being, divisible and changeable, and a body, and, in so far as it depends on them, the God without a body is subject to the limitations of a body.' And since we must now renew our attack upon this explanation of the most godless heresy from the statements in the Gospels, we have judged it expedient to include the complete text of this heresy here in Book 6, which we have already transcribed in our first Book,[3] in order that by reading it again, and by examining each of its articles with the additional answers provided by a comparison with the teachings of the Gospels and the Apostles, we may draw from them a recognition of the truth in spite of their unwillingness and resistance. Hence, they say:

(5) 'We know the one God, alone unmade, alone everlasting, alone without a beginning, alone true, alone possessing immortality, alone the best, alone powerful, the Creator of all, the unchangeable, immutable, just, and best regulator and ordainer of the Law, the Prophets, and the New Testament. This God gave birth to the only-begotten Son before all the ages, through whom He also made the world and all things, born not in appearance but in truth, obedient to His will. He is unchangeable and immutable, the perfect creature of God, but not just as one of His creatures; He was the handiwork, but not as the other things that were made. The Son is not, as Valentinian asserted, an emanation of the Father, nor is the Son, as Mani taught, a portion of the one substance of the Father, nor as Sabellius, who divides the union and calls the same one the Son whom he also called the Father, nor, as Hieracas declares, is He a lamp from a lamp, or a torch divided into two parts.'

'Nor is He one who previously was, and then was born or created anew into the Son, but, as even you yourself, O most blessed Father, in the presence of the Church and the council of the brethren have frequently condemned those who introduce such doctrines. But, as we have stated, He was created by the will of God before all times and ages, and has received both His life and His being from the Father, and the Father makes His own glorious qualities exist in Him. For, the

---

3 Cf. above 4.12-13.

Father, in conferring the inheritance of all things upon Him, has not deprived Himself of those which have not been made and are still in His possession; He is still the origin of all things.'

(6) 'Wherefore, there are three substances: the Father, the Son, and the Holy Spirit. Truly, God is the cause of all things, completely alone, without a beginning; the Son, however, has been brought forth from the Father without time, and has been created and has been formed before the world; still, He was not before He was born, but was born without time before everything, and He alone has the same substance as the Father alone. For He is not eternal or co-eternal, nor was He uncreated at the same time with the Father, nor, as certain individuals say, does He possess His being at the same time with the Father, or according to some who advance two unborn principles, but as the oneness or principle of all things, in this manner God is also before all things. Therefore, He is likewise before the Son, as we have also learned from you when you taught publicly in the church.'

'In so far as God confers upon Him His being, His glory, His life, and everything that has been given to Him, in so far God is His principle. But He is His principle, that is to say, His God, since He is before Him. For, if the expressions "from Him," and "from the womb," and "I came forth from the Father and have come," are understood as if He were a part of this one substance and as if He were the extension of an emanation, then, according to them, the Father would be a composite being, divisible and changeable, and a body, and in so far as it depends on them, the God without a body is subject to the limitations of a body.'

(7) Who does not recognize in these words the slippery windings of the serpent's tracks, and who does not perceive in its crooked contortions the coiled snake in which the tremendous power of its poisonous mouth is concealed when

its twisted body is rolled together in a circle? But, when it has been stretched out and uncoiled, all the venom hidden within its head will be revealed. In the first place, it offers us the true names, so that the poison of error may gain admission. There is goodness in their mouth, so that the evil in their heart may creep in. And among all their words I never hear them give the name of God to the Son of God; I never hear them teach about the Son in such a manner that He is the Son. They introduce the name of the Son in order to pass over His nature in silence; they take away the nature in order that the name may be foreign to Him. They bring forth other heresies as a pretext for disguising the lies of their own heresy. They offer us the one God alone and the one true God alone, in order to deprive the Son of the true and proper attributes that belong to God.

(8) Therefore, although we learned in the preceding Books from the teaching of the Law and the Prophets about God and God, about the true God and the true God, and of the one true God, who is to be conceived as being in the true God the Father and in the true God the Son by a unity of nature, not by a union of person, we must cite the doctrines of the Gospels and the Apostles for a complete explanation of this faith, in order that we may understand that the Son of God is God, not by a nature alien to or different from that of the Father, but that He belongs to the same Godhead, since He exists by a true birth.

I do not imagine that anyone can be so unreasonable as not to understand God's revelations about Himself when he has become aware of them, or who does not wish to understand them when he has learned to know them, or who believes that they should be improved by the theories of human wisdom. Before beginning to speak about the subjects themselves that are connected with these salutary mysteries, we must unmask the complete disguise of this cunning malice so that the heretical belief may not flatter itself in any way by its exposure of the names of the heretics, so that the hidden poison may be betrayed and revealed by the very same means that it has used to conceal itself, and so that the comprehension of the public consciousness may move forward to the knowledge of this honeyed poison.

(9) Therefore, since the heretics did not wish the Son of God to be from God, nor born as God from the nature and in the nature of God from God, and since they had spoken of the 'one God alone true' without adding 'the Father,' after thus disposing of the attribute of birth, and in order to deny the one true nature of the Father and the Son, they stated: 'Nor is the Son, as Valentinian asserted, an emanation of the Father,' in order to reject the birth of God from God by condemning the term 'emanation' as it appeared in the heresy of Valentinian.

Valentinian invented certain absurd and disgusting things, when, in addition to the principal God, he introduced a family of deities, and the numerous powers of the aeons, and then asserted that our Lord Jesus Christ came into existence as an emanation according to a mystery of a sacred will. The evangelical and apostolic faith of the Church, therefore, knows nothing about this pretended emanation, which owes its origin to a rash and idiotic author. It is unaware of the 'highest aeon,' the 'silence,' and the 'thirty aeons' of Valentinian, and is familiar with nothing else than the one God the Father from whom are all things, and our one Lord Jesus Christ through whom are all things, and who has been born as God from God. But, because God is born from God, and His birth has not taken away from God what God is, but He is born as God from God, and, since what is born, according to the understanding of our human nature, seems to have come into existence as an emanation so that the emanation itself may be regarded as a birth, they therefore have attempted to do away with the term 'emanation' by joining it to the heresy of Valentinian so that the nature of the birth might not remain, because the idea of an emanation, according to our human way of thinking, does not differ much from an earthly birth.

The slowness and difficulty whereby our human nature grasps divine things makes it necessary to remind ourselves frequently of what we have formerly stressed,[4] that we should not look upon human analogies as completely satisfactory in explaining the mysteries of the divine power, but that the illustrations of an earthly nature are only employed in order to direct our mind in a spiritual way to heavenly things, in order that we may move forward along this step of our nature to the comprehension of the divine majesty. But, the birth of God is not to be judged according to the emanations of human births. Where one is born from one, and God is born from God, an earthly birth only hints at the meaning. Moreover, the origin of those who are born is not entirely suitable as a means of comparison, since in it there is the intercourse, the conception, the time, and the delivery, while in the birth of God we are to understand nothing else except that He was born. We shall treat of the true nature of the divine birth according to the faith of the Gospels and the Apostles in its proper place.[5] Meanwhile, we must expose the character of the heretical deceit whereby they suppressed the term 'emanation' in order to destroy the true nature of His birth.

(10) They also practise the same kind of malicious deceit in other matters when they declare: 'Nor is the Son, as Mani taught, a portion of the one substance of the Father.' Previously, they had rejected the doctrine of emanation in order to do away with the birth, while now they likewise repudiate

---

4 Cf. above, 1.10; 4.2.
5 Cf. below, 6.23-52.

the portion of the one substance by invoking the name of Mani in order that we may not believe that God is from God. For, in his unbridled fury, Mani refused to accept the Law and the Prophets and, in so far as it depended upon him, was an avowed champion of the Devil, and an ignorant worshiper of his sun, and taught that a portion of the one substance was in the Virgin. He meant us to understand by the Son a portion of some part of the substance of God that had appeared in the flesh. Accordingly, in order to do away with the birth of the only-begotten Son and the name of the one substance, a portion of the one substance is extended in the birth of the Son so that, since it would be blasphemous to assert that the birth has resulted from a portion of one substance, first of all, the birth, which had been condemned in the Manichaean doctrine of the portion, never actually took place, then the name and the faith of the one substance would be taken away, because this would correspond to a portion among the heretics, and, consequently, God would not be from God, because the true property of the divine nature would not be present within Him.[6]

Why does this blasphemous rage simulate such absurd worries under the hypocritical pretext of giving worship to God? The pious faith of the Church condemns Mani as one of the proponents of heretical insanity. She does not know of a portion in the Son, but is aware that the whole God is from the whole God, not cut off, but born; she realizes that the birth of God does not mean a diminution of the begetter nor the weakness of the one begotten. If her knowledge comes from herself, then direct your criticism against her boldness in using such knowledge which she has unjustly appropriated, but, if she has learned of it from her God, then concede that

---

6 Christ would not be the true God if He were composed of only a portion of the divine substance. To be the true God He must possess the entire divine substance.

the one begotten is aware of His own birth. The only-be-gotten God has thus instructed her that the Father and the Son are one and that the fullness of the Godhead is in the Son. Hence, she also detests this portion of the one substance in the Son, and worships the true Godhead in the Son because of the true nature of His birth. But, we wish to examine the rest of this section briefly while we postpone for the time being a more detailed answer to these specific charges.

(11)   These words come next: 'Nor as Sabellius, who divides the union and calls the same one the Son whom he also called the Father.' If this is the belief of Sabellius, he does not know the mysteries of the Gospels and the Apostles. But the heretics are not without guile in this condemnation of a heretic. Since they do not wish the Father and the Son to be one, they reproach Sabellius for his guilt in dividing the union; this division of the union does not result in the birth but divides Him in the Virgin.[7] But we acknowledge the birth; we detest the union and hold fast to the unity of the Godhead, namely, that as God from God they are one in nature, while that which was formed by a true birth from God into God did not receive its being from anywhere else except from God.

That which does not exist from anywhere else than from God must continue in that true nature by which it is God, and thereby they are one, since He who is from God is Himself neither anything else than God nor is He from anywhere else than from God. But, the union of Sabellius is

---

7 Sabellius taught that there is a unicity of Persons in the Trinity, i.e., the Father and the Son are one Person under two different names. A corollary of his teaching is that there was a divine and human Person in Christ. The Arians reproached Sabellius for creating a division in the one Person of God the Father, who is indivisible, and for also teaching that there are two Persons in Christ, since, according to them, Christ is a purely human person. The purpose of the Arians, of course, was to condemn the Catholics, who were regarded as reviving the errors of Sabellius.

only advanced for the purpose of uprooting the pious belief of the Church in this unity. I shall, therefore, expose the other cunning devices of heretical ingenuity so that no one may believe that I am acting perhaps through groundless fear rather than from genuine concern, and thus am a malicious interpreter of another man's simplicity. At the conclusion of this complete profession of faith, I shall indicate the consequences to which the logical outcome of these cunning words have inevitably led.

(12) The words that follow are: 'Nor, as Hieracas declares, is He a lamp from a lamp, or a torch divided into two parts. Nor is He one who previously was, and then was born or created anew into the Son.' Since Hieracas did not know about the birth of the Only-begotten, and did not penetrate into the depths of the mysteries of the Gospel, he taught that there were two lights from one lamp, so that the twofold division of the lights resembled the substance of the Father and the Son, which had been enkindled into light by the oil of one vessel, just as if there were an external substance of oil in a lamp which contained the essence of two kinds of lights, or as if it were indeed a candle which had the same wick throughout and which was burning at both ends, and as if there were some matter between them from which a twofold light was diffused.

The error of human folly has given rise to these theories because the wisdom which they possess is a wisdom that comes from themselves rather than from God. But, because the profession of the true faith is that God is born from God in the manner of a light from a light, which sends forth its substance without suffering any loss, so that it gives what it has and has what it gives, and that which is is born—for nothing else is born except that which is, and the birth has received that which was, and has not taken away that which it has received, and both are one, while it is born from that which is, and what is born does not come from anywhere else nor is it anything else, for it is a light from a light—for this reason they seek to prevent us from comprehending this faith by citing the light from the light, in order that we may not regard as a pious doctrine what they have condemned, now and formerly, in an impious sense.

Desist, desist, O groundless fear of the heretics, and do not lie as if you wished to protect the faith of the Church by falsely pretending that you are oversolicitous about this statement! According to our explanation there is nothing corporeal, nothing lifeless in the things of God. What is God is wholly God. In Him there is nothing but power, life, light, blessedness, and spirit. His nature is incompatible with the dull elements of matter, nor is it composed of different things that it may survive. God, as He is God, always remains what He is, and the God who remains as He is has begotten God. They are not held together as a torch and a torch, or as a lamp and a lamp, by some external nature. The birth of the only-begotten God is not a lineage but a begetting; it is not an extension, but a light from a light. Light is not the diffusion of something that has been joined together, but unity is characteristic of the nature of light.

(13) Now, what remarkable craftiness and cunning there are in this heretical formula of faith: 'Nor is He one who previously was, and was then born or created anew into the Son.' God, who was born from God, was certainly not born from nothing, nor was He born from non-existing things, but He had a living nature for His birth. He is not the same God who was, but He was born as God from the God who was, and His birth has the nature of His origin in His very birth. If we speak of ourselves, we are arrogant, but, if we shall show that we have been instructed by God to speak, then you must acknowledge His birth in accordance with the teaching of God. The heretical madness attempts,

therefore, to do away with the unity of nature in the Father and the Son and with this ineffable mystery of the living birth, and declares: 'Nor is He one who previously was, and was then born or created anew into the Son.' For, who will be so bereft of reason as to imagine that the Father has destroyed Himself in order that the same one who had been should afterwards be born and created anew into the Son, and then there would be an annihilation of God in order that the birth should follow from this annihilation, since the birth bears witness to the permanent existence of the author? Or who will be so demented as to believe that the Son was endowed with life in any other way except by birth? Furthermore, who will be so simple-minded as to dare preach that God did not exist from the fact that God is born?

The God who existed[8] was not born, but God was born from the God who existed, and preserves in Himself the nature of His begetter in the birth of the nature. But the birth of God, which proceeded from God to God, does not possess things which were not, but by the true nature of the birth obtains those things which were and are the property of God. Hence, He who was was not born, but the God who was born exists from and in those things which belong to God. All the above statements about the deceitfulness of the heretics, therefore, have prepared the way for their most godless doctrine, so that, while denying the only-begotten God, as if they had previously argued in defence of the truth, they might teach that He was born from nothing rather than from God, and connect His birth with the will of a creation from non-existing things.

(14) Then, after many words, which prepared the way, as it were, for their approach, they rushed forward with:

---

8 St. Hilary often uses the word 'God' alone when he is referring to the Person of God the Father. By 'existed' he here means the eternal existence of God.

'The Son, however, has been brought forth without time, and has been created and has been formed before the world; still, He was not before He was born.' The heretics in their statement have exercised as much restraint as they believed possible, to strengthen their godlessness as well as to justify their false accusation if a closer examination should be made, when they declare 'He was not before He was born,' in order to deny that the nature of a subsistent[9] origin is in Him, and that He was not before He was born, and in order that He should come into being from nothing to whom no pre-existing origin had been given before His birth; then, if such a statement should be regarded as blasphemous, an immediate defense would be ready at hand, because He who was could not be born, and He who already existed would not have been obliged to be born in order to exist, since birth brings it about that He who is born begins to exist.

O foolish and godless man, who will expect Him to be born who exists without birth? Or how can we believe that He who is is born, since birth is the process by which one is born? But, while you are seeking to deny the birth of the only-begotten Son of God from God the Father, you would like to escape from your dilemma by slyly asserting that 'He was not before He was born,' because God was, from whom the Son of God was born, and the nature of God remained from which the Son of God derived His existence by means of His birth. Therefore, if He was born from God, we must acknowledge the birth of a subsistent nature, not that the God who was was born, but that we might understand the birth of God from the God who was.

(15)   The impetuous heretics cannot restrain their godless fury, and because of what was said: 'He was not before He was born,' they seek to prove that He was born from non-existing things, that is to say, He was not born from

---

9 *subsistentis*: here equivalent to 'eternal.'

God the Father into God the Son by a true and perfect birth, and at the conclusion of their complete explanation they break forth into the most extreme and most sacrilegious outburst of their godless rage when they declare: 'If the expressions, "from Him" and "from the womb" and "I came forth from the Father and have come," are understood as if He were a part of this one substance, and as if He were the extension of an emanation, then, according to them, the Father would be a composite being, divisible and changeable, and a body, and in so far as it depends on them, the God without a body is subject to the limitations of a body.'

It would be a burdensome and very formidable task to defend religious truth against the impiety of heresy, if godlessness were as prudent in its deliberations as it is reckless. But it is fortunate that the will of godlessness proceeds from a lack of wisdom. And for this reason, while it is easy to draw up a reply to folly, it is difficult to effect an improvement in fools, first of all because in their folly they do not seek for knowledge, and then they do not grasp what has been made known to them by one who understands. But, if there are some who are being held captive in error out of reverence for God and through a lack of knowledge and not because of a godless will, which results from the knowledge of folly, I hope that they will be amenable to correction, since the explanation of the truth will clearly expose the folly of impiety.

(16) You have said, O foolish men, and you repeat the same thing today, while you do not understand how to be wise according to God: 'If the expressions, "from Him" and "from the womb" and "I came forth from the Father and have come." ' In regard to the phrase, 'I came forth from the Father and have come,' I ask you whether God spoke all these words or did He not speak them? Certainly God spoke them, and, since He was speaking about Himself,

you must understand them only in the way in which He used them. We shall discuss these words in the proper place, after we have explained the meaning of each phrase.

Meanwhile, I ask each one's opinion about the interpretation of 'from Him.' Are we to understand these words in the sense of coming from another person, or from no one else, or are we to believe that He Himself was the one to whom He was referring? They are not from another person, because they are 'from Him,' that is, in the sense that God does not come from anywhere else except than from God. They are not from nothing, because they come 'from Him,' for a nature is revealed from which the birth is derived. He Himself is not meant, because 'from Him' refers to the birth of the Son from the Father. Moreover, when it is pointed out that He is 'from the womb,' I ask whether it is possible to believe that He was born from nothing, since the true nature of the birth is revealed by applying the terminology of bodily functions? God was not composed of bodily members when He spoke of the generation of the Son in these words: 'From the womb before the day star I begot thee.'[10] He spoke in order to enlighten our understanding while He confirmed that ineffable birth of the only-begotten Son from Himself with the true nature of the Godhead, in order that He might impart to the faculties of our human nature the knowledge of the faith concerning His divine attributes in a manner adapted to our human nature, in order that He might teach us by the expression 'from the womb' that the existence of His Only-begotten was not a creation from nothing, but a natural birth from Himself. Finally, has He left us in any doubt whatsoever that His words, 'I came forth from the Father and have come' are to be understood in the sense that He is God, that His being does not come from anywhere else except from the Father? When He came forth from the Father He

---

10 Ps. 109.3.

did not have a different nature or no nature, but He bears testimony to the fact that He is His author from whom, as He says, He has gone forth. But I shall speak later on about these matters which have to be made known and understood.

(17)   In the meantime, let us see the self-assurance of these men who will not concede that these things should be understood about God when they do not deny that God was referring to Himself when He uttered them. Oh, the measureless shame of human folly and insolence for not only finding fault with God by not believing His own statements about Himself but even condemning Him by correcting them! By its human doctrines it defiles and attacks that indescribable mystery of the nature and power within Him and dares to speak in this manner: 'If the Son is from God, then God is changeable and corporeal, since He allowed an emanation from Himself or an extension of Himself to be made into His Son.' Why are you so anxious that God be not changeable? We, who have been taught by God, acknowledge His birth and we proclaim the Only-begotten. But you object by alleging the nature of an immutable God which cannot be extended or projected, in order to do away with the birth, and to make the Only-begotten disappear from the faith of the Church.

O unhappy error, even in earthly affairs I could offer you the example of certain natures which are born that you should not consider birth as an extension, or believe that the natures of those who are born are a loss for their begetters, so that there are also many instances of living beings begetting living beings without intercourse, if it were not unlawful not to believe God's testimony about Himself, and if it were not regarded as the height of madness and fury to deny the authority of Him in matters of faith whom you profess to worship for eternal life. If there is no life except through Him, how can we possess the faith of life if not through

Him? How can the faith of life depend upon Him who is considered an unreliable witness about Himself?

(18)   O godless heretics, you wrongly assume that the birth of the Son was due to the creative will, so that He was not born from God, but received existence by creation through the will of Him who created Him. Therefore, in your opinion He is not God because, since God remains one, the birth of the Son did not preserve the nature of its author. He is a creature[11] of a different substance, although He Himself as the Only-begotten is more exalted than everything else that has been created and made. He has been endowed with life so that He may take upon Himself the place of the creation that has been granted to Him,[12] but has not received the nature of God by His birth. And you declare that He was born because He received existence from nothing, but you give Him the name of Son, not because He was born from God, but because He was created by God, since, as you are aware, God also considered devout men as deserving of this name, and for this reason you confer the title of God upon Him in accordance with the same qualification of the words: 'I have said: You are gods and all sons of the Most High,'[13] so that He shares in this dignity because He has received this name from the one who designated Him, not because He has a right to this name by possessing the true nature. According to you, He is the Son by adoption and God in name, He is the Only-begotten by favor; He is the first-born in the order of succession, He is wholly a creature, and in no sense is He God, because His procreation is not a natural birth from God, but the begetting of a created substance.

---

11 *conditio*: in the sense of creature or man; cf. Kinnavey, *op. cit.* 19.
12 *ut creationis indultae sibi habeat substitutionis*: this phrase seems to refer to the Redemption of Christ, who took the place of the human race in order to appease the justice of God. *Ibid.* 262.
13 Cf. Ps. 81.6.

(19)   And while, first of all, I beseech You, O almighty
God, to pardon me for my overwhelming grief, permit me
to speak before You and allow me, who am dust and ashes,
but united to You by the sacred bond of charity, to speak
these words courageously. I, unfortunate one, was formerly
nothing, I was devoid of all the consciousness of life, and,
without any knowledge of myself, was lacking that which I
now am. But in Your mercy You have caused me to live,
and I do not doubt that because You are God You have
considered it as something good for me that I should be born.
You, who have no need of me, would not have caused me
to exist in order to make me the source of evil. But, when
You breathed the breath of life into me, and endowed me
with the gift of reason, You taught me the knowledge of
Yourself through what, I believe, are the sacred books of
Your servants, Moses and the Prophets, where You have made
known that we should not pay worship to You in your isolation.

I have learned to know that there is a God with You, not
different in nature, but one in the mystery of Your substance.
I have found out that You are God in God, not by a confused
mingling together, but by the power of Your nature, while,
because You are God, You dwell within Him who is from
You, not that You are the same person as the one in whom
You dwell, but the true nature of the perfect birth teaches
us that You dwell in Him who is from You. The statements
of the Gospels and the Apostles repeat this same doctrine,
and the words from the sacred mouth of Your Only-begotten
Himself, as they have been recorded in the books, testify that
Your Son, as the only-begotten God from You, the unborn
God, was born as man from the Virgin for the mystery of
my salvation, and the true nature of the birth from You
would contain You in Him, and the nature of the eternal
birth from You would retain You in Him.

(20)   Into what depths You have plunged me, I beseech
You, so that I have lost all hope of returning. Thus have I
learned these doctrines, thus have I believed them, thus do
I cling to them with the faith of an unshaken mind, so that
I can neither believe nor will in any other manner. Why
have You deceived me, a wretched man, concerning Yourself
and ruined my unfortunate body and soul by teaching a
doctrine that imparts an alien doctrine about Yourself? After
the parting of the Red Sea I was deceived by the splendor
of Moses as he descended from the mountain where, in company with You, he had gazed upon the secrets of the heavenly
mysteries. I believed him when he uttered these words about
Yourself. I was destroyed by David, a man according to
Your own heart; by Solomon, who was deserving of the gift
of divine wisdom; by Isaias, who prophesied after beholding
the Lord of hosts; by Jeremias, who was sanctified before
his formation in the womb, and who uttered predictions about
the nations that were to be uprooted and planted; by Ezechiel, the witness of the mystery of the resurrection; by Daniel,
the man of desires who was aware of the times; by the con-
secrated company of the Prophets; by the entire revelation
of Gospel teaching;[14] by Matthew the publican, who was
chosen to be an Apostle; by John, who was deemed worthy
of receiving the revelation of the heavenly mysteries because
of his intimate association with the Lord; by blessed Simon,
who after the profession of the revealed doctrines became
the foundation for the building of the Church and received
the keys to the kingdom of heaven; by all the others who
preached in the Holy Spirit; by Paul, who from a persecutor
became an Apostle, the vessel of election who lived in the
depths of the sea, the man raised up to the third heaven, in

---

14 According to Coustant, this phrase includes all the preachers of the
    Gospel.

paradise before his martyrdom, and by his martyrdom making a complete offering of perfect faith.

(21)   These men have taught me the doctrines which I maintain and which have been irrevocably impressed upon my mind. O almighty God, forgive me for not being able to improve upon them and for being able to die with them. It is the present age of the world, in so far as I can judge, that has gradually given rise to these most godless teachers. My faith, in which You have instructed me, has found out too late about these teachers. Before I had heard these names, thus did I believe in You, thus was I reborn through You, and, accordingly, I have thus become Your possession. I realize that You are omnipotent and I do not expect an explanation of the ineffable birth, which is a secret known only to You and to your Only-begotten Himself. Nothing is impossible to You, and I have no doubt that the Son has been born from You by means of your omnipotence. Should I become incredulous, I shall at that moment deny that You are all-powerful.

By my own birth I have learned that You are good, and for this reason I am confident that You are not envious of your goods in the birth of Your Only-begotten. I believe what is Yours in His, and that what is His is Yours. The creation of the world itself has also shown me that You are wise. I am aware that You have begotten Your own wisdom from Yourself, and not one that is unlike Yours. To me, indeed, You are also the true and only God, but I shall not believe that there is anything than what is Yours in Him who is God from You. And pass judgment upon me in this matter if it is a crime for me to have placed too much trust in the Law, the Prophets, and the Apostles for the sake of your Son.

(22)   But let us put an end to these rash statements and leave these subjects into which we plunged because we had

to expose the folly of the heretics, and apply ourselves more to the task of setting forth our proofs in order that, if any can still be saved, they may continue on the journey to the faith of the evangelical and apostolic doctrine and may understand the true Son of God, not by adoption, but by nature. In our reply it will be fitting for us to follow this order first, to teach that He is the Son of God, so that He possesses the nature of the Godhead in its fullness because He is the Son. For, the heresy that we are now discussing endeavors especially to show that our Lord Jesus Christ, who is truly a Son of God, is not the true God.

We have learned in many ways that our Lord Jesus Christ, as the true and only-begotten Son of God is God, and that He has been proclaimed as such, while the Father bears testimony to Him, while He Himself asserts it in regard to Himself, while the Apostles preach it, while devout men believe it, while the devils acknowledge it, while the Jews deny it, while the pagans recognize it in His Passion. It is not a sharing in the name that our faith teaches in regard to His true nature.[15] And, since all that the Lord said or did surpasses everything that has been done by those who are called the sons of God, consequently, of all the names peculiar to Christ, this is considered the most excellent that He is the Son of God, and does not bear the name of Son because others have it in common with Him.

(23) I do not defile the faith about the true nature in order to justify it by my own words. Let the Father speak about His only-begotten Son, as He was often wont to do, in order that He might not remain unknown because of His body when the mystery of the baptism was about to be fulfilled: 'This is my beloved Son, in whom I am pleased.'[16] I

---

15 Christ has a right not only to the name of God but also to the true nature of God. Such is the meaning of *proprietas* in this context. Cf. Beck, *op. cit.* 13.

16 Cf. Matt. 3.17.

ask where does the true nature suffer any injury, and where
is there any weakness in the assertion? Neither the birth from
the Holy Spirit through the Virgin, which the angel announced, nor the star which guided the Magi, nor the dignity
of the one worshiped in the cradle, nor the power of the
one to be baptized which the Baptist acknowledged are regarded as sufficient to reveal His majesty. The Father speaks
from heaven and speaks thus: 'This is my Son.' What does
our faith indicate, not about the surnames, but the pronouns? Surnames are added to the names, but pronouns
possess in themselves the power of the names. The meaning
of the real nature is signified wherever you hear the words
'this is' and 'is my.' Grasp the true nature and significance
of the words. You read: 'I have begotten sons, and exalted
them,'[17] but you do not read 'my sons,' for he begot them
through the division among the Gentiles and from the people
of the inheritance. In order that the name of son, therefore,
might not be added to the Only-begotten by reason of a
participation in the inheritance, which was obtained through
adoption, His true nature is shown by indicating that it is
proper to Him. You may, if you like, ascribe the name of
Christ as Son to a mutual participation, if you will find
anyone else of whom it was said: 'This is my beloved Son.'
But, if these words, 'This is my beloved Son,' are proper and
unique, why do we criticize God the Father for acknowledging
the real nature of His Son? Does it not seem to you that in
this instance the words 'this is' seem to have the following
meaning: 'I have indeed called others by the name of son,
but this is my son. I have given the name of adoption to
many, but this is a son for me. Seek for no other. Believe
that this is the one. This is the one I point out, as it were,
by my index finger and by the meaning of the words when
I say "is my" and "this is" and "is a son." ' After these

17 Cf. Isa. 1.2.

words, how can we still make the matter comprehensible so that you may not be skeptical about who He is? And the designation by the voice of the Father was done for this reason, that He who was to be baptized in order to fulfill all justice might not remain unknown, and that He who was to be seen as man in the mystery of our salvation might be recognized as the Son of God by the voice of God.

(24)   Because the life of the believers would depend upon the confession of this faith (for there is no other eternal life if we do not know that Jesus Christ, the only-begotten God, is the Son of God), the Apostles again hear the voice from heaven, which reiterates the same message, in order that they might believe more firmly in the doctrine which leads to life, and which it would be death not to believe. For, when the Lord had appeared on the mountain in the garment of His majesty with Moses and Elias at His side and the three pillars of the Churches had been chosen as witnesses to verify the vision and the voice, the voice of the Father comes from heaven: 'This is my beloved Son, in whom I am pleased; hear this one.'[18] The glory that was seen did not suffice to establish His majesty; He is designated by the words 'This is my Son.' The Apostles do not endure the glory of God, their mortal eyes are dimmed by the vision, and the faith of Peter, James, and John is overwhelmed with fear and sinks to the ground. Then follows the confession with the Father's sanction and it is revealed that this one who is pointed out is His Son by reason of His true nature. The true nature of the Son is indicated not only by the words 'this' and 'is my,' but by those that are added, 'hear this one.' The testimony of the Father comes, it is true, from heaven, but the testimony of the Son is confirmed on earth, for it is made known that He must be heard. And, although the Father's statement leaves no room for doubt, it is determined that the Son's avowal

---

18 Cf. Matt. 17.5.

about Himself must also be believed. And the true nature of the Son in Him is taught to such an extent that the ratification by the voice of His Father demands that we obey the one who must be heard. Accordingly, since the voice expresses the will of the Father that we listen to His Son, let us hear what the Son Himself asserts about Himself.

(25)   I do not believe that there is anyone so devoid of ordinary intelligence, who—when he learns in all the books of the Gospel about the assumption of our bodily lowliness from the Son's confession, as when He says: 'Father, glorify me,'[19] and the words which are very frequent: 'You shall see the Son of man,'[20] and these words: 'The Father is greater than I,'[21] and these: 'Now my soul is very troubled,'[22] or even these: 'My God, my God, why hast thou forsaken me?'[23] and many statements of this kind, which we shall discuss in their proper order[24]—will still accuse Him of arrogance in spite of such repeated declarations of humility, because He calls God His Father, as when He says: 'Every plant that my Father has not planted will be rooted up'[25] or 'You have made the house of my Father a house of business,'[26] and because, wherever He always calls God His Father, this proceeds from a rash presumption rather than from a confident nature, which is aware of its birth and preserves the name of the true nature in the Father.

Nor is He, who called God His Father, guilty of a similar presumption when He declares that He is His Son, saying:

---

19 John 17.5.
20 Matt. 26.64.
21 John 14.28. This text is applied here to Christ in His human nature, though elsewhere it is applied to Him in His divine nature (cf. above, 3.12).
22 Cf. John 12.27.
23 Matt. 27.46.
24 These texts are discussed in Book 10.
25 Cf. Matt. 15.13.
26 Cf. John 2.16.

'For God did not send his Son into this world in order to judge the world, but that the world may be saved through him,'[27] or again: 'Dost thou believe in the Son of God?'[28] If we only admit the name of adoption in Christ, what are we to do now, since we also accuse Him of a similar presumption when He calls God His Father? The voice of the Father is from heaven: 'Hear him.'[29] I hear: 'Father, I give thee thanks.'[30] I hear: 'You say that I have blasphemed, because I said, "I am the Son of God." '[31]

If I do not believe the names, if I do not understand the nature from the words, I ask what shall I believe and understand? No other meaning is left to me. The authority of the Father is from heaven: 'This is my Son.' The confession of the Son regarding Himself is: 'The house of my Father' and 'My Father.' The confession of the name is salvation, since the question demands faith in the words: 'Dost thou believe in the Son of God?'[32] The names of things that are truly mine follow where 'my' is used. I ask you, O heretic, whence do you derive a different supposition? You do away with the faith in the Father, the confession of the Son, the nature of the names. You do violence to the words of God in order that they may not proclaim what they are. It is only the boldness of your godlessness that causes you to accuse God of lying about Himself.

(26) Although the mere confession, therefore, reveals the names of the nature so that He of whom it was said: 'This is my Son' and He to whom it was said: 'My Father' are what they are called, still, in order that the Son's name may not be one of adoption, or the Father's name one of

---

27 Cf. John 3.17.
28 John 9.35.
29 Matt. 17.5.
30 John 2.41.
31 John 10.36.
32 John 9.35.

honor, let us see what attributes are attached to the name of
son by the Son. He says: 'All things have been delivered to
me by my Father; and no one knows the Son except the
Father; nor does anyone know the Father except the Son,
and him to whom the Son wills to reveal him.'[33] Do not the
words already cited 'This is my Son' and 'My Father,' agree
with 'No one knows the Son except the Father nor does
anyone know the Father except the Son'? For, it is only by
a mutual attestation that the Son could be known by the
Father or the Father by the Son. The voice comes from
heaven and the statement comes from the Son. The Son is
just as unknown as the Father. All things have been delivered
to Him, and by all is meant that nothing is excepted. If they
are equal in power and in the secret of knowledge, if the
nature is in the names, I ask in what way are they not what
they are called, when in regard to the strength of their omnipotence and to the difficulty in being known there is no
distinction? God is not guilty of deception in these words and
the Father and the Son do not lie about themselves; learn
how reliable are these names!

(27) He says: 'For the works which the Father has given
me that I accomplish them, these very works that I do bear
witness to me, that the Father has sent me. And the Father
himself, who has sent me, has borne witness to me.'[34] The
only-begotten God teaches that He is the Son not only by
the testimony of His name, but also of His power, for the
miracles which He performs testify that He has been sent
by the Father. I ask to what do His miracles bear testimony?—to this, that He has been sent. Accordingly, in the
one who is sent we learn of the obedience of the Son and
the authority of the Father, for the miracles which He performs cannot be done by anyone else except by Him who has

---

33 Cf. Matt. 11.27.
34 Cf. John 5.36,37.

been sent by the Father. But, for the unbelievers, the miracles do not offer sufficient proof that the Father sent Him. Then come the words: 'And the Father who sent me has borne witness to me. But you have never heard his voice, nor seen his figure.'[35] And what was the testimony of the Father about Him? Unroll the volumes of the Gospels and examine the entire work. Give the testimony of the Father besides that which we have already heard. 'This is my beloved Son, in whom I am pleased'[36] and 'Thou art my Son.'[37] John in the desert was certainly deserving of hearing this voice, but the Apostles, also, were not to be deprived of this authoritative testimony. The same voice comes to them from heaven but they learn more than John. John, who already prophesied from the womb, did not need these words, 'Hear him.'

I shall hear Him by all means and I shall hear no one else besides Him, except the one who heard in order that he might teach. If no other testimony of the Father about the Son is found in these books except that this is His Son, the truth of this testimony is borne out by this fact, that the miracles of the Father which He performs corroborate the truth of this testimony. What a calumny is being circulated at the present time that this name comes from adoption, that God is a liar, and that the names are useless! The Father became a witness for the Son; the Son places Himself on an equality with the testimony of His Father by means of His miracles. Why should we not believe that He possesses what He mentions and proves, that is, the true nature of the Son? The name of the Son does not belong to Christ as a result of an adoption through the generosity of the Father, nor did He merit this name by His holiness, as many became the sons of God by their profession of the faith. In their case there

---

35 Cf. John 5.37,38.
36 Cf. Matt. 3.17.
37 Mark 1.11.

is no indication that this is a personal attribute, for, in a manner worthy of Him, God merely bestowed the dignity of the name upon them. 'This is' is something different from 'This is my' and 'hear him.' Herein is the truth, the nature, the faith.

(28) In regard to Himself, the Son indeed testifies to nothing less than the real nature which the Father pointed out. For, as the revelation of the nature is contained in the Father's words: 'This is my Son,' and the hearing of the mystery and the faith on account of which He came down from heaven in those which He added: 'hear this one,' since we are admonished to hear Him for the salutary instruction in the confession of the faith, in a similar manner the Son taught the true nature of His birth and coming, when He declared: 'Neither do you know me, nor do you know where I am from, for I have not come of myself, but he is true who has sent me, whom you do not know; but I know him because I am from him, and he has sent me.'[38]

No one knows the Father, and the Son often reminds us of this. He states that He is known to Him alone because He comes from Him. But I ask whether that which comes from Him reveals the work of creation in Him or the nature of His birth? If it is the work of creation, then, everything else that is created comes from God. And why is it that everything does not know the Father, since He is known to Him for this reason, because He comes from the Father? If He is created rather than born, we shall see in Him whatever comes from God, and, since everything comes from God, why is not the Father unknown to Him as in the case of the other things which come from Him? Accordingly, if it is proper for Him to know Him because He comes from Him, why will that not be regarded as proper to Him which comes from Him, that is, that He is the true Son from the nature

---

38 A combination of the sense of John 7.28, 29 and 8.19.

of God, since He is the only one, therefore, who knows God because He alone comes from Him? Hence, you derive the true nature of the knowledge from the true nature of the birth, and because He comes from Him you do not find the power of a creature in Him (for all things exist through Him by the power of creation), but the true nature of the birth whereby He alone knows the Father, while the other things which are from Him do not know Him.

(29) In order that heresy might not pounce upon the phrase 'from him' and perhaps apply it to the time of His arrival,[39] He immediately added: 'because I am from him, and he has sent me.' He follows the order of the Gospel revelation when He stated that He was born and sent into the world, in order that we might know from the above sentence who He was and whence He came. The words, 'I am from him,' are not the same as 'He sent me,' just as there is a distinction between 'neither do you know me' and 'nor do you know where I am from.' For, according to the commonly accepted opinion, is not every man from God, although He is born in the flesh? And how can He assert that it is not known who He is or whence He is, unless the words, 'whence he is,' referred to the author of His nature, who, accordingly, would be unknown, because He Himself was not recognized as the Son of God.

O unhappy folly, explain what these words mean: 'neither do you know me, nor do you know where I am from.' All things are, of course, from nothing, and they are from nothing to such a degree that you even have the audacity to lie about the only-begotten God as coming into existence from nothing. What is the reason why these godless men do not have any knowledge of who Christ is or whence He is? For, the fact that it is not known whence He is reveals the nature from

---

39 The heretics might apply these words to the Son's arrival on earth in human flesh.

which He is, while it is not known whence He is. Where that is from, which has come into the world from nothing, cannot be unknown, because this very fact, that its coming into existence from nothing is not unknown, does not permit any ignorance in regard to where it is from. He who has come is not from Himself, but He who sent Him is true, and the godless men do not know Him. Consequently, in regard to Him who sent, He Himself is no longer known as the one who sent. He who was sent, therefore, is from Him who sent, and He is from Him from whom He is without this fact being known, and therefore they do not know who He is because they do not know from where He is. He does not know Christ who does not know whence Christ is; and he does not acknowledge the Son who denies that He was born, and He does not recognize Him as one born who believes that He is from nothing. But, so little is He from nothing that the godless men do not know from where He is.

(30) They are wholly ignorant, they are ignorant, who take away the nature from the name, who in their ignorance have no desire to know. And let them listen to the Son as He rebukes them for their lack of this knowledge at the moment when the Jews said that God was their Father, for He declares: 'If God were your Father, you would surely love me. For from God I came forth and have come; neither have I come of myself but he sent me.'[40] The Son of God did not condemn the assuming of a religious name by those who acknowledge Him as the Son of God and call God their Father, but He reproves the reckless usurpation of the Jews in presuming that God was their Father because they did not love Him. 'If God were your Father, you would surely love me. For from God I came forth.' All who have God for their Father through faith have Him as their Father through that faith whereby we profess Jesus Christ as the Son of God.

---

40 Cf. John 8.42.

But, what kind of faith is it to acknowledge the Son as possessing the ordinary names of holy persons, so that we say He is not the Son? Are not the others also sons in this weakness of their created nature? What special excellence distinguishes a faith that confesses Jesus Christ as the Son of God when it belongs to Him as to other sons, not by nature, but by name?

This infidelity does not love God and this godless profession does not appropriate God as its Father in a pious manner, because, if God were their Father, they would love Christ for this reason, that He came forth from God. I do not ask for the meaning of the words, to have come forth from God. Assuredly, it cannot be said that to have come forth from God is the same as to have come, for He refers to both of them: 'For I came forth from God and have come.' And He shows the meaning of 'I came forth from God' and 'I have come' by adding at once: 'for neither have I come of myself but he sent me.' He taught that He was not the cause of His own origin when He says: 'for neither have I come of myself,' and when He again testifies that He came forth from the Father and was sent by Him. But, when He declared that He must be loved by those who said that God was their Father, because He came forth from God, He taught that the reason for loving Him arose from His birth.

He connected the words, to have come forth, with the name of His incorporeal birth because the faith to profess God as His Father would have to be merited by loving Christ, who was born from Him. For, when He says: 'He who hates me hates my Father also,'[41] by the word 'my' He excluded a mutual sharing of this name by indicating that it was proper to Him. Besides, He condemns one who confessed God as His Father, and does not love Him for usurping the name of Father, because whoever hates Him will also hate the

---

41 John 15.23.

Father, nor will he have any veneration for the Father who does not love the Son, since there is no other reason for loving the Son except that He comes from God. The Son, therefore, is from God not by His coming but by His birth, and in this case the love for the Father will be complete if the Son is believed to come from Him.

(31)   The Lord bears testimony to this when He says: 'I will not say to you that I will ask the Father for you, for the Father Himself loves you because you love me, and believe that I came forth from God. And I have come from the Father into this world.'[42] The perfect faith concerning the Son, which believes and loves that which has come forth from God, does not need to intercede with the Father, and such faith by itself already deserves to be heard and loved, since it admits that the Son was born from and sent by God. His birth and His coming, therefore, are shown together with the most absolute truth in the true nature which was designated. He says 'I came forth from God' in order that no one might believe that there is any other nature in Him except that arising from His birth, for what else can it be but God? And He declares: 'I have come into this world from the Father.' In order that we might realize that that going forth from God signified His birth from the Father, He declared that He came into this world from the Father.

Accordingly, the one refers to the plan of salvation, the other to the nature.[43] And He does not allow His coming forth to be regarded as a coming to earth, since He informs us of His coming from the Father, after He had mentioned His coming forth from God. For, 'to have come from the Father' and 'to have come forth from God' do not have the same meaning; the difference between having been born and

42 Cf. John 16.27,28.
43 His birth in time takes place in the plan of salvation; His eternal birth expresses His true nature.

having come is as great as the difference between these two expressions. It is one thing to have come forth from God in the substance of birth; it is something else to have come from the Father into the world in order to complete the mysteries of our salvation.

(32)   And, in keeping with the order of the answers upon which we have determined, this is certainly the most suitable place to teach now for the third time that the Apostles have believed that our Lord Jesus Christ was the Son of God, not according to name, but according to nature; not by adoption, but by birth. Although there are many and, indeed, important declarations of the only-begotten God about Himself, in which He offered evidence for the true nature of His birth without giving even the slightest pretext for a false accusation, still, because the mind of the readers should not be burdened with a great collection of texts, and many things about that true nature have already been shown, all the other statements will be reserved for future discussions. But, since we have fixed upon this arrangement in our treatise, that after the testimony of the Father and the declaration of the Son we should also be taught by the faith of the Apostles about the true Son of God, admitting Him as such according to birth, we must now see whether they found in the Lord's words, 'I came forth from God,' any other meaning besides the nature of His birth.

(33)   After the many ambiguities of the proverbs, when He spoke in the form of parables, they already knew Him as the Christ announced long before by Moses and the Prophets, after Nathaniel had also acknowledged Him as the King of Israel and the Son of God; similarly, after He had rebuked Philip, when he asked about the Father, why he did not recognize that the Father was in Him and He in the Father from the power of His miracles, and after He had often asserted on previous occasions that He was sent by the

Father—still, when they heard Him declare that He had come forth from God, this was their reply (for it immediately follows His statement): His disciples say to Him, 'Now thou speakest plainly and utterest no parable. Now, therefore, we know that thou knowest all things, and thou dost not need that any one should question thee. For this reason we believe that thou hast come forth from God.'[44]

What reason is there, I ask, for such admiration of this statement in which He declares that He came forth from God. O holy and blessed men, who had witnessed deeds so great and so suitable to God, which were performed by our Lord Jesus Christ, the Son of God, who because of the merit of your faith received the keys of the kingdom of heaven and obtained the right to bind and to loose in heaven and on earth! And now, when He declares that He came forth from God, do you assert for the first time that you have grasped the knowledge of the truth? You had certainly seen the water at the wedding being made into wine at the wedding, either by a change, or a development, or a creation of a nature into a nature. You had also broken the five loaves of bread as food for a large number of people, and, when all had been fully satisfied, the remains of the bread filled twelve baskets, and the insignificance of the nature which drives away hunger has grown into an abundance of the same nature. You had gazed upon the withered hands recovering their strength, the tongues of the dumb being loosed and they spoke, the feet of the paralytics becoming eager for the journey, the eyes of the blind recovering their sight, and the dead returning to life.

The ill-smelling Lazarus arose at the sound of the voice; when he was called from the tomb, he came forth swiftly without any interval between the voice and life, and, while the air still brings the odor of death to the nostrils, he now

---

44 Cf. John 16.29,30.

stands alive before them. I pass over in silence the other great and divine miracles. And therefore, do you now realize for the first time who He is that was sent from heaven, after you hear the words: 'I came forth from the Father'? And is it now for the first time that He spoke to you without a proverb, and you perceive the truth that He came forth from God, when He silently looks into your thoughts and desires, when He asks as if He did not know anything, when He knows all things? For, by all these things which He performs by the power and the nature of God, it must be believed that He has come forth from God.

(34) The holy Apostles did not understand the words, 'to have come forth from God,' as being synonymous in this instance with 'to have been sent by God,' for in all His previous discourses they had frequently heard Him declaring that He was sent, but, when they hear that He came forth from God, when they discern the nature of God in Him by His miracles, they recognize His true nature by that which came forth from God when they declare: 'Now, therefore, we know that thou knowest all things, and dost not need that anyone should question thee. For this reason we believe that thou hast come forth from God.' They believe that He came forth from God because He is able to do and to perform those things which are characteristic of God. For, the perfection of the nature of God is not that it has come from the Father, but that it has come forth from God.

Finally, that which they now hear for the first time confirms them in the faith. Since the Lord had expressed two thoughts: 'I have come forth from God' and 'I have come from the Father into this world,' they were not startled by what they had often heard: 'I have come from the Father into this world,' but their response bears testimony to their faith in and understanding of these words: 'I have come forth from God.' To this only did they reply: 'For this reason we believe that thou hast come forth from God,' and they do not add: 'You have come from the Father into the world.' While they acknowledge the one, they are silent about the other. The novelty of the expression was the cause of their confession, but the knowledge of the true nature elicited the declaration of their confession. They knew, indeed, that as God He could do all things, but they had not as yet heard the subject of His birth, and they knew that He had been sent by God, but did not know that He had come forth from God. By virtue of these words they now understand this ineffable and perfect birth of the Son, and declare that He now spoke to them without proverbs.

(35) God is not born from God after the manner of a human birth, nor does He develop through the elements of our origin as a man from a man. For this birth is unimpaired, perfect, and immaculate, and is rather a procession from the Father than a birth. It is one from one. It is not a part, not a withdrawal, not a diminution, it is not an emanation, it is not an extension, it is not a suffering, but it is the birth of a living nature from a living nature. It is God proceeding from God, not a nature selected for the name of God. He does not begin to be from nothing, but comes forth from Him who remains, and to have come forth signifies the birth, not the beginning. And, although the knowledge of this birth cannot be expressed in words, since it is ineffable, we have a sure guarantee of our faith in the doctrine of the Son, who reveals that He has come forth from God.

(36) It is not the evangelical or apostolic faith to believe that He is the Son of God in name rather than in nature. If this name is one of adoption and He therefore is not the Son because He came forth from God, I ask why did the blessed Simon make this confession: 'Thou art Christ, the Son of the living God.'[45] Do not all have the power to be born

45 Matt. 16.16.

as sons of God through the sacrament of regeneration? If Christ is the Son of God according to this designation, then, I ask, what is this that flesh and blood did not reveal to Peter, but the Father who is in heaven? What merit is there in a general confession?[46] Or what glory is there in the revelation of what is publicly known? If He is a son by adoption, why is this confession of Peter blessed when he offers the Son what is common to holy persons? But the apostolic faith extends beyond the limits of human understanding. He had, of course, often heard: 'He who receives you, receives me; and he who receives me, receives him who sent me.'[47] Hence, at that time he knew that he had been sent, and he had often heard the statement from Him whom he knew had been sent: 'All things have been delivered to me by the Father; and no one knows the Son except the Father, nor does anyone know the Father except the Son.'[48]

What is it that the Father now reveals to Peter which merits the glory of the confession that is blessed? Did he not know the name of the Father and the Son? Yet, he had often heard it. He speaks, however, what a human voice had not as yet announced: 'Thou art Christ, the Son of the living God.' Although, while abiding in the flesh, He declared Himself the Son of God, this is the first time that the faith of the Apostle recognizes the nature of the Godhead within Him. Glory was rendered to Peter not only for his confession of praise, but for his recognition of the mystery, and because he did not acknowledge Christ alone but confessed that He was the Son of God. If he had said: 'Thou art Christ,' surely this would have been sufficient for a confession of praise, but it would have been useless for him to have acknowledged

---

46 What merit is there in St. Peter's confession if he acknowledges Christ as the Son of God only in the sense that other men have the title of sons of God?
47 Matt. 10.40.
48 Cf. Luke 10.22.

Christ if he had not acknowledged Him as the Son of God. For, by the words 'Thou art' he made known the power and the significance of the Godhead which was His by nature. And the Father, by declaring 'This is my Son,' revealed to Peter that he should say: 'Thou art the Son of God.' The one who reveals is indicated by the words 'This is,' but the knowledge of the one who confesses by the words 'Thou art.' It is upon the rock of this confession that the building of the Church rests. But the sense of flesh and blood does not reveal the knowledge of the confession. This is the mystery of the divine revelation not only to call Christ the Son of God, but to believe it. Or was it the name rather than the nature which was disclosed to Peter? If the name, he had often heard it from the Lord, who declared that He was the Son of God. In what, then, does the glory of the revelation consist? Of the nature, surely, and not of the name, for the confession of the name had frequently been made.

(37) This faith is the foundation of the Church, and therefore the gates of hell are powerless against her. This faith possesses the keys of the kingdom of heaven. What this faith bound and loosed on earth will also be bound and loosed in heaven. This faith is the gift which the Father has revealed, not to misrepresent Christ as a creature made from nothing, but to confess Him as the Son of God in accordance with a nature that is truly His own. Oh, the godless rage of pitiable folly! It does not recognize the witness of a venerable age and faith, and Peter, the witness for whom the Father was asked that his faith might not fail in temptation, who, after he had repeated the profession of faith that had been requested of him, grieved that he was still being put to the test by a third question, as if he were wavering and uncertain, and, therefore, after this threefold purification of the weaknesses of his temptation, also merited to hear the threefold declaration of the Lord: 'Feed my sheep,' who, amid the silence of all

the Apostles, recognized the Son of God by the revelation of the Father, for this is beyond the limits of human weakness, and deserved the supereminent glory by the confession of his blessed faith. What conclusion must we now necessarily draw from a study of his words?

He confessed Christ as the Son of God, but, today, you, the lying priesthood of a new apostolate, force Christ upon me as a creature made from nothing. What violence you use against these glorious words! He confessed the Son of God, on which account he was blessed. This is the revelation of the Father, this is the foundation of the Church, this is the pledge of eternity. Therefore he had the keys of the kingdom of heaven; therefore his judgments on earth are judgments in heaven. Through a revelation he learned the mystery hidden from eternity; he proclaimed the faith; he disclosed the nature. He, on the contrary, who denies this by acknowledging Him as a creature must first repudiate the apostleship, faith, blessedness, priesthood, and testimony of Peter, and after doing so learns that he has become estranged from Christ, because Peter merited these things by confessing Him as the Son.

(38)   O wretched heretic, whoever you are today, are you of the opinion that Peter would have been more blessed if he had said: 'You are Christ, the perfect creature of God and the handiwork superior to everything that has been made; you have had your beginning from nothing; and you have merited the name of adoption from the goodness of God who alone is good—but you have not been born from God'? I ask you what he would have heard if he had spoken in this manner, he who, when he had learned of the Passion, declared: 'May He be merciful to thee, O Lord, that will not be,'[49] and received this reply in return: 'Get behind me,

---

49 Cf. Matt. 16.22.

Satan, thou art a scandal to me.'[50] Human ignorance, however, was not responsible for Peter's guilt, for the Father had
not yet revealed the complete mystery of the Passion to him,
but his little faith drew upon him the sentence of condemnation. Why did not the Father, therefore, reveal this faith of
the confession to Peter, namely, that He is a creature and an
adoption?

This God, I believe, was envious of Peter so that by practising concealment until these latter times He might now
reserve these doctrines for you, the new preachers! It may
well be that there is another faith if there are other keys to
the kingdom of heaven. It may be that there is another
faith, if there will be another Church against which the gates
of hell shall not prevail. There may be another faith, if there
will be another apostleship that binds and looses in heaven
that which has been bound and loosed by it on earth. There
may be another faith, if there is a Christ, other than He who
is, who will be proclaimed as the Son of God. But, if this
faith alone which confesses Christ as the Son of God merited
for Peter the glory of all the beatitudes, then that faith which
will confess Him rather as a creature made from nothing,
since it has not received the keys of the kingdom of heaven,
is outside of the faith and power of the Apostle, and is not
that Church and does not belong to Christ.

(39)   Let us, therefore, bring forth all the statements
of the apostolic faith in which they acknowledge the Son of
God, and confess that the name belongs to Him not by
adoption but by the reality of the nature; nor do they bear
testimony to His lowly origin by creation but to the glory of
His birth. Let John speak who remains thus until the coming
of the Lord, for, in the mysterious decrees of the divine will,
he was to be left behind and to be kept apart, while it was
not said of him that he was not to die but that he was to

---

50 Cf. Matt. 16.23.

remain. Let him, therefore, speak to us, as he is wont to do, in his own words: 'No one has at any time seen God, except the only-begotten Son who is in the bosom of the Father.'[51] It seemed to him that the faith in the nature was not satisfactorily explained until he had also added the attribute of the real nature by indicating that it belonged to Him exclusively. For, in addition to 'Son' he also called Him the 'only-begotten,' and in this way removed any suspicion of adoption, since the nature of the Only-begotten guarantees the truth of the name.

(40) For the time being I shall not make any inquiries into the meaning of 'who is in the bosom of the Father.' This question will be treated in the proper order. I would like to know what conclusion we have to draw from His designation as the Only-begotten? Let us see whether this means what you profess, that is, that He is the perfect creature of God in the sense that 'perfect' refers to the unbegotten, but 'creature' to the Son. But, John declared that the only-begotten Son was God, and not a perfect creature. He was not unaware of the blasphemous names, since he said: 'He who is in the bosom of the Father,' and he heard from his Lord: 'For God so loved the world that he gave his only-begotten Son that those who believe in him may not perish, but may have life everlasting.'[52]

If the pledge of His love arises from the fact that He has bestowed a creature upon creatures, and that He has given to the world what belongs to the world, and that He has offered Him who came into existence from nothing for the redemption of those who were made from nothing, this small and insignificant loss did not merit such a great reward. But, those gifts are precious which are a manifestation of love, and great things are measured by great things. God who loves the

---

51 Cf. John 1.18.
52 John 3.16.

world has not given an adopted son but His own Son, His
only-begotten Son. Here is the real nature, here is the birth,
here is the truth. He is not a creation, He is not an adoption,
He is not a falsehood. From this arises our faith in His love
and benevolence, that He has offered His Son, His own Son,
His only-begotten God for the salvation of the world.

(41)   I pass over all the titles of the Son in silence. Such
an omission will do no harm where there is so much from
which to choose. There is always a reason for progress in
everything, and every work has an evident compulsion for
whatever it undertakes. Since he unquestionably composed
a Gospel, he must explain why he wrote it and let us see the
reason that he has made known in the words: 'But these
things are written that you may believe that Jesus is Christ,
the Son of God.'[53] He adduced no other reason for writing
the Gospel than that all might believe that Jesus Christ is
the Son of God. If it is sufficient for salvation to believe in
Christ, then why did he add 'Son of God'? Finally, if that is
the faith in Christ not only to believe in Christ, but to believe
in Christ as the Son of God, then Christ, the only-begotten
God, does not possess the name of the Son, which is necessary
for salvation, after the manner of adoption. If, therefore,
we are saved by confessing the name, I ask why is not the
true nature included in the name, and by what authority is
He said to be a creature, since it is not the confession of a
creature but of the Son that will guarantee our salvation?

(42)   This, therefore, is the true salvation, this is the
reward of perfect faith, to believe in Jesus Christ as the Son
of God. We possess the love of God the Father only through
our faith in His Son. Let us hear him as he speaks in his
Epistle: 'Everyone who loves the Father, loves him who is
begotten from him.'[54] What is it, I ask, to be born from Him?

53 John 20.31.
54 Cf. 1 John 5.1.

Is it the same as being created by Him? Or why does the Evangelist lie in saying that He was born from Him, since the heretic teaches more correctly that He was created by Him? Let all of us hear who this teacher is. It is said: 'This is the Antichrist who denies the Father and the Son.'[55] What are you doing, O champion of the creature, you who have formed Christ anew from non-existing things? If you cling to your confession, then recognize the name of him who makes this confession.[56] Or, when you shall teach that the Father and the Son are the Creator and the creature, do you believe that you can escape being recognized as the Antichrist by the words in which you have disguised the names?[57]

If, according to your faith, He is the Father by nature, and He is the Son by nature, then I am a slanderer, then I am burdening you with the disgrace of a name that you do not deserve. But, if all of these attributes are mere pretenses, and are names rather than realities, then learn the surname which the Apostle applies to your faith, and hear what is the nature of the faith that believes in the Son of God. For, there follow the words: 'He who denies the Son does not have the Father; he who confesses the Son has the Son and the Father.'[58] He who denies the Son is deprived of the Father. He who confesses and possesses the Son has the Father. I ask you: What place is there here for adopted names? Is not this whole matter concerned with the nature? Learn how closely it is related to the nature!

(43) For he said: 'Because we know that for our sake the Son of God has come, has taken our flesh, has suffered, and rising from the dead has assumed us, and given us an

---

55 1 John 2.22.
56 If you persist in denying that Christ is the Son of the heavenly Father, remember that the Antichrist has taught you this doctrine.
57 The Arians used the names, Father and Son, but interpreted them in the sense of Creator and creature.
58 Cf. 1 John 2.23.

excellent understanding, that we may know the true [God] and may be in Jesus Christ, his true Son. This one is the true [God], and the eternal life and our resurrection.'[59] O unhappy understanding that is lacking in the spirit of God, that is moving forward to the spirit and the name of Antichrist, that does not know that the Son of God has come for the mystery of our salvation (for which reason you are unworthy of gaining an insight into this sublime knowledge), that has confessed that Jesus Christ has the adopted name of a creature rather than of the true Son of God, by what secrets of the hidden mysteries have you learned this? Or who is the new author today of this knowledge of yours? Or did the Lord reveal this to you when in the intimacy of love you reclined on His bosom? Or did you alone follow the cross, and, besides the other command, to take Mary as your mother, did you also learn these things as a mark of His special love for you? Or, when you also outraced Peter and arrived first at the sepulchre, did you then receive it? Or was it amid the assembly of the angels and the unbreakable clasps of the sealed books, and the manifold powers of the heavenly signs, and the everlasting hymns of the new and incomprehensible canticles, that this so pious doctrine was revealed to you by the Lamb, your leader, that the Father is not the Father, that the Son is not the Son, that the nature is not the nature, and that the truth is not the truth? For, you have changed all these things into falsehoods. After the Apostle had been granted this sublime knowledge, he calls him the Son of God; you affirm His creation, you preach His adoption— you deny His birth. And, since He is for us the true Son of God, the eternal life, and the resurrection, there is no eternal life nor resurrection for him to whom He is not the true God.

59 Cf. 1 John 5.20,21. The words about Christ taking our flesh, suffering for us, rising from the dead, and becoming our resurrection are not found in the original Greek text.

Such is indeed the teaching that we learn from John, the beloved disciple of the Lord.

(44)   He who from a persecutor became an apostle and a vessel of election did not preach a different doctrine than this. In what sermon has he not confessed the Son of God? Which of his Epistles does not begin with a reference to the majesty of this truth? In what name does he not indicate the true nature? It is said: 'We were reconciled to God by the death of his Son.'[60] And again: 'God sent his Son in the likeness of sinful flesh.'[61] And again: 'The trustworthy God by whom you have been called into fellowship with his Son.'[62] Where do the heretics find an opportunity for their theft in these passages? He is His Son; He is the Son of God; He is not His adoption; He is not His creature. The name expresses the nature; the true nature proclaims the divinity, the confession bears testimony to the faith. I do not know what can be added to the nature of the Son.

For, in this matter, that He is the Son of Him who is believed to be His Father, the vessel of election has proclaimed nothing uncertain or trivial. Nor has the Teacher of the Gentiles and the Apostle of Christ tolerated any lack of clarity that might make his doctrine ambiguous. He knows those who are the sons of adoption, and who by reason of their faith have deserved to be so and to be given this name, for he says: 'For as many as are led by the Spirit of God, they are the sons of God. For you have not again received a spirit of bondage so as to be again in fear, but you have received a spirit of adoption, by virtue of which we cry, "Abba! Father." '[63] This is the name of our faith in the mystery of the regeneration, and our profession of faith confers adoption upon us. Actions that are performed according to the spirit

60 Cf. Rom. 5.10.
61 Cf. Rom. 8.3.
62 1 Cor. 1.9.
63 Cf. Rom. 8.14,15.

of God bestow the name of the sons of God upon us, and
'Abba, Father' proceeds from us as an exclamation rather
than from the essence of our nature, for the function of the
voice is outside the essence of our nature, and to be called
and to be are not one and the same thing.

(45)   But let us grasp what the Apostle teaches about
the Son of God. Although in all of the sermons which he
preached on the doctrine of the Church he never spoke of
the Father without acknowledging the Son, still, in order
to show us the true nature of the name, in so far as it could
be expressed in human language, he declared: 'What to
these things? If God is for us, who is against us? He who has
not spared his own Son but delivered him for us.'[64] Will the
title of adoption still be His even now, He to whom the name
of true Son properly belongs? For, the Apostle, wishing to
manifest the love for us, in order that we might appreciate
its sublimity from some sort of a comparison, taught that
God did not spare His own Son, that is to say, not an adopted
one for those to be adopted, not a creature for creatures,
but His for strangers, His own for those who were to bear
this name.[65]

Seek for the meaning of these words, that you may realize
the greatness of the love! Weigh the significance of 'his own,'
that you may not be ignorant of the true nature! The Apostle
now says that He is 'his own Son,' whereas in many places
he had referred to Him as 'his Son' or 'the Son of God.' And
although this passage in many of the manuscripts was written
as 'his Son' instead of 'his own Son,' because of the trans-
lators' lack of critical knowledge, the Greek language, which
the Apostle spoke, here used 'his own' rather than 'his.'
Notwithstanding the fact that in our ordinary manner of
thinking we do not sufficiently distinguish between 'his own'

---

64 Cf. Rom. 8.31,32.
65 I.e., for those who were only to be called the sons of God.

and 'his,' the Apostle—since he had mentioned 'his Son' in other places, which in Greek is *tòn eautoū uiòn,* but in this instance he expressed the truth of the nature in a very striking manner, inasmuch as he said *hos ge toû idíou uioû oùk èpheísato* ('who has not spared his own Son'), so that he who had already pointed out that there were many sons through the spirit of adoption—now revealed that the only-begotten God was a son according to the real significance of this word.

(46) There is no human error here, nor is the denial of the Son due to a lack of knowledge, since it is impossible to be ignorant of that which is denied. A creature who comes into existence from nothing is called the Son of God. If the Father did not speak of this, if the Son did not give any evidence in its favor, if the Apostles did not preach it, then to dare speak in such a manner is not only not to know Christ, but to hate Him. Since the Father says of Him: 'This is,'[66] and the Son declares in reference to Himself: 'I who speak with thee am he,'[67] and Peter confesses: 'Thou art,'[68] and John testifies: 'This is the true [God],'[69] and Paul does not cease to proclaim Him as 'his own Son,' I cannot understand how there can be anything else except hatred in this denial where the guilt cannot be excused on the plea of ignorance.

The very one who will later express these doctrines through Antichrist speaks of them in the meantime, and speaks very plainly through the prophets and the messengers of his coming.[70] He disturbs the salutary confession of faith by these new temptations in order to uproot all the knowledge of the Son of God from our minds, because this is our belief, and then excludes any other name by that name itself which will

---

66 Matt. 3.17.
67 John 4.26.
68 Matt. 16.16.
69 1 John 5.20.
70 Satan denies the divinity of Christ through the Antichrist, and through his agents, i.e., the heretics.

be called adopted.[71] Among those to whom Christ is a creature, among them Christ must be Antichrist himself, for a creature does not possess the true nature of the Son, and that one falsely represents himself as the Son of God. Accordingly, for those who already deny that this one [Christ] is the Son of God, for them that one [Antichrist] must be believed to be the Christ.

(47) O senseless fury, what, I pray you, are the things for which you hope and seek to obtain? And what assurance do you have of being saved, when your blasphemous mouth claims that Christ is a creature rather than the Son? You should have known from the Gospels and should have clung fast to the revelation of this faith. For, while the Lord can do all things, it was His will that each one of those who besought Him for the efficacy of His operation[72] should receive the merit of this confession. The confession of the suppliant did not increase the power of Him who is the power of God, but was merited as a reward for faith. When He asked Martha, who was interceding for Lazarus, whether she believed that those who had faith in Him would not die forever, she expressed the convictions of her faith when she declared: 'Yes, Lord, I have believed that thou art Christ, the Son of God, who has come into the world.'[73] This confession is eternal life, and that faith does not die. When Martha, pleading for the life of her brother, was asked whether she had this faith, she had this faith. What life does he expect and from whom does he expect it, who denies this, since life consists in nothing else than believing in this manner? For, great is the mystery of this faith, and perfect is the blessedness of confessing it.

(48) The Lord gave sight to the man who was blind

---

71 I.e., by saying that Christ is adopted they hoped to prevent the Catholics from asserting that Christ was the true God or even a Son of God.
72 A reference to those who begged Christ to perform a miracle.
73 John 11.27.

from birth, and the Lord of nature did away with a defect of nature. And because the man had been born blind for the glory of God, in order that the work of God might be recognized in the work of Christ, the confession of faith was not expected of him, but he who was ignorant of the Author of such a great favor when he received his sight was afterwards deemed worthy of learning about this faith. The removal of blindness did not bring him eternal life. Hence, the Lord questions him, when he had already been cured and expelled from the synagogue: 'Dost thou believe in the Son of God?'[74] in order that he might not regard his exclusion from the synagogue as a misfortune since the confession of this faith would restore him to immortality. And when that man, who was doubtful even at that moment, made this reply: 'Who is he, Lord, that I may believe in him?' He did not wish that this man, upon whom He had bestowed the knowledge of such great faith after the recovery of his sight, should continue in his ignorance, and so He said to him: 'And thou has both seen him and he it is who speaks with thee.' Does the Lord demand a confession of faith from this man and from others who begged Him to cure them, in order that they might prove themselves worthy of being cured? Certainly not. He spoke these words to the blind man who could now see, but only that he might reply: 'I believe, Lord.' But, because this name would be on the lips of almost all the heretics, so that they would confess Christ but would not recognize Him as the Son, he is required to make his profession of faith in what is proper to Christ, that is, to believe in Him as the Son of God. But, what profit is there in believing in the Son of God if we regard Him as a creature, since we are required to have faith in Christ, not as a creature, but as the Son of God?

(49)   Did not the devils know the real nature of this

---

74 This text and those immediately following are from John 9.35-38.

name? It is fitting that the heretics should be found guilty,
not by the teachings of the Apostles, but by the mouth of
demons. The latter exclaim and often exclaim: 'What have
I to do with thee, Jesus, Son of the most high God?'[75] The
truth drew forth this reluctant confession, and their grief at
being forced to obey testifies to the strength of this nature.
This power overcomes them, since they abandon bodies which
they have possessed for a long time. They pay their tribute of
honor when they acknowledge the nature. In the meantime,
Christ testifies that He is the Son by His miracles as well as
by His name. O heretic, where among those words by which
the demons admit who He is do you find the name of a
creature or the favor of an adoption?

(50)   At least allow yourselves to learn from those who
are ignorant of what Christ is in order that that confession
itself, which came unwillingly from those who do not recognize it, may expose your impiety. For, while the Jews did not
recognize Christ in the body, they knew that He who was the
Christ was the Son of God. Thus, when the false witnesses
whom they had hired against Him did not make any true
statements, the priest thus interrogates Him: 'Art thou the
Christ, the Son of the most high God.'[76] They do not know
the mystery, but they are not ignorant of the nature. They
do not inquire whether Christ is the Son of God, but whether
this one is the Christ, the Son of God. They were mistaken
about the person, but not about the Son of God. There is
no doubt that Christ is the Son of God; thus, while they
ask whether this one is He, they do not deny that Christ is
the Son of God.

Finally, I ask you, how can you deny with assurance that

75 Luke 8.28.
76 Cf. Mark 14.61, interpreted in the sense that the Jews of our Lord's
   time took it for granted that Christ, the Messias, would also be the
   Son of God. But, L. Fillion, *The Life of Christ* (St. Louis 1929)
   3.468 says: 'the divinity of the Messias was not commonly held in the
   Jewish world of that time.'

which is not denied by these very men who do not know it? Since it is the perfection of knowledge to know that Christ, who existed before the ages, was also born from the Virgin, even they who are unaware that He was born from Mary still realize that He is the Son of God. And take note that by your denial of the Son of God you have entered into partnership with the blasphemy of the Jews. They reveal the reason why they condemned Him when they declare: 'And according to that law he must die, because he has made himself Son of God.'[77] Is not this also the taunt of your own blasphemous voice in asking why He calls Himself the Son who, as you assert, is only a creature? These men judge that He is worthy of death for acknowledging that He is the Son; what, pray, is your verdict when you deny that He is the Son of God? His confession is just as displeasing to the Jews as it is to you. I would like to know if your opinion is different from theirs, since your intention is not different from theirs? For, with the same godlessness you deny that He is the Son of God. But they are guilty of a lesser crime, for they are ignorant of the fact that Christ is from Mary, but they are not at all doubtful that Christ is the Son of God. But, although it is impossible for you not to be aware of the fact that Christ came from Mary, you do not proclaim that Christ is the Son of God.

By reason of their ignorance their salvation can still be secured if they believe, but all the gates of salvation are closed to you because you already deny that of which you cannot be uninformed. You know that Christ is a son of God, so much so that you favor Him with this name by way of adoption, in order that you may falsely claim that a creature has received the name of Son. Since you take away His nature, in so far as it is within your power, you would also rob Him of the name, if you could. But, since this is impossible, you do

---

77 John 19.7.

not allow the nature to be a part of the name, so that, because He is called the Son, He is not the true Son of God.

(51) You should have remained in the confession of
those for whom the word of command restored tranquility to
the violent wind and the angry sea, so that you, too, would
have acknowledged the true Son of God and made use of
their words: 'Truly thou art the Son of God.'[78] But a raging
spirit is carrying you on to the shipwreck of life, and rules
over the emotions of your soul as a threatening storm over a
turbulent sea.

(52) If this faith of the sailors appears unreliable because you consider it as that of the Apostles, still, even
though it may cause me less surprise, it affords me all the
greater certainty. However, accept the faith of the Gentiles
in Him; listen to the soldier of the Roman cohort, who in the
midst of the heartless custodians of the cross was won over
to the faith. For, when the centurion saw the mighty deeds
that were performed, he exclaimed: 'Truly he was the Son
of God.'[79] After He had given up His spirit the veil of the
temple that was rent, the earthquake, the rocks that were
split, the graves that were opened, the dead who rose again
bore testimony to this truth. The man from among the unbelieving Gentiles acknowledged it. He recognized the nature
of the divinity by the deeds and confessed the nature of the
name. So great was the reasonableness of truth, and so great
was the power of faith, that the irresistible truth conquered
the will, and even he who had crucified Him did not deny
that the Lord of eternal glory was truly the Son of God.

---

78 Matt. 14.33.
79 Matt. 27.54.

BOOK SEVEN

E ARE WRITING this seventh Book against the insane audacity of the new heresy. In number, it is true, it comes after the others that have preceded, but it is the first or the greatest in regard to the understanding of the mystery of the complete faith. In it we realize how difficult and how arduous is the journey of the evangelical doctrine which we are ascending. Although the consciousness of our weakness inspires us with fear and seeks to call us back, we are inspired by the ardor of faith, aroused by the fury of the heretics, and disturbed by the peril of the ignorant, and we cannot remain silent about those matters of which we do not dare to speak.

The fear of a twofold danger overwhelms us, that either by our silence or by our preaching we shall be guilty of betraying the truth. The cunning heretics have girded themselves with the unbelievable devices of a depraved ingenuity in order that they may claim, first of all, to possess the true worship of God; then, to disturb the confidence of all the uneducated by means of their words; next, to adapt themselves to the wisdom of the world; and finally, to hinder the comprehension of the truth by the specious reasons which they allege. By expressing their belief in the one God they have misrepresented the true worship of God; again, by acknowledging the Son they have deceived the hearers by the name; they have also gratified the wisdom of the world by stating that He was not before He was born; and by asserting that God is immutable and incorporeal they have excluded the birth of God from God by the subtle manner in which they have explained their arguments. They have employed our doctrines against us, have fought the faith of the Church with the faith of the Church, and have brought us into the gravest danger, whether we make a reply or remain silent, because they preach those doctrines which are denied by means of those doctrines that are not denied.

(2)   We recall, of course, the warning that we addressed to our readers in the preceding Books that, while perusing the manifesto of the entire blasphemy,[1] they should take note that it has no other aim than to inculcate the belief that our Lord Jesus Christ is neither the Son of God nor God, and, while conceding to Him only the names derived from a sort of adoption, they deny that He has the nature of God and the nature of a son, since they assert, therefore, that God is immutable and incorporeal in order that the Son to whom He gave birth may not be God; hence, in their confession only God the Father is the one God, in order that Christ may not be God in our faith, for an incorporeal nature does not admit the idea of a birth, and the confession of only one God destroys our faith in God from God.

In the preceding Books, where we have already taught, in accordance with the Law and the Prophets, that this teaching of theirs was both deceitful and futile, we mapped out that plan in our reply which, in the explanation of God from God and in our confession of the one true God, would not be found wanting by creating a union in the one true God, nor would it go too far by professing our faith in a second God, since in our confession God is neither alone, nor are there two

---

1 The Arians' profession of faith, already mentioned above, 4.12-13; 6.4-5.

gods. Meanwhile, as we neither denied nor affirmed that He is one, we preserved the perfection of faith. For, that they are one in nature is referred to both of them, and both are not one person. Accordingly, we who are about to give a complete explanation of this indescribable mystery of the perfect faith in conformity with the teaching of the Gospels and the Apostles must in the first place bring to our readers' attention nothing else than the nature of the Son of God, who subsists by a true birth, and to make known that the Son is not from anywhere else or from anything except from God. In accordance with that which we have brought out in the preceding Books, there is no doubt that He is the Son of God by the true nature of His birth, and that the name of adoption may not be applied we shall now prove these same things from the Gospels so that we may also recognize Him as the true God, because He is the true Son, for He will not be a true Son unless He is also the true God, nor will He be the true God unless He is also the true Son.

(3) There is nothing more oppressive to human nature than the consciousness of danger (for those things which take place unknown to us, or suddenly, leave our peace of mind in a truly pitiable state, but no fear of the future accompanies them), because the anxiety itself brings the pain of suffering with it to one who is aware of the coming misfortunes. I do not now set sail from port without being familiar with shipwreck, nor do I enter upon the journey unaware that the forests are infested with robbers, nor do I pass across the deserts of Libya without realizing that scorpions, asps, and basilisks are present everywhere. Nothing eludes my care or my knowledge. I speak under the watchful eyes of all the heretics who hang upon every word from my mouth, and the entire journey of my treatise is either difficult to ascend because of the narrow passages, or is filled with pitfalls, or covered with traps. I do not complain very much about the

fact that the journey is already arduous and difficult, because I am ascending not by own steps but by those of the Apostles. I am, however, always in danger, ever fearful of going aside from the narrow paths, or of falling into the ditches, or of being ensnared by the traps. For, as I am about to explain the one God according to the Law, the Prophets, and the Apostles, Sabellius confronts me; if I proclaim this term, his most savage bite will devour me completely as a choice morsel. Again, if I oppose Sabellius, deny the one God and acknowledge the Son of God as the true God, a new heresy[2] is ready to accuse me of teaching that there are two gods. If I shall say that the Son of God was born from Mary, then Ebion, that is, Photinus,[3] will derive prestige for his lie from the confession of the truth. I pass over the others in silence, because everyone knows that they are outside of the Church.

Although this one has been frequently condemned and rejected, it is a deeply rooted evil even at the present day. Galatia has nourished many who have made this impious confession of God.[4] Alexandria has maliciously proclaimed throughout almost the whole world the two gods whom it denies.[5] Pannonia offers a damaging defense of the doctrine that Jesus Christ has been born from Mary.[6] And amid these arguments the Church is in peril of not clinging to the truth

---

2 Arianism.

3 Photinus (d. 376), Bishop of Sirmium in Pannonia, was often condemned as a heretic, but because of the attachment of the people to him was not deposed from his see. It is interesting to note that St. Hilary did not mention Photinus by name when drawing up his synopsis of *De Trinitate* in Book 1.

4 By Galatia he is probably referring to Marcellus, Bishop of Ancyra, one of the controversial figures of the fourth century, whom the Arians accused of Sabellianism.

5 This is a reference to Arius, who claimed that there is only one God, although his doctrine led to the inevitable conclusion that there are two gods, and the Son is an inferior God to the Father.

6 Photinus did not admit the permanent incarnation of the Son of God, but taught that God dwelt for a time in the child born of the Virgin Mary.

by means of the truth, since those doctrines by which the true worship of God is confirmed and destroyed are introduced for the sake of godlessness. We cannot teach about the one God in a pious manner if we teach that He is alone, because God the Son will not belong in the faith of a God who is in isolation. But, if we acknowledge that the Son of God is God, as He truly is, we are in danger of not preserving the faith in the one God, and it is as equally dangerous to deny the one God as it is to admit a solitary God. The folly of the world does not grasp these things, since it does not believe that He can be designated as one unless He is alone, nor can it conceive how He is not alone if He is one.

(4)   But the Church, as I hope, shall cast that light of her doctrine even upon the folly of the world so that, although it may not accept the mystery of faith, it realizes that we are teaching the mystery of faith to the heretics. For, great is the power of truth which, although it can be comprehended by itself, shines forth by the very teachings which are opposed to it, so that, while it remains steadfast in its nature, its nature daily acquires strength while it is being attacked. It is characteristic of the Church that she conquers when she is undergoing assault, that she is then understood when she is blamed, and that she gains then when she is abandoned. She desires, of course, that all should persevere with her and within her, nor is it her wish either to cast the others from her most peaceful bosom or to destroy them, when they become unworthy of dwelling with so great a mother. But, when the heretics have left her, or when they have rejected her, inasmuch as she loses the opportunity for dispensing her salvation, she gains confidence that blessedness is to be sought from her.

This is perceived most readily from the endeavors of the heretics themselves. Since the Church, instituted by the Lord and strengthened by the Apostles, is the one Church of all men, from which the raging error of the different blasphemous teachings has cut itself off, and it cannot be denied that the separation from the faith has come about as the result of a defective and perverted understanding, while that which was read was adapted to one's views rather than one's views being submissive to what was read, still, while the individual groups contradict one another, she is to be understood not only by her own teachings but also by those of her adversaries, so that, while all are directed against her alone, she refutes the most godless error of all of them by the very fact that she is alone and is one. All the heretics, therefore, rise up against the Church, but, while all the heretics mutually conquer themselves, they gain no victories for themselves. Victory in their case is the triumph of the Church over each of them, while one heresy wages war against that teaching in another heresy which the faith of the Church condemns in the other heresy (for there is nothing which the heretics hold in common), and, meanwhile, they confirm our faith while they contradict one another.

(5) By doing away with the birth of the Son, Sabellius proclaims the one God, while he does not doubt that the power of the nature which produced its effect in the man is God. Since he does not know the mystery of the Son, he has lost the faith in the true generation of the Son through his admiration for the deeds, and while he hears: 'He who has seen me has seen also the Father,'[7] he grasps at the union of the undivided and indistinguishable nature in the Father and the Son, not perceiving that a natural unity is revealed by the designation of a birth, since from the fact that the Father is seen in the Son we have a confirmation of the divinity and not the abolition of the birth.

Accordingly, the knowledge of the one is in the other, because the one does not differ from the other in nature, and,

---

7 Cf. John 14.9.

where there is no difference between them, then the study of the true essence of the nature does not reveal any distinction. There can be no doubt that He who remained in the form of God caused the outward appearance of the form of God to be recognized in Himself. Even this saying of the Lord: 'I and the Father are one,'[8] also leads to the absurd madness of this sinful opinion. For, the unity of the identical nature has developed in a godless manner into the error of a union, and by understanding this passage in the sense of power alone they have lost sight of its meaning. For, 'I and the Father are one' does not indicate one who is in isolation. The conjunction 'and' which designates the Father does not permit us to think of one, and the word 'are' is incompatible with a single person, but, while this phrase, 'are one,' does not do away with the birth, it does not make any distinction in the nature, since 'one' is not a suitable word where there is a difference, nor 'are' where one person is concerned.

(6) Join the rage of the present heretics to the rage of this man in order that they may defend themselves against Sabellius! They will declare that they have read: 'The Father is greater than I,'[9] and, since they understand nothing either of the mystery of the birth or the mystery of the God who emptied Himself and assumed our flesh, they effect a lessening of the nature by acknowledging a greater nature. They contend that He is a Son to such an extent that He is less than the Father, that He demands a restoration of His former glory, that He is afraid to die, and has died. On the contrary, that one defends the nature of God from His deeds, and since this new heresy will not now deny the one God in order that it may not believe that the Son is God, Sabellius will retain the one God in his profession in order that the Son may not exist at all. This one [Arius] will introduce the

8 John 10.30.
9 John 14.28.

Son as working, and this one [Sabellius] will contend that
God is present in the works. The latter [Sabellius] will speak
of the one God, the former [Arius] will deny the one God.

Sabellius will defend himself in this manner: 'Nothing
except the nature of God produces the miracles which have
been performed. From God alone come the forgiveness of
sins, the cure of diseases, the walking of the paralytics, the
sight of the blind, the dead coming back to life. No other
nature, except that which is conscious of what it is, would
say: "I and the Father are one." Why do you force me into
another substance? Why do you endeavor to make me another God? The one God has performed the deeds which are
characteristic of God.' But, with a mouth that is no less
venomous, these men will cry out against these things, and
proclaim that the Son is unlike God the Father: 'You do
not know the mystery of your salvation. We must believe
that He is the Son, through whom the worlds were made,
through whom man was formed, who gave the Law through
the angels, who was born from Mary, who was sent by the
Father, who was crucified, died, and was buried, who rose
from the dead, is at the right hand of God, and who is the
judge of the living and the dead. We must be born again into
this one, we must acknowledge this one, we must merit this
one's kingdom.' Each enemy of the Church is doing the work
of the Church, and, while Sabellius preaches that He is God
by nature because of His works, these men, on the other hand,
acknowledge that He is the Son of God in accordance with
the mystery of faith.

(7)   Furthermore, what a victory it is for our faith when
Ebion, that is, Photinus, either conquers or is conquered,
while he reproves Sabellius because he denies that the Son of

God is man, and while the Arian fanatics[10] refute him because he knows nothing about the Son of God in man. In
opposition to Sabellius he claims the Gospels for the Son
of Mary, but Arius does not concede to him that the Gospels
belong to the Son of Mary alone.[11] In opposition to him
[Sabellius] who denies the Son, he [Photinus] unlawfully assumes a man into the Son. He [Photinus] who does not
know that the Son exists before the world is contradicted by
this one [Arius] who denies that the Son of God is only from
man.

Let them conquer, as they will, because they are conquered
by mutually conquering one another. While these men of the
present time are also refuted by the nature of God, Sabellius
is overthrown by the mystery of the Son, and Photinus is
blamed either for his ignorance or his denial of the Son of
God who was born before the world. Meanwhile, the faith
of the Church, that rests upon the doctrines of the Gospels
and the Apostles, clings to the confession of the Son against
Sabellius, to the nature of God against Arius, and to the
creator of the world against Photinus, and she does so with
all the more right because these men are not in mutual agreement about their denial of these doctrines. Sabellius teaches
that the nature of God is in the miracles, but he does not

---

10 This is the first explicit mention of the followers of Arius in this
   work. The word used here, *Ariomanitae*, is also found in the writings
   of St. Athanasius and other opponents of Arianism. It probably arose
   from Ares, the war god whose chief characteristic was fury; thus, the
   word was regarded as being singularly appropriate to the name and
   temperament of Arius.
11 Sabellius claimed that the Son of Mary was only God the Father in
   human flesh, but Photinus asserted that the work of salvation was
   completed by the Son of Mary. Arius rejects the deeds that are
   ascribed to Christ in the Gospels.

recognize the Son who works in them. On the other hand, these men give Him the title of Son, but they do not acknowledge that the nature of God is within Him. Photinus, however, refers to the man, but he is unaware that the man of whom he speaks has been born from God. Thus, while they are either defending or condemning they manifest the truth of our faith, which defends or condemns these doctrines in a God-fearing manner, just as they really are.

(8) I have made these things known in a few words, not from any desire to be diffuse, but for safety's sake, in order that we should realize, first of all, that all the assertions of the heretics are ambiguous and false, since it is to our advantage when they mutually disagree, and furthermore, when I contradict the blasphemous statements of these men of the present day, and proclaim God the Father and the Son of God as God, and next confess that by the identical kind of divinity the Father and the Son have the same name and nature, no one may believe that I have been ensnared either by the error of two gods, or the contrary error of a God who is unique and alone, since no union will be found in our teaching about God the Father and God the Son, and no diversity of gods will result from our explanation of the undivided nature. Since in the preceding Book we based our reply to those who deny that the Son of God subsists from God on the true nature of the birth, we must now prove that He who is truly the Son of God by His nature is also truly God by His nature, but in such a manner that our faith may not deteriorate into an unique God nor into a second God, since it will not teach about the one God in such a manner as if He were alone, nor will it confess the God who is not alone as if He were not one.

(9) We know, therefore, that our Lord Jesus Christ is God in these ways: by His name, birth, nature, power, confession. And in regard to His name I do not believe that

there is any ambiguity, for we read: 'In the beginning was the Word and the Word was with God; and the Word was God.'[12] What kind of a slander is it that He should not be what He is called? Or does not the name designate the nature? Since there is a motive behind every contradiction, I shall now inquire into the reason for this denial of God. It is a simple word and nothing strange is added that might be a stumbling-block. For, the Word that was made flesh is nothing else than God. Here we find no indication that this title was assigned to or assumed by Him, so that the name that is God is not His by nature.

(10)   Look at the other names that were either bestowed or appropriated. It was said to Moses: 'I have given thee as the God of Pharao.'[13] But is not the reason for the name brought out when 'Pharao' is mentioned? Or has He bestowed the nature of God upon him and not, rather, the power to inspire terror, when the serpent of Moses, which became a rod shortly afterwards, devours the serpents of the magicians, when he drives away the plague of flies which he had brought in, when he puts a stop to the hail with the power with which he had called it upon them, when he drives away the locusts with the strength with which he had admitted them, when the magicians acknowledge that the finger of God is present.[14]

In this manner Moses was given as the God of Pharao, while He is feared, while petitions are addressed to him, while he punishes, and while he cures. It is one thing to be given as God, and it is another thing to be God. God was given to Pharao. Besides, the nature and the name do not belong to Him in such a manner that He is God. I also recall another use of this title, where it is stated: 'I have said: you

---

12 John 1.1.
13 Cf. Exod. 7.1.
14 Cf. Exod. 9-10.

are gods.'[15] Here the meaning indicates a name that has been conferred. And when the expression 'I have said' is used, the words refer to the speaker rather than to the name of the thing,[16] because the name of the thing brings us an understanding of the thing, but the title is dependent on the will of another. And where the author of the title reveals himself, there the title comes from the pronouncement of the author, and not as a true name derived from the nature.

(11)   But, here, the Word is God; the thing exists in the Word; the thing of the Word is expressed in the name. The name 'Word' belongs to the Son of God from the mystery of the birth just as do the names of wisdom and power. And even if they have been transmitted to the Son of God with the substance of the true birth, they are not wanting to God[17] as attributes that are proper to Him, although they have been born from Him into God. As we have often declared, we do not teach the mystery of a division in the Son, but the mystery of the birth. There was not an imperfect separation but a perfect begetting, for the birth does not lead to any loss on the part of the begetter, while it includes a gain for the one who is born. For this reason, the surnames of those things[18] are suitable to the only-begotten God which still inhere in the Father by the power of His unchangeable nature, while they perfect Him who subsists by the birth. The only-begotten God is the Word, but the unborn God is never wholly without the Word, not that the nature of the Son is the utterance of a voice, but He was designated as the Word, while He subsists as God from God with the true

---

15 Ps. 81.6.
16 The word *res*, which is used here, indicates a permanent nature in contradistinction to *accidens,* which is something that is merely added to the nature.
17 That is, to God the Father.
18 By 'those things' are meant such attributes of God the Father as wisdom and power.

nature of the birth, in order that we might proclaim Him as the proper Son of the Father and inseparable from Him by the identity of nature.

As Christ is the wisdom and power of God, so He is not that efficacious movement of an internal power or thought, as He is wont to be understood, but His nature, which preserves the truth of His substance by His birth, is indicated by these names of the internal natures. For, it is impossible for that which derives its existence by birth to be regarded as the same as that which is always internal for everyone.[19] But, in order that we may know that He is not a stranger to the nature of the Father's divinity, the only-begotten Son, who has been born from the eternal God the Father into a God of the same substance, has been revealed as subsisting in the names of these attributes, which are not wanting to Him from whom He subsists.[20] When I hear: 'And the Word was God,' I understand that He is not only called God, but is shown to be God. As we have pointed out above, the name has been added as a title to Moses and to those who are called gods, but here the nature of the substance is indicated. Being is not an accidental name, but a subsistent truth, an abiding principle, and an essential attribute of the nature.

(12)   Let us see whether the confession of the Apostle Thomas agrees with this teaching of the Evangelist, when he says: 'My Lord and my God.'[21] He is therefore his God whom he acknowledges as God. And certainly he was aware that the Lord had said: 'Hear, O Israel, the Lord thy God is one.'[22] And how did the faith of the Apostle become un-

---

19 *Semper internum* is here synonymous with *semper inhaerens*; that is, what is born is not a mere inherent quality of the begetter, but is a being that subsists by itself.
20 Such names as wisdom, and power, which are proper to the Son and reveal His nature, have come to Him from the Father, and the latter has not lost these attributes by the birth of the Son.
21 John 20.28.
22 Cf. Deut. 6.4.

mindful of the principal commandment, so that he confessed Christ as God, since we are to live in the confession of the one God? The Apostle, who perceived the faith of the entire mystery through the power of the resurrection, after he had often heard: 'I and the Father are one' and 'All things that the Father has are mine' and 'I in the Father and the Father in me,'[23] now confessed the name of the nature without endangering the faith. For, the true religion, which acknowledges the Son of God as God, does not conflict with the confession of the one God the Father, since it believes that nothing except the true nature of the Father is in the Son of God, nor is the faith of the one nature imperiled by the impious confession of a second God, because the perfect birth of God does not lead to the nature of a second God.

Since Thomas, therefore, comprehended the true nature of the mystery of the Gospel, he acknowledged Him as his Lord and his God. This is not an honorary name, but the confession of a nature, for he believes that He was God because of the things and the powers themselves. And the Lord taught that this God-fearing confession was not a matter of honor, but of faith, when He said: 'Because thou hast seen, thou hast believed. Blessed are they who have not seen, and yet have believed.'[24] Thomas believed when he saw. But you ask: What did he believe? And did he believe anything else than what he confessed: 'My Lord and my God'? He could not rise from the dead into life by Himself except through the nature of God, and the faith of the orthodox religion has believed and has confessed that He is God. And will not the name of God, therefore, be regarded as the essence of the nature, since the confession of the name follows the faith of the nature that is believed? For, the God-fearing Son, who would do not His own will but the will of Him who sent

23 Cf. John 10.30; 16.15; 14.11.
24 John 20.29.

Him, and who would not seek His own honor but that of
Him from whom He had come, would surely have rejected
the glory of the name for Himself in order that He might
not contradict what He Himself had preached about the one
God. But, since He has indeed confirmed the mystery of the
apostolic faith, and has admitted that the name of the Father's
nature was in Him, He taught that those were blessed who,
even though they had not seen Him rising from the dead,
believed that He was God because they knew of His resurrection.

(13) The name of the nature, therefore, is not wanting
in the profession of our faith. For, the name, which designates
everything, also makes known a thing of the same nature,
and there are no longer two things but a thing of the same
nature. The Son of God is God, since that is what the name
indicates. One name does not add up to two gods, for God
is the one name of a nature that is one and identical. Since
the Father is God and the Son is God and the name of the
divine nature is proper to each, the two of them are one, for,
although the Son subsists by the birth of the nature, the unity
is preserved in the name, nor does the birth of the Son, which
claims that the Father and the Son have the one name just
as they have the one nature, force the faith of the believers
to acknowledge two gods. Hence, the name of God belongs
to the Son by His birth. This is the second step in our
exposition, that He is God by reason of His birth. Although
the authority of the Apostle about the true nature of the
name is still available to me, nevertheless it is my intention
for the time being to discuss the statements of the Gospel.

(14) First of all, I raise the question: What new element
could the birth have introduced into the nature of the Son
so that He is not God? The judgment of the human mind
rejects this opinion, that anything by its birth is distinct from
the nature of its origin, unless, perhaps, it has been conceived

by natures that are different and something new comes into the world (and thus that which comes from two natures belongs to neither one), a thing that is customary among animals and wild beasts. But, even that new element is in it only because of the qualities that have been born together with it from the distinction of the natures, and their birth did not cause but accepted the distinction, and from the two of them it held fast to that which it combined into one in itself. Since these things are so in these corporeal processes and occurrences, what madness is it, I ask, to connect the birth of the only-begotten God with a spurious nature, since birth comes only from the essence of the nature, and there will no longer be a birth if the essence of the nature is not in the birth?

Hence, the purpose of all that heat and fury is that there may not be a birth but a creation in the Son of God, and that He who subsists may not preserve the origin of His nature, but may receive from non-existing matter a different nature from God. Since God is a Spirit, there is no doubt that the one born from Him has nothing in Him that is different from or alien to Him from whom He has been born, in accordance with the saying: 'That which is born of the flesh is flesh; and that which is born of the Spirit is spirit.'[25] Consequently, the birth of God perfects God, so that we realize that God is not one who has begun to be but one who has been born, for that which has begun cannot be the same as that which has been born, since that which has a beginning either begins to exist from nothing into something or it develops from one thing into something else and ceases to be, as gold from the earth, as liquids from solids, as heat from cold, as red from white, as animate creatures from water, as living beings from those that are lifeless. The Son of

---

25 Cf. John 3.6.

God, however, does not begin to be God from nothing, but was born, nor was He anything else before He was God. Thus, He who is born into God did not begin to be, nor did He develop into that which God is. The birth, therefore, maintains the nature from which it subsists, and the Son of God does not subsist as anything else than that which God is.[26]

(15) If anyone raises doubts at this point, let him learn the knowledge of the nature from the Jews, or, rather, let him recognize the true nature of the birth from the Gospel, wherein it is written: 'This is why the Jews were seeking the more to put him to death; because he was not only breaking the Sabbath, but was also calling God his own Father, making himself equal to God.'[27] The words of the Jews are not recorded here, as generally happens in other places; rather, this is the explanation by the Evangelist, who points out the reason why the Jews wanted to kill Him.

Hence, the excuse of an inadequate knowledge no longer holds for the godless blasphemers, since, according to the testimony of the Apostle, the true meaning of His nature is revealed when His birth is indicated, 'but he was also calling God his own Father, making himself equal to God.' Is there not a natural birth where the equality of the nature is manifested by the name of His own Father? There is no question regarding the fact that they do not differ in equality. Besides, will anyone deny that a birth gives rise to an identical nature? From this alone can come that which is true equality, because only birth can bestow an equality of nature. But, we shall never believe that equality is present where there is a union; on the other hand, it will not be found where there is a distinction. Thus, the equality of likeness does not admit

---

26 The Arians argue that in spiritual things a birth is impossible, for they realize that, if Christ is recognized as the true Son of God by His birth, then He must also be recognized as the true God.
27 John 5.18.

either of solitude or of diversity, because in every case of equality there is neither a difference nor is it by itself.

(16) Although the judgment of our reasoning, therefore, agrees with universal opinion of men, that birth brings about an equality of nature, and where there is equality there can be nothing strange nor can it be alone, still, the faith of our testimony should be ratified by the words of the Lord Himself, so that the reckless spirit of contradiction, by its lack of restraint in comprehending differences in the names, may not dare oppose the assertions of the divine testimony about Himself. The Lord replied: 'The Son can do nothing of himself, but only what he sees the Father doing. For whatever he does, the Son also does the same in like manner. For the Father loves the Son and shows him all that he himself does. And greater works than these he will show him that you may wonder. For as the Father raises the dead and gives them life, even so the Son also gives life to whom he will. For neither does the Father judge any man, but all judgment he has given to the Son, that all men may honor the Son even as they honor the Father. He who does not honor the Son, does not honor the Father who sent him.'[28]

The order of what we have proposed[29] required us, it is true, to discuss every single aspect of every single subject, so that, because we have learned that our Lord Jesus Christ is God in accordance with His name, birth, nature, power, and confession, our exposition should consider the specific steps in the proposed arrangement, but the nature of the birth, which embraces within it the name, the nature, the power, and the confession, does not allow this. For, without these there will be no birth, because by being born it contains all these things in itself. Accordingly, when we treat this subject we are necessarily placed in such a position that it is impossible

28 Cf. John 5.19-23.
29 That is, that Christ is the true God.

to postpone the above-mentioned subjects in accordance with
our plan of devoting a special treatise to each of them.

(17)   In replying to the Jews, who were the more eager
to kill Him on this account, because He made Himself equal
to God by calling God His Father, He explained the complete
mystery of our faith while He rebuked their sinful passions.
He had previously declared, after He had cured the paralytic
and been judged worthy of death for this violation of the
Sabbath: 'My father works even until now, and I work,'
and by these words all were inflamed with hatred, because
He had placed Himself on an equality with God by using
the name of Father. And since He wished, therefore, to confirm His birth, and to confess the power of His nature, He
stated: 'This Son can do nothing of himself, but only what
he sees the Father doing.' The beginning of His answer was
directed toward the godless fury of the Jews by which they
were so aroused that they even determined to put Him to
death.

To their accusation that He was guilty of violating the
Sabbath He had declared: 'My Father works even until now,
and I work,' in order that it might be understood that He
acted thus by the authority of His example, but He indicated
that what He had done was to be regarded as the work of
His Father, because the latter Himself was working in whatever He did. Again, He added these words in reference to
that hatred which He had stirred up by placing Himself on
an equality with God when He gave Him the name of
Father: 'Amen, amen I say to you, the Son can do nothing
of himself, but only what he sees the Father doing.' In order
that that equality, therefore, which was derived from the
name and the nature of the Son might not do away with the
faith in His birth, He said that the Son can do nothing of
Himself except what He sees the Father doing. And that the
salutary order of our confession in the Father and the Son

might remain, He revealed the nature of His birth, which was the power to work not by an increase of strength, that would be granted for each specific task, but would be possessed beforehand by reason of His knowledge. He possesses it beforehand, however, not after the example of a material work, so that the Father would first do something that the Son would do later on, but He had come into existence with the nature of God into the nature of God, that is to say, the Son had been born from the Father. Because He was aware of the Father's power and strength that was with Him, the Son asserted that He could do nothing by Himself except what He saw the Father doing. And since the only-begotten God would do His work through the operations of His Father's power, He would claim that He could do as much as he was conscious of, that He could do it by His nature which was inseparable from that of God the Father, and which He had received by His legitimate birth. God does not see in a material way, but sees everything by the power of His nature.

(18)   Then He continued: 'For all things that the Father does, the Son also does the same in like manner.' He added 'in like manner' to indicate the birth, but He mentioned 'all things' and 'the same' when He was referring to the truth of the nature that He was to reveal. In these words, 'all things whatever' and 'the same,' there can be no distinction, nor can there be anything that is passed over.[30] Thus, He to whose nature it belongs to do all the same things possesses the same nature. But, where all the same things are done by the Son 'in like manner,' the similarity of the works excludes the solitude of the one who does the work, so that all the things that the Father does the Son does in like manner. This is the understanding of the true birth and the most complete mystery of our faith, which confesses the true nature in the Father

---

30 Hilary is referring here to the fact that everything that the Son has He has received from the Father, and retains as His own.

and the Son, and that arises from the unity of the divine nature and the one and identical Godhead, so that the Son, while He is doing the same things, does them in like manner, and that, while He is doing them in like manner, He is doing the same things, because by the designation of the things that are done in like manner He bears witness to the birth, and by the designation of the same things that are done He bears witness to the nature.

(19) The order of the Lord's response, therefore, keeps intact the order of the Church's faith, so that it does not make any distinction in the nature, and indicates the birth. These words follow: 'For the Father loves the Son, and shows him all that he himself does. And greater works than these he will show him, that you may wonder. For as the Father raises the dead and gives them life, even so the Son also gives life to whom he will.'[31] Does the manifestation of the works in this instance point out anything else to us than the faith in His birth so that we believe that the Son subsists from the Father who subsists? Unless, perhaps, we are to believe that the only-begotten God needed to be instructed in the doctrine that was to be made known because of His ignorance, but the rashness of this godless opinion is not permissible. It is not necessary for Him to be taught who knows whatever He must teach. He said later on: 'The Father loves the Son and shows him all that he himself does,' in order to make known that this complete manifestation of the Father was the doctrine of our faith, that is to say, that we should acknowledge the Father and the Son. And in order that no ignorance might be here attributed to the Son, to whom the Father would show everything that He would do, He immediately continued: 'And greater works than these he will show him, that you may wonder. For as the Father raises the

---

31 John 5.20-21.

dead and gives them life, even so the Son also gives life to whom he will.'

Hence, the revelation of the coming work is not unknown to the Son, to whom this was to be shown in order that He might bring back the dead to life in accordance with the example of His Father's nature. He declares that the Father will show these things to the Son which they will admire, and He at once taught us what these same things were: 'For as the Father raises the dead and gives them life, even so the Son also gives life to whom he will.' The power is made equal through the unity of an indistinguishable nature. And the manifestation of the works is not for the instruction of ignorance but for our faith. This did not acquaint the Son with the knowledge of things unknown, but acquainted us with the confession of His birth, while it confirms it by the fact that all things would be shown to Him that He could do.

The heavenly statement was not lacking in caution in order that the meaning of a distinct nature might not creep in under the pretext of ambiguous words. It declared that the works of the Father were shown rather than that the nature of the power was added in order to perform them, to teach us that the manifestation was the substance of the birth itself, and because of the Father's love there would be born with it the knowledge of the works of the Father which He wished Him to perform. Furthermore, in order that no one might conclude from this reference to the manifestation that there was a difference of nature in Him who did not know, He already knows the things themselves which, as He asserts, are to be made known. So far removed is He from having to act by the authority of an example[32] that He gives

---

32 This statement does not contradict what was said above in Ch. 17. There he wished merely to point out that the Son's right to act according to the example of the Father comes from His birth from the Father. Here he uses the same phrase to indicate the service that a servant renders to his master, and, since the Son is equal in nature to His Father, He does not perform such a service.

life to those to whom He wills. For, to will is the liberty of a nature, which subsists together with the freedom of choice for the blessedness of perfect omnipotence.

(20) And, then, in order that it might not appear, because He gives life to those whom He wills, that He does not possess the nature of a birth in Him, but that He subsists rather by the permission of the unborn power, He immediately declared: 'For neither does the Father judge any man, but all judgment he has given to the Son.' And from the fact that all judgment has been given to Him, His nature and His birth are shown, for on the one hand only an identical nature can possess everything, and on the other hand birth cannot have anything unless it is given.

But all judgment has been given, because He vivifies those whom He wills. Nor can it be claimed that all judgment has been taken away from the Father, since He Himself does not judge, because the judgment of the Son comes from the judgment of the Father, for from Him all judgment has been given. But the reason why the judgment has been given is not passed over in silence. For there come the words: 'But all judgment he has given to the Son, that all men may honor the Son even as they honor the Father. He who does not honor the Son, does not honor the Father who sent Him.'[33] Is there anything left to us, I ask, that might give grounds for suspicion, or is there anything remaining here that might afford a pretext for impiety? For, neither does the Father judge any man, but all judgment He has given to the Son. The reason why the judgment was given, however, was that the Son might be equally honored with the Father, so that he who does not honor the Son does not honor the Father. And after these words, how can the nature of the birth be understood as being different, which has been made equal not only by the work, the power, the honor, but also

33 John 5.23.

by the insult, if the honor is denied? Accordingly, the statement in the Lord's reply now reveals nothing else than the mystery of the birth. Nor can we, nor must we, distinguish the Son from the Father in anything except that we teach that He is born, but is not distinct.

(21) The Father, therefore, works even until now, and the Son works. You have the names of the nature, since both the Father as well as the Son work. Grasp the fact that the nature of God also works through which God works! And in order that you may not believe that the operation of two unlike natures is perhaps to be understood, recall what was said about the blind man: 'But that the works of God were to be made manifest in him. I must do the works of him who sent me.'[34] Accordingly, in the work that the Son does there is the work of the Father, and the work of the Son is the work of God. And the words that follow are still on the subject of these works. Meanwhile, the reply in this instance has had no other aim than to refer every work to the two of them, but the nature of the operation would not be different in either of them, since from the fact that the Father works even until now the Son also works, in order that He who is the Lord of the Sabbath (for the Son of Man is the Lord of the Sabbath) might not be regarded as working in a godless manner on the Sabbath, and the sanction for His work would be the Father, who works in Him through the nature of His birth.

Accordingly, there is no confusion or destruction of nature so that He is not the Son, but, again, the nature is not taken away so that He is not God. They are not separated by any distinction so that they are not one, and the fact that they are one cannot bring it about that there are not two of them.[35] In the first place, recognize the Son when it is said:

---

34 John 9.3,4.
35 The fact that the Father and Son are one in nature does not prevent them from having their own distinct manner of existence, that is, the Father is unborn and the Son is the only-begotten.

'The Son can do nothing of himself, but only what he sees the Father doing.' You have the birth of the Son, who can do nothing of Himself except that which He sees. But from the fact that He can do nothing of Himself He does away with the error that He has not been born, for birth cannot come from itself, but the fact that He sees indicates that He possesses in Himself the knowledge of a nature that is aware of what it is. And from this fact now recognize the true nature of God: 'For, whatever He does, the Son also does the same in like manner.' But after the power of the nature, then learn from it about the unity of the identical nature: 'that all men may honor the Son even as they honor the Father who sent him.' And in order that the unity of the nature may not involve you in the union of one who is alone, learn about the mystery of faith from the words: 'He who does not honor the Son, does not honor the Father who sent him.'

Everything is sealed against the ingenuity of heretical fury. He is the Son because He can do nothing of Himself; He is God because He Himself does the same things that the Father does. They are one because they are equal in honor; He does the same things, not other things. He Himself is not the Father, because He was sent. Hence, the mystery belongs to the birth alone, so that it includes the name, the nature, the power, and the confession, because the entire birth cannot but have that nature from which it was born. It does not offer the substance of an extraneous nature, because a nature alien to it does not come into existence from one. But, that which is not different from it is one in nature. Whatever is one by birth does not include solitude, because solitude pertains to a single individual, and the unity of birth refers to both of them.

(22) Besides, let the evidence of the divine teaching be its own defense! It states: 'Those who are my sheep hear my voice, and I know them and they follow me. And I give them everlasting life; and they shall never perish, neither

shall anyone snatch them out of my hand. What the Father
has given me is greater than all; and no one will be able to
snatch anything out of the hand of my Father. I and the
Father are one.'[36] What dullness of the sluggish mind, I ask,
deadens our understanding so that these words so clearly
expressed do not penetrate our consciousness? Or what vain
and arrogant spirit deludes our human infirmity so that,
although they have received the knowledge of God from
these words, they imagine that God is not to be recognized
by the words whereby He is known? For, either other Gospels
must be produced which are to teach us, or, if these alone
have taught us, why do we not believe them as we are taught?
And if our knowledge has been received from them alone,
why does not our faith come from these words whence our
knowledge is derived?

But, if the faith is found to be contrary to the knowledge,
that faith no longer proceeds from knowledge, but from sin,
since it arrogates a godless faith to itself in opposition to the
orthodox teaching about the knowledge that is confessed.
Hence, the only-begotten God, conscious of His nature in
Himself, nevertheless reveals the ineffable mystery of His
birth in words as clear as possible for the confession of our
faith, so that we may know that He was born, and may
believe that the nature of God is in Him, and that He is one
with the Father, and, while he acknowledges Himself as one
with the Father, He is not one in such a way that we may
regard Him as being only alone, and as the Father Himself,
and that He ceases to be that which the Son is. In the first
place, He bears witness to the power of His nature when He
says of His sheep: 'Neither shall anyone snatch them out
of my hand.' This is the voice of a self-reliant power, to confess the independence of an invincible strength because no
one may snatch the sheep out of His hands. Although in the

---

36 Cf. John 10.27-30.

nature of God, still, in order that we might realize that this is the birth of the nature from God, He added: 'What the Father has given me is greater than all.' He does not conceal His birth from the Father, for what He has received from the Father 'is greater than all.'

And He who has received is in that which He has received from His birth, not later on, and still He is from the other while He has received. But He who is from the other has received and in order that no one may believe that He is something else and that He does not exist in the nature of Him from whom He has received, He said: 'No one will be able to snatch anything out of the hand of my Father.' No one snatches from His hand, because that which He has received from the Father is greater than all. What is the meaning of so different a statement that again no one can snatch anything from the hand of His Father? It is the hand of the Son which has received from the Father; it is the hand of the Father which has given to the Son, and how is that which is not taken from the hand of the Son not taken from the hand of the Father? If you ask how, then learn: 'I and the Father are one.'

The hand of the Son is the hand of the Father. The nature does not lose its nobility by its birth, so that it would not be the same, and, again, since it is the same, there is no obstacle to the understanding of a birth, because a birth does not admit anything alien to itself. But, that you may be able to recognize the power of the same nature by means of a corporeal illustration, He mentions that the hand of the Son is the hand of the Father, because the nature and the power of the Father would be in the Son. Finally, that you may become acquainted with the truth of an identical nature by the mystery of the birth, it was said: 'I and the Father are one,' so that because they are one you should believe that they are not different or solitary, and that the same nature exists in both of them through the true significance of birth and generation.

(23) The determination of the insane spirits remains, in so far as we can perceive, even though it has not attained its goal, and the desire of malevolence does not desert the evil mind when the occasion for the performance of an evil work is not present. Although the raging heretics cannot now lead Him to the cross after the example of the Jews, since the Lord is already seated in heaven, they are equally guilty of unbelief in denying that He is what He is. And since they cannot deny what has been said, still, since they are not submissive to His words, they reveal their hatred of God, cast the stones of words, and, if they could, would again drag Him from His throne in heaven to the cross.

Thus, it is written concerning the Jews, who were indeed enraged by the novelty of these words: 'The Jews therefore took up stones to stone him. He answered them, "Many good works have I shown you from the Father. For which of these works do you stone me?" The Jews answered him, "Not for a good work do we stone thee, but for blasphemy, and because thou, being a man, makest thyself God." '[37] But you, O heretic, take note of what you are doing and acknowledging, and realize that you are the companion of those whose unbelieving example you are copying. For, when the words were spoken: 'I and the Father are one,' the Jews took up stones, and their godless sorrow, which could not endure the mystery of the salutary faith, burst forth with such violence that they were ready to put Him to death. Are you who cannot stone Him doing anything less by your denial? Your will does not differ, but the heavenly throne renders your will ineffective. And how much greater is your godlessness than that of the Jew! He raises his stones against the body, you against the soul; he against One whom he considers

---

37 Cf. John 10.31-33.

as a man, you against God; he against One living on earth, you against One seated on the throne of power; he against One whom he does not acknowledge, you against One whom you know; he against One who will die, you against the Judge of the ages. He says: 'because thou art a man,' you say: 'because thou art a creature'; both of you declare in unison: 'thou makest thyself God.' This is the customary taunt that comes from your godless mouth. For, you deny that He is God by His birth from God; you deny that He is the Son by a real birth. You deny that these words, 'I and the Father are one,' are an avowal of the one and similar nature in both of them. You set up in His place a God of a new, strange, and alien substance, so that He is either a God of another nature or no God at all, because He does not subsist by His birth from God.

(24) Because you are enraged at the mystery of the words, 'I and the Father are one,' so that, as the Jew declares: 'Because thou, being a man, makest thyself God,' you assert with equal impiety: 'Because thou, being a creature, makest thyself God' (for you declare: 'Thou art not the Son by thy birth, thou art not God by thy true nature, thou art a creature more excellent than the others, but thou hast not been born into God, because I do not admit the birth of a nature from an incorporeal God, not only art thou and the Father not one, but neither art thou the Son, nor art thou like Him, nor art thou God').

The Lord indeed replied to the Jews, but this entire response is better suited to your impiety: 'Is it not written in the Law, "I said you are gods"? If he called them gods to whom the Word of God was addressed (and the Scripture cannot be broken), do you say of him whom the Father has made holy and sent into this world, "Thou blasphemest," because I said, "I am the Son of God'? If I do not perform the works of the Father, do not believe me. But if I do perform them, and if you are not willing to believe me, believe the works, that you may know and believe that the Father is in me and I in Him.'[38] The charge of blasphemy that was brought against Him caused Him to make this reply. For, it was regarded as a crime that, since He was a man, He made himself God. He was accused of making Himself God, therefore, because He had said: 'I and the Father are one.' Accordingly, since He will prove that He employed these words by reason of the nature of His birth, He first refutes the absurdity of this ridiculous reproach of which He was alleged to be guilty, that He, being a man, made Himself God. Since the Law decided upon the designation of this name for holy persons, and the indestructible Word of God ratified this statement about the name that was bestowed, how will this one whom the Father had sanctified, and whom He had sent into the world, be a blasphemer for asserting that He was the Son, since the Word of God, which cannot be broken, had established through the Law that they should be given the name of God?

Hence, it can no longer be regarded as a reproach that He, being a man, makes Himself God, since the Law declares that those who are men are gods. And if the use of this name by others is not blasphemous, then it seems that that man whom the Father has sanctified (for the entire discourse centers about the man because the Son of God is also the Son of Man) is not guilty of any rashness in making use of it when He said that He was the Son of God, since He excels the others, who may call themselves God in a reverential manner, by the fact that He was sanctified into the Son, for blessed Paul imparts the knowledge of this sanctification when he says: 'Which he promised beforehand through his prophets in the holy Scriptures, concerning the Son who was born according to the flesh of the offspring of David; who was ordained Son of God by an act of power in keeping with the

---

38 Cf. John 10.34-38.

holiness of his spirit.'[39] The charge of blasphemy, that He, being a man, makes Himself God, comes to an end, since the Word of God has bestowed this name upon many, and He who was sanctified and sent by the Father confessed that He was nothing else than the Son of God.

(25)   There is no longer any reason to doubt, I believe, that the words, 'I and the Father are one,' were spoken in reference to the birth. For, since the Jews had based their accusation against Him on these words, that He Himself, who was a man, made Himself God, His reply corroborates the revelation of Himself as the Son of God from the fact that 'I and the Father are one,' first by the name, then by the nature, and finally by the birth. For, 'I and the Father' are the names of things, but 'one' is the acknowledgment of a nature, because the two of them do not differ in that in which they are, but 'are' does not permit a union. And where there is no union, because they 'are one,' it is the birth that has caused them to be one. All this proceeds from the fact that He who was sanctified by the Father confesses that He is the Son of God, and this assertion of the Son of God is ratified by the words, 'I and the Father are one,' because birth cannot bring any other nature with it except that from which it subsists.

(26)   But the discourse of the only-begotten God has completed the mystery of our entire faith. After He had made His reply to the accusation why He, who was a man, made Himself God, in order that the words, 'I and the Father are one,' might provide us with a clear and complete knowledge, He added the following words: 'You say, "Thou blasphemest" because I said, "I am the Son of God"? If I do not perform the works of the Father, do not believe me. But, if I do perform them, and if you are not willing to believe me, believe the works, that you may know and believe that the Father

---

39 Cf. Rom. 1.2-4.

is in me and I in Him.' Unrestrained audacity now follows when people despair of salvation because of their evil conscience, and every profession of godlessness is beyond the reach of shame. For, when the true religion is lost, no one blushes any longer at his folly; it is not ignorance but madness to oppose these words.

The Lord had said: 'I and the Father are one.' This is the mystery of the birth that the Father and Son possess a unity of nature. And because the claim of nature would be cited as an accusation, the reason for the lawfulness of the claim is offered as proof. For He said: 'If I do not perform the works of the Father do not believe me.' If He does not perform the works of the Father, we should not believe Him when He asserts that He is the Son of God. Hence, His birth does not bring Him a new and alien nature, because we must believe that He is the Son from the fact that He carries out the works of His Father. How can an adoption or the bestowal of the name occur here so that He would not be the Son of God by nature, since we are to believe in Him as the Son of God by the works of the paternal nature?

A creature is not made equal or similar to God; no power of an alien nature is compared to Him; we believe without any blasphemy that only the birth of the Son is similar to or equal to Him. For, whatever is outside of Him will be made equal to Him by a mockery of the power honored in Him. If anything can be found which is not from Him and is similar to Him and possesses the same power, He has lost the privilege of God by the partnership of one who is His co-equal, and there will no longer be one God since there is another God who is His equal. But the equality proceeding from His own true nature does not lead to any insult, because that which is similar to Him is His, and that which is compared to Him by reason of its likeness is from Him, and that which can complete what is His is not outside of

Him, and it is an exaltation of the divinity to have begotten the power and not to have changed the nature.

The Son carries out the works of the Father and therefore He asks us to believe in Him as the Son of God. This is no arrogant presumption, which asks that He be tested only by those deeds that He performs. He testifies, however, that He does not perform His own works, but those of His Father, in order that the birth of His nature may not be taken away by the splendor of His deeds. And because the Son of God was not understood in the mystery of the assumed body and in the man born from Mary, the faith in His name was taught by His deeds, since He said: 'But if I do not perform them, and if you are not willing to believe me, believe the works.' First of all, He does not wish that we believe in Him as the Son of God except through the works of the Father which He does. And if He performs the works, and is regarded as unworthy of what He professes because of the abasement of His body, He asks us to believe His actions. For, why should the mystery of Him who is born as man be an obstacle to the understanding of the divine birth, since the divine birth fulfills its entire work during the ministry of the body which He assumed? If, therefore, you do not believe that the man is the Son of God because of the works,[40] then believe that the works are indicative of the Son of God, because it cannot be denied that they are characteristic of God. For, by His birth the Son of God possesses everything in Himself that is God, and, as a consequence, the work of the Son is the work of the Father, because the birth is not outside of the nature from which it subsists, and includes that nature within itself from which it subsists.

(27) Since He therefore performs the works of His Father and asks that, if we do not believe Him, at least we should believe His works, He must show us what we are to

---

40 That is, because they appear to be only human works.

believe from the works, and He does so surely in the words that follow: 'But if I do perform them, and if you are not willing to believe me, believe the works, that you may know and believe that the Father is in me and I in Him.' To this statement belong the words: 'I am the Son of God'; to it belong these words: 'I and the Father are one.' This is the nature of the birth, this is the mystery of the salutary faith, not to make a division because they are one, nor to take away the nature from the birth, and to confess the truth of the living God from the living God. God, who is the life, does not subsist by tangible and inanimate things, nor is He who is the power limited by weak things, nor is He who is the light composed of what is dark, nor is He who is a spirit formed out of disparate things.

Everything that is in Him is one, so that what is spirit is also light, power, and life, and what is life is light, power and spirit. He who says: 'I am and I change not,'[41] cannot be changed by parts, nor become different in nature. All these things, which have been pointed out above, are not found within Him as portions, but all are one and perfect within Him, for everything is the living God. Accordingly, there is the living God, and the eternal power of the living nature, and that which is born from Him with the mystery of His own knowledge could not be born as anything else than from a living being. Since He says: 'As the living Father has sent me, and as I live because of the Father,'[42] He taught that life was in Him by the living Father. Hence, when He states: 'For as the Father has life in himself, even so he has given to the Son also to have life in himself,'[43] He gives evidence that everything living within Him is from the living. But that which was born alive from the living has the advantage

---

41 Cf. Mal. 3.6.
42 John 6.58.
43 John 5.26.

of birth without the novelty of nature. That is not new which is generated from the living one into the living one, because life was not sought for among non-existing things to bring about the birth, and the life which receives its birth from life by reason of the unity of nature and the mystery of the perfect and unutterable birth must live in the living and have the living life in itself.

(28)   We recall the warning that we issued at the beginning of our treatise,[44] that human analogies do not afford an adequate description of their divine counterparts; yet it is through material images that our mind acquires some knowledge of them. I turn for guidance to those who have knowledge of human birth, whether the origin of those who are born does not remain in their parents. For although these inanimate and ignoble elements, which are the primary causes of birth, are passed on to another man, they remain mutually in themselves by the power of nature, while he who begets follows him who is begotten through the origin of the same nature that has been given, and he who is born remains in him who begot him through the birth that has been received, for the power, although transmitted, has not been lost. Of course, we have merely stressed these facts for the sake of understanding a human birth; we do not offer them as an explanation of the perfect example of a birth in the only-begotten God, because the weakness of human nature takes its origin from unlike things, and its life is maintained by lifeless matter.

And that which is begotten does not live in it at once, nor does the whole live from the life because there are many parts in it, which, when they have grown, are cut off without their nature being conscious of it. But in God everything that is lives. God is the life, and nothing can come from life except what is alive. And His birth does not come about through

---

44 Cf. above, 1.19; 4.2.

an emanation, but through power. Thus, while everything that is lives, and while everything that is born from Him is power, He possesses the birth and does not experience any change, and He bestows an increase but does not lose His nature, while He follows the birth, which He has given by the similarity of an indistinguishable nature, and the birth, which is the living one from the living one, does not abandon its nature when it is born.

(29)   But fire, which is fire in itself and which remains in fire, offers us a partial understanding of this faith. For, while in it there is the brightness of light, the natural warmth, the power of burning, and the fluctuating movement of the flame, it is totally a fire, and this totality is one nature. It has, of course, this weakness, that matter provides it with its sustenance and life, and it dies out with that through which it has received life. But by means of a comparison we have a partial knowledge of that which admits of no comparison in God, so that which is found to some extent in the elements of earth is not incredible when applied to God. I now raise the question whether there is any division and separation when there is a fire from a fire? Or is the nature cut off so that it does not endure, or is it that the nature does not follow so that it is not present within it, since, when a light is enkindled from a light by a sort of increase, as if it were a birth, there is no separation from the nature and yet a light is from a light? Or does it not remain in that which has come into existence from it, without any separation? Or is it not present within that from which it has not been cut off, but has proceeded from it with the unity of the natural substance? And I ask whether they are not one since a light from a light cannot be separated either by a division or by nature?

(30)   These things, as I have stated, are only brought in for the sake of a comparison, in order to impart to us a knowledge of the faith, and not as things suitable to

the dignity of God, in order that we may the more easily
derive our understanding of invisible things from those
that are material, not, indeed, that any comparison does
adequate justice to the nature of God, since it is fitting
and just to believe God when He testifies regarding Himself.
But, because the rage of the heretics disturbed the faith of
the unlearned so that they should not believe these things
about God, which could not be grasped without difficulty
except through a material illustration, therefore, in harmony
with the saying of the Lord which we have already mentioned
in a previous place: 'That which is born of the flesh is flesh;
and that which is born of the Spirit is spirit,'[45] because
God is a spirit, we have judged it useful to insert these
examples as a partial illustration in order that no one may
believe that He is guilty of any deception in His assertions
about Himself, since the natural examples of created objects
would provide us with some insight into this divine confession.

(31) Hence, when the living Son of God from the
living one and the God from God revealed the unity of the
inseparable and identical nature, as well as the mystery of
the birth, He said: 'I and the Father are one.' And because
a false accusation arose on account of this statement, as if
it were presumptuous, in order to manifest even more emphatically the consciousness of His nature when He uttered
these words, He said: 'You say that I have blasphemed
because I said, "I am the Son of God," while He thereby
affirmed that the unity of nature proceeded from His birth.
But, in order that an unmistakable declaration might strengthen the faith in the birth, and the confession of the birth
might not cause any conflict with the nature, He concluded
this whole response in the following manner:'Believe the
works that the Father is in me, and I in the Father.' Is
there anything here in the mystery of the birth that is not

---

45 John 3.6.

natural and proper? They are mutually contained in each
other, while there is no birth except from the Father, while
He does not subsist as a second God, either outside of Him
or unlike Him in nature, while the God who exists from
God is that which God is from nowhere else.

Bring two gods into the faith, if occasion offers, or at
least invent a solitary God by offering a false claim! Separate
the Son from the Father, if you can, excepting only the
truth of the birth which you confess! The Son is in the Father
and the Father in the Son, not by a mutual transfusion
and flowing, but by the perfect birth of a living nature.
Thus, in God the Father and God the Son you will not
count either two gods because both are one, nor will you
proclaim a unique God because the two are not one[person].
The apostolic faith, therefore, does not have two gods, because
it does not have two fathers and two sons. When it acknowledges the Father it has acknowledged the Son. When it
believes in the Son it has also believed in the Father, because
the name of the Father likewise contains the name of the
Son in itself. There is no father except through a son; the
designation of a son reveals the father to us because there
is no son except from a father. There is not one person,
therefore, in the confession of the one God, while the Son
also completes the Father and the birth of the Son is from
the Father. The nature, however, is not changed by the
birth so that it would not be the same according to the
likeness of the nature. It is the same in such a manner that
by reason of the birth and generation we must confess the
two as one [nature] and not as one [person].

(32) Let him, therefore, proclaim the two gods who
can proclaim the one God without proclaiming the unity,
or let him teach that there is a unique God who can deny
that the one is in the one by the power of nature and the
mystery of the generation and birth! Let him also ascribe a

different nature to the two who does not know that in our teaching the Father and the Son are one! Let the heretics suppress the statement of the Son about Himself in the Gospel: 'I and the Father are one,' so that they may teach either that there are two gods or a unique God! For, there are no designations of natures in the proper meaning of one nature, nor does the truth of God from God result in two gods, nor does the birth of God admit of a unique God, nor are they not one who are interchangeable. But they are interchangeable since the one is from the one, because the one has not given anything else to the one by generation except that which is His own, nor has the one obtained by His birth from the one anything else except that which belongs to the one. Consequently, if the apostolic faith will proclaim the Father it will proclaim the Son, or if it will confess the Son it will confess the one God, because the same and identical nature of God is in both, and because the one denotes **both** while the Father is God and the Son is God, and the **nature** of both has the one name. The God from God or the God in God does not result in two gods, since the one from the one remains in the nature and the name of the one, nor does it go astray into a solitary God, since the meaning of one and one is not one who is alone.

(33) The Lord has not left us an uncertain or dubious doctrine about so great a mystery, nor has He abandoned us in a labyrinth of hazy ideas. Let us hear Him as He reveals the complete knowledge of his faith to His Apostles, for He says: 'I am the way, and the truth, and the life. No one comes to the Father but through me. If you know me, you would also know my Father. And henceforth you do know him, and you have seen him.' Philip said to him, 'Lord, show us the Father and it is enough for us.' Jesus said to him, 'Am I so long a time with you and you do not know me? Philip, he who has seen me has seen also the Father.

How canst thou say, "Show us the Father?" Do you not believe me that I am in the Father and the Father in me? The words that I speak to you I speak not on my own authority. But the Father dwelling in me, it is he who does his works. Believe me that I am in the Father and the Father in me; otherwise believe because of the works themselves.'[46]

He who is the way does not guide us to the wrong roads or to those that are impassable, nor does He who is the truth deceive us by falsehoods, nor does He who is the life leave us in the error of death. Since He Himself has determined upon the gracious names of His dispensation for the sake of our salvation, so that He might be as the way that would lead us to the truth and as the truth that would lead us to life, we must grasp what that mystery is which He has revealed to us for obtaining life. 'No one comes to the Father but through me.' The road to the Father is through the Son. And we must ascertain whether this is to be found in the doctrines of which He warns us or in the faith of His nature, because it might appear as if we are to go to the Father through the doctrine of the Son rather than reach Him by acknowledging the Godhead of the Father in Him. Let us seek for the sense in which this is to be understood in the words that follow. For, we must enter the faith not by our own decisions, but by the meaning of what has been said.

(34) These words follow: 'If you know me, you would also know my Father.' The man Jesus Christ is seen. And if they know Him, how will they know His Father, since the Apostles recognize the outer form of His nature, that is, the nature of man in Him, and since God is not subject to a material body, He cannot be recognized in the weakness of a human body? But, when the Lord confirmed the nature of the Father's divinity in Him in the mystery of the body

---

46 Cf. John 14.6-12.

which He had assumed, He followed this order: 'If you know
me, you would also know my Father. And henceforth you
do know him, and have seen him.' He draws a distinction
between the time of seeing him and the time of knowing
Him. In regard to Him whom, as He said, they should know,
He also declared that the same one had already been seen,
in order that now, from the time of this revelation, they
might receive the knowledge of the nature which they had
seen in Him for a long time.

(35) The novelty of the expression, however, disturbs
the Apostle Philip. A man is seen and confesses that He is
the Son of God. He asserts that when He is known the Father
must be known. He says that the Father has been seen, and
therefore must be known since He has been seen. The weakness of the human spirit does not grasp this and a statement
about natures so different does not gain acceptance, so that
He who was then seen must now be known since the sight
is knowledge, so that if the Son is known the Father is also
known, since the mere bodily sight and contact had brought
the knowledge of the Son according to His human nature,
but the knowledge of the Father that comes from Him was
not granted by the nature itself of the visible man that
differed from His [the Father's],[47] and the Son often testified
that no one had seen the Father.

Hence, Philip, with the informality and confidence of an
Apostle, blurted out and asked the Lord: 'Lord, show us the
Father and it is enough for us.' His faith does not waver
now, but here the mistake is the result of ignorance. The
Lord declared that the Father had already been seen and
therefore must be known, but the Apostle had not realized
that He had been seen. Finally, he did not deny that He

---

47 Hilary argues that to know Christ only in His human nature is not
to know the Father. Hence, since the Father is known through
Him, there must be in Christ another nature, which is concealed from
human eyes and is not different from that of the Father.

had been seen, but asked that He might be revealed to him, nor did he desire the manifestation, as it were, of a bodily appearance but he asked for such a manifestation that would enable him to comprehend Him who had been seen. He had indeed seen the Son under the appearance of man, but he does not understand how he had thereby seen the Father. For, when uttering the words, 'Lord, show us the Father,' he had added 'and it is enough for us,' in order that that revelation might make known how He was to be comprehended rather than how He was to be seen. He did not refuse to believe His words, but asked for a manifestation of Him who was to be known that would be sufficient to place reliance upon His words, because there would be a certain guarantee of the faith from the Lord's assertion. From this arose the request to make the Father known, because He said that He had been seen, and as a consequence must be known because He had been seen. Nor was he guilty of insolence in asking for a revelation of Him who had been seen.

(36) The Lord, therefore, made this reply to Philip: 'Am I so long a time with you, and you do not know me?' He rebukes the Apostle's lack of knowledge in not comprehending Him, because He had previously stated that when He was known the Father would also be known. But, what is the meaning of His complaint that He has not been known for a long time? That is to say, because, if He were known, the divinity of the Father's nature within Him must be understood. For, since those things which He did were proper to God—to walk upon the waters, to command the winds, to perform actions in the changing of water into wine and in the multiplication of the loaves that were incomprehensible and completely credible,[48] to put the demons to flight, to

---

48 The manner in which the miracles of Christ were performed is incomprehensible, yet they were credible because of the persons who witnessed them.

drive out disease, to repair bodily injuries, to correct the defects of birth, to forgive sins, to restore the dead to life, and to do these things in the flesh, and meanwhile to declare that He was the Son of God—the whole basis of His accusation and complaint arose from this fact that in the deeds which were performed during the mystery of the human birth the divine nature was not perceived in the manhood which He had assumed.

(37) Consequently, while He blames him for not knowing Him, since He had been performing these deeds for so long a time, in order to manifest the Father to those who asked Him, He said: 'He who has seen me has seen also the Father.' He is not referring here to His bodily appearance, to that which their earthly eyes gazed upon, but to those of which He had said: 'Do you not say, "There are yet four months, and then comes the harvest"? Well, I say to you, lift up your eyes and behold that the fields are already white for the harvest.'[49] The time does not allow, nor does the allusion to the fields white for the harvest justify us in believing that anything earthly and material was intended here, but He commanded them to lift up the eyes of their soul in order to gaze upon the blessedness of the perfect fruits, so that, as He now says: 'He who has seen me has seen also the Father.'

For this, which is carnal from the birth of the Virgin, does not help us to contemplate the divinity and the image of God within Him, nor is the form of man which He assumed an example of the nature of the immaterial God which we are to behold. God is recognized in Him, if, indeed, He will be recognized by anyone at all, by the power of His nature, and when God the Son is perceived He allows us to perceive the Father, while He is the image in such a manner that He does not differ in nature, but manifests His author.

49 John 4.35.

Other images of different colors or materials of different kinds and classes reproduce the appearance of those whose images are placed before them. But, in order that you may have true images, can those that are lifeless be placed on equality with those that are living, or can those that are painted, carved, or molten equal those that are natural? The Son is not the image of the Father after the manner of these things, because He is the living image of the living One, and He who has been born from Him does not have a different nature, and He who does not differ in anything preserves the power of His nature from whom He does not differ. That He is the image, therefore, proceeds from the fact that the birth of the only-begotten God points to God the Father, but it points to Him in such a manner that He Himself is the form and the image of the invisible God; hence, He does not lose the united similarity[50] of the nature, because He is not lacking in the power of the nature.

(38)   Therefore, we have those words: 'Am I so long a time with you, and you do not know me? Philip, he who has seen me has seen also the Father. How canst thou say, "Show us the Father"? Do you not believe me that I am in the Father and the Father in me?' Human language has been left with no other choice than to express the things of God in the words of God. Everything else is restricted, confined, cumbersome, and obscure. If anyone should wish to make this known in any other words than those in which God has spoken, either he himself does not understand it or he does not offer an intelligible explanation of it to his readers.

When He was asked to show the Father, the Lord said: 'He who has seen me has seen also the Father.' It is characteristic of Antichrist to change this, of the Jew to deny this, of the Gentile to be ignorant of this. But perhaps the

---

50 By the words, *unitam similitudinem,* Hilary means that the Father and the Son possess a oneness of nature.

perception of our intelligence is at fault. It may be that the
defect lies with our faith, if the words of God are involved
in obscurity. His statement does not designate a solitary God,
yet His revelation teaches that there is no difference in nature.
The Father, who is seen in Him, cannot be unique or unlike
Him, because that one who is seen through this one cannot
but be one nature in the confession of the mystery, nor can
they be one person. And I ask what are we to believe was the
meaning of the Lord's words when He said: 'He who has
seen me has seen also the Father?' You do not have a union
where the addition of the Father's name is indicated by
the conjunction. For when you say 'also the Father' you
exclude the idea of one who is isolated and unique. And
what else is there left except that the Father is seen through
the Son by means of the united likeness of their nature?
And in order that our faith in this matter might not remain
uncertain, the Lord continued: 'How canst thou say, "Show
us the Father"?' What compelling reason was still left for
not knowing the Father, or for revealing Him to those who
were ignorant of Him, since the Father was seen in the Son?

(39)   But, He was seen to such an extent in the property
of His nature, while, as a consequence of the identity and the
nature of the Godhead, the one who was born and the one
who begot are one, that this statement of the Lord follows:
'Do you not believe that I am in the Father and the Father
in me?' We cannot teach that the Father and the Son are
inseparable because of their natural likeness in any other
words except those of the Son. For, by changing His name
and appearance, this Son, who is the way, the truth, and
the life, is not playing a theatrical role here, so that in the
manhood which He assumed He calls Himself the Son of
God, but He calls Himself God the Father in His nature,
and He who is one and alone now falsely represents Himself
as someone else by a change of disguise.

Accordingly, He Himself is not isolated: now He is a Son to Himself, now he acknowledges Himself as His own Father, and He brings in the names of the nature when the nature is not present. Here the candor of the words is quite different, for the Father is also the Father, and the Son is also the Son. These names and natures do not contain within them anything that is new, or different, or strange. The truth of the nature retains its proper meaning, so that what is from God is God and the birth does not bring about any lessening or distinction, while the Son does not subsist in a nature outside of or unlike that of God the Father, nor does the Father acquire anything alien to Himself by the birth of the Son; rather, He has granted everything that is His without any loss to the giver.

Thus, He is not in want of the nature of God, while He is God from nowhere else than from God, nor does He differ from God while He Himself is nothing else than God, because the birth of God takes place in the Son, nor has the nature of God deprived itself of that which God is by the birth of God. The Father, therefore, is in the Son, the Son is in the Father, and God is in God, not by a twofold union of natures that are in harmony, nor through the superimposed nature of a larger substance, because through bodily necessity things that are within cannot be outside of those things by which they are enclosed, but through the birth of a living nature from a living nature, while the nature does not differ, while birth does not deprive the nature of God of its nobility, while God is born as nothing else than God from God, while there is nothing new, nothing strange, nothing separable in these things, while it is impious to believe that there are two gods in the Father and the Son, while it is sacrilegious to preach that the Father and the Son are one unique God, and while it is blasphemy to deny that they are one in the likeness of nature as God from God.

(40) And in order that the evangelical faith might not look upon this mystery as uncertain and ambiguous, the Lord followed this plan in His instruction: 'Do you not believe me that I am in the Father and the Father in me? The words that I speak to you I speak not on my own authority. But the Father dwelling in me, it is he who does his works.' By what other words, I ask, could and can the true significance of the nature in the Father and the Son be revealed than by these very words, while the reference to the birth shines forth prominently in all of them? Since He declares: 'The words that I speak to you I speak not on my own authority,' He does not exclude the person nor does He deny that He was the Son, nor does He conceal the nature of the Father's power within Him. For while He Himself is speaking (and this is indicated by the pronoun 'I') He speaks while He abides in the substance, but, while He does not speak of Himself, He bears testimony to the birth of God in Him from God the Father.

He Himself is inseparable from Him and indistinguishable from Him by the unity of nature, because, although He speaks by His authority, it is He Himself who speaks. He, who does not speak by His own authority, yet speaks, cannot but be while He is speaking, and while He does not speak of Himself He reveals that it is not He alone who speaks. For, He added: 'But the Father dwelling in me, it is he who does His works.' For the Father to remain in the Son does not denote a being that is alone and unique, but for the Father to work through the Son is not characteristic of a nature that is different from or outside of Him—just as it is a sign of one who is not alone not to speak by His own authority on the subjects whereof He speaks, and again it is not an indication of one who is alien to or separable from Him to speak through Him who is speaking, but this is the mystery of those who are one. Both, who are in each other by the

property of their nature, are not something else. Their unity
consists in this, that the speaker does not speak of Himself,
nor does He not speak, who does not speak of Himself. And
because He had taught that the Father speaks and works in
Him, He established the faith of this perfect unity when He
declared: 'But the Father dwelling in me, it is he who does
His work. Believe me, that I am in the Father and the Father
in me. Otherwise believe because of the works themselves.'
The Father works in the Son, but the Son also performs the
work of the Father.

(41) Consequently, in order that no one might believe
that the Father works and speaks in the Son through the
energy of His own power and not through the property of
the nature, which is in accordance with the birth, He said:
'Believe me, that I am in the Father and the Father in me.'
What, I ask, does the phrase 'believe me' mean? It refers, of
course, to what had been said: 'Show us the Father.' The
faith is strengthened by the command to believe, and it was
that faith that had asked that the Father be shown to it. It
was not sufficient to declare: 'He who has seen me has seen
also the Father,' if He did not increase our knowledge to
such an extent that, since we know the Father in the Son,
we would still remember that the Son was in the Father, in
order that we might not look upon it as a transfusion of one
into another rather than as the unity of the same nature in
both of them through the generation and birth.

Hence, the Lord wishes us to believe Him in order that
our consciousness of the faith might not be imperiled, perhaps,
through the dispensation of the man who was assumed.
Indeed, if the flesh, the body, and the passion should give
rise to any doubts, then at least we should believe from His
works that God is in God and God is from God, that they are
one, while by the power of the nature each one is in Himself,
and neither one is without the other, while the Father loses

nothing of Himself in the Son, and the Son takes everything from the Father that a son is. Material natures are not so constituted that they mutually inhere in one another, that they possess the perfect unity of a subsistent nature, and that the abiding birth of the Only-begotten is inseparable from the true nature of the Godhead in the Father. That is proper only to the only-begotten God, and that faith is rooted in the mystery of the true birth, and it is to the spiritual power that this work belongs, so that there is no distinction between to be and to inhere, but to inhere not as one thing in another as a body in a body, but to be and to subsist in such a manner that He inheres in Him who subsists but inheres in such a manner that He Himself subsists.[51] Hence, we have those sayings: 'I and the Father are one,' and 'He who has seen me has seen also the Father,' and 'I in the Father and the Father in me,' because the birth did not bring about any distinction or loss of nobility, because the nature of the birth completes the mystery of the Godhead in the Father and the Son, while the Son of God is nothing else than that which God is. For this reason, the generation of the Only-begotten does not result in a separation into two gods, because, when the Son of God was born into God, He revealed in Himself the nature of the God who begot Him.

---

51 He who subsists according to generation, that is, as the begetter, does not have a different nature from Him who subsists according to birth, that is, who has been born.

BOOK EIGHT

The blessed Apostle Paul, when drawing the portrait of one who was to be appointed bishop and raising up an entirely new man of the Church by his precepts, taught that this was, as it were, the epitome of all the virtues that were to perfect him when he declared: 'Holding fast the word according to the doctrine of faith that he may be able both to exhort in sound doctrine and to confute opponents. For there are also many disobedient, vain babblers, and deceivers.'[1] He thus indicated that whatever pertains to discipline and morals is useful to the dignity of the priesthood if, in addition to other things, those are also present which are necessary for the knowledge of the faith that must be taught and defended, because it is not an immediate indication of a good and useful priest merely to live a sinless life, or merely to teach learnedly, since he who is holy helps no one but himself unless he is learned, and knowledge gives no authority to one who is learned unless he is holy.

The statement of the Apostle does not merely equip a man for life in the world through its teaching about uprightness and honesty, nor, again, does it direct the scribe to the Law by means of the knowledge of doctrine, but it represents the perfect ruler of the Church with the perfect goods of the

---

1 Cf. Tit. 1.9-10.

273

highest virtues so that his life might be adorned by his learning and his learning by his life. Finally, it instructed Titus, the very one to whom the words were addressed, about attaining perfection in the practice of the true religion, by the following admonition: 'Showing thyself in all things an example of good works, teaching the sound and blameless word with dignity, so that anyone opposing may be put to shame, having nothing disgraceful or evil to say of us.'[2] This teacher of the Gentiles and the chosen teacher of the Church, conscious of Christ who spoke and dwelt within him, knew that the plague of a deadly eloquence would rise up about him, and that the corruption of a contagious disease would rage against the health of the faithful words, which, while spreading the epidemic of its godless doctrine even to the very abode of the soul, would slink about with its immeasurable wickedness. He says of these persons: 'Whose speech spreads like a cancer,'[3] while its secret and stealthy contagion is ever poisoning the health of the souls which it infects. For this reason, he wished the bishop to possess learning, the consciousness of the faith, and the knowledge of exhortations, which would withstand these godless, lying, and insane objections. There are many who make a pretense of the faith without being obedient to it, and they suit the faith to themselves rather than receive it. They are puffed up with the sentiments of human vanity, while they are wise in those things that they will, and have no desire to be wise in those things that are true, since this is the true kind of wisdom: to be wise at times about those things that you do not desire.

But the words of folly follow the wisdom of one's own will; what is foolishly wise is foolishly taught. How great the evil is that the preaching of folly now does to the hearers when they are enticed into the teaching of folly under the

2 Cf. Tit. 2.7,8.
3 Cf. 2 Tim. 2.17.

guise of wisdom. Consequently, the Apostle followed this order in regard to these persons when he said: 'For there are many disobedient, vain babblers, and deceivers.' We must therefore oppose the insolent godlessness, the boasting insolence, and the treacherous boastfulness, and we must oppose them by soundness of doctrine, the truth of faith, and by the sincerity of preaching, so that the sincerity of the truth is present as well as the truth of sound doctrine.

(2) The reason, of course, that led me to mention the teaching of the Apostle at this point was that men who were evil-minded, deceitful in their belief, vain in their hope, and venomous in their speech forced us into the necessity of contradicting them when they insinuated their deadly doctrine, their fatal ideas, and their perverted wills into the guilelessness of their hearers under the disguise of the true religion; they act thus in their presence without any regard for the purity of the apostolic teaching, so that the Father is not the Father, the Son is not the Son, God is not God, and the faith is not the faith. In opposing their insane lies we have already come so far in the words of our response that, after we proved from the Law that there is God and God and the true God in the true God, we then made known the perfect and true birth of the only-begotten God from the teachings of the Gospels and the Apostles, and, finally, in the same series of our instructions we taught that the Son of God is the true God and does not differ in nature from the Father, so that the faith of the Church does not acknowledge a unique God nor two gods, since the birth of God excludes a God who is alone, and the perfect birth does not admit the names of distinct natures in two gods.

But, a twofold care weighed upon us while refuting their idle talk, that, in the first place, we might teach what is holy, perfect, and sound, and that, while our language was wandering about, as it were, in the winding and twisting roads, and extricating itself from the false and deceptive snares, it might not be groping for the truth rather that making it known, so that in the sight of everyone we might then expose as ridiculous and out of place the very things which the subtlety of their futile and misleading principles had invested with the outward appearance of an enticing truth. It is not sufficient for us to teach doctrines that are pious, if we do not realize from doing so that they are the most pious of all, while at the same time we are refuting those that are impious.

(3) As it is characteristic of the nature and endeavor of good and prudent men to apply themselves wholeheartedly to the attainment of the reality or the opportunity of some blessed hope in order that the preparation may measure up in every respect to the expectation, so these insane men in their heretical fury are most solicitous to devote all the talents of their godlessness against the truth of the pious faith in order that they may gain the victory by their impiety over those who are God-fearing, and may surpass the hope of our life by the hopelessness of their own life, and may apply more thought to their falsehoods than we do to the truths of our doctrine. They have taken great pains with these objections of their infidelity against the pious professions of our faith, so that they want to know in the first place whether we believe in the one God, then, they continue, whether Christ is also God, and lastly, whether the Father is greater than the Son, in order that, when they hear that there is one God in our profession of faith, they may exploit it so that Christ is not God.

In regard to the Son, they do not wish to know whether He is God, but in their questioning about Christ their only desire is that He be not the Son, in order that, while they ensnare a man of simple faith in the one God, they may drive him away from recognizing Christ as God, since there is no longer one God if we are also to acknowledge Christ as God. But how great is the subtlety of the wordly ingenuity which they employ by stating: 'If He is one, then whoever that other one may appear to be He will no longer be. And if there is another, then there will no longer be one, since nature does not admit that where there is another, there is one, or where there is one, there is another.'[4]

Then, when they have deceived those who are quick to believe and to hear by the skillful wording of this statement, they next lay plans for that which they may attain, so to speak, by a less difficult approach: namely, that Christ is God in name rather than in nature, because this common name, which belongs to Him, in no wise destroys the faith in the one God which is the only true faith; and that the Father, therefore, is greater than the Son, because, by their difference in nature and since there is only one God, the Father is greater through the real essence of the nature; and that this one is called the Son and subsists as a creation by the will of God, because He is also less than the Father, and He is not God because the one God does not tolerate a second God, and He who is the lesser must be of a different nature from Him who is the greater. Indeed, how ridiculous they are in this matter when they give orders to God and assert that nothing can be born from one because the birth of all things comes about through the union of two beings, but that the immutable God can communicate no birth from Himself to one who is born, because that which is unchangeable is not subject to an increase nor does the nature of one who is solitary and unique find itself in a position where it can give birth!

(4)   But, we who have acquired the faith of the Gospels and the Apostles by means of spiritual doctrines, and who seek for the hope of a blessed eternity in the confession of the Father and the Son, have made known the mystery of

---

4 According to the Arians, to say that another one is God is to deny that there is one God.

God and God from the Law, nor do we go beyond the faith of the one God, nor do we preach that Christ is not God, but have maintained this order in our reply from the answers of the Gospels, so that we may teach the true birth of the only-begotten God from God the Father, because by reason of it He is also the true God, nor is He different from the nature of the true God, and thus it can neither be denied that He is God, nor can He Himself be called another God, because birth bestowed the Godhead upon Him, and the nature of the one God from God in Him did not separate Him into another God.

Although the ordinary reasoning of our mind impelled us to this conclusion, that the names of natures do not fit in with the same nature, and that they are one between whom there is no distinction of nature in regard to that which they are, we determined that this should be manifested by the statements of the Lord Himself, who—when He often made known the one God of our faith and hope in order to confirm the mystery of the one God, while He asserted and proved at the same time that He was God—spoke as follows: 'I and the Father are one,' and 'If you know me, you also know my Father,' and 'He who has seen me has seen also the Father,' and 'But the Father dwelling in me, it is he who does his works,' and, 'Believe me that the Father is in me and I in the Father; otherwise believe because of the works themselves.'[5] He expressed His birth by the name Father. He teaches that the Father is known in Him when He is known. He reveals the unity of nature, since the Father is seen in Him when He is seen. He testifies the He is inseparable from the Father, since He remains in the Father who remains in Him. He possesses a confident assurance, since He asks that His words be believed because of the operation of His

---

5 Cf. John 10.37; 14.7-12.

power. Thus, in this most blessed faith of the perfect birth, every error, whether of two gods or of a unique God, is removed, since those who are one nature are not one person, and thus He who is not one person does not differ in any way from Him who is, so that the two are not one.

(5) Accordingly, because the heretics cannot deny these things, since in fact they are so clearly expressed and understood, they distort them by the most foolish lie of their godlessness in order to deny them. They seek to refer the words, 'I and the Father are one,' to an agreement of unanimity, so that there is a unity of will and not of nature in these words, that is, they are one not because of what they are but because they will the same thing. And in defense of their position they apply those words, from the Acts of the Apostles: 'But the multitude of the believers were of one heart and soul,'[6] so that the difference of souls and hearts leads to a unity of one heart and soul because of the agreement of the same will. Or those words, which were written to the Corinthians: 'Now he who plants and he who waters are one,'[7] so that, since there is no disagreement in the office of salvation and in the performance of the same mystery, there is a unity of will in the two of them. Or those words, in which the Lord prays for the salvation of those people who will believe in Him: 'Yet not for these only do I pray, but for these also who through their word are to believe in me, that all may be one even as thou, Father, in me and I in thee, that they also may be one in us,'[8] so that, because men cannot be poured back to God and cannot themselves be mutually united into one indistinguishable group, the fact that they are one proceeds from the unity of will, since all of them do the things that are pleasing to God, and unite together while the

6 Cf. Acts 4.32.
7 Cf. 1 Cor. 3.8.
8 John 17.20,21.

sentiments of their minds are in harmony, and thus it is not the nature but the will that makes them one.

(6)   He is completely ignorant of wisdom who is ignorant of God. And, since Christ is wisdom, he who does not know Christ or does not hear Him must be outside of wisdom, as they are who wish the Lord of majesty, the King of the ages, and the only-begotten God to be a creature of God rather than the Son of God, and while they practice their deception in a foolish manner, they are, however, even more foolishly wise in defending their deception. We now must delay for a few moments our discussion of the true nature of the unity which is in God the Father and God the Son, and refute them from these very words which they employ.

(7)   In regard to those who were one soul and one heart, I ask whether they were one through their faith in God? Of course they were one by their faith, for, by that, all of them were one soul and one heart. And I raise the question whether there is one faith or a second faith? There is one, by all means, as the Apostle himself testifies who taught that there is one faith just as there is one Lord, one baptism, one hope, and one God. If, therefore, all are one through faith, that is, through the nature of the one faith, why do you not recognize a natural unity among those who are one by the nature of the one faith? For, all have been born again to innocence, to immortality, to the knowledge of God, and to the assurance of hope. And if these cannot be distinct from one another because there is one hope and one God, just as there is one Lord and one baptism of rebirth, if these are one by consent rather than by nature, then attribute a unity of will to those who have also been reborn to these things. But, if they have been reborn into the nature of the one life and the one eternity whereby they are one soul and one heart, then the unity of consent ceases to apply in the case of those who are one in the regeneration of the same nature.

(8)   We do not express our own theories, nor do we forge any lies from these words by distorting their meaning in order to deceive the ears of our listeners, but we hold fast to the norm of sound doctrine, and know and preach what is honest. The Apostle teaches us that this unity among the faithful proceeds from the nature of the sacraments when he writes: 'For as many as you have been baptized into Christ have put on Christ. There is neither Jew nor Greek; there is neither slave nor freeman; there is neither male nor female. For you are all one in Christ Jesus.'[9] In regard to the fact that they are one amid so great a diversity of peoples, states in life, and sexes, does this arise from the agreement of the will or from the unity of the sacrament, for all have the one baptism and all have put on the one Christ? What purpose, therefore, will harmony of minds serve here, since they are one because they are clothed in the one Christ by the nature of the one baptism?

(9)   Or, since he who plants and he who waters are one, are they not one by the fact that they themselves have been reborn in the one baptism and have the one administering of the one regenerating baptism? Do they not perform the same actions? Are they not one in one? Therefore, those who are one by the same thing are also one in nature, and not only in will, because they themselves have become the same thing and are dispensers of the same thing and the same effect.

(10)   The objection of fools, however, always helps to reveal their folly, because the arguments which they employ against the truth, in the spirit of a foolish and perverted knowledge, must be recognized as false and ridiculous, because they are contrary to it, while it remains firm and unshaken. The heretics endeavor to deceive because of what was said: 'I and the Father are one,' in order that we might not believe

---

9 Cf. Gal. 3.27,28.

that there is unity between them as well as the identical substance of the Godhead, but that they are one from their mutual love for each other and the harmony of their wills, and, as we have pointed out above, they have even cited the words of our Lord as an illustration of that unity: 'That they all may be one, even as thou, Father, in me and I in thee, that they also may be one in us.' Whoever is outside their faith is outside the promises of the Gospels, and the understandable hope has been destroyed by the guilt of a godless knowledge. For, not to know what you believe does not deserve pardon as much as it does a reward, because the highest recompense of faith is to hope for what you do not know. But the rage of the most unbridled godlessness is not to believe what is understood, or to distort the meaning of what must be believed.

(11)   Although impiety may change the meaning itself in accordance with its own ideas, the ideas contained in the words cannot be set aside. The Lord prays to His Father that those who will believe in Him may be one, and, as He Himself is in the Father and the Father in Him, so all may be one in them. Why do you bring in unanimity here, why a unity of soul and heart resulting from an agreement of the will? There was an abundance of suitable words, so, if the will had made them one, the Lord would have prayed thus: 'Father, just as we will the one thing, so let them also will the same thing, in order that all of us may be one in harmony.' Or perhaps He who is the Word was unaware of the meaning of the word, and He who is the Truth did not know how to speak the truth, and He who is Wisdom went astray in foolish talk, and He who is Power was so helpless that He could not express what He wanted us to understand? He spoke plainly of these true and candid mysteries of the evangelical faith. Nor did He proclaim them merely to explain their meaning; He

also taught them for the faith when He spoke thus: 'That all may be one, even as thou, Father, in me and I in thee; that they also may be one in us.' In the first place, His prayer is for these of whom He says: 'That all may be one'; then an inducement for growing in unity is revealed by an example of unity, when He declares: 'As thou, Father, in me and I in thee; that they also may be one in us,' in order that, as the Father is in the Son and the Son in the Father, all are thus to be one in accordance with the form of this unity in the Father and the Son.

(12)   But, because it is proper only to the Father and the Son to be one by their nature, for the God from God and the Only-begotten from the unborn can alone possess the nature of His origin, so He who is born exists in the substance of His own birth, and the birth of the divinity does not have another and different God than that from which it has come. The Lord, who has left nothing uncertain in the faith, taught the nature of this complete unity in the whole discourse that follows, for these words come next: 'That the world may believe that thou hast sent me.' The world therefore, will believe that the Son has been sent by the Father because all who will believe in Him will be one in the Father and the Son. And He at once teaches us how they will be one: 'And the glory that Thou hast given me, I have given to them.'[10]

I now ask whether the glory is the same as the will, since the will is an emotion of the soul, but glory is an appearance or an adornment of the nature. Hence, the Son has given the glory that He has received from the Father to all who believe in Him, and certainly not the will, for, had that been given, then faith would have no merit, since the compulsion of the will that had been fastened upon us would bring us

10 John 17.21,22.

the faith.[11] He reveals, however, the gain that will result from the bestowal of the glory that He has received. 'That they may be one even as we are one.' Consequently, the glory that has been received was given for this reason, that they all may be one. All are, therefore, one in glory, because no other glory except that which has been received has been given, nor has it been given for any other reason than that they all may be one. All are, therefore, one in glory, because no other glory except that which has been received has been given, nor has it been given for any other reason than that they may be one.

And, since all are one through the glory that has been given to the Son and that the Son confers on those who believe in Him, I ask how is the glory of the Son different from that of the Father, since the glory of the Son elevates all the believers to the unity of the glory of the Father? As a matter of fact, the declaration of human hope in the present instance may well be arrogant, but it will not be unbelieving, for, although it may be rash to hope for this, it is not godless to believe it, since the same one is the author of our faith as well as of our hope.[12] As it becomes fitting, we shall discuss this matter more fully and in greater detail in its proper place.[13] In the meantime, even our present explanation will show that this hope of ours is neither futile nor rash. All are one by the glory that has been received and given. I hold fast to the faith and I apprehend the cause of the unity; still, I do not grasp the manner in which the glory that has been given causes all to be one.

(13)   But the Lord, who leaves nothing vague in the

---

11 In Ch. 30 of this Book, St. Hilary says that faith is one of the gifts of the Holy Spirit. Here he is only concerned with showing that the act of faith proceeds from our freedom of the will.

12 From a purely human standpoint it would be rash to hope for union with God, but it is not rash when the hope is based on the promise of God Himself.

13 Cf. Book 11.

consciousness of the faithful, has informed us about that
very result that is produced by the power of nature, when
He says: 'That they may be one, as we are one: I in them
and thou in me; that they may be perfected in unity.'[14] I
now ask those who introduce a unity of will between the
Father and the Son, whether Christ is in us by the truth of
His nature or by the harmony of the will? If the Word has
indeed become flesh, and we indeed receive the Word as
flesh in the Lord's food, how are we not to believe that He
dwells in us by His nature, He who, when He was born as
man, has assumed the nature of our flesh that is bound
inseparably with Himself, and has mingled the nature of His
flesh to His eternal nature in the mystery of the flesh that was
to be communicated to us?

All of us are one in this manner because the Father is in
Christ and Christ is in us. Therefore, whoever will deny that
the Father is not in Christ by His nature let him first deny
that he[15] is not in Christ by his nature, or that Christ is not
present within him, because the Father in Christ and Christ
in us cause us to be one in them. If, therefore, Christ has
truly taken the flesh of our body, and that man who was
born from Mary is truly Christ, and we truly receive the
flesh of His body in the mystery (and we are one, therefore,
because the Father is in Him and He is in us), how can you
assert that there is a unity of will, since the attribute of the
nature in the sacrament is the mystery of the perfect unity?[16]

(14) We should not talk about the things of God in a
human or worldly sense, nor should the perversity of a strange
and impious knowledge be extorted from the soundness of
the heavenly words by a violent and imprudent manner of

---

14 Cf. John 17.22,23.
15 That is, the one who denies the unity of nature between the Father
and the Son.
16 Through the reception of the Body and Blood of Christ in the
Eucharist we share in His nature and, through Him, with that of
His Heavenly Father.

teaching. Let us read what has been written and hold fast to
what we have read, and then we shall fulfill the duty of
perfect faith. We speak in an absurd and godless manner
about the divinity of Christ's nature in us—the subject which
we are discussing—unless we have learned it from Him. He
Himself declares: 'For my flesh is food indeed, and my blood
is drink indeed. He who eats my flesh and drinks my blood
abides in me and I in him.'[17] It is no longer permitted us to
raise doubts about the true nature of the body and the blood,
for, according to the statement of the Lord Himself as well
as our faith, this is indeed flesh and blood. And these things
that we receive bring it about that we are in Christ and
Christ is in us. Is not this the truth? Those who deny that
Jesus Christ is the true God are welcome to regard these
words as false. He Himself, therefore, is in us through His
flesh, and we are in Him, while that which we are with Him
is in God.

(15)   How deeply we are in Him through the sacrament
of the flesh and blood that has been communicated to us is
evident from His own testimony, when He declares: 'And
this world no longer sees me. But you shall see me, for I live
and you shall live, since I am in the Father, and you in me,
and I in you.'[18] If He wished us to understand only a unity
of will, why did He explain, as it were, the steps and the
order of the unity that was to be brought about, unless it
were that, while He was in the Father by the nature of the
Godhead, we, on the other hand, should be in Him by His
corporeal birth, and again that we should believe that He
would dwell in us by the mystery of the sacraments, and thus
the perfect unity would be taught by means of the mediator,
since He Himself remains in the Father while we remain in
Him, and while He remains in the Father He remains in us,

17 John 6.56,57.
18 Cf. John 14.19,20.

and in this manner we would arrive at the unity of the Father, since we would also be in the nature of Him [the Son], who is in the nature of Him [the Father] by birth, while He Himself [the Son] ever remains in us by His nature.

(16) He Himself thus testifies how natural is this unity in us: 'He who eats my flesh, and drinks my blood, abides in me and I in him.'[19] No one will be in Him unless He Himself has been in Him, while He has assumed and taken upon Himself the flesh of Him only who has received His own. Previously, He had already given an explanation of the perfect unity when He declared: 'As the living Father has sent me and as I live through the Father, so he who shall eat my flesh shall live through me.'[20] Consequently, He lives through the Father, and, as He lives through the Father, we live in the same manner through His flesh. Every illustration is adapted to the nature of our understanding in order that we may grasp the matter under discussion by means of the example that is set before us. Accordingly, this is the cause of our life, that we, who are carnal, have Christ dwelling in us through His flesh, and through Him we shall live in that state in which He lives through the Father. Hence, if we live through Him by His nature according to the flesh, that is, have received the nature of His flesh, why should He not possess the Father in Himself by His nature according to the Spirit, since He Himself lives through the Father? But He lives through the Father while His birth has not brought Him an alien and a distinct nature, while that which He is, is from Him and yet is not removed from Him by any hampering dissimilarity of nature, while through His birth He possesses the Father in Himself in the power of the nature.

(17) Accordingly, we have mentioned these facts because the heretics, who have misrepresented the unity between the

19 John 6.57.
20 John 6.59.

Father and the Son as one merely of will, have used the example of our unity with God just as if we were united to the Son, and through the Son to the Father, only by our obedience and agreement in the true religion, and the reality of a mutual participation in the nature has not been conferred upon us through the sacrament of the body and blood, although we are to proclaim the mystery of the true and natural unity both because of the glory which the Son has given to us as well as because of the Son who remains in us, while at the same time we are united to Him in a corporeal and inseparable manner.

(18)   Hence, we have replied to the folly of these raging men merely to expose the absurdity of their empty falsehoods in order that they might not deceive the unlearned by the error of their vain and ridiculous pronouncements. Besides, the faith of the Gospel did not necessarily demand our response. The Lord prayed for our unity with God, but He preserves His own and remains in it. Nor are they one through the mystery of the dispensation but through the birth of the nature, while God, by giving birth to Him from Himself, is not reduced to an inferior state in Him. They are one while those things that are not snatched from His hands are not snatched from the hands of His Father, while the Father is known when the Son is known, while the Father is seen when He is seen, while those things which He speaks the Father who remains in Him speaks, while the Father works when He works, while He Himself is in the Father and the Father in Him. This is not granted by creation, but by birth; it is not brought about by the will, but by the power. Harmony does not speak, but nature does, because to be created and to be born are not the one thing, nor is to will the same as to be able, nor is to agree the same as to abide.

(19)   We do not deny, therefore, the harmony between the Father and the Son, for the heretics are wont to lie about

this matter and declare that we are affirming their lack of harmony when we reject harmony alone as the basis of their unity. But let them hear how little we deny the lack of harmony. The Father and the Son are one by nature, power, and glory, nor can the same nature desire different things. Furthermore, let them listen to the Son as He testifies about the unity of the Father with Him: 'When that Advocate has come, whom I will send you from the Father, the Spirit of truth who proceeds from the Father, He will bear witness concerning me.'[21] The Advocate will come and the Son will send Him from the Father, and He is the Spirit of truth who proceeds from the Father. Let the entire school of the heretics hurl all the sophistries of their clever wit, and let them invent something which may at least deceive the uninformed, and let them teach what it is that the Son sends from the Father! He who sends manifests His power in that which He sends. But, what are we to understand by that which He sends from the Father? Is it something received, or sent forth, or begotten? That which He sent from the Father must mean one or the other of these things. And He who proceeds from the Father will send that Spirit of truth from the Father. Hence, there is no longer an adoption where a procession is revealed. Nothing remains but for us to corroborate our teaching on this point, whether we are to understand here the going forth of one who exists or the procession of one who has been born.

(20) Nor will I now infringe upon any one's liberty of thought in this matter, whether they may regard the Paraclete Spirit as coming from the Father or from the Son.[22] The Lord has left nothing uncertain, since He spoke as follows in the same discourse: 'Many things yet I have to say to you,

21 Cf. John 15.26.
22 St. Hilary declares above (2.4) that the Son of God is the *largitor* and *auctor* of the Holy Spirit.

but you cannot bear them now. But when he, the Spirit of truth, has come, he will direct you into all the truth. For he will not speak on his own authority, but whatever he will have heard he will speak, and the things that are to come he will declare to you. He will glorify me, because he will receive of what is mine and will declare it to you.'[23] Consequently, He receives from the Son who has been sent by Him and who proceeds from the Father. And I raise the question whether it is the same to receive from the Son as to proceed from the Father? But, if we must hold that there is a difference between receiving from the Son and proceeding from the Father, then, certainly, we shall have to admit that it is one and the same to receive from the Son as it is to receive from the Father. The Lord declares: 'Because he will receive of what is mine and declare it to you. All things that the Father has are mine. That is why I have said that he will receive of what is mine and will declare it to you.'

That which He will receive (whether it is power, or strength, or doctrine) the Son states that it will be received from Him, and again He lets it be understood that the same thing must be received from the Father. For, since He asserts that everything that the Father has is his, and has, therefore, said that they must be received from Him, He likewise teaches that what is to be received from the Father must still be received from Him, because everything that belongs to the Father is His. This unity does not admit any difference, nor is there any distinction in regard to Him from whom it is received, because what is given by the Father is also represented as given by the Son. Or shall a unity of will be also added here? Everything that the Father has is the Son's and everything that the Son has is the Father's. He Himself says: 'And all things that are mine are thine, and thine are mine.'[24]

23 Cf. John 16.12-15.
24 John 17.10.

This is not a suitable place to explain why He spoke as follows: 'Because he will receive of what is mine,' for this refers to a later date where it is revealed that He shall receive.

Hence, He now clearly asserts that He will receive from Him because everything that belongs to the Father is His. If you are able to do so, separate the unity of this nature, and bring forth some compelling reason for a dissimilarity as a consequence of which the Son will not be in the unity of nature! The Spirit of truth proceeds from the Father, but He is sent by the Son from the Father. Everything that belongs to the Father belongs to the Son; hence, whatever He who is to be sent will receive He will receive from the Son, because everything that the Son has the Father has. Accordingly, nature adheres to its own law in everything, and because the two are one the reference to the same Godhead in both is indicated by the birth and generation, since the Son declares that what the Spirit of truth will receive from the Father will be given by Him. Hence, the impiety of heresy is to be granted no liberty for its godless knowledge so that it may claim that this saying of the Lord—that everything that the Father has is His, and therefore the Spirit of truth will receive from Him—does not have any reference to the unity of nature.

(21) Let him speak who is the vessel of election and the teacher of the Gentiles, when he had already praised the faith of the Romans for being in accord with the understanding of the truth. When he wished to teach the unity of nature in the Father and the Son, he spoke thus: 'You, however, are not carnal but spiritual, if indeed the Spirit of God is in you. But if anyone does not have the Spirit of Christ, he does not belong to Christ. But if Christ is in you, the body, it is true, is dead by reason of sin, but the spirit is life by reason of justice. But if the Spirit of him who raised Jesus from the dead dwells in you, then he who raised Jesus Christ from

the dead will also bring to life your mortal bodies because of his Spirit who dwells in you.'[25]

We are all spiritual if the Spirit of God is in us. But, this Spirit of God is also the Spirit of Christ. And, since the Spirit of Christ is in us, the Spirit of Him who raised Christ from the dead is in us, and He who raised Christ from the dead will also give life to our mortal bodies because of the Spirit of Him who dwells in us. We are vivified, however, because of the Spirit of Christ that dwells in us through Him who raised Christ from the dead. And since the Spirit of Him who raised Christ from the dead is in us, the Spirit of Christ is in us; nevertheless, it is the Spirit of God that is in us. Hence, O heretic, separate the Spirit of Christ from the Spirit of God, and the Spirit of Christ that was raised from the dead from the Spirit of God that raises Christ from the dead, since the Spirit of Christ that dwells in us is the Spirit of God, and since the Spirit of Christ that was raised from the dead is, nevertheless, the Spirit of God that raises Christ from the dead!

(22) And now I ask, whether you believe that the Spirit of God indicates a nature or a thing belonging to the nature? For, the nature is not the same as the thing belonging to the nature,[26] just as man is not the same as that which belongs to man, nor is fire the same as that which belongs to fire, and, accordingly, God is not the same as that which belongs to God.

(23) I am well aware that the Son of God is signified in the Spirit of God in such a manner as to make us realize that God the Father is revealed in Him,[27] that the expression,

---

25 Cf. Rom. 8.9-11.
26 A. Palmieri, 'Esprit, Saint,' *DTC* V 747 thus explains the meaning of *res naturae* as applied to the Holy Spirit, the third Person of the Trinity: 'Le Pére est la nature principielle, la source primordiale; le Saint-Esprit est la nature communiquée, c'est à dire l'être qui appartient à Dieu le Père comme à sa source.'
27 That is, by the use of the term, 'Spirit of God.'

the 'Spirit of God,' may serve to designate either one, and that we can prove that this is authorized not only by the Prophets but also by the Gospels when they declare: 'The Spirit of the Lord is upon me; therefore he has anointed me,'[28] and again: 'Behold, my servant, whom I have chosen, my beloved in whom my soul is well pleased: I will put my Spirit upon him.'[29] And He Himself bears testimony concerning Himself: 'But if I cast out devils by the Spirit of God, certainly the kingdom of God has come upon you.'[30] These words seem to refer clearly either to the Father or the Son, yet they manifest the power of the nature.

(24)   I think that the term, the 'Spirit of God,' is applied to both, therefore, in order that we may not conclude that the Son is in the Father or the Father in the Son in a corporeal manner, that is to say, that we may not believe that God remains in a place and never seems to be anywhere else apart from Himself. For, when man, or anything else that is similar to him, is in one place, he will not be in some other place, because that which is there is restricted to the spot where it is, for the nature of him who is firmly rooted in some place is incapable of being in every place. But God, the living power of incalculable strength, who is present everywhere and is absent from nowhere, shows Himself completely through His own, and gives us to understand that His own is nothing else than Himself, so that where His own are present we know that He Himself is present. We should not imagine, however, that like a body, when He is present in some place He is not also present in every place through His own, since those things that are His own are, nevertheless, nothing else than what He Himself is. We have mentioned these facts, of course, in order that we may understand the meaning of the nature.

---

28 Cf. Luke 4.18.
29 Cf. Matt. 12.18.
30 Matt. 12.28.

(25) We must conclude, I believe, that the Spirit of God means God the Father because the Lord Jesus Christ asserted that the Spirit of the Lord was upon Him, and therefore He anoints Him and sends Him to preach the Gospel. The power of the Father's nature is manifested in Him, while through the spiritual anointing He also reveals that the Son, who was born in the flesh, has a share in His own nature, since after the birth that took place in the baptism, this designation of the true nature was also heard at that time when the voice testifies from Heaven: 'Thou art my son: this day have I begotten thee.'[31] We must not understand this in the sense that He Himself was over Himself, or that He was present with Himself from heaven, or that He gave Himself the name of Son, but this entire manifestation was for the benefit of our faith so that through the mystery of the perfect and true birth we might recognize the unity of the nature remaining in the Son who also began to be man. Thus we discover that the Spirit of God refers without doubt to the Father. But we perceive that the Son has been revealed in this manner when He declares: 'But if I cast out devils by the spirit of God, then the kingdom of God has come upon you,' that is, when He reveals that through the power of His own nature He cast out the devils, who cannot be cast out except by the Spirit of God. There is also a reference to the Spirit Paraclete in the Spirit of God, not only by the testimony of the Prophets, but also by that of the Apostles, when it is said: 'But this is what was spoken through the prophet: And it shall come to pass in the last days, says the Lord, that I will pour forth of my Spirit upon all flesh. And their sons and daughters shall prophesy.'[32] And we are taught that these words were completely fulfilled in the Apostles, when all of them spoke in the languages of the Gentiles after the Holy Spirit had been sent.

31 Ps. 2.7.
32 Cf. Acts 2.16,17.

(26) It was necessary to reveal these facts, therefore, in order that, no matter where the heretical error might turn, it would still be confined within the limits and the command of the evangelical truth. For, Christ dwells in us, and while Christ dwells God dwells. And since the Spirit of Christ dwells in us, still, while the Spirit of Christ dwells in us, no other Spirit dwells except the Spirit of God. If we realize that Christ is in us through the Holy Spirit, we still recognize that the latter is just as much the Spirit of God as the Spirit of Christ. And, since the nature itself dwells in us through the nature of the thing, we must believe that the nature of the Son does not differ from that of the Father, since the Holy Spirit, who is the Spirit of Christ and the Spirit of God, is made known as the thing of one nature.

Accordingly, I now raise the question: in what manner are they not one by nature? The Spirit of truth proceeds from the Father; He is sent by the Son and receives from the Son. But, everything that the Father has belongs to the Son. He who receives from Him, therefore, is the Spirit of God, but the same one is also the Spirit of Christ. The thing belongs to the nature of the Son, but the same thing also belongs to the nature of the Father. It is the Spirit of Him who raises Christ from the dead, but the same one is the Spirit of Christ who has been raised from the dead. Let the nature of Christ and the nature of God differ in something, that it may not be the same, if it can be shown that the Spirit which is the Spirit of God is not at the same time the Spirit of Christ!

(27) O heretic, you who rage and are surrounded by the spirit of a deadly doctrine, the Apostle holds you fast and restricts you when he places Christ as the foundation of our faith. You are also unaware of this saying of the Lord: 'If anyone love me, he will keep my word, and my Father will love him, and we will come to him and make our abode with

him.'[33] He thus testified that, while the Spirit of Christ remains in us, the Spirit of God remains in us, and that the
Spirit of Him who was raised from the dead and the Spirit
of Him who raises Christ from the dead are not distinct from
each other. For, they come and dwell in us, and I ask whether
they will come in the company of differences and take up
their abode, or whether they will come in the unity of nature.
But the teacher of the Gentiles objects that there are not two
spirits present in the believers, that is, of God and Christ,
but the Spirit of Christ who is also the Spirit of God. This
is not a co-indwelling, but a dwelling; the dwelling, however,
is in the mystery of the co-indwelling, while there are not two
spirits who dwell, nor is the one dweller different from the
other. The Spirit of God is in us, but the Spirit of Christ is
also in us, and when the Spirit of Christ is in us then the
Spirit of God is in us. Thus, since that which is God's is
Christ's, and since that which is Christ's is God's, Christ
cannot be anything different from that which God is. Christ,
therefore, is God, one Spirit with God.

(28)   In regard to those words of the Gospel: 'I and the
Father are one,'[34] the Apostle teaches that there is a unity
of nature, not the solitude of a union, when he writes to the
Corinthians: 'Wherefore I give you to understand that no
one speaking in the Spirit of God says "Anathema" to Jesus.'
Do you realize, O heretic, in what spirit you speak of Christ
as a creature? Since they are accursed who have served the
creature rather than the creator, understand what you are
when you call Christ a creature, you who are aware that you
are accursed in worshiping a creature! And take note of that
which comes next: 'And no one can say: "Lord Jesus" except
in the Holy Spirit.' Do you realize what is wanting to you
when you deny to Christ that which is His? If Christ is your

33 John 14.23.
34 John 10.30.

Lord through the nature of God, you possess the Holy Spirit, but if this one is the Lord through an adopted name, then you are wanting in the Holy Spirit, you are inspired by the spirit of error, because no one can say 'Lord Jesus' except through the Holy Spirit. And when you say that He is a creature rather than God, although you give him the title of Lord, you still do not say that He is the Lord, because for you He is the Lord by a common nature and an ordinary name. But learn the nature from Paul.

(29)   These words follow: 'Now there are varieties of gifts, but there is the same Spirit; and there are varieties of ministries but the same Lord; and there are varieties of workings but the same God, who works all things in all. Now the manifestation of the Spirit is given to everyone for that which is profitable.' There is a fourfold meaning in the words that lie before us, since there is the same Spirit in the varieties of the gifts, and there is the same Lord Himself in the varieties of the ministries, and there is the same God in the varieties of the works, and there is a manifestation of the Spirit in the bestowal of what is profitable. And that the bestowal of what is profitable might be recognized in the manifestation of the Spirit, it was added at once: 'To this one through the Spirit is given the utterance of wisdom; and to another the utterance of knowledge, according to the same Spirit; but to another faith, in the same Spirit; to another the gift of healing, in the one Spirit; to another the working of miracles; to another prophecy; to another the distinguishing of spirits; to another various kinds of tongues; to another interpretation of tongues.'[35]

(30)   We have without doubt a clear knowledge of what we have called the fourth point, that is, the manifestation of the Spirit in the bestowal of that which is profitable. For, mention has been made of the profitable gifts, in the bestowal

---

35 Cf. 1 Cor. 12.3-11.

of which there is a revelation of the Spirit. There is an unquestioned demonstration of this gift in the varieties of these powers, to which the Lord referred when He commanded His Apostles: 'not to depart from Jerusalem, but wait for the promise of the Father, "of which you have heard," said he, "by my mouth; for John indeed baptized with water, but you shall be baptized with the Holy Spirit not many days hence." ' And again: 'But you shall receive power when the Holy Spirit comes upon you, and you shall be witnesses for me in all Judea and Samaria and even to the very ends of the earth.'[36]

He orders them to await the promise of the Father, which has been heard from His mouth. Certainly, the discourse even now[37] is concerned with the promise of His Father. Consequently, the manifestation of the Spirit is through the effects which these powers produce. The gift of the Spirit is not hidden where there is the word of wisdom and the words of life are heard, or where there is the perception of the divine knowledge in order that we may not be like the animals, unaware of the Author of our life through our ignorance of God; or through faith in God in order that we may not be outside the Gospel of God by not believing the Gospel of God; or through the gift of healing in order that by the cure of infirmities we may render testimony to the grace of Him who has granted these gifts; or through the performance of miracles in order that the power of God may be recognized in what we are doing; or through prophecy in order that through our knowledge of the doctrine it may be known that we have been taught by God; or through the distinguishing of spirits in order that we may perceive whether anyone speaks through a holy or an evil spirit; or through the various kinds of languages in order that the sermons in these lan-

36 Acts 1.4,5,8.
37 That is, the words just quoted from Acts 1.8.

guages may be offered as a sign of the Holy Spirit who has
been given; or in the interpretation of the languages in order
that the faith of the hearers might not be endangered through
ignorance, since the interpreter of a language makes it intelligible for those who are not familiar with the language.
Hence, in all the diversities of these gifts, which have been
granted for the profit of everyone, there is a manifestation of
the Spirit. That is to say, through the miracles that have
been granted for the profit of everyone the gift of the Holy
Spirit does not remain hidden.

(31)   The blessed Apostle Paul, however, has displayed a
blameless manner of argumentation as well as a judicious
caution in this mystery of the heavenly revelations, that is
most difficult for our human comprehension, in order to
prove that these various gifts are bestowed by the Spirit and
in the Spirit (for to be given through the Spirit is not the same
as to be given in the Spirit), because this bestowal of the
gift which is obtained in the Spirit is, nevertheless, granted
through the Spirit. He brings together the varieties of these
gifts in the following manner: 'But all these things are the
work of one and the same Spirit, who divides to everyone
according as he will.'[38]

Hence, I now ask what Spirit performs these actions,
dividing to everyone as He wills, whether this division of the
gifts is by the Spirit through whom or by the Spirit in whom?
If anyone will dare to assert that they are the same, the
Apostle will contradict him, because the reader has not understood him correctly, for he had previously stated: 'And there
are varieties of gifts, but the same God who works all things
in all.' There is one, therefore, who divides, and there is
another upon whom the division has been conferred. And
realize that God is always performing all of these works, but
in such a manner that Christ performs them, so that the Son

---

38 1 Cor. 12.11.

who works does the work of the Father. If you admit that Jesus the Lord is in the Holy Spirit, then grasp the threefold meaning of the Apostle's words, since there is the same Spirit in the varieties of the gifts, and the same Lord in the varieties of the ministries, and the same God in the varieties of the miracles, and again it is the one Spirit who works in all, dividing to everyone according as He wills. And if you can, grasp the fact that the Lord in the varieties of the ministries and the God in the varieties of the miracles is the one and the same Spirit, who works with them and divides to everyone as He wills, because there is the one Spirit in the varieties of the gifts, and the same Spirit works and distributes.

(32) Or, if this one Spirit of the same Godhead and the Lord through the mystery of the birth displeases you, then make known what Spirit works in us and divides, and in what Spirit He does so! But you will point out nothing except what is in our faith, because the Apostle reveals which one is to be understood when he says: 'For as the body is one and has many members, and all the members of the body, many as they are, form one body, so also is it with Christ.'[39] He indicates, therefore, that the divisions of the gifts are from the one Lord Jesus Christ, who is the body of all, because, when he made the Lord known in the ministry, he likewise made God known in the miracles, but revealed that the one Spirit effects and divides all these gifts, distributing these members of graces in the perfection of the body.

(33) Unless, perhaps, some believe that the Apostle did not preserve the idea of unity in this passage because he said: 'And there are varieties of ministries but the same Lord, and there are varieties of workings but the same God,' so that, because he referred the ministries to the Lord and the workings to God, it would appear that we are not to understand them as one and the same in the ministries and the workings.

---

39 1 Cor. 12.12.

Learn to what an extent these members of the ministries are members of the workings when he says: 'Now you are the body of Christ and the members. And God indeed placed some in the Church, 'first apostles' in whom there is the word of wisdom, 'secondly prophets,' in whom there is the gift of knowledge, 'thirdly teachers' in whom there is the instruction in the faith; 'after that miracles,' in which are 'the healing of infirmities, the services of help, the administrations of the prophets,' and the gifts of 'various tongues'[40] either of speaking or interpreting. These are, of course, the ministries and the workings of the Church in which the body of Christ is, and God has instituted these things. Or declare that they have not been instituted by Christ because God has instituted them! But you will hear him saying: 'But to each one of us grace was given according to the measure of Christ's bestowal.' And again: 'He who descended, he it is who ascended also above all the heavens, that he might fill all things. And he himself gave some men as apostles, and some as prophets, some again as evangelists, and some as pastors and teachers, in order to perfect the saints for a work of the ministry.'[41] Are not the gifts of the ministries, then, the gifts of Christ, while they are, nevertheless, the gifts of God?[42]

(34) But, if godlessness has unlawfully made this claim in its own defense, that they do not possess unity of a nature because he spoke of the 'same Lord and the same God,' I will add what you consider the stronger bulwarks for your understanding of this matter. The Apostle himself declared: 'Yet for us there is one God, the Father from whom are all things, and we unto him; and one Lord, Jesus Christ, through whom are all things, and we through him.'[43] And again:

40 Cf. 1 Cor. 12.27,28.
41 Cf. Eph. 4.7,10-12.
42 That is, of God the Father. The fact that the *charismata,* which St. Paul had just mentioned, may be attributed either to God the Father or God the Son is an additional proof of their unity of nature.
43 Cf. 1 Cor. 8.6.

'One Lord, one faith, one baptism; one God and Father of all, and through all, and in us all.'[44] When he speaks of the 'one God and the one Lord' he seems to regard that which God is as proper only to God, as if He were the one God, since the correct significance of one does not admit companionship with another. O gifts of the divine graces, how undeniably rare and difficult you are! And how truly is the manifestation of the Spirit based upon this bestowal of the profitable gifts!

And he has rightly maintained this arrangement in the distribution of the graces, so that the first one should be the utterance of wisdom, for true indeed are those words: 'And no one can say "Lord Jesus" except in the Holy Spirit,' because only by this word of wisdom can Christ be understood as the Lord. Then follows the utterance of knowledge in order that we may speak knowingly of those things which we understand so that we may understand the word of wisdom. The third gift consists of faith, for, unless we believed in God, the first and more important graces would cease to be profitable gifts, so that now in the mystery of this greatest and most elegant statement of the Apostle there is not the utterance of wisdom among all the heretics, nor the utterance of knowledge, nor faith in the true religion, because impiety, which does not perceive knowledge, is outside the knowledge of the word and the simplicity of faith.

No one speaks about that which he does not understand, nor does anyone believe that which he cannot express. The Apostle, therefore, who comes from the Law and is called to the Gospel of Christ, remained faithful to the confession of the perfect faith in his teaching about the one God. In order that the simplicity of his language, as if He were lacking in caution, might not provide the heretics with any pretext for denying the birth of the Son through their teaching about the one God, he acknowledged the one God by indicating His

---

44 Cf. Eph. 4.6

essential attributes when he spoke thus: 'One God, the Father
from whom are all things, and we unto him,' in order that we
might believe that He who is God is also the Father. Hence,
because this truth alone, to believe in the one God the Father,
would not bring us salvation, he added: 'And one Lord,
Jesus Christ through whom are all things, and we through
him,' and thus makes known that the purity of the salutary
faith consists in teaching the one God and the one Lord, so
that in our faith there would be the one God the Father
and the one Lord Jesus Christ. The words spoken by the
Lord were not unknown to him: 'For this is the will of my
Father that whoever beholds the Son and believes in him
shall have everlasting life.'[45] But, when he arranges the order
of the Church's faith and defines the faith in the Father and
the Son, he expresses the mystery of the inseparable and
indissoluble unity of faith when he said 'one God and one
Lord.'

(35)   In the first place, O heretic, you who are living outside of the apostolic spirit, recognize your folly! For, if you
usurp the profession of faith in the one God in order that
Christ may not be God, because where there is one He must be
regarded as solitary, and the fact that anyone is one must be
considered as proper and peculiar to Him who is one, what
will you assert about Christ being the one Lord? If in your
opinion, because the one Father is God, He has left nothing
for Christ to be God, then it must also follow according to
you that the one Lord Christ does not leave anything for
God to be the Lord, because you wish what one is to be the
exclusive property of Him who is one. If, therefore, you will
deny that the one Lord Jesus Christ is also God, you will
likewise deny that the one God the Father is also the Lord.
Of what will the power of God consist if He is not the Lord,
and the strength of the Lord if He is not God, since the fact

45 John 6.40.

that He is God causes Him to be the Lord and the fact that He is the Lord enables Him to be what God is?

(36) But the Apostle, while holding fast to the mystery of the Lord's words, which are: 'I and the Father are one,' while confessing that both are one, thus indicates that both are one, not to teach us the solitude of a single person, but the unity of the spirit, because the one God the Father and the one Christ the Lord, although each is the Lord and God, do not allow two gods and two lords in our faith. Consequently, each is one and, since each is one, each is not alone. Nor are we able to speak of the mystery of faith except in the words of the Apostle. For, there is one God and there is one Lord, and from the fact that God is one and the Lord is one the Lord is revealed in God just as God is revealed in the Lord. You do not cling to a union in order that God may be unique; neither do you divide the Spirit in order that both may not be one. Nor will you be able to make a distinction between the power in the one God and the one Lord so that He who is the Lord is not also God, or that He who is God is not also the Lord. In expressing the names, the Apostle has seen to it that we do not proclaim two gods or two lords. For this reason he employed that manner of teaching so as to make known that the one God is also in the one Lord Christ, and to point out that the one Lord is also in the one God the Father; yet he has not offered us a godless union in order to do away with the birth of the only-begotten God, and he acknowledged the Father as well as Christ.

(37) Unless, perhaps, the rage of final despair may dare to break forth into such violent speech that, since the Apostle spoke of Christ as the Lord, no one may venture to recognize Him as anything else than the Lord, and while possessing what is proper to the Lord He does not have the true nature of God. But Paul knew that Christ was God when he said: 'Who have the fathers and from whom is Christ,

who is over all things, God.'[46] Here a creature is not likened
to God, but He is the God of creatures who is God over all
things.

(38)   Learn also from this statement of the Apostle which
we are now discussing how much He is the God over all things
and the Spirit inseparable from the Father. Since he acknowledged the one God the Father from whom are all things and
the one Lord Jesus Christ through whom are all things, I
ask what distinction has he introduced by declaring that all
things are from God and all things are through Christ? Or,
are we to suppose that He from whom and He through whom
are all things are composed of a nature and spirit that can be
separated from themselves? For, through the Son all things
have come into being and the Apostle referred to God as the
one 'from whom all things' and to the Son as the one 'through
whom are all things.' I do not find what difference there is,
since the work of the same power is done through each one.
If, in bringing all things into being, it would be proper to
and sufficient for creatures to be from God, what reason
compelled him to mention that the things which are from
God are through Christ, except that it is one and the same
to be through Christ as it is to be from God? But, just as
'Lord' and 'God' are ascribed to each so that the terms are
interchangeable, so 'from whom' and 'through whom' are
referred to each one to reveal the unity between the two
and to prevent us from believing that there is an isolated
person.

His words do not afford a pretext for impiety and the
apostolic faith does not fail in the preciseness of its teaching.
He has confined himself to the exact meaning of the terms
so that we would realize that he was referring neither to two
gods nor to a unique God, and while detesting the union he
does not divide the unity. For, these words, 'from whom are

---

46 Cf. Rom. 9.5.

all things' and 'through whom are all things,' although
they do not assign the power of the Godhead to a unique
person, do not reveal that they are different in what is produced, since 'from whom are all things' and 'through whom
are all things' indicate that the author of this work has the
same nature. He declares, however, that it is proper for
each one to possess the same nature. After he had borne
testimony to the depths of the riches and the wisdom and
the knowledge of God, and had admitted his lack of knowledge about the inscrutable judgments, and had revealed his
ignorance about the unsearchable ways, he exercised the
function of human faith and paid this tribute of honor to
the depths of the heavenly mysteries that are incomprehensible
and inscrutable when he said: 'For from him and through
him and unto him are all things. To him be the glory forever,
amen.'[47] He now cites as an indication of one nature that
which can only be the work of one nature.

(39)   Since he has attributed to God as something distinc-
tive that all things are from Him, and has recognized as
proper to Christ that all things are through Him, and now
renders homage to God because all things are from Him, in
Him, and through Him, and since the Spirit of God is the
same as the Spirit of Christ, or since in the ministry of the
Lord and in the working of God the one Spirit works and
divides, they cannot but be one whose essential attributes
belong to one, since in the same Lord the Son and in the
same God the Father the one and the same Spirit distributes
in the same Spirit and brings everything to completion.

What a one, worthy of knowing the exalted and heavenly
mysteries, who was raised aloft and chosen as a sharer in
the divine secrets, who must be silent about those very things
of which it is forbidden to speak, and truly an Apostle of
Christ, who has put an end to the sophistries of human

47 Rom. 11.36.

perversity by the teaching of his complete message, while he acknowledges the one God the Father and the one Lord Jesus Christ so that in the meantime no one might be able to proclaim that there are either two gods or a unique God, since he who is not unique does not develop into two, nor can they who are not two be considered as solitary, and meanwhile through the manifestation of the Father he revealed the perfect birth of the Son!

(40) Now stretch forth your hissing tongues, O heretical serpents, whether Sabellius, or Photinus, or those who now proclaim the only-begotten God as a creature! Whoever denies the Son shall hear of the one God the Father, for, since the Father is not the Father except through the Son, the Son is therefore revealed in the Father. Whoever deprives the Son of unity in the identical nature, let him acknowledge the one Lord Jesus Christ. For, unless He is the one Lord through the unity of the Spirit, nothing will be left for God the Father to be the Lord. But, whoever thinks of the Son as being in time and in the flesh, let him know that all things are through Him and we are through Him, and that the eternal infinity which established all things is outside of time. Meanwhile let him read again that there is one hope of a calling, one baptism, and one faith. If he then contradicts the teaching of the Apostle, he has made himself accursed, since by following his own judgment he has learned a different kind of wisdom, and he is neither called, nor is he baptized, nor is he a believer, because there is one faith of one hope and one baptism in one God the Father and in one Lord Jesus Christ; nor can a contrary doctrine boast of being among those which possess the one God, Lord, hope, baptism, and faith.

(41) It is, therefore, one faith to confess the Father in the Son and the Son in the Father through the unity of an inseparable nature, not intermingled but undivided, not

blended together but identical, not cohering but existing, not incomplete but perfect. It is a birth, not a division. He is a Son, not an adoption. He is God, not a creature. Nor is he a God of another nature, but the Father and the Son are one; the nature has not been changed by the birth so that He would be alien to the true nature of His origin. Hence, the Apostle holds fast to this faith of the Son remaining in the Father, and the Father remaining in the Son, and proclaims that for him there is the one God the Father and the one Lord Jesus Christ. For, God is also in the Lord Christ, and, similarly, the Lord is in God the Father, and both are one because each is God and both are one because each is the Lord, for it would be regarded as an imperfection in God if He were not the Lord, and in the Lord if He were not God. Thus, since both are one and one is indicated in both, and both are not without the one, the Apostle does not go beyond the teaching of the Gospel, and Christ, who speaks in Paul, does not teach anything different from that which the Incarnate One spoke while He remained in the world.

(42)   The Lord had said in the Gospels: 'Do not labor for the food that perishes, but for that which endures unto life everlasting, which the Son of Man will give you. For upon him the Father, God himself, has set his seal. They said therefore to him, "What are we to do in order that we may perform the works of God?" In answer Jesus said to them, "This is the work of God, that you believe in him whom he has sent." '[48] When the Lord explained the mystery of His Incarnation and divinity, He also spoke of the doctrine of our faith and our hope, so that we should labor not for the food that perishes, but for that which remains forever, that we should bear in mind that this eternal food was given to us by the Son of God, that we should know that God the Father had set His seal upon the Son of Man, and that we

---

48 John 6.27-29.

should recognize this as the work of God: to believe in Him whom He has sent. And who is He whom the Father has sent? It is He upon whom the Father has set His seal. And who is it upon whom the Father has set His seal? It is, of course, the Son of Man, that is, He who offers the food of eternal life. And finally, who are they to whom He offers it? It is they who will labor for the food that does not perish. Thus, the labor for this food is at the same time the work of God, namely, to believe in Him whom He has sent. But the Son of Man tells us of these things. And how will the Son of Man give the food of eternal life. At this point I now raise the question: In what sense, finally, are we to understand the words that God the Father has set His seal upon the Son of Man?

(43) First of all, we must realize that God did not speak to Himself, but to us, and adapted the words of His discourse to our power of comprehension, so as to enable the weakness of our nature to grasp His meaning. When, on a previous occasion, the Jews had rebuked Him because He had made Himself the equal of God by asserting that He was the Son of God, He had answered that He does everything that the Father does, and that He has received all judgment from the Father, and also that He must be honored like the Father.[49] And in all these things, when He had already asserted that He was the Son, He had placed Himself on an equality with the Father in glory, power, and nature. Then He had declared that, as the Father has life in Himself, so He had given to the Son to have life in Himself, and by these words indicated the unity of the same nature through the mystery of His birth. For, by what the Father has, He meant that He has the latter Himself, for God is not made up of composite things in a human fashion, so that what He has within Him is one thing and what He Himself is is

49 Cf. John 5.18-23.

something else, but everything that He has is life, that is to say, a perfect, complete, and infinite nature: one not consisting of unlike parts, but one that lives entirely by itself. Since what He possesses as such He has also given as such, even though we understand that His birth is being referred to, this does not bring about a distinction of nature in Him to whom it is given, since it was given in such a manner as it was also possessed.

(44) Accordingly, after this designation, so manifold and so appropriate for revealing the nature of the Father within Him, He used these words: 'For upon this one God the Father has set his seal.' The nature of seals is such as to manifest the entire form of the figure that has been impressed on them, and nothing is wanting to them of that which has been transmitted by the sealing, and while they receive the entire object that is impressed, they reproduce in themselves the entire object that has been impressed. This does not serve as a true type of the divine birth, because in seals we find matter, distinction, and the impression whereby the images of stronger substances are impressed on substances that are weaker.

The only-begotten God, and the Son of Man through the mystery of our salvation, wishing to indicate the likeness of the Father's real nature in Him, said that God had set His seal upon Him, and had done so because the Son of Man would give the food of eternal life, in order thereby to let us know that in Him was the power to give food for eternal life, because He possessed in Himself the complete fullness of the paternal nature of the God, who had set His seal upon Him, so that upon which God had set His seal would reproduce in itself nothing else than the nature of the God who had set His seal upon Him. The Lord indeed addressed Himself to the Jews, who were incapable of grasping these words because of their unbelief.

(45)   But the preacher of the Gospel instructs us in the knowledge of the real nature by the Spirit of God that speaks through Him when he declares: 'Who though he was by nature God, did not consider being equal to God a thing to be clung to, but emptied himself, taking the nature of a slave.'[50] He upon whom God had set His seal could not be anything else than the form of God, and that which had been sealed in the form of God must preserve in itself the complete image of that which God is. Accordingly, the Apostle taught that He upon whom God has set His seal is the God who abides in the form of God. When He was about to speak of the mystery of the body, which had been assumed and born together with Him, he says: 'He did not consider being equal to God a thing to be clung to, but emptied himself, taking the nature of a slave.' That which He was in the form of God He continued as God through the God who had set His seal upon Him. But, because He was to receive the form of a slave, He would be obedient unto death, while He does not consider being equal to God a thing to be clung to, and through His obedience He emptied Himself of the form of God, that is, of that by which He was equal to God.[51] He does not, however, consider Himself as equal to God because of something that He has clung to, although He was in the form of God, equal to God, and sealed as God by God.

(46)   At this point I now raise the question whether He who abides as God in the form of God is a God of a different nature, as in seals we distinguish the likenesses according to whether they are stamped on the seal or on the instrument used in the sealing, since the iron impressed upon the lead and the gem upon the wax either form the likeness of their

---

50 Phil. 2.6-7.
51 As is clear from later passages in *De Trinitate,* the *kenosis* meant that the Son of God in becoming man stripped Himself only of the glory that was rightfully His by reason of His divine nature. Cf. 9,7; 10,7; 11,18.

own concave image or bring forth the likeness of a raised impression of themselves. But, if there is anyone so foolish and insane as to believe that God forms anything else from Himself into God except God, and that He Himself, who is in the form of God, is in His entire being anything else than God, after the mysteries of the man that was assumed and of the abasement that was to reach its consummation through obedience even to the death of the cross, then he will hear every tongue in heaven, on earth, and under the earth confessing that Jesus is in the glory of God the Father. If, therefore, He shall remain in this glory when He already had the form of a slave, I ask: What did He remain when He was in the form of God? Was not Christ the Spirit in the nature of God which is signified by 'in the glory' when Christ Jesus, that is, He who was born as man, will exist in the glory of God the Father?[52]

(47) The blessed Apostle holds fast to the unchangeable teaching of the evangelical faith in everything, while he proclaims the Lord Jesus Christ as God in such a manner that the apostolic faith does not lapse into two gods through the God of another nature, nor does God the Son, who is inseparable from the Father, offer a godless pretext for teaching that God is unique and solitary. For, when he says: 'in the nature of God and in the glory of God the Father,' he teaches that there is no distinction and does not allow us to regard Him as non-existing. For, He who was in the form of God does not develop into another God, and He Himself is also God. He cannot be separated from the form of God, since He is in it, nor is He not God who is in the form of God. Just as He who is in the glory of God cannot be anything else than what God is, and while God is in the glory of God He cannot be proclaimed as another God and as a God

---

52 'Christ the Spirit' refers to the divine nature, while 'Christ Jesus' refers to the Son of God after He had assumed our human nature.

different from God, because by reason of His being in the glory of God He possesses the nature of God in Himself from Him in whose glory He is.

(48) There is no danger of the one faith not being the one faith because it teaches many things. The Evangelist had reported that the Lord has said: 'He who has seen me has seen also the Father.'[53] But, has Paul, the teacher of the Gentiles, been unaware of or silent about the meaning of these words, when he said: 'Who is the image of the invisible God?'[54] I ask whether there is a visible image of the invisible God, and whether the infinite God can be brought together in an image so that He is visible through the image of a limited form? An image must express the form of Him whose image it is. Let those who wish the Son to have a different kind of nature decide upon what kind of an image they wish the Son to be of the invisible Father. Do they desire it to be bodily and visible, one that wanders from place to place by its movement and walking? Let them bear in mind that Christ is a Spirit and God is a Spirit, according to the Gospels and the Prophets. And if they will circumscribe this Spirit Christ within the bounds of that which may be formed and is corporeal, then the Incarnate One will not be the image of the invisible God and a finite limitation will not be the form of Him who is infinite.

(49) Neither has the Lord left anything uncertain: 'He who has seen me has seen also the Father,' nor has the Apostle been silent about the nature of Him 'who is the image of the invisible God.' The Lord has declared: 'If I do not perform the works of my Father do not believe me.'[55] Hence, He teaches that the Father is seen in Him because He performs His works so that the power of the nature that was perceived would reveal the nature of the power that

53 Cf. John 14.9.
54 Col. 1.15.
55 John 10.37.

was perceived, wherefore the Apostle, indicating that this is the image of God, says: 'Who is the image of the invisible God, the firstborn of every creature. For in him were created all things in the heavens and on the earth, things visible and things invisible, whether Thrones, or Dominations, or Principalities, or Powers. All things have been created through and unto him, and he is before all creatures, and in him all things hold together. Again, he is the head of his body, the Church; he, who is the beginning, the firstborn from the dead, that in all things he may have the first place. For it has pleased God the Father that in him all his fullness should dwell, and that through him he should reconcile to himself all things.'[56] Accordingly, He is the image of God by the power of these works. Certainly, the creator of invisible things is not compelled by any necessity of nature to be the visible image of the invisible God. And in order that we might not regard Him as the image of the form rather than of the nature, He is therefore the image of the invisible God, because by the power of His nature we are to understand that in Him there is not an invisible attribute but the nature of God.

(50)   He is the first-born of every creature, because all things have been created in Him. And in order that no one may dare to refer to anyone else but Himself that all things were created in Him he said: 'All things have been created through him and unto him, and he is before all creatures, and in him all things hold together.' All things hold together in Him who is before all things and in whom are all things. These facts, indeed, pertain to the beginning of creatures. Moreover, because of the dispensation of our body, he said: 'And he is the head of his body, the Church, he, who is the beginning, the firstborn of the dead, that in all things he may have the first place. For it has pleased God the Father that

---

56 Col. 1.15-20.

in him all his fullness should dwell, and that through him
he should reconcile to himself all things.'

The Apostle added the corporeal actions to the spiritual
mysteries. He who is the image of the invisible God is also
at the same time the head of His body, the Church, and He
who is the first-born of every creature is the same one who
is the beginning, the first-born of the dead, so that He may
have the first place in all things, while He who is the image
of God is for us a body, while He who is the first-born of
creatures is at the same time the first-born to eternal life, so
that He to whom the spiritual beings, created in the first-born,
are indebted for their existence, to Him human beings are
similarly indebted, because they have been born again in the
first-born to eternal life. He Himself is the beginning who,
since He is a Son, is an image, and, since He is an image,
He is an image of God. He is also the first-born of every
creature who contains within Himself the beginning of every
creature. Again, He Himself is the head of His body, the
Church, and the first-born of the dead, so that He Himself
may have the first place in all things. And because all things
hold together in Him, the well-pleased fullness lives in
Him, while in Him all things are reconciled through Him
and unto Him in whom all things were created through Him
and unto Him.

(51) Do you now know what it is to be the image of
God? It surely means that all things were created through
Him and unto Him. Since all things are created in Him, then
understand that He whose image He is also creates all things
in Him. But, since these things which are created in Him are
created through Him, then realize that in Him who is the
image there is also the nature of Him whose image He is.
He creates through Himself what is created in Him, just as
all things are reconciled in Him through Himself. Since they

are reconciled in Him, grasp the nature of the paternal unity in Him that reconciles all things to Himself in Him! Since all things are reconciled in Him, recognize that fact that He reconciles all things to the Father in Himself, which He will reconcile through Himself. The same Apostle says: 'But all things are from God, who has reconciled us to himself through Christ and has given to us the ministry of reconciliation. For God was truly in Christ, reconciling the world to himself.'[57] Compare the entire mystery of the evangelical faith with these words! He who is seen in Him who is seen, He who works in Him who works, He who speaks in Him who speaks is the same one who will reconcile in Him who reconciles. Accordingly, there is the reconciliation in Him and through Him, because the Father Himself, who remains in Him through the identical nature, restored the world to Himself through Him and in Him by this reconciliation.

(52) Accordingly, God, who takes our human weakness into consideration, has not taught our faith by ambiguous and barren words. Although the mere authority of the Lord's statement compelled us to believe, He aided our powers of reasoning by informing us of the manner in which it was produced, in order that we might know what was said: 'I and the Father are one'[58] by means of the very thing that was the basis of the unity that had been revealed. When He declares that He speaks through Him who speaks, works through Him who works, judges through Him who judges, is seen through Him who is seen, reconciles through Him who reconciles, and remains in Him who remains in Him, then I ask what expressions better adapted to our power of comprehension could He have used in His explanation to make us understand that they are one than those whereby

57 2 Cor. 5.18,19.
58 John 10.30.

through the true nature and the unity of nature whatever
the Son did and said the Father said and did in the Son?

This is not characteristic, therefore, of a nature alien to
His own, nor of a nature which has been made equal by
creation, nor of a nature that has been formed from a portion
of God into God, but of the divinity that has been begotten
into the perfect God by the perfect birth, and which possesses
such conscious assurance of its own nature that it can say:
'I in the Father and the Father in me,'[59] and again: 'All
things that the Father has are mine.'[60] For, nothing is wanting
to Him from God in whom, when He works, speaks, and is
seen, God works, speaks, and is seen. There are not two in
the work, speech, or sight of one.[61] Nor is the God solitary
who in the God who works, speaks, and is seen has also
worked, spoken, and been seen as God. The Church understands this, the synagogue does not believe this, philosophy
does not know this, that one is from the one, that the whole
is from the whole, that the God and Son has not taken away
anything that belongs to the completeness of the Father,
nor has He not held fast to this very completeness that has
come to Him by His birth. Whoever will be imprisoned in
this folly of unbelief is either a follower of the Jews or the
pagans.

(53)   To grasp this statement of the Lord when He
says: 'All things that the Father are mine,' study also the
doctrines and faith of the Apostle who declares: 'See to it
that no one seduces you by philosophy and vain deceit,
according to human traditions, according to the elements of
the world and not according to Christ. For in him dwells
the fullness of the Godhead bodily.'[62] He is of the world, he is

---

59 John 14.11.
60 John 16.15.
61 That is, there are not two gods distinct in nature, where the Father
   and Son work, speak, and are seen together.
62 Cf. Col. 2.8,9.

learned in the teachings of men, and is a victim of philosophy who does not know that Christ is the true God, and who does not recognize the fullness of the Godhead in Him.

The human spirit is wise only in that which it understands, and the world believes only what is possible, since in accordance with the elements of nature it regards as possible only that which it either sees or does. The elements of the world have come into existence from nothing, but Christ does not receive His being from things that do not exist, nor did He have any beginning in His origin, but received an eternal origin from His origin. The elements of the world are either lifeless, or else they have been given life, but Christ is the life who has been born from the living God into the living God. The elements of the world have been established by God, but they are not God. Christ as God from God is Himself this fullness that God Himself is. Since the elements of the world are within, they cannot exist outside themselves so that they are not within;[63] Christ is in God while He has God in Himself in the mystery. When the elements of the world give life to the offspring of their own kind, they indeed produce the beginnings of birth from themselves by means of bodily functions, but they themselves are not present as living beings in those that are born from them; the entire fullness of the Godhead, however, is in Christ bodily.

(54)   I ask what fullness of the Godhead is in Him? If it is not that of the Father, what other God, O false teacher of the one God, do you force upon me, the fullness of whose Godhead dwells in Christ? But, if it is that of the Father, teach me how this fullness dwells in Him bodily. If you believe that the Father is in the Son in a bodily manner, then the Father while dwelling in the Son will not exist in Himself. But if, what is more likely, the God who dwells in

---

63 On the contrary, Christ is not only within the Father but also outside of the Father; cf. above, 3.1.

Him bodily refers to the truth of the nature in Him of God from God, then God is in Him not by an abasement, nor by the will, but dwells in the bodily fullness truly and completely just as He is, while that which He Himself is has also been generated by the birth of God into God, nor is there anything contrary or different in God except that which dwells in Christ bodily, and whatever dwells bodily is itself in harmony with the fullness of the Godhead. Why do you seek after human things? Why do you remain attached to the doctrines of useless deceptions? Why do you offer me unanimity, concord, and a creature? The fullness of the Godhead is in Christ bodily.

(55)   The Apostle also maintained the law of his faith in this matter so that he taught that the fullness of the Godhead dwells bodily in Christ, in order that the statement of the faith might not fall into the godless union and that an irreligious fury might not burst forth into a knowledge of another nature. The fullness of the Godhead that dwells bodily in Christ is neither unique nor separable, while the bodily fullness does not allow itself to be kept apart from the bodily fullness, nor can the Godhead itself that dwells be conceived as the dwelling of the Godhead. And Christ is such that the fullness of the Godhead is in Christ bodily, but the fullness of the Godhead is in Christ in such a manner that the fullness which dwells in Him may not be conceived as anything else than as Christ. Grasp at any favorable meaning of the words that you like, and stir up the stinging retorts of your godless talent! At least invent something about Him whose fullness of the Godhead dwells bodily in Christ! For He is Christ. There is the fullness of the Godhead that also dwells bodily in Him.

(56)   And if you ask what the corporeal dwelling is, then consider what it is to speak in one who speaks, to be seen in one who is seen, to work in one who works, to be God in God,

to be the whole from the whole, to be one from one, and thus learn the fullness of the corporeal Godhead! And remember that the Apostle is not silent about Him in whom this fullness of the Godhead dwells bodily, when he says: 'For since the creation of the world the invisible attributes of him are clearly seen—his everlasting power also and divinity—being understood through the things that are made.'[64] The bodily Godhead of this one, therefore, is in Christ, not in part, but in its entirety; not as a portion, but as the fullness. It remains bodily in such a way that they are one; they are one in such a way that God does not differ from God; God is not different from God in such a way that the perfect birth has brought the perfect God into being; but the perfect birth subsists in such a way because in the God, who has been born from God, the fullness of the Godhead dwells bodily.

---

64 Cf. Rom. 1.20.

BOOK NINE

N THE PRECEDING Book we discussed the identical
nature of God the Father and God the Son, and
proved that the words, 'I and the Father are one,'
did not lead to a solitary God but to the unity of the undivided
Godhead, since God has been born from nowhere else than
from God, and the God from God cannot be anything else
than that which God is. Even if we did not examine all the
divine and apostolic statements in which the inseparable
nature and power of the Father and Son was proclaimed,
we did examine a sufficient number to clarify our meaning
until we came to this passage of the apostolic faith which
declared: 'See to it that no one seduces you by philosophy
and vain deceit, according to human traditions, according to
the elements of the world and not according to Christ. For
in him dwells all the fullness of the Godhead bodily.'[1]

In accordance with these words, through the fullness of
the Godhead that dwells in Him bodily, we taught that He
was the true and perfect God, who possesses the nature of
the Father, so that the fullness that dwelt in Him did not
mean a different or a unique God, since the corporeal dwelling of the incorporeal God manifested the real nature of the
natural unity in the God who derived His being from God,
while the God dwelling in Christ proclaimed the birth of

---

1 Cf. Col. 2.8,9.

the subsisting Christ, since He dwells in Him. By these words, I think, we have more than answered those who referred the sayings of the Lord: 'He who has seen me has seen also the Father,' and 'The Father in me and I in the Father,' and 'I and the Father are one,' and 'All things that the Father has are mine,' to a unity and harmony of will so that the lying religion of a deceitful doctrine distorted the meaning of the words, because the credibility of the words was not open to question, and, while it could not deny that harmony of will was to be found in those whose unity of nature was acclaimed, it believed only in an alliance, based on mutual agreement, in order to destroy the unity which proceeds from the birth.

After many clear references to the truth of the nature, the blessed Apostle, while manifesting the fullness of the Godhead that dwells bodily in Christ, did away with every assertion of the godless rashness since the corporeal dwelling of the incorporeal God brought about the unity of nature. Accordingly, when it is stated that the Son is not alone but that the Father remains in Him, and not only remains but also works and speaks, and not only works and speaks but is seen, these are not mere titles but true names, while, as a consequence of the mystery of the birth the power has the power in itself, the strength has the strength, and the nature has the nature.[2] Through the birth He Himself possesses that which is His, and in so far as He is the image which comes from Him He reveals what is in Him, while He is the image and the true nature of His origin, for the perfect birth bestows the perfect image, and the fullness of the Godhead, which dwells bodily, preserves the truth of the nature.

(2) Although these things remain indeed as they are,

_____
[2] The power, strength, and nature of the Son are also the power, strength, and nature of the Father.

because the natural God from God can only have that nature in His birth that God has,[3] and the identical unity of the living nature cannot be separated from itself by the birth of a living nature, still, by means of the salutary confession of the evangelical faith the heretics secretly plot the destruction of the true nature in order to deprive the Son of the natural unity, while words which were spoken in one context and for one purpose are so arranged by them as to be understood in a different context for a different purpose. When denying the Son of God, therefore, they cite as proof the words that He spoke: 'Why dost thou call me good? No one is good but God only,'[4] so that, because He mentioned the one God in His statement, everything else will henceforth merely enjoy the name of God and will no longer preserve the nature of God, because God is one.

Hence, when He Himself is called God, they seek to show that this is a title rather than a true description, because He declared: 'But this is everlasting life, that they may know thee, the only true God.'[5] And in order to exclude Him from the reality of the true Godhead they add these words: 'The Son can do nothing of himself, but only what he sees the Father doing.'[6] Similarly, they cite that passage: 'The Father is greater than I.'[7] Finally, they now boast, as if they have overturned the faith of the Church by an incontestable argument, that is a denial of the divinity when they again read: 'But of that day or hour no one knows, neither the angels in heaven, nor the Son, but the Father only.'[8] For, it does not seem that the birth produces an equality of nature, since the lack of knowledge necessarily supposes

---

3 The Son, whose nature comes from the Father, has the nature of the Father.
4 Mark 10.18.
5 John 17.3.
6 John 5.19.
7 John 14.28.
8 Mark 13.32.

a distinction, and the Father by knowing and the Son by not knowing manifest a difference in the divinity, because God should know everything, and one who is ignorant cannot be compared to one who is not ignorant. But they speak of all these matters in their foolish and unintelligent rage against the nature of the Godhead, while they do not grasp their significance, or take into consideration the circumstances of time, or perceive the mysteries of the Gospel, or realize the force of the words, while they mention only these bare statements in order to fill the ears of the uneducated, and pass over in silence either the explanations or the reasons that prompted them, for the meaning of words is to be ascertained either from those that precede or from those that follow.

(3) Since we shall, of course, explain these words which we have just mentioned, in accordance with the statement of the Gospels or the Apostles themselves, we think that all should be reminded of the universal faith so that in the confession in which eternal life consists we should recognize the knowledge of eternity at the same time. He is completely unacquainted with his own life, he does not know, who is ignorant of the fact that Christ Jesus is the true God as well as the true man. And it is equally dangerous to deny that Christ Jesus is God the Spirit as it is to deny that He is flesh of our body. 'Therefore, everyone who acknowledges me before men, I also will acknowledge him before my Father in heaven. But whoever disowns me before men, I in turn will disown him before my Father in heaven.'[9] The Word made flesh spoke these words, and the man, Jesus Christ the Lord of majesty, taught them. He Himself has been appointed as the mediator in His own person for the salvation of the Church, and by the mystery itself of the mediator between God and man He alone is both, while He

9 Matt. 10.32,33.

Himself, by reason of the two natures that are united in Him, is the same person in both natures, but in such a manner that He is not wanting in anything that belongs to either, so that He does not cease to be God by His birth as man, and again, He is man even while He remains God. Hence, this is the true faith of human blessedness: to acknowledge Him as God and man, to proclaim Him as the Word and as the flesh, to know of God that He is man, and to know of the flesh that it is the Word.

(4) If it is contrary to the nature of our comprehension that He who remains as God is born as man, it is not contrary to the nature of our hope that He who is born as man remains as God, since the higher nature, which has been born into the lower nature, is a guarantee that the lower nature can be born into the higher nature. Indeed, in accordance with the law and the custom of the world, it is easier for us to grasp the realization of our hope than the realization of the divine mystery.[10] The world possesses the power of growth in these things that are born, but it does not possess the power of growing smaller. Behold the trees, the seeds, the animals! Gaze upon man himself who enjoys the power of reason! He always develops by growth, but never shrinks by becoming smaller, nor does he lack that which has grown in himself. Even though he may shrivel with age, or become a victim to death, there is indeed a change of time in him or an end to his manner of existence, but it does not lie within his power not to be that which he is in such a manner that by growing smaller he may form a new man in himself, that is, from an old man to pass over into a child.

Our nature, which in accordance with the law of the world, is ever increasing, is not foolish in looking forward

---

10 That is, it is easier for us to understand how we can be united with God, in whom we place our hope, than it is for us to understand how the Son of God can abase Himself and become the Son of Man.

to its growth into a higher nature, since an increasing is in harmony with its nature, as shrinking is contrary to its nature. Accordingly, it was proper for God to be something else than what He was, and still to be what He had been, to be born as God in man and still not cease to be God, to diminish by means of the conception, the cradle, and the infancy, yet to remain in the power of God. This is a mystery not for Him, but for us. Nor is it a gain for God to assume our nature, but His voluntary abasement is our exaltation, while He does not lose that which God is, and He obtains for man that He be God.

(5) Consequently, the only-begotten God, who was born as man from the Virgin and who in the fullness of time was to raise man to God in Himself, usually followed this procedure in expressing the doctrine of the Gospel: He taught us to believe in Him as the Son of God and exhorted us to proclaim Him as the Son of Man. As man He spoke and performed all those actions that are characteristic of God, and then as God spoke and performed all those actions that are characteristic of man, but in such a way that even in this twofold manner of speaking He never spoke without indicating that He was man as well as God. But, while He always reveals the one God the Father and asserts that He possesses the nature of the one God because He was truly born, He is subject to the Father in His dignity as Son and in His condition as man, since every birth must be referred to its author and all flesh must recognize its weakness when compared to God. Hence, an opportunity is here offered to the heretics of practising their deception upon the simple and the uneducated, so that they may misrepresent those statements which He made as man as being spoken because of the weakness of His divine nature, and they contend that

since it is one and the same speaker who expressed all these things, He was speaking in all of them about Himself.[11]

(6) We do not at all deny that whatever He says in His own name proceeds from His own nature. But, if Jesus Christ is man and God, and neither is He not God first of all when He is man, nor when He is also man is He not also God, nor after the man in God[12] is not the whole man the whole God, it necessarily follows that the mystery of His words must be one and the same as the mystery of His nature. And when you make a distinction in Him between the man and God according to the periods of time, then make a distinction also between the words God and the man. Again, when you are referring to the time when the man and God was the whole man and the whole God, if He said anything to reveal that time, apply it to that time so as not to confuse the mystery of salvation in its times and natures, since God is one thing before man, another thing when man and God, and something else again after the man and God was the perfect man and the perfect God. For, in keeping with the qualities of His various natures, He must speak in one way in the mystery of the man who was not yet born, in another way in the man who is to die, and in still another way in the man who is already eternal.[13]

(7) Jesus Christ, therefore, who became all these things for our sake, and who was born as the man of our flesh, spoke in accordance with the custom of our nature, but does not forget that He is God in accordance with His own nature. Even though He performed the deeds of our nature in the birth, passion and death, He did all these very things

---

11 That is, about His divine nature.
12 The phrase, *post hominem in Deo,* refers to the glorified body of Christ, as is evident from the context of this section.
13 Hilary distinguishes three period in the life of the Son of God: before the Incarnation, during the Incarnation, and after He rose from the dead. Accordingly, to understand His words correctly we must bear in mind the period of His life to which He refers.

by the power of His own nature, while He Himself is the cause of His own birth, while He wills to suffer what He could not suffer, while He who dies lives. While God did all these things through the man, while He was born from Himself, suffered through Himself, and died of Himself, He performed them as man while He was born, suffered, and died. But these secrets of the heavenly mysteries were already ordained before the creation of the world, so that the only-begotten God willed to be born as man and man would remain eternally in God, so that God willed to suffer in order that the Devil in his rage might not retain the law of sin in us through the passions of human weakness, since God had taken our weakness upon Himself, so that God willed to die in order that no power might become arrogant toward God, nor be able to obtain under false pretenses the nature of the created strength in it, since the immortal God had been made subject to the law of death. Hence, God is born for the sake of our adoption, suffers for the sake of our innocence, and finally dies for the sake of our revenge, while our man remains in God, while the passions of our infirmities are allied with God, while the spiritual powers of wickedness and malice are conquered by the triumph of the flesh, when God dies through the flesh.

(8) Consequently, the Apostle, who was aware of this mystery and who received the knowledge of the faith from the Lord Himself, since he realized that the world, men, and philosophy would be incapable of grasping it, said: 'See to it that no one seduces you by philosophy and vain deceit, according to human traditions, according to the elements of the world and not according to Jesus Christ. For in him dwells all the fullness of the Godhead bodily, and in him who is the head of every Principality and Power you have received of that fullness.'[14] Hence, when he had explained

---

14 Col. 2.8-10.

the fullness of the Godhead, which dwells in Him bodily, he at once added the mystery of our adoption when he says: 'In him you have received of that fullness.' For, as the fullness of the Godhead is in Him, so we have received of that fullness in Him, nor does he indeed say: 'You have received of that fullness,' but: 'In him you have received of that fullness,' because all those who have been or are to be reborn through the hope of faith into eternal life now remain in the body of Christ, while later on they themselves will no longer receive of that fullness 'in him' but in themselves, at that time of which the Apostle says: 'Who will transfigure the body of our lowliness in conformity with the body of his glory.'[15]

Now, therefore, we have received of that fullness in Him through the assumption of His flesh, in whom the fullness of the Godhead dwells bodily. And for this hope of ours He possesses no insignificant power. In that fullness which we have received in Him is the head and the beginning of every power: 'So that in his name every knee bends of those in heaven, on earth and under the earth, and every tongue confesses that the Lord Jesus is the glory of God the Father.'[16] This confession will therefore be 'Jesus in the glory of God the Father,' who was born as man, and who no longer remains in the weakness of our body but in the glory of God. And every tongue will confess this. Since all who are in heaven and on earth bend the knee, this is the head of every Principality and Power, so that all by bending the knee are subject to Him of whose fullness we have received, and we must confess that He, through the fullness of the Godhead dwelling in Him bodily, is in the glory of God the Father.

(9) But after he had made known the mystery of His nature and of our adoption, since we receive of that fullness

15 Cf. Phil. 3.21.
16 Cf. Phil. 2.10-12.

in Him by His birth as man, because the fullness of the Godhead remains in Him, he proceeds with the remaining plan of man's salvation when he says: 'In him, too, you have been circumcised with a circumcision not wrought by hand, but through putting off the body of the flesh, a circumcision which is of Christ. For you were buried together with him in baptism, and in him also rose again through faith in the working of God who raised him from the dead.'[17] We are circumcised, therefore, not by a carnal circumcision, but by the circumcision of Christ, that is, we have been born again into the new man. Since we are buried together by His baptism, we must die to the old man, because the regeneration of baptism is the power of the resurrection. And this circumcision of Christ is not by having the flesh of the foreskin removed, but by dying entirely with Him and thereby living afterwards entirely with Him. We rise again in Him through faith in His God, who raised Him from the dead. Hence, we must believe in God through whose operation Christ has been raised from the dead, because that faith rises at the same time with Christ.

(10) Then the whole mystery of the assumed manhood is completed in this manner: 'And you, when you were dead by reason of your sins and the uncircumcision of your flesh, he brought to life along with him, having forgiven you all your sins, cancelling the handwriting that was written against us in the ordinances, which was hostile to us. Indeed, he has taken it completely away, nailing it to the cross. When he put off the flesh, he exposed the Powers to mockery, having triumphed over them in himself.'[18] The man of the world does not grasp the apostolic faith, nor do any other words except his own explain the meaning of his words. God raises Christ from the dead, that is to say, the Christ in whom

17 Col. 2.11,12.
18 Cf. Col. 2.13-15.

the fullness of the Godhead dwells bodily. But He has brought us to life with Himself, forgiving our sins, cancelling the handwriting of the law of sin, which was hostile to us by reason of the former ordinances, taking it away completely, nailing it to the cross, stripping Himself of the flesh, and exposing the Powers to mockery, after He had triumphed over them in Himself.

We have previously discussed the triumph over the Powers in Himself, the exposing of them to mockery, the handwriting that was cancelled, and about ourselves who were brought to life with Him.[19] But who will comprehend or express this mystery? The work of God raises Christ from the dead, and this same work forgives sin, cancels the handwriting, and nails it to the cross; He strips Himself of the flesh, exposes the Powers to mockery, and triumphs over them in Himself. You have the work of God, who raises Christ from the dead; you also have Christ doing these very same things in Himself which God does. For, Christ died, stripping Himself of the flesh. Hold fast, therefore, to Christ the man, whom God has raised from the dead! Hold fast to Christ the God, who accomplishes the work of our salvation when He shall die! Thus, since God does these things in Christ, although God works, Christ, who strips Himself of the flesh, will die, and, since Christ died, although He worked as God before His death, the work of God raises the dead Christ to life, since it is He Himself, who raised Christ from the dead, who worked as Christ before His death, and He who will die is the same one who strips Himself of the flesh.

(11) Do you already understand the mystery of the apostolic faith? Do you now comprehend who Christ is? I ask you who is He who puts off the flesh, and what is that flesh that is put off? On the authority of the Apostle I hold fast to two ideas: the flesh that is put off and He

---

19 Cf. above, 1.13.

who puts off the flesh, and meanwhile I hear of Christ, who was raised from the dead by the work of God. And since there is the God, who raises Christ from the dead, and since there is Christ, also, who has been raised from the dead, I ask the question: Who is He who puts off the flesh, and who is He who raises Christ from the dead and vivifies us with Christ? If the dead Christ is not the same as He whose flesh has been put off, then make known the meaning of the flesh that has been put off, and again explain the nature of Him who has put off the flesh. For, I discover that the God Christ who was raised from the dead is the same one as He who put off the flesh, and, again, that the Christ who was raised from the dead is the flesh that was put off, and then I see Him holding up the Principalities and the Powers to mockery and triumphing over them in Himself. Do you perceive that the flesh that has been put off and He who puts off the flesh are not distinct from each other? He triumphs in Himself, that is to say, in that flesh which He has put off. Do you realize that it is in this manner that He is proclaimed as God and man, so that the death is ascribed to the man and the resurrection of the flesh to God, but not that He who died is one and He through whom the dead one rises again is someone else? The flesh that is put off is the dead Christ, and, again, He who raises Christ from the dead is the same Christ who puts off the flesh. Grasp the nature of God in the power of the resurrection! Recognize the dispensation of the man in the death! While each action is done in accordance with its proper nature, bear in mind that it is the one Christ who is present in each of them.

(12) Although I am aware that the Apostle frequently refers to God the Father as raising Christ from the dead, the Apostle does not contradict the evangelical faith, nor does he teach anything contrary to his own words, especially since the Lord says: 'For this reason the Father loves me,

because I lay down my life that I may take it up again. No one will take it from me, but I lay it down myself. I have the power to lay it down, and I have the power to take it up again. This command I have received from the Father.'[20] Or, when He was asked to make known a sign that He might be believed, He spoke of the temple of His body: 'Destroy this temple, and in three days I will raise it up.'[21] Since by the power of taking up His life as well as by the power of raising up the temple He teaches that He Himself is the God of His own resurrection, and, nevertheless, He refers all these things to the authority of His Father's command, we perceive that the Apostle does not teach anything to the contrary when he proclaims Christ as the power of God and the wisdom of God, and thereby attributes the entire magnificence of His work to the glory of the Father, because whatever Christ does, the power and wisdom of God does, and whatever the power and wisdom of God does, undoubtedly God does, whose wisdom and power Christ is. Now, finally, Christ has been raised up from the dead by the work of God, because He Himself has performed the works of God the Father by a nature that does not differ from that of God. And the faith of the resurrection rests on that God who has raised Christ from the dead.

(13) The blessed Apostle adhered to this doctrine about the twofold designation of the person of Christ so as to teach that in Him was the weakness of man as well as the power and the nature of God, according to those words to the Corinthians: 'For though he was crucified through weakness, yet he lives through the power of God,'[22] while he revealed that His death was due to human weakness but His life to the power of God; and in those words to the Romans: 'For

20 Cf. John 10.17,18.
21 John 2.19.
22 2 Cor. 13.4.

the death that he died, he died to sin once for all, but the life that he lives, he lives unto God. Thus do you consider yourselves also as dead to sin, but alive to God in Christ Jesus,'[23] while he attributed death to sin, that is, to our body, but life to God to whose nature it belongs that He lives, so that we accordingly must die to our body that we may live in Christ Jesus, who, while assuming the body of our sin, already lives wholly for God, since He has united the nature that He shared with us into a mutual participation of the divine immortality.

(14) Consequently, I had to explain these doctrines in a few words in order to keep before your mind that in our Lord Jesus Christ we are discussing a person of two natures, because He who was in the form of God received the form of a slave in which He was obedient unto death. The obedience unto death is not in the form of God, just as the form of God is not in the form of a slave. According to the mystery of the Gospel's plan of salvation, however, He who is in the form of a slave is no different from Him who is in the form of God; still, since it is not the same thing to receive the form of a slave as it is to remain in the form of God, He who was in the form of God could not receive the form of a slave except by emptying Himself, since the combination of two forms is incongruous.

But, He who emptied Himself is not another person or a distinct person from Him who receives the form of a slave. To be able to receive does not belong to Him who does not exist, since to receive is characteristic of Him who subsists. Hence, the emptying of the form is not the destruction of the nature, because He who empties Himself is not wanting in His own nature and He who receives remains. And since it is He Himself who empties and receives, we find indeed a mystery in Him, because He empties Himself and receives

23 Rom. 6.10,11.

Himself, but no destruction takes place so that He ceases to exist when He empties Himself or does not exist when He receives. Hence, the emptying brings it about that the form of a slave appears, but not that the Christ who was in the form of God does not continue to be Christ, since it is only Christ who has received the form of a slave. Since He who emptied Himself that the abiding Spirit Christ might be the same Man Christ, the change of the outer appearance in the body and the assumption of a nature did not remove the nature of the Godhead that remains, because it is one and the same Christ who changes and assumes the outward appearance.

(15) Accordingly, since we have explained the plan of salvation in the mysteries by which the heretics would deceive all of the unlearned in attributing everything that was said and done through the nature of the man who was assumed to the weakness of the Godhead, and ascribed what is appropriate to the form of a slave to the form of God, we must now draw up our answer to the questions which they themselves have proposed. Since the faith only requires us to confess the Word and the flesh, that is, Jesus Christ both as God and as man, we shall now be able to make a safe judgment about the different specific statements. The heretics believe, therefore, that we must deny that our Lord Jesus Christ is God because He said: 'Why dost thou call me good? No one is good but God only.'[24] A complete understanding of the replies must come from the reasons that prompted the questions, for the answer will be directed to the matter that led to the inquiry.

First of all, I ask him who distorts this statement if he imagines that the Lord objected to being called good and preferred to be called bad? That seems to be the meaning of the words: 'Why dost thou call me good?' I cannot believe

---

24 Mark 10.18.

that anyone is so devoid of reason as to wish to attribute a confession of guilt to Him who said: 'Come to me, all you who labor and are burdened, and I will give you rest. Take my yoke upon you, and learn from me, for I am meek and humble of heart; and you will find rest for your souls. For my yoke is easy and my burden light.'[25] He declares that He is meek and humble; shall we believe that He is angry at being called good? These different assertions are contradictory, in that He who bears witness to His own goodness disapproves of the name of goodness in Himself. Consequently, we perceive that He is not irritated at being called good. And since we are not to believe that He condemns the name of goodness in Himself, we must find out to what other statement about Himself does He object.

(16) Let us see what else the questioner said besides the word 'good,' for he declares: 'Good master, what good thing shall I do?'[26] Two things, therefore, are mentioned together—'good' and 'master'—and, since He does not find fault with being called 'good,' His criticism must be against the term 'good master.' But, He voiced His objection to the title of good master in such a way as to blame the faith of the questioner rather than the designation of Himself as a master or as good. The young man, who had become arrogant through the observance of the Law and did not know the consummation of the Law which is Christ, who believed that He was justified by works, and who was not aware that He had come for the lost sheep of the house of Israel, and that the Law could not save those who believed through the faith of justification, questions the Lord of the Law and the only-begotten God as if He were the teacher of precepts that were ordinary and written down in the Law. Hence, the Lord rejected this declaration of a godless faith about

25 Matt. 11.28-30.
26 Cf. Mark 10.17.

Himself, because the question was put to Him as if He were a teacher of the Law, and replied: 'Why do you call me good?' And, in order to make known how much He was to be recognized and acknowledged as good, He declared: 'No one is good but God only,' since He does not find fault with the attribute of goodness when this is given to Him as God.

(17) Finally, He made known that He censured the name of a good master because of the faith of him who questioned Him as if He were a man, and thus replied to the young man who prided himself and gloried in fulfilling the Law: 'One thing is lacking to thee; go, sell whatever thou hast, and give to the poor, and thou shalt have treasure in heaven; and come, follow me.'[27] He who promises a heavenly treasure does not avoid the name of goodness in reference to Himself, nor is He unwilling to be looked upon as a master who offers Himself as a guide to this perfect beatitude. He finds fault with a worldly estimate of Himself, while He teaches that goodness is in God alone. And to emphasize that He is God as well as good, He exercises the duties of goodness when He opens the treasures of heaven and proposes Himself as a guide to them. Thus, on the one hand, he abhors whatever was offered to him merely as a man, and, on the other, He declared that He was not a stranger to these qualities which He attributed to God, since, while recognizing the one God as good, He Himself spoke of and performed those actions which are associated with the power, the goodness, and the nature of God.

(18) How He rejected the name of goodness, therefore, and did not repudiate the glory of a master, but the faith of him who recognized in Him only what was corporeal and carnal is seen from this fact, that He spoke differently to the Apostles, who acknowledged Him as their master when He

---

27 Mark 10.21.

said: 'You call me Master and Lord, and you say well, for so I am,'[28] and when He declared in another place: 'Do not be called masters, for your master is Christ.'[29] Where He is a master in harmony with the faith, there He praises so highly that He even acknowledges this name, but, here, He does not recognize the name of a good master, where He is not looked upon as the Lord nor as the Christ. While He proclaims the one God as alone good, He by no means separates Himself from God, since He asserts that He is the Lord and the Christ and reveals Himself as the guide to the treasures of heaven.

(19)   The Lord always adhered to this arrangement of the faith of the Church, so that, while He proclaims the one God the Father, He does not separate Himself from the mystery of the one God, while He asserts that through the nature of His birth He is neither another God nor is He Himself,[30] because the nature of the one God in Him does not permit Him to be a God of a different nature, nor is it compatible with a birth that he who is a son is not a perfect son. Thus, He can neither be kept apart from God nor is He Himself. Therefore, He carefully prepared all the statements in His sermons in such a manner that, whatever honor He claimed for God the Father, He revealed in a most unassuming confession as also proper to Himself. For, when He says: 'Believe in God and believe also in me,'[31] I ask in what way does He make any distinction in the nature who does not make any distinction in the glory? When He who declares: 'And believe in me,' after He had said: 'And believe in God,' are we not to understand by the words 'in me' that He meant His own nature?

---

28 John 13.13.
29 Cf. Matt. 23.10.
30 That is, He is not the person of God the Father under a different name.
31 Cf. John 14.1.

Separate the nature altogether, if you separate the faith!
If it is life to believe in God without Christ, then take away
from Christ both the name and the real nature of God. But,
if it produces life for those who believe in God to believe also
in Christ, then let the diligent reader weigh the meaning
of the saying: 'Believe in God, and believe also in me.' When
He says: 'Believe in God, and believe also in me,' He who
joins Himself to the faith of God has also joined Himself
to His nature, since, after mentioning the God in whom we
are to believe, He also taught that we are to believe in
Him, thereby teaching that He is God, since those who
believe in God must believe in Him. Christ obviated any
pretext of a godless union, because, when He declared that
we must believe in God and believe in Him, He did away
with the possibility of believing in Him as a solitary person.

(20) Hence, although He offered an explanation of this
mystery in very many, in fact in almost all, of His statements,
that He might not separate Himself from His unity after
speaking of God as His Father, and that He might not
acknowledge Him as one and solitary when He had placed
Himself in unity with Him, we also realize that the revelation of the unity and the birth was being taught in a very
special way from these words when He said: 'The witness,
however, that I have is greater than that of John. For the
works which my Father has given me to accomplish, these
very works that I do bear witness to me, that the Father has
sent me. And the Father himself, who has sent me, has borne
witness to me. But you have never heard his voice, or seen
his form. And you do not have his word abiding in you,
since you do not believe him whom he has sent.'[32]

How do we truly know that the Father has given testimony
to the Son, since He Himself has not been seen nor has His
voice been heard? I am, of course, aware that the voice from

---

32 Cf. John 5.36-39.

heaven was heard saying: 'This is my beloved Son, in whom I am well pleased, hear this one.'[33] And how was not the voice of God heard, since the voice that was heard indicated that it was the Father's voice? But, perhaps those who were in Jerusalem did not hear it, because John alone heard it in the desert? We must therefore ascertain how the Father gave testimony in Jerusalem? He does not appeal any longer to the testimony of John, who heard the voice from heaven, but He has a greater testimony than John, and He immediately added what this was: 'For the works which my Father has given me to accomplish, these very works that I do bear witness to me, that the Father has sent me.' I recognize the force of the testimony, for no one except the Son who was sent by the Father did these things. Consequently, the work is His testimony. What follows after this? 'And the Father himself, who has sent me, has borne witness to me. But you have never heard his voice, or seen his form. And you do not have his word abiding in you, since you do not believe him whom he has sent.'

Are they guiltless, therefore, who do not recognize the testimony of the Father, since He has never been heard or seen among them, and in them His word does not remain? But, they cannot excuse themselves on the plea that the testimony is unknown to them, because He declares that the testimony of His own works is the testimony of the Father about Him. Hence, His works give evidence that He has been sent by the Father, but this testimony of the works is that of the Father. And, since the work of the Son is the testimony of the Father, we must grasp the fact that that nature works in Christ through which the Father is also a witness. Thus it is revealed that Christ who works and the Father who bears witness in His work have an inseparable nature as a con-

---

33 Cf. Matt. 3.17.

sequence of the birth, since that very work of Christ is designated as the Father's testimony about Him.

(21) Consequently, they are not free from blame because they did not know the testimony, since the work of Christ is the testimony of the Father about Him. Hence, they are not kept in ignorance of the testimony, because they have not heard the voice of Him who testifies, or seen His form, or because His word does not remain in them. For, to that which was said: 'But you have not heard his voice, or seen his form. And you do not have his word abiding in you,' in order that they might still understand why they had not heard His voice, and why they had not seen His form, and why His word had not remained in them, He at once added: 'Since you do not believe him whom he has sent,' showing thereby that, if they believed in Him, the voice of God would be heard, His form would be seen, and His word would be in those who believed, since, as a consequence of the unity of nature, the Father would speak in Him, would be seen in Him, and would be possessed in Him. Does He not also designate the Father, since He has been sent by Him? Does He separate Himself from the Father by any difference of nature, when the Father, who bears witness to Him, is therefore not heard, nor seen, nor perceived, because they do not believe that He has been sent by the Father? The only-begotten God, therefore, does not dissociate Himself from God, when He acknowledges God as His Father, but, while He reveals that God is His Father by using the title of Father, He also attributes the glory of God to Himself.

(22) In this very same sermon, where He teaches that His works testify that He has been sent by the Father, and points out that the Father gives evidence that He has been sent by Him, although He had declared: 'And you do not seek the glory of him, who is the only God,'[34] still, He did

---

34 Cf. John 5.44.

not leave us this bare statement without any previous preparation for the faith of the unity. Just before, He had spoken thus: 'You are not willing to come to me that you may have life. I do not receive glory from men. But I know that you have not the love of God in you. I have come in the name of my Father, and you have not received me. If another comes in his own name, him you will receive. How can you believe who receive glory from men, and do not seek the glory of him, who is the only God?'[35]

He rejects the glory from men, because we should rather seek glory from God, and it is characteristic of unbelievers to seek glory from one another. For, what glory will a man give to a man? Hence He says that He is aware that the love of God is not found in them, and teaches that this is the reason why the love of God does not remain in them, because they do not receive Him who comes in the name of His Father. What does it mean, I ask, for Him to come in the name of the Father? Is it something different from the name of God? Or is it, therefore, that the love of God is not in them, because He has not been received as one who comes in the name of God? Or did He not indicate that the nature of God is in Him when He says: 'You are not willing to come to me that you may have life.' He Himself had already stated in the same discourse: 'Amen, amen, I say to you, the hour is coming, and now is here, in which the dead shall hear the voice of the Son of God, and those who hear shall live.'[36]

When He comes in the name of the Father, He Himself is not the Father; nevertheless, He possesses that nature of the Godhead which the Father possesses, because it is proper to Him who is the Son as well as God to come in the name of God the Father. Furthermore, another who comes in the same name is to be received. But, this one is a man from

35 Cf. John 5.40-44.
36 Cf. John 5.25.

whom men will hope to obtain glory for themselves, and to whom they will again render honor, since this same one, however, will deceive them as if he had come in the name of the Father. And it is indeed evident that by this man is meant the Anti-christ, who glories in the deceitful use of the Father's name. Since they will honor this one and be honored by him (for they will receive this spirit of error), they will not seek the honor of Him who is the only God.

(23) Since this is the reason why they do not possess the love of God, because they have not received Him who comes in the name of the Father, and again receive another who comes in the same name, and do not seek for the glory of Him who is the only God while they accept glory from one another, is it possible for us to believe that Christ is separating Himself from the glory of the one God, since the glory of the only God, therefore, is not being sought, because they have received the Anti-christ but have not received Him? For, if in rejecting Him they neglect the glory of the only God, then in honoring Him they must pay honor to the only God, since, if they had not refused to receive Him, they would have sought the glory of the only God.

This very same discourse is a witness in our favor, for it states in the beginning: 'That all men may honor the Son even as they honor the Father. He who does not honor the Son, does not honor the Father who sent him.'[37] Unless things are of the same nature, they are never accorded equal honor, and equality of honor does not bring about a separation in those who are to be honored. But, the mystery of the birth demands equality of honor. Since we must honor the Son just as we do the Father, and since the honor of Him who is the only God is not being sought, He is not excluded from the honor of the only God, whose honor is also one and the same with that of God. For, as he who dishonors the Son

---

37 John 5.23.

also dishonors the Father, He who does not seek the honor of the only God is also not seeking that of Christ. As a consequence, the honor of Christ is inseparable from the honor of God. And He also teaches how much the two are one and the same when, after hearing the news of the sickness of Lazarus, He declared: 'This sickness is not unto death, but for the glory of God, that through it the Son of God may be glorified.'[38] Lazarus dies for the glory of God in order that the Son of God may be glorified through Lazarus. Is there any doubt that the glory of God is in the glory of the Son of God, since the death of Lazarus, which is glorious for God, shall bring glory to the Son of God? Thus, the natural unity of God the Father in Christ is taught by means of the birth, since the sickness of Lazarus is for the sake of God's glory, and the mystery of the faith is retained, since the Son of God is to be glorified through Lazarus. While we perceive from this that the Son of God is God, we are not to conceive of Him as God in such a manner that we do not also acknowledge Him as the Son of God, since by the glorification of God through Lazarus the Son of God is glorified.

(24) By the mystery of the divine nature the birth of the living one is inseparable from the living one, nor does the Son of God suffer any change in His nature so that the truth of the Father's nature does not abide in Him. Even in these expressions where He has acknowledged the one God and appears to repudiate the nature of God in Him by His emphasis upon the word 'only,' He has identified Himself with the unity of the Father's nature without destroying the faith in the one God. When He was asked by the Scribe what was the principal commandment in the Law, He replied: 'Hear, O Israel! The Lord our God is one Lord; and thou shalt love the Lord thy God with thy whole heart, and with thy whole soul, and with thy whole spirit, and with

---

38 John 11.4.

thy whole strength! This is the first commandment. The
second is like it, Thou shalt love thy neighbor as thyself.
But there is no commandment greater than these.'[39]

They imagine that He has excluded Himself from the
nature and the worship of the one God, since this is the
confession of the principal commandment: 'Hear, O Israel!
The Lord our God is one Lord,' and, furthermore, He does
not even include Himself in the obligation of the following
commandment when the Law calls us to the love of our
neighbor as it does to the faith in the one God. We certainly
should not overlook the answer of the Scribe when he declares: 'Well answered, Master, thou hast said truly that
God is one and there is no other besides him; and so he is
to be loved with the whole heart, and with the whole strength
and with the whole soul. This is greater than all holocausts
and sacrifices.'[40] The response of the Scribe seems to be in
agreement with the words of the Lord, since he recognizes
the intimate and interior love of the one God, but measures
the love of one's neighbor in accordance with the true love
of one's self, and believes that the love for God and man
is superior to the burnt offerings of sacrifices. But we must
examine that which follows.

(25) Jesus, seeing that he had answered wisely, said to
him: 'Thou art not far from the kingdom of God.'[41] What
is the meaning of so gracious a reply that this Scribe is not
yet in the kingdom of God but is not far from the kingdom
of God, if to believe in the one God and to love Him with
your whole soul, with your whole strength, and with your
whole heart, and also to love your neighbor as yourself is the
faith that makes us ready for the kingdom of heaven? In
another statement, this is bestowed upon those who clothe

---

39 Cf. Mark 12.29-31.
40 Cf. Mark 12.32,33.
41 Mark 12.34.

the naked, feed the hungry, give drink to the thirsty, visit the sick, and come to those in prison: 'Come, blessed of my Father, take possession of the kingdom prepared for you from the foundation of the world.'[42] Or to those who receive this as a reward for being poor in spirit: 'Blessed are the poor in spirit, for theirs is the kingdom of heaven.'[43] This is the perfect fruit, the complete possession, and the clear handing over of a kingdom that is already prepared. Or did the young man confess anything that was less noble than any of these? Since he made the love of his neighbor equal to the love of himself, what was wanting to him in order that a good work might be perfect? To be courteous and obliging at times is not the mark of perfect love, but perfect love satisfies every obligation of a universal charity, since he who bestows upon another as much as he does upon himself does not remain indebted to anyone for anything.

But, while the Lord praises the Scribe, who has lived in ignorance of the perfect mystery, for his profession of faith, and replies that he is not far from the kingdom of God, He does not confer upon him the possession of the blessed hope itself. He was journeying along a favorable course, even though unaware of it, since he made the love of God superior to everything else, and placed the love of his neighbor on an equal level with the love of himself. Since he had preferred the love of God even to this love of his neighbor, he was no longer confined by the commandments regarding holocausts and sacrifices. This was not far removed from the revelation of the Gospel.

(26) We must learn from the Lord's own words why He tells him that he is not far from the kingdom of God rather than that he will be in the kingdom of God. For, this is followed by: 'And no one after that ventured to ask

---

42 Matt. 25.34.
43 Matt. 5.3.

him questions. And while Jesus was teaching in the temple
he addressed them, saying, How do the Scribes say that
Christ is the Son of David? For David himself says, by the
Holy Spirit, The Lord said to my Lord: Sit thou at my right
hand, till I make thy enemies the footstool of thy feet. David
himself calls him Lord; how then is he his son?'[44] The Scribe,
therefore, is not far from the kingdom of God when he
acknowledges the one God who is to be loved above all
things. But he is warned by his own confession why he does
not know the mystery of the Law and does not realize that
Christ the Lord, the Son of God by the nature of the birth,
is to be acknowledged in the faith of the one Lord. And
because in accordance with the Law's confession of faith in
the one God it did not seem possible for the Son of God to
be included in the mystery of the one Lord, He asks the
Scribe how David can call Christ his son, since David had
called Him his Lord, and nature does not allow the son of
so great a patriarch to be his Lord at the same time.

Consequently, this should remind the Scribe, who only
recognized Him according to the flesh and the birth from
Mary, who was descended from David, that He was the
Lord rather than the son of David according to the Spirit,
and that the words, 'Hear, O Israel! The Lord our God is
one Lord,' did not exclude Christ from the mystery of the
one Lord, since so great a patriarch and prophet had recognized Him as the Lord, who was begotten from the womb of
God before the day-star. He is not unmindful of the Law
by any means, nor is he ignorant of the fact that we must
not acknowledge another God, but, without doing any
violence to the faith of the Law, He gives us to understand
that He is the Lord who has come into being by the mystery
of the natural birth from the womb of the incorporeal God,
since the one from the one through the nature of the one

44 Cf. Mark 12.34-37.

Lord would possess that nature in Himself which belongs to the Lord.

(27) Accordingly, what room is there left for doubt? When the Lord Himself teaches that the principal commandment consists in the confession and love of the one Lord, He did not make use of His own testimony, but that of the Prophet, to prove that He is the Lord, yet He indicated that He is always the Lord, because He is the Son of God. He remains, therefore, in the mystery of the one God through the birth, because He does not become a second God by a difference in nature, for the birth from God preserves the nature of God in Him. The true nature of the birth does not deprive the Father of being the Lord; similarly, it does not result in the Son not being the Lord. Thus, the Father does not lose His attribute as the originator nor does the Son not cling to the nature. Wherefore, God the Father is not the one Lord, nor is the only-begotten God the Lord separated from the one, since He Himself subsists as the one Lord from the one Lord, while, in accordance with the Law, He proclaims the one Lord in such a manner that the Prophet also testifies that He is the Lord.

(28) Let the answer of the evangelical faith be directed to the other assertions of the godless rage; let it repulse them by these very means by which it is attacked, and, while it conquers with the weapons destined for its destruction, let the words of the one Spirit be a proof for the doctrine of the one faith! There is no other Christ than He who is proclaimed, that is to say, the true God who also abides in the glory of the one true God, and, just as He declared that He was the Lord in accordance with the Law while He seemed to deny it, so He also revealed Himself as the true God in the Gospels, while He appeared to assert the opposite opinion. In order that they may refuse recognition to Him as the true God, the heretics allege this saying of His

as a pretext: 'But this is everlasting life that they may know thee, the only true God, and him whom thou hast sent, Jesus Christ.' When He uses the words, 'Thee, the only true God,' they imagine that He is separating Himself from the true nature of God by restricting it to one who is alone, since the only true God does not allow Himself to be considered as anything else than a solitary God. Certainly the apostolic faith forbids us to believe in two true gods, because nothing alien to the nature of the one God should be placed on an equality with the truth of the same nature. For, there will not be one God in the true nature of the one God, if, outside the nature of the one true God, there exists a true God of a different nature whose nature does not belong to Him by birth.

(29) In order that we may realize that by this very same statement He asserted in no ambiguous fashion that He was the true God in the nature of the one true God, we shall explain the faith step by step, proceeding from His previous utterances, which are connected and bound up with it, so that the assurance of our liberty may then establish Christ at the summit of the true God. Hence, after the mystery of His pronouncement in which He had declared: 'He who has seen me has seen also the Father,' and 'Do you not believe me that I am in the Father and the Father in me? The words that I speak to you I speak not on my own authority. But the Father dwelling in me it is He who does his works. Believe me, that I am in the Father and the Father in me; otherwise believe because of the works themselves,'[45] and after this discourse on the sublime mysteries the disciples, therefore, gave their answer in the following words: 'Now we know that thou hast known all things, and dost not need that anyone should question thee. For this reason we believe

45 Cf. John 14.9-12.

that thou camest forth from God.'[46] From the power of God in Him they also became aware of the nature of God that was in Him, for to know all things and to be familiar with the thoughts of the hearts is characteristic of the Son of God rather than of His messenger. Accordingly, they express it as their belief that He has come forth from God because the power of God's nature was in Him.

(30) The Lord replied by praising their understanding, and certainly it was not in regard to His being sent but to His coming forth from God, for by designating it as a procession He bore witness to the coming forth which took place through the birth from the incorporeal God. He Himself also referred to His birth by pointing out that it was a procession, when He declared: 'You love me and believe that I came forth from God, and have come from the Father into this world.'[47] He comes from the Father into this world because He has come forth from God. To make us realize that by the procession He was referring to His birth, He added that He had come from the Father. Since He had come from the Father, therefore, because He had come forth from God, this procession from God is the perfect birth to which the confession of the Father's name has been joined. Hence, He addressed these words to the Apostles who understood this mystery of the procession: 'Now you believe. Behold the hour is coming, and has now come for each one to be dispersed to his own house, and to leave me alone. But I am not alone, because the Father is with me.'[48]

In order to teach that this procession was not an alienation from God the Father, but a birth which preserves the nature of God the Father in Him by His being born, He added that He is not alone, but that the Father is with Him,

---

46 Cf. John 16.30.
47 Cf. John 16.27,28.
48 Cf. John 16.31,32.

by the power certainly and by the unity of nature, since the
Father would abide with Him, working and speaking in Him
while He speaks and works. Then, to reveal the reason for
this whole discourse of His, He continued: 'These things
I have spoken to you that in me you may have peace. In
this world, however, you will have affliction. But be consoled,
because I have overcome the world.'[49] He spoke these words,
therefore, in order that they might remain tranquil and might
not differ through an eagerness for quarrels over questions of
faith, since He who would be left alone would not be alone,
and He who had come forth from God would possess in
Himself the God from whom He had come forth. Moreover,
when they met with persecutions in the world, they would
persevere, remembering the promises of Him who had conquered the world by proceeding from God and having God
with Him.

(31)   Finally, when He was about to speak about the
faith of the entire mystery, after raising His eyes to heaven,
He said: 'Father, the hour has come! Glorify thy Son, that
thy Son may glorify thee, even as thou hast given him power
over all flesh, in order that to all thou hast given him he
may give everlasting life.'[50] In your opinion, does He appear
helpless in asking to be glorified? Let Him be completely
helpless if He does not ask to be glorified, therefore, in order
that He may glorify the one who has glorified Him. We
have discussed the glory that is to be received and to be
returned in another Book,[51] and it would be wholly superfluous to repeat these same remarks. There is clearly no
doubt, therefore, that He is asking for glory in order that He
who bestows it may be glorified.

But, perhaps He is weak because He has received power

49 Cf. John 16.33.
50 John 17.1,2.
51 Cf. above, 3.9-16.

over all flesh. Let the acceptance of power be also a weakness, if He is unable to grant eternal life to those whom He has received. But, He is accused of having a certain weakness of nature by the very fact that He has also received. The acceptance may indeed be a weakness if Christ is not the true God by reason of the birth rather than by reason of not being born. If the acceptance of power indicates the birth in which He has received that which He is, then the bestowal is not to be ascribed to weakness, since it produces this effect, that the one born is everything that God is. Since the unborn God is the author of the divine blessedness in the perfect birth of the only-begotten God, the mystery of the Father is to be the author of the birth.

Besides, there is no degradation associated with that which results in Him being the image of His author by a real birth. To have given power to all flesh and to have given it in order that it may have eternal life brings it about that the bestower is that which the Father is, and the receiver is that which God is, since He is designated as the Father inasmuch as He has given, and the Son remains God inasmuch as He has received the power of conferring eternal life. Accordingly, all power is natural to and congenital with the Son of God. And, since it has been given, it does not alienate Him from the author because it has been given, since what has been given belongs to the author, namely, to bestow eternal life and to change corruption into incorruption. Hence, the Father has given all things and the Son has received all things. Nor is there any doubt about this, since He has said: 'All things that the Father has are mine.'[52] Here, it is true, the present discourse does not point to any species of creatures or any material changes in the elements, but, while it reveals the glory of the blessed and complete Godhead to us, it makes known that God is to be recognized in those

---

52 John 16.15.

things that are His own, in the strength, in the eternity, in the providence, and in the power, not that we are to believe that God possesses these attributes in such a manner that they are, as it were, something outside of Himself, but that our power of reasoning can comprehend Him to some extent by reason of the attributes which belong to Him. Hence, the Only-begotten, who taught that He had come into existence with the qualities that are characteristic of His Father and who declared that the Holy Spirit would receive them from Him, added: 'All things that the Father has are mine. That is why I have said that he will receive of what is mine.' All that the Father has is His, has been certainly handed over to Him, and has been received. But these attributes which have been given, and which assign to Him those which the Father has, do not weaken the divinity.

(32)   These are the steps, therefore, which He followed in giving us advance knowledge about Himself: He taught that He had come forth from the Father, asserted that the Father was with Him, testified that He had overcome the world, and that He who was to be glorified by the Father would glorify the Father, and would make use of the power which He had received in bestowing everlasting life upon all flesh. Then He summed up all these teachings in this concluding explanation: 'But this is everlasting life, that they may know thee, the only true God, and him whom thou hast sent, Jesus Christ.' O heretic, learn either to speak of or to believe in the faith of eternal life! And, if you can, detach Christ from God, the Son from the Father, the God over all things from the true God, the one from the only one (for there is one Lord Jesus Christ), if it is eternal life to believe in the one true God without Christ! But, if you do not obtain eternal life by the confession of the only true God, after you have separated Christ from the only true God, then I fail to understand how we are to separate Him from

the true God for our faith, who does not allow Himself to be separated for salvation.

(33) Hence, although I realize that the leisurely solution of difficult questions does not meet with the wishes of my readers, I think that it will produce no little gain if I pause for a while in my exposition of the complete faith and engage in a struggle with you, O heretic, about the very words of the Gospel. You hear the statement of the Lord who says: 'But this is everlasting life, that they may know thee, the only true God, and him whom thou hast sent, Jesus Christ.' What is it, I ask, that causes you to understand that Christ is not the true God? No other expression has now been added to make known to you what you should believe about Christ. You possess nothing else except 'Jesus Christ,' not the Son of Man, as He was wont to call Himself, nor the Son of God, as He generally referred to Himself, nor the living bread, which comes down from heaven, a phrase that He often used about Himself to the scandal of many. But, when He says: 'Thee, the only true God, and him whom thou hast sent, Jesus Christ,' He has passed over all the customary names and titles, whether by birth or adoption, so that we have no hesitation in singling out Jesus Christ as God, since we are to acknowledge the only true God and Christ Jesus as the givers of eternal life.

(34) Perhaps the words 'thee, the only' are incompatible with His partnership and unity with God. They may indeed be incompatible, if to the words, 'thee, the only true God,' He did not immediately add: 'and him, whom thou hast sent, Jesus Christ.' I appeal to the judgment of the hearer about what we are to believe about Jesus Christ, since in addition to our belief that the Father is the only true God we must also believe in Christ. But, perhaps the Father as the only true God has left nothing for Christ to be God. It may well be that He has left nothing, if the one God the Father has

left nothing for Christ to be the Lord. But, if the one God the Father does not deprive Christ of being the one God, so the only God the true Father does not take anything away from Christ so that He is not the true God, since this leads us to the reward of eternal life that while believing in the only true God we also believe in Christ.

(35)   O heretic, I now ask you this question. In accordance with the opinion of your folly, what are we to hold about Christ, about Christ who has bestowed eternal life, who has overcome the world, who is not alone, even though He is to be left alone, but has the Father with Him, and who has come forth from God and has come from the Father? What nature and divinity will you confer upon Him, who has been born with such great powers of God? It is useless for us to believe in the only true God the Father if we do not also believe in Christ whom He has sent. Why do you hesitate? Teach us what we are to confess about Christ! For you who deny what has been written, what is there left for you but to believe what has not been written. O unhappy will and falsehood that resists the truth! If Christ is joined to the faith and confession of the true God the Father, I ask you by what faith will He be designated as a creature whom you refuse to accept as the true God, since there is no faith in believing in the true God without Christ? The meaning of the heavenly words does not gain admission into you who are narrow and incapable of the divine Spirit; urged on by the error of the Serpent, you do not realize that you must recognize Christ as the true God in the faith of the only true God in order that you may obtain eternal life.

(36)   But, the faith of the Church, which acknowledges the only true God the Father, also acknowledges Christ. When it acknowledges Christ as the true God it also acknowledges the Father as the only true God, and, again, when

acknowledging the Father as the only true God it also acknowledges Christ as such. By acknowledging Christ as the true God it acknowledges the Father as the only true God. Thus, the fact that God the Father is the only true God is also a confirmation of Christ as the true God. The natural birth has not brought about any change of nature in the only-begotten God, and He who subsists as God from the subsisting God, in accordance with the nature of the divine birth, cannot be separated from the divinity of His nature who is the only true God. But, the nature of the divinity has preserved its own order, so that the divinity of the nature might gain admission for the divinity of the birth, and the one God will not bring forth a God of another nature from Himself.

Thus, the mystery of God does not consist in solitude or in divinity, since He will not be looked upon as another God who subsists from God with the attributes of His own nature, and He does not remain in a union, since the divinity of the birth teaches that we are to acknowledge Him as the Father. Hence, the God who has been born has not renounced the qualities of His own nature and they are in Him by the natural birth from Him whose nature He preserves in Himself by the natural birth. In Him there is not a God who has been either changed or of a lower category, since, if the birth has produced any defect, it would bring disgrace rather upon the nature which brought Him into being by the birth, while that which is from Him would cease to be that which is His own, and thus a change would not weaken Him who had been formed into a new substance by the birth, but Him who was unable to preserve the strength of His own nature in the birth of the Son and had begotten something foreign or alien to Himself.

(37)   As we have already mentioned on many occasions,

the unity of God the Father and God the Son is not to be understood in accordance with the insufficiency of our human concepts, so that it is either an extension, or a lineage, or an emanation, or like a fountain that pours forth a stream from its source, or like a tree which fastens the branch to the trunk, or like a fire that sends forth heat into the atmosphere. These objects are an inseparable extension of themselves and bound together rather than existing by themselves, since the heat is in the fire, the branch in the tree, and the river in the fountain. And this thing itself is alone by itself rather than a thing that has received its being from an existing thing, because the tree cannot be something different from the branch, nor the fire from the heat, nor the fountain from the stream. But, the only-begotten God is the God who subsists by a perfect and indescribable birth, and is the true offspring of the unborn God, the incorporeal birth of an incorporeal nature, the living and the true God from the living and the true God, and the God who is inseparable from the nature of God, while the subsisting birth has not brought about a God of a different nature, nor has the generation which produced the substance changed the nature of the substance in its kind.

(38) By the dispensation of the assumed flesh and the obedience of Him who emptied Himself of the form of God, Christ who was born as man has taken a new nature upon Himself, not by any loss of His power or His nature but by a change in His appearance. Hence, He who emptied Himself of the form of God received the form of a slave when He was born. But, that nature of the Father, which was joined to His own by a natural unity, did not experience this assumption of the flesh, and, although the temporal newness continued in the power of the nature, it lost the unity of nature with the form of God in the man who was as-

sumed.[53] The sum total of the economy of salvation was this, that the complete Son, namely, He who was both man and God, would now inhere in the nature of the Father through a concession of the Father's will, and He who remained in the power of the nature also remained in the genus of the nature.

That was acquired that man should be God. But, the man who was assumed could in no way remain in the unity of God unless He ascended to the unity of the natural God through the unity with God, so that from the fact that God the Word was in the nature of God, the Word made flesh would also again be in the nature of God, and thus the man Jesus Christ would remain in the glory of God the Father if the flesh were united with the glory of the Word, and then the Word made flesh, even in its manhood, would return to the unity of the Father's nature, since the flesh that was assumed had taken possession of the glory of the Word. Hence, His own unity with the Father must be restored to Him,[54] in order that the birth of His nature, which is to be glorified, might take up its abode in Him, because the newness of the plan of salvation had brought about an obstacle to the unity and there could not be a perfect unity, as there had been formerly, if the flesh that had been assumed were not glorified with Him.

(39) Therefore, after He had previously prepared their minds in so thorough a manner for the understanding of this faith, when He had said: 'But this is everlasting life, that they may know thee, the only true God, and him whom

---

53 The preceding Book had clearly shown that Hilary believed in the unity of the divine and human natures in the Son of God in the Incarnation. From the words that immediately follow it seems indisputable that his unusual terminology means that the Son of God renounced the glory that was due to His divine nature when He became man and this glory was restored to Him when He rose from the dead.

54 That is, to the Son.

thou hast sent, Jesus Christ,' He added, in accordance with
the obedience of His own plan of salvation: 'I have glorified
thee on earth; I have accomplished the work that thou hast
given me to do.' Then, in order that we might realize the
reward of obedience and the mystery of the whole dispensation, He continued: 'And now do thou, Father, glorify me
with thyself, with the glory that I had with thee before the
world existed.'[55]

He who denies that Christ remains in the nature of God
and does not believe that He is inseparable from and identical
with the only true God, let him explain the purpose of this
petition: 'And now do thou, Father, glorify me with thyself.' On what grounds should the Father glorify Him with
Himself? Or what is the meaning of this statement? And
what effect follows from it? The Father does not need glory,
nor has He emptied Himself, and how will He glorify Him
with that glory which He had with Him before the foundation of the world? Furthermore, what is the significance of
the words, to have with Him? He does not say: 'The glory
that I had before the world existed when I was with you,'
but: 'The glory that I had with you.' For, 'to be with you'
means to be at your side, but 'to have with you' reveals the
mystery of the nature. But, 'glorify me with thyself' is not
the same as 'glorify me.' He does not merely ask to be glorified
with Him in such a manner that He may have some glory
that is peculiarly His own, but He prays to the Father that
He may glorify Him with Himself. The Father was to glorify
Him with Himself in order that He might remain in His
unity as He had remained, because the unity of His glory
had departed from Him through His obedience in the plan
of salvation, that is to say, through His glorification He
might be once again in that nature wherein He was united
through the mystery of the divine birth, and be glorified by

---

55 John 17.4,5.

the Father with Himself, so that He might remain what He had formerly enjoyed with Him and that the assumption of the form of a slave might not estrange Him from the nature of the form of God, but that He might glorify the form of a slave with Himself, so that it might continue to be the form of God, because He who was in the form of God was the same one as He who was in the form of a slave. And, since the form of a slave was to be glorified in the form of God, it was to be glorified with Him in whose form the appearance of the form of a slave was to be honored.

(40) These words of the Lord are not new, nor are they now mentioned for the first time in the teachings of the Gospel, and He bore testimony to this very fact, the mystery of God the Father who is to glorify the Son with Himself, in that most sublime joy of His own hope, when, after Judas had gone forth to the betrayal, He expressed His happiness at the consummation of the plan of salvation in these words: 'Now is the Son of Man glorified, and God is glorified in him. If God has been glorified in him, and God has glorified him in himself, and God has glorified him at once.'[56] Why are our souls, weighed down by a body made of dust, our souls, polluted and stained with the foul consciousness of sin, puffed up with pride to such an extent that we pass judgment on the confession of God about Himself? How can we who regard ourselves as judges of the heavenly nature rebel against God with our impious and slanderous debates? The Lord expressed the faith of the Gospel in words as simple as possible, and adapted them to our understanding in so far as the weakness of our nature could grasp them, yet He did not say anything that was unbecoming the majesty of His nature.

I certainly regard the first part of His words as free from ambiguity when He declares: 'Now is the Son of Man glorified.' All the glory was acquired not for the Word but

---

56 Cf. John 13.31,32.

for the flesh, that is, not for the birth of God, but for the dispensation of Him who was born as man. But I ask what is the meaning of these words that follow: 'And God has been glorified in him.' I hear that God has been glorified in Him, and, O heretic, I am unaware of what meaning you attach to this statement. God has been glorified in Him, in the Son of Man, of course, and I raise the question: Is the Son of Man the same as the Son of God? Since there is no other Son of Man and no other Son of God (for the Word was made flesh), and since He who is the Son of God is also Himself the Son of Man, I ask what God has been glorified in this Son of Man who is also the Son of God?

(41) Because God has been glorified in the Son of Man who is also the Son of God, let us see what is added in the third place: 'If God has been glorified in him and God has glorified him in himself.' What, I ask, is the mystery of this secret revelation? In the glorified Son of Man, God glorifies the glorified God in Himself. The glory of God is in the Son of Man and the glory of God is in the glory of the Son of Man. God gives glory in Himself. Assuredly, man is not glorified by himself. Again, it is God Himself who is glorified in man; although He will receive glory, He Himself is not anything else than that which God is. But, after the glorification of the Son of Man, the God who glorifies God glorifies in Himself, I discover that the glory of the nature is assumed into the glory of the nature that glorifies the nature.[57] God does not glorify Himself but glorifies in Himself the God who has been glorified in man. That which He glorifies in Himself, although He does not glorify Himself, He who glorifies the nature assumes it into the glory of His own nature. And since God glorifies God, because He has been glorified in man, He

---

57 The nature which glorifies the nature of the Son is the nature of the Father, and the nature of the Father is glorified by the glory of the Son.

glorifies Him in Himself and proves that the God is in Him whom He has glorified, since He glorified Him in Himself.

O heretic, whoever you are, bring forth the unsolvable questions of your tortuous doctrine, and, though they may be twisted together with their own knots, still, no matter how they are arranged, they will not keep us in the embarrassing situation of being unable to extricate ourselves. For, the Son of Man is glorified and God is glorified in Him, and God, who has glorified Him in the man, has glorified Him in Himself. It is not the same thing for the Son of Man to be glorified as it is for God to be also glorified in the Son of Man, or for God to glorify in Himself Him who has been glorified in the man. Tell us in your own words, and in keeping with your godless interpretation, what meaning you wish to place on the words: God is glorified in the Son of Man. Evidently, it must be either Christ, who is glorified in the flesh, or the Father who is glorified in Christ. If it is Christ, then Christ is certainly the God who is glorified in the flesh. If it is the Father, then it is the mystery of the unity, since the Father is glorified in the Son. By admitting that it is Christ you will also speak of Him as God even though you do so reluctantly. Or, if you understand that God the Father is meant, you will not deny that the nature of God the Father is in Christ. And may these words about the Son of Man who was glorified and the God who was glorified at the same time in Him be sufficient.

But, in regard to the fact that God glorifies in Himself the God who has been glorified in the Son of Man, are you of the opinion that here at last you have an opportunity for manifesting your godlessness, so that Christ is not the true God according to His real nature? God glorifies in Himself Christ who was born as man. Is it, then, something outside of Himself that He glorifies in Himself? He will restore to

Christ in Himself the glory that He had with Himself, and when the adoption of the form of a slave is assumed into the form of God, the God who was in Him before He emptied Himself in the plan of salvation, and who has been glorified in the man, is glorified in Himself, and has become united to Him both by the form of a slave and the nature of the birth. The birth has not produced a God of a new or an alien nature, but the natural Son has been brought into existence by the birth from the natural Father. And when He who was glorified in the man after the birth of the man again shines forth in the glory of His own nature, God glorifies Him in Himself, while He is assumed into the glory of the Father's nature, of which He had emptied Himself in the plan of salvation.

(42) The apostolic faith raises a barrier to the most insolent rage of your godlessness, in order that you may not roam about freely with your uncontrolled knowledge, when it declares: 'And every tongue will confess that the Lord Jesus Christ is in the glory of God the Father.'[58] We must confess that He whom the Father has glorified in Himself is in His glory. And in regard to Him whom we must confess as being in the glory of the Father and whom the Father has glorified in Himself, we must have no hesitation in believing that He possesses those things which the Father has, since He has glorified Him in Himself and we must acknowledge that He is in His glory. Now, He is not only in the glory of God, but in the glory of God the Father. Nor did He glorify Him with an external glory, but glorified Him in Himself. By restoring Him to that glory which is proper to Him, and to that glory which He had with Him, He also glorified Him with Himself and in Himself.

Thus, we perceive that He is inseparable from the union

---

58 Cf. Phil. 2.11.

of this faith even under the lowly form of man, when He states as follows: 'But this is everlasting life that they may know thee, the only true God, and him whom thou hast sent, Jesus Christ,' since, on the one hand, there is no everlasting life if the Father is recognized as the only God without Christ, and, on the other hand, Christ has been glorified in the Father. Finally, if this is eternal life, to know the only true God and Jesus Christ whom He has sent, then, surely, we may not look upon Christ as the true God if it is life to believe in God without Christ. And that God the Father is the only true God does not affect the God Christ except in so far as all the glory of Christ is in the only true God. For, if the Father glorifies Him in Himself and the Father alone is the true God, then Christ is not excluded from being the only true God, because the only true God the Father glorifies in Himself Christ who has been glorified into God. And if He is glorified in Himself by the only true [God], He is not estranged from the only true [God] because He is glorified in Himself alone by the true [God].

(43)　But, perhaps you will oppose this pious faith of ours with the declaration of your godless infidelity that the following admission of something that is needed does not harmonize with the concept of the true God: 'Amen, amen, I say to you, the Son can do nothing of himself, but only what he sees the Father doing.'[59] If the twofold indignation of the Jews did not require a twofold answer, then the Son is clearly acknowledging His weakness in being unable to do anything except what He sees the Father doing. And if the same statement contains His answer to the double accusation of the Jews, who judged Him guilty of violating the Sabbath and who could not tolerate Him for placing Himself on an equality with God by asserting that God is His Father, do you imagine that the truth of what He said can be obscured

59 John 5.19.

by the confession which He made in His reply? Although we have discussed this passage in another Book,[60] yet, since the reconsideration of our faith will not only offer no obstacle but will prove a positive aid to the true religion, we shall now return to this very same question because the case requires it.

(44) But, first of all, the necessity of making a reply came about as follows: 'And this is why the Jews kept persecuting Jesus and sought to kill him, because he was doing these things on the Sabbath.' Hence, their anger was aroused to such an extent that they sought to kill Him because of the deeds that He had performed on the Sabbath. But let us see what the Saviour answered: 'My Father works even until now, and I work.'[61] I ask you, O heretic, to reveal what that work of the Father is. All things, both visible and invisible, are through the Son and in the Son. And you, who are wiser than the Gospels, must have obtained a knowledge of the Father's work by some other secret doctrines so that you may make us acquainted with the Father who works! And if the Father works in the Son, as He Himself says: 'The words that I speak to you I do not speak, but the Father, who dwells in me, it is he who does his works,'[62] do you now perceive what these words mean: 'My Father works even until now'? He spoke these words, therefore, in order that we might understand the power of the Father's nature in Him, which had employed the nature of His power in the work of the Sabbath. For, since the Father works in Him when He works, He Himself must work when the Father works; hence, He declares: 'My Father works even until now,' in order that even this present work of His words and deeds may be regarded as the work of the Father's nature in Him. For, when He states that He 'works even until now,'

60 Cf. above, 7.15.
61 Cf. John 5.16,17.
62 Cf. John 14.10.

the words and the time are included in one and the same moment, in order that we may not believe that this work that He is doing is some other work of the Father and not His own, since, from the fact that the Father works even until now, this very work of the Father is a work that takes place at the same time as His words.

And lest the faith fail in its hope of eternal life, because it was restricted only to the knowledge of the Father, He at once added: 'And I work,' so that the Son is also engaged in the very work that the Father is now doing. Thus, He taught the perfect faith, since 'now' refers to what is going on at the same moment, and the union of a single person is excluded by the fact that the work that is being done by the Father is also being done by the Son. But, the grief of the listeners was twofold, for these words follow: 'This, then, is why the Jews were seeking the more to put him to death; because he was not only breaking the Sabbath, but was also calling God his own Father, making himself equal to God.'[63] At this point I again remind you that, in accordance with the judgment of the Evangelist and the common consent of all mankind, a son possesses equality with the nature of his father, but the equality is derived from the same nature, because a birth cannot come about in any other way, and every birth bears a relationship with that which begot it, since it has been formed from the same into that which it is. Hence, let us see what the Lord replied to this twofold indignation: 'Amen, amen, I say to you, the Son can do nothing of himself, but only what he sees the Father doing. For whatever he does, the Son also does the same in like manner.'

(45) If these words do not refer to the question that has been raised, then we are doing violence to the words by presumptuously placing upon them our peculiar and unbeliev-

---

63 John 5.18.

ing meaning. But, if the response takes into consideration the reasons that aroused their anger, then our faith can claim to be expressing what is taught more than the godless perversity can defend the error of its own impiety. Hence, let us see whether the following answer is applicable to the work of the Sabbath: 'The Son can do nothing of himself, but only what he sees the Father doing.' He had previously stated: 'My Father works even until now, and I work.' If what He does by the authority of the Father's nature in Him, He does in such a manner that the Father does it, who works even until now on the Sabbath, then the work of the Son is free from blame, since the authority of the Father's work is revealed in it. The phrase 'can do nothing' did not refer to any weakness, but to the source of His authority, for He can do nothing by Himself except what He sees. For, to see does not confer any power, and, since the sight does not confer the power, it does not weaken the nature if He can do nothing without seeing, but he points out the source of His authority by what is seen. The words which He uses, 'but only what he sees,' indicate that His consciousness comes from what He sees, just as He had said to the Apostles: 'Well, I say to you, lift up your eyes and behold that the fields are already white for the harvest.'[64] Consequently, from the consciousness of the Father's nature in Him which works while He works, in order that no one might believe that the Lord of the Sabbath had broken the Sabbath, He declared: 'The Son can do nothing of himself, but only what he sees the Father doing,' so that He proved that the work which He did was dependent upon the consciousness of the nature that was working in Him, since the Father was working even until now on the Sabbath, while He was likewise working on the Sabbath.

The second cause of their ill will prompted Him to issue the following statement: 'For whatever the Father does, the

---

64 John 4.35.

Son also does the same in like manner.' Reproach the Son of God for His weakness, do away with the equality of nature, if the Son does not also perform the same things in a manner similar to that of the Father, if He admits any distinction between the power and the work of the Father, if He does not demand the equality of glory that is befitting the equality of power and nature! He Himself says later on: 'That all men may honor the Son even as they honor the Father. He who does not honor the Son does not honor the Father who sent him.'[65] Separate the equality where the glory is equal! Weaken the nature in which the same power is at work!

(46)   Why do you assail the incident that prompted the reply in order to disparage the divinity? Concerning the work on the Sabbath, He answered that He could do nothing unless He saw the Father doing it, but to bring out the equality He declared that He did everything that the Father did. Hold fast to that which pertains to the Sabbath in order to heap ridicule on the weakness, if everything that the Father does the Son does not also do in like manner! But, if 'everything' admits of no exception, where at length will a weakness be found, since there is nothing that the Father can do that the Son likewise cannot do? Or, finally, why do you allege the weakness as a pretext for denying the equality, since He demands that one and the same honor be accorded to each of them? And last of all, if the same power of working is present as well as the same obligation for paying worship, I do not understand what reasons are left for accusing Him of a weak nature, since there is the same power of the Godhead and the same equality of glory in the Father and the Son.

(47)   Although we have indeed discussed these texts with the greatest thoroughness, still, in order that the Lord's words: 'The Son can do nothing of himself, but only what he sees

---

65 John 5.23.

the Father doing,' may not lead to the impiety of weakening His nature, but, rather, to His awareness of the Father's nature in Him through whom and by whose authority He worked on the Sabbath, we must also point out the significance of the Lord's statement, which refers to this matter, in which He says: 'And of myself I do nothing: but even as the Father has taught me, I speak these things. And he who sent me is with me; he has not left me alone, because I do always the things that are pleasing to him.'[66]

Do you realize what it means for the Son to be unable to do anything unless He sees the Father doing it, and the mystery that is contained in the words: 'And of myself I do nothing,' and again: 'He has not left me alone, because I do always the things that are pleasing to him?' If He does nothing of Himself, therefore, because the Father remains in Him, how can He again declare that the Father has not left Him alone, therefore, because He is always doing the things that are pleasing to Him? According to your interpretation, O heretic, the differences in these statements cannot be reconciled, namely, that He does nothing of Himself unless He has been instructed by the Father who remains in Him, and, again, the Father remains in Him, therefore, because He always does the things that are pleasing to Him. If He does nothing of Himself because of the Father who remains in Him, how did He deserve to have the Father remain in Him by doing the things that are pleasing to Him? There is no merit unless He does by Himself whatever He does. And on the contrary, how does the Son do the things that are pleasing to the Father, since the Father who remains in the Son does these very things? O impiety, you are in a difficult position and the well-fortified piety of our faith presses upon you from every side. The Son either does something or He does not do it. If He does not do it, how is He pleasing to Him in

66 John 8.28,29.

these things that He does? But if He is active how is He active in these things which He does not do by Himself? It is proper to Him to have done the things that are pleasing to Him, and it brings Him no merit if what He has done He has not done by Himself.

(48)   But, my opponent, this is the unity of nature, that He acts through Himself in such a way that He does not act by Himself, and that He does not act by Himself in such a way that He acts through Himself. Grasp the fact that the Son is active and the Father is active through Him! He does not act by Himself, since we have to make known how the Father remains in Him. He acts through Himself when He Himself does the things that are pleasing to Him in accordance with the nature of His birth as the Son. In not acting by Himself He may appear as weak, unless He Himself is active to such an extent that what He does is pleasing to Him. He may seem, however, to be outside the unity of nature, if the things that He Himself does, and in which He is pleasing to Him, He does not by Himself, but the Father, who remains in Him, teaches Him what He is to do. Thus, the Father by remaining imparts instructions and the Son by His activity does not act by Himself, and the Son who does not act by Himself is Himself active, since He does the things that are pleasing to Him. Thus, the unity of nature is preserved in the activity, while He Himself who works does not work by Himself, and He Himself who has not worked by Himself works.

(49)   With these words also join those which you unlawfully seize upon for the sake of discrediting Him for His weakness: 'All that the Father gives to me shall come to me, and him who comes to me I will not cast out. For I have come down from heaven, not to do my own will, but the will of him who sent me.'[67] Perhaps the Son is without freedom

---

67 John 6.37,38.

of will, so that the weakness of His nature forces this necessity upon Him! Therefore, He is subject to necessity rather than to freedom of will, so that He may not reject those who have given to Him and who come to Him from the Father! But, while the Lord revealed the unity of the mystery in these matters, while He does not cast aside those who have been given to Him, while He does not His own will but that of Him who sent Him, after repeating this same statement to the Jews who murmured against Him, He confirms our interpretation of His meaning when He says: 'Everyone who listens to the Father, and learns, comes to me; not that anyone has seen the Father except him who is from God, he has seen the Father. Amen, amen, I say to you, he who believes in me has life everlasting.'[68]

First of all, I ask where has the Father been heard, where has He taught those who listen to Him? No one has seen the Father except Him who is from God. And how has anyone heard Him whom no one has seen? Consequently, he who listens to the Father comes to the Son. Since the Son is heard and teaches, the reality of the Father's nature, which is heard and which teaches, is revealed in Him, so that by the hearing of the Father's doctrine is understood whatever is taught and heard from the Son. For, since no one has seen the Father and he who comes to the Son listens to the Father and learns to come, we find it easier to realize what it means for the Father to teach in the Son who speaks, and for the Father, whom no one has seen, to be in the Son who is seen, because the perfect birth of the Son includes the attributes of the Father's nature. While the Only-begotten, therefore, wished to bear testimony to His origin from the Father, but without sacrificing the unity of nature with Him, He does not reject those who have been given to Him by the Father, and does not His own will but that of Him who sent Him, not as

68 Cf. John 6.45-47.

if He does not will that which He does or as if He Himself is not heard, since He teaches, but to let it be known that He who sent Him and He who is sent possess the reality of the identical nature, for what He wills, does, and says are the will, the works, and the saying of the Father.

(50) He reveals in no uncertain language that He possesses freedom of will when He declares: 'For as the Father raises the dead and gives them life, even so that Son also gives life to whom he will.'[69] When the Father and the Son are shown as equal in the power of the Godhead as well as in the splendor of glory, there the freedom is also revealed, but when the unity is shown, there the love for the Father's will is pointed out. The Son does what the Father wills. But, to do the will is more than to obey the will, because to obey the will implies an external necessity, while to do the will is proper to the unity, since it is an act of the will. And, since the Son does the will of the Father, He teaches that He has a natural will with the Father that proceeds from their identity of nature, since His will is everything that He does.

The Son clearly wills everything that the Father wills, nor does the natural will give rise to any contradiction. Since this is the will of the Father which He reveals in the words: 'For this is the will of my Father, that whoever beholds the Son, and believes in him, shall have everlasting life, and I will raise him up on the last day,'[70] hear now whether the will of the Son is in opposition to that of the Father when He says: 'Father, I will that where I am, they also whom thou has given me may be with me.'[71] Consequently, there is no doubt that the Son wills. Since the Father wills that the faithful should have eternal life in the Son, so the Son wills that the believers should be there where He Himself is.

---

69 John 5.21.
70 John 6.40.
71 John 17.24.

Perhaps it is not eternal life to dwell together with Christ, or perhaps He does not grant what is perfect and blessed in Himself to those who believe in Him when He speaks as follows: 'No one knows the Son except the Father; nor does anyone know the Father except the Son, and him to whom the Son chooses to reveal him.'[72] Does He not enjoy freedom of will who desires to impart to us the knowledge of that mystery of the Father? And is His will not free to such an extent that He grants the knowledge of Himself and His Father to whomsoever He wills? Thus the nature of the birth and the unity between the Father and the Son are revealed, since the Son is free in this sense, that what He does freely is an act of His Father's will.

(51) He who is totally unaware of the plan of salvation is excluded from the knowledge of the mysteries, and he who has not received the doctrine of the Gospel is wandering from the hope of the Gospel. We must believe that the Father is in the Son and the Son in the Father by the power of the Godhead, by their equality in glory, and by the generation of the birth. Perhaps the testimony of the Lord contradicts this assertion of ours when He says: 'The Father is greater than I.' Is this, then, O heretic, the weapon of your impiety? Are these the arms of your fury? Has it escaped your memory that the Church knows nothing of two unborn persons, and does not admit that there are two Fathers? Have you forgotten the mediator of the dispensation and the birth, cradle, age, passion, cross, and death which took place during it? And you who have been born again, have you not confessed that the Son of God was born from Mary?

If, while all these things were proper to Him, the Son declared: 'The Father is greater than I,' do you believe that you must remain in ignorance of the fact that this dispensation of your salvation was the emptying of the form of God, and

---

72 Matt. 11.27.

that the Father was not affected by this assumption of human passions and continued in that blessed eternity of His own unspotted nature without taking our flesh?[73] We confess that the only-begotten God, who remains in the form of God, has remained in the nature of God, nor do we at once pour back the unity of the form of a slave into the nature of the divine unity, nor do we again proclaim that the Father is in the Son by a bodily incorporation, but that the nature of the same kind, which was begotten by Him, possesses within it in a natural way the nature of Him who begot it, and that, while it remained in the form of the nature of Him who begot it, it received the form of our nature and bodily weakness. For, He had the essence of the nature, but no longer had the form of God, because by His emptying the form of a slave was received. The nature has not disappeared so that it no longer existed, but, while it still remained in Him, is submitted to the humiliation of an earthly birth, while it employed the power of its own nature in the habit of the humility which it had assumed. And the God born from God, and found as man in the form of a slave, while He works as God by His powers, was not only the God whom He revealed by His deeds, but also remained as the man in whose habit he was found.

(52)   We have the reason for His previous assertion in this same discourse where He bore testimony to the unity of nature between Him and the Father: 'He who has seen me has seen also the Father,' and 'The Father in me and I in the Father.' Assuredly, by reason of the equality of nature there is no distinction between them, since the appearance of the Son is also a guarantee that the Father has been seen, and the one who remains in the one does not bring about any separation of the one from the one. And lest it be

---

73 Hilary is here refuting the doctrine of Sabellius that the Son was merely a name assumed by the Person of God the Father.

imagined that the bodily appearance was by itself a reflection of the image of the Father's appearance, He added: 'Believe me that I am in the Father and the Father in me. Otherwise believe because of the works themselves,' in order that, since the power was a thing of the nature and the work itself was the strength of the power, the unity of the Father's nature might be recognized in Him, for, in so far as anyone recognized Him as God in the strength of the nature, in so far they would recognize God the Father in the power of the nature, and, because He is just as great as the Father, the Son would enable us to see the Father in Himself by means of His deeds, and the Father would thereby be known as identical with the Son by the realization that there is an indistinguishable nature in the exercise of the power.

(53) Hence, when the only-begotten God was about to fulfill the plan of salvation in the flesh, and to complete the mystery of the servile form which He had assumed, He uttered a statement which was to be a proof of our faith when He said: 'You have heard me say to you, "I go away and I am coming to you." If you loved me, you would rejoice that I am going to the Father, for the Father is greater than I.'[74] Since He had explained these matters pertaining to the nature of the Godhead in the earlier part of the same sermon, does this declaration, therefore, deprive the Son of the equality of nature which the true birth completes? Or is it a disgrace for the only-begotten God to have the unbegotten God as His Father, since the only-begotten birth from the unbegotten God has brought an only-begotten nature into being? The Son is not the source of His own origin, nor did He Himself produce His birth from nothing, since He did not exist, but as a living nature He possesses the power of the nature in Himself and acknowledges the source of His nature, in order to render testimony to the honor as well as His gratitude for

---

74 Cf. John 14.28.

the honor that He had received with the birth. And while He indeed repays this debt to the Father, inasmuch as He attributes His obedience to the will of Him who sent Him, but not in the sense that this humble obedience weakens the unity of the nature, He who became obedient to death is, nevertheless, above every name after His death.

(54) If He appears, therefore, to be unequal because this name is given to Him after the emptying of the form of God, this defamation ignores the mystery of the humiliation which He took upon Himself. For, if the birth of the man brought about a new nature, and the abasement changed the form through the assumption of a slave, the bestowal of the name now restores equality to the form. Examine what was given. If this which is given is a property of God, the gift of this nature does not lead to any degradation of the divine nature. Finally, even if this name which is now given to Him possesses the mystery of the gift, it does not include a strange name in the bestowal of the name. It is given to Jesus in order that those in heaven, on earth, and under the earth may bend the knee and every tongue may confess that the Lord Jesus is in the glory of God the Father. The glory of the confession, therefore, is given so that we must acknowledge Him in the glory of God the Father. Hence, if you hear Him say: 'The Father is greater than I,' know that it is He of whom it was said as a reward for the merit of His obedience: 'And he gave him a name which is above every name.' Again hear Him: 'I and the Father are one.' And: 'He who has seen me has seen also the Father.' And: 'I in the Father and the Father in me.'

Appreciate the glory of the confession that has been given to him, that the Lord Jesus is in the glory of God he Father! When, therefore, did He declare: 'The Father is greater than I'? Precisely at the time when a name above every name is given to Him. On the other hand, when did He say:

'I and the Father are one?' At that moment, namely, when every tongue confesses that the Lord Jesus is in the glory of God the Father. If the Father, therefore, is greater by reason of His prerogative as the donor, is the Son less by His acknowledgment of the gift? The donor, therefore, is greater, but at the same time He is not less to whom it is given to be one. If this is not given to Jesus so that we are to acknowledge Him in the glory of God the Father, He is less than the Father. But, if it is given to Him so that He may be in that glory in which the Father is, then in the name of the donor you find that He is greater, and in the acknowledgment of what is given that they are one. Hence, the Father is greater than the Son, and surely greater, since He allows Him to be as great as He Himself is, since He bestows the image of His unbegotten nature upon Him by the mystery of the birth, since He begets Him from Himself into His own form, since He again renews Him from the form of a slave into the form of God, and since He permits Him who was born in His glory as the God Christ according to the Spirit to be again in His glory after He died as the God Jesus Christ according to the flesh. Consequently, He makes known the reason why they should rejoice, if they loved Him, that He is going to the Father, because the Father is greater than He.

(55) As a consequence, when teaching that this joy proceeds from love, because love is glad that Jesus is to be confessed in the glory of God the Father, He immediately added how He should again acquire this glory which He had merited when He said: 'For the prince of this world is coming, and in me he has nothing.' The prince of this world has nothing in Him, because He who was found in His appearance as man was not included in the sin of the flesh, while as a sin-offering in the likeness of sinful flesh He condemned sin in the flesh. But, since He regarded all this as an act of obedience to the command of His Father, He continued:

'But that the world may know that I love the Father, and
that I do as the Father has commanded me. Arise, let us go
from here.'[75] To complete the mystery of the bodily passion
He hastens to rise because of His love for carrying out the
command of His Father, but He immediately reveals the
mystery of His assumption of a body, whereby we are in
Him like the branch in a vine, since we as the branches would
produce no useful fruit if He had not become the vine.

And for this reason He exhorts us to remain in Him by our
faith in the body which He had assumed, in order that we
might be in the nature of His flesh as branches in the vine,
because the Word was made flesh. Then, while He keeps the
form of His Father's majesty separate from the assumption
of His bodily abasement by asserting that He is the vine that
gives unity to the branches, He reveals that His Father is the
careful cultivator of this vine, who prunes away the useless
and barren branches and puts them aside to be burned.
Consequently, in order to reveal the secret of the birth as
well as the mystery of the body that He had assumed, He
says: 'He who has seen me has seen also the Father,' and:
'The words that I speak I do not speak on my own authority.
But the Father dwelling in me, it is he who does his works,'
and: 'Believe me, that I am in the Father and the Father in
me.' Then, in accordance with the logical meaning of these
words, He arrives at the point when He declares: 'Because
the Father is greater than I.' And to clarify the meaning of
His words He at once added the illustration of the farmer,
the vine, and the branch, and by so doing made known the
assumption of the bodily abasement. And He taught us that
this is the reason why He must go to the Father and why
they must rejoice at such love in going to the Father, because
the Father is greater than He. That is to say, He would again
receive glory, since He is to be glorified with Him and in

75 Cf. John 14.30,31.

Him not by a new but by a former glory, not by a different glory but that which He had with Him. If, therefore, He is not to be glorified in Him, that is, He is not to be in the glory of God the Father, then place the blame for this insult upon the nature; but, if it is His origin that is being glorified by Him, then recognize the Father as greater, because He is the origin of Him who is to be glorified.

(56) Why do you seize upon the plan of salvation to proclaim your godlessness? Why do you attack the mystery of salvation to cause destruction? The Father who is to glorify the Son is greater. The Son who has been glorified in the Father is not less. Or, how is He less who is in the glory of God the Father? Or why is not the Father greater? Hence, the Father is greater while He is the Father, but the Son is not less while He is the Son. The birth of the Son establishes the Father as the greater, but the nature of the birth does not allow the Son to be less. The Father is greater while He is asked to restore glory to the man who was assumed; the Son is not less while He again acquires glory with the Father. Thus, both the mystery of the birth and the dispensation of the Incarnation are fulfilled. The Father, while He is the Father and while He now glorifies the Son of Man, is greater; and the Father and the Son are one while the Son, who has been born from the Father, is glorified in the Father after the assumption of an earthly body.

(57) Consequently, the birth does not lead to an inferior nature, because it is in the form of God and because it is born from God. Although we believe that the very meaning of innascibility differentiates it from birth, the birth is not outside the nature of innascibility. Even if it has not succeeded in being likewise unborn, it has obtained that which God is for the only-begotten God. Although our faith, therefore, does not perceive the beginning of the birth, it always confesses that there is an only-begotten God, because nature does not allow

it to assert that He whose birth transcends every beginning of time has had His beginning at any time. But it does not doubt that He of whom it confesses that He always was and was before all time has, nevertheless, been born from a timeless infinity, and it proclaims that His birth is to be looked upon as without any beginning.

(58) But the heretics quote these passages to heap insults upon His nature, because in them He said: 'The Father is greater than I,' and: 'But of that day or hour no one knows, neither the angels in heaven, nor the Son but the Father only.' Accordingly, the lack of knowledge about the day and the hour is thus cited as an objection to the only-begotten God, so that the God born from God does not possess that perfection of nature which God has, since, if He is subject to ignorance, then there is some external force stronger than Himself against which He is helpless, and which, so to speak, imprisons Him in the weakness of ignorance. Yes, the rage of the heretics even seeks to compel us to the godlessness of this belief, as if it were in strict justice a confession that is unavoidable and which we must admit as such, both because the Lord spoke thus and also because it may be looked upon as the height of blasphemy to distort a statement from His own testimony about Himself by arbitrarily giving it a different meaning of our own.

(59) First of all, before explaining the meaning of and the reason for this statement we must decide in accordance with the principles universally accepted whether He who is the origin of everything that is and that is to be can possibly be ignorant of anything. If all things are through Christ and in Christ, and through Him in such a manner that all things are in Him, why is that which is in Him and through Him not included within the range of His knowledge, since by the power of His perceptive nature His knowledge is continually comprehending things that are not in Him or through Him?

In regard to that which derives its origin only from Him and which receives its impetus for what it is and will be in Him alone, how is it beyond the knowledge of His nature, through which and in which everything is included that is to be brought into being? The Lord Jesus is aware of the thoughts of men, not only those flashing through their minds at the present moment, but also those which will be aroused by the promptings of their will in the future, as the Evangelist testifies: 'For Jesus knew from the beginning who they were who did not believe, and who it was who should betray him.'[76]

Are we to believe, then, that the power of His nature, which grasps the knowledge of non-existing things and which knows the temptations of those whose minds are still at peace, did not know what is in itself and through itself? And is He who possesses power over things foreign to Himself impotent in those things pertaining to Himself, He about whom, as we recall, these words were said: 'All things have been created through and unto him, and he is before all creatures,' or those: 'For it has pleased him that in him all fullness should dwell, and that through him all things should be reconciled in him?'[77] Since, therefore, all the fullness is in Him, and all things are reconciled through Him and in Him, and that day is the expectation of our reconciliation, is He ignorant of this day when its time depends on Him and when it is connected with mystery of the dispensation? That is the day of His coming about which the Apostle declares: 'When Christ, your life, shall appear, then you too will appear with him in glory.'[78] Consequently, no one is unaware of what takes place through Himself and in Himself. Christ will appear, and is He ignorant of the day of His own coming? It is His day according to the same Apostle: 'Because the day of the

---

76 John 6.65.
77 Col 1.16,19.
78 Col. 3.4. The Son of God will appear in His glorified body to judge the living and the dead.

Lord is to come as a thief in the night,'[79] and are we to suppose that He is being kept in ignorance of it?

Human natures know beforehand what they are to do, in so far as it depends on them, and the knowledge of what is to be done follows upon the will to act. Is He who was born as God unaware of what is in Him and through Him? The times are through Him, and the day is in Him, because the determination of future things comes about through Him and the dispensation of His own coming takes place in Him. Will He be the victim of such stupidity that the perception of a sluggish nature does not realize what is dependent upon Him, like those wild and untamed animals that, although alive, are not aware of the very thing they are doing, because they lack the capacity of prudent foresight, but, when aroused, by what we may call the impulse of a senseless will, are driven ahead to some object along an unforeseen and aimless course?

(60) Granting that the day of His coming is unknown to Him, how can we believe that the Lord of glory also possesses a discordant and imperfect nature that is subject to the necessity of coming and that has not received the knowledge of His coming? In such a case it would be more preferable for God to be a victim of ignorance which would deprive Him of the power of knowledge.[80] But, now, how enormously the opportunity for godlessness is increased if in addition to the weakness of Christ we also attribute an imperfection to God, since He has kept back the knowledge of that day from the only-begotten God and the Son of His love, and motivated by ill will has begrudged Him the knowledge of His future achievement! And although He wills that the day and the hour of His passion should be revealed to

---

79 Cf. 1 Thess. 5.2.
80 That is, it would be better to ascribe ignorance to God rather than to accuse Him of withholding knowledge from the Son through a motive of jealousy.

Him, He has refused to inform Him about the day of His power and the hour in which He will be glorified in His saints, and has deprived Him of the knowledge of His blessedness to whom He has granted a prevision of His death. The timidity of the human conscience cannot dare to be so presumptuous in its judgment of God as to impute to Him the defects of human changeableness so that the Father either denies something to the Son, or else that He who was born as God is ignorant of anything.

(61) God does not know how to be ever anything else than love, nor to be anything else than the Father. He who loves does not envy and he who is a father is at the same time wholly a father. This name does not admit of any parts, so that in one respect He is the Father and in another respect He is not the Father. The Father is the Father of everything that is in Him and all that He has, and not merely a part of what a father is is present in Him—not in the sense that the Father Himself is present in those things that are His own, but that in regard to those things that are His own He is wholly the Father of Him who receives His being from Him. According to the nature of human bodies, which are formed of unlike elements and consist of parts, a father can only be a father of all those things that are His own, while the perfect birth of the sons preserves the elements and parts that each one has. Hence, every father is the father of all his own, since the birth proceeds from the whole of himself and remains in the whole of the child. In God there are no material, but simple, things, nor are there any divisions; everything is whole and entire. There is nothing in Him that needs to be made alive; everything is alive. The complete God is wholly alive and is one. He is not composed of parts, but is perfect by reason of His simplicity. Hence, in so far as He is the Father, He must be the whole Father of all His own attributes which are in the one whom He

has begotten from Himself, while the perfect birth of the Son, with all of these attributes, completes Him as the Father.

If, therefore, He is the proper Father of the Son, the Son must remain in the true nature which the Father possesses. But how shall we regard Him as remaining, if the attribute of foreseeing coming events is denied to Him, and if something is wanting to His birth from the author? Almost everything will be wanting to Him if He does not have that which is proper to God. But, what else is proper to God than the knowledge of the future, so that a nature that is capable of possessing invisible and non-existing things embraces those that do not yet exist, but will exist later on.

(62)   Paul, the teacher of the Gentiles, does not allow us to teach this godless error of looking upon the only-begotten God as ignorant of anything, for he declares: 'Being well equipped in charity and in all the riches of complete understanding, so as to know the mystery of the God Christ in whom are hidden all the treasures of wisdom and knowledge.'[81] The God Christ is a mystery and all the treasures of wisdom and knowledge are hidden in Him. But, a part and everything cannot be together in the same object, because we may not conceive the part as everything, nor does everything permit us to conceive it as a part. If the Son does not know the day, then all the treasures of knowledge are not in Him, since He who knows the day contains all the treasures of knowledge in Himself. It is well for us to recall that these treasures of knowledge are hidden in Him, nor are they, therefore, not in Him because they are hidden, since they are in Him by the fact that He is God, but hidden by the fact that there is a mystery. The mystery of the God Christ, in whom are hidden all the treasures of knowledge, is not concealed from us or unknown to us. Because He Himself is the mystery, let us see whether He is ignorant in these matters

---

81 Cf. Col. 2.2,3.

which He does not know. If He declares in other places that He does not know, this does not mean that the matter in question is unknown to Him, and so He is not ignorant even now of what He does not know. His ignorance is rather the plan of salvation than the lack of knowledge, inasmuch as all the treasures of knowledge are hidden in Him. Therefore, you perceive the reason for His ignorance without being obliged to conclude from this that anything is unknown to Him.

(63) In all the passages where God represents Himself as ignorant He admits His ignorance, it is true, but He is not subject to ignorance, because the helplessness of ignorance is not present where something is unknown to Him, but it is either the time for not speaking or the plan of salvation causes Him to refrain from action. When addressing Abraham, God said: 'The outcry against Sodom and Gomorrha is full, and their sins are very great. I will go down, therefore, and see if they are acting in accordance with the outcry against them, and if not, that I may know.'[82] Hence, we have a God who does not know something that is, nevertheless, not unknown to Him. Since He knows that their sins are very great, and again comes down to see whether they have been done, or if they have not been done that He may know, we may conclude that He is not ignorant because He does not know, but that He does not know at that moment because it is the time for action. Consequently, for God to know is not a change from ignorance but the fullness of time. He is still waiting to know, and, since we cannot suppose that He does not know, yet, since He is still waiting to know, it must be that what He, though knowing, does not know and what He, though not knowing, does know is nothing else than the divine economy of salvation in its relation either to speech or to action.

---

82 Cf. Gen. 18.20.

(64)   Hence, we are not permitted to doubt that the knowledge of God is adapted to the time rather than to the result of a change, since in connection with that which God knew it is a question of the opportune moment to divulge what is known rather than to acquire it, as we are also taught by the words which were spoken to Abraham: 'Do not lay your hand on the boy, and do nothing to him, for I know now that you fear your God, and have not spared your beloved son for my sake.'[83] Accordingly, God knows now, but to know something now is an admission of previous ignorance. Since it is a contradiction for God not to know that Abraham had been previously faithful to Him, and of whom it had been said: 'Abraham believed God, and it was credited to him as justice,'[84] that which He knew at this moment is the time when Abraham received this testimony, and not the time when God also began to acquire this knowledge. By bringing his son as a holocaust, Abraham manifested the love which he had for God. God was aware of it then when He speaks. And, since we are not to believe that He had been ignorant of it up to that moment, we must understand that He knew of it then because He speaks of it. Of the many passages in the Old Testament which contain references to the knowledge of God, we have cited only this one as an example that we may realize that God's ignorance of anything does not arise from a lack of knowledge, but from the occasion.

(65)   In the Gospels we find many instances where the Lord knows what He does not know. He does not know the workers of iniquity and those who glory in their many virtues and in their own name when He declares: 'And then I will swear, "I did not know you. Depart from me, all who work iniquity." '[85] He affirms even by the taking of an oath that He

---

83 Cf. Gen. 22.12.
84 Cf. Gen. 15.6; Gal. 3.6.
85 Cf. Matt. 7.23.

did not know them, yet He knows that they are the workers of iniquity. He did not know them, therefore, not because He did not know, but because they are unworthy of His knowledge by reason of their sinful actions. He even confirms the truth of His words by the holiness of an oath, and it lies within the power of His nature to know, and He retains the right of not knowing in the mystery of His free choice.

Similarly, the only-begotten God does not know the foolish virgins, because they were careless about procuring oil for themselves, and He does not know them after He has entered the bridal chamber of His glorious coming. They come forward and implore Him, and He knows them only to such an extent as to answer: 'Amen I say to you that I do not know you.' Their coming together and their request do not allow them to remain unknown, but His reply about not knowing is characteristic not of His nature, but of His will, since they are unworthy of being known by Him who is aware of everything. Finally, in order that they might not consider His lack of knowledge as a weakness, He immediately spoke to His Apostles in the following manner: 'Watch therefore, for you know neither the day nor the hour,'[86] in order that, when He warns them to be vigilant because of their ignorance of the day and the hour, they might therefore realize that He did not know the virgins, since they were drowsy and careless and unfit for the entrance into His bridal chamber because of the oil that was missing.

(66) The Lord Jesus Christ, therefore, who is the God that searches the hearts and reins, is not subject to such a weakness of nature as not to know, since we perceive that the very thing that He does not know springs from the knowledge of His nature. But, if there are some, perhaps, who attribute ignorance to Him, let them take heed lest He who knows their thoughts say to them: 'Why do you harbor evil

---

86 Cf. Matt. 25.12,13.

thoughts in your hearts?'[87] When He who knows the thoughts
and deeds sometimes asks about the thoughts and deeds as if
He were ignorant of them, as, for example, when He asked
the woman about touching the hem of His garment, or the
Apostles about dissensions among them, or those who were
weeping at the tomb of Lazarus, we are to understand His
lack of knowledge as due not to ignorance, but to His manner
of speaking. It is contrary to nature for Him who was absent
to know that Lazarus was dead and buried but to be ignorant
of the place of burial, and for Him who sees the thoughts
not to recognize the faith of the woman, and for Him who
does not need to ask anyone to be unaware of dissensions
among the Apostles.

But, in accordance with the economy of salvation, He who
knows all things sometimes refers to these very things that
He knows as if He did not know them, while in the case of
Abraham He concealed His knowledge for a time, or in
regard to the foolish virgins and the workers of iniquity He
refuses to know them because they are unworthy, or in the
mystery of the Son of Man the questions of the one who does
not know come from the man, while in all these instances
where the weakness of our nature is limited, He acts in
accordance with the true nature of the bodily birth, not that
He who is God is weak according to His own nature, but
that God, who was born as man, took upon Himself the
weakness of men, but did not take them upon Himself in
such a way that His immutable nature would be reduced to
a weak nature, but that there would be the mystery of the
adoption in the immutable nature, while He who was God is
man, nor does He who is man cease to be God.

Accordingly, while He acts as one who was born as man
and confirms the fact that He is such, the Word that is the
abiding God very often expresses Himself in His character as

---

87 Matt. 9.4.

man, but even His statements as God are often couched in the language of men, since He does not know those things which are not to be divulged at that moment, or He does not recognize them when it is a question of their worthiness.

(67) Hence, we must understand why He declared that He did not know the day. If there are any who believe that He is wholly ignorant, the Apostle thus contradicts them: 'In whom are hidden all the treasures of wisdom and knowledge.' Consequently, the knowledge is hidden, and because it must be hidden it is expressed at times as a lack of knowledge, in order that it may remain hidden. If it is proclaimed, it will not remain a secret at the same time. Hence, He denies that He knows, in order that the knowledge may be hidden. If He does not know, therefore, in order that the knowledge may be hidden, His lack of knowledge does not come from His nature, since He knows all things and, consequently, He is only ignorant for the sake of keeping it hidden. The reason why the knowledge of the day is hidden is obvious. Since He warns us to be always ready, even while persevering in the faith, He has deprived us of the assurance of a certain knowledge, so that our soul, made uneasy by the uncertainty of anxious waiting, may press forward and be ever on the alert for the day of His coming; by means of this unceasing watchfulness He would strengthen our hope, and the uncertainty regarding the time itself, that is, however, certain to arrive may keep us ready and watchful. Thus the Lord declares: 'Therefore you must also be ready, because at an hour that you do not expect, the Son of Man will come.' And again: 'Blessed is that servant whom his master, when he comes, shall find doing so.'[88] The ignorance was necessary, not for the purpose of deception, but for perseverance. That which is denied does not harm us, but that which is unknown has contributed to our gain, so that the assurance of knowl-

---

88 Matt. 24.44,46.

edge would not lead us to the carelessness of an inactive faith, but the indefinite expectation would keep us ever ready, since we would be like the vigilant father of a household, who is ever fearful of loss, yet is constantly on his guard against the dreaded thief who selects the time of sleep to commit his robbery.

(68) Although it is clear, therefore, that the ignorance of God is not ignorance, but a mystery, since in accordance with the dispensation for working, asserting, or revealing, He does not know in such a manner that He does know, and knows in such a manner that He does not know, we must ascertain whether, perhaps, He is not weak in such a way that He cannot know those things that the Father knows. He could indeed become aware of the thoughts of the human hearts, because a more powerful nature has united itself with the movements of a lower nature, and by the strength of its power passes through it, as through one that is weak, but the weak nature by itself is unable to penetrate the stronger nature. So light objects can be penetrated by heavy ones, rare objects by dense ones, and liquids by solids, and, on the contrary, heavy objects do not yield to light one, or dense to rare ones, or solids to liquids, because strong objects are impervious to those that are weak, but the weak objects are penetrated by those that are strong. Consequently, the blasphemers declare that the Son does not know the thoughts of God the Father, for, since He Himself is weak, He may not enter into an alliance with one who is stronger and penetrate Him, nor may one who is feeble pass through one who is strong.

(69) If anyone will not only dare to say such things about the only-begotten God in his reckless mouth, but even allow such thoughts in his godless heart, let him learn from the Apostle who expressed his belief when he wrote as follows to the Corinthians: 'But to us God revealed them through his Spirit. For the Spirit searches all things, even

the sublime things of God. For who among men knows the things of a man, that are in him, save the spirit which is in him. Even so, the things of God no one knows but the Spirit of God.'[89] Let us despise these useless examples of material things, and let us judge the God from God, the Spirit from the Spirit, by their own powers rather than by material creatures. Let us judge them, not according to our way of thinking, but according to God's own statement, and let us believe Him who said: 'He who has seen me has seen also the Father.' And let us not ignore Him who declared: 'Or believe my works that the Father is in me and I in the Father.' Nor let us neglect Him who declared: 'I and the Father are one.'

If the names of things, when they are used in conformity with our human understanding, confirm our knowledge of them, then He is not different in nature in whom our mind perceives that there is someone else, nor is He distinct in nature who, while He possesses Him who abides in Him, is within Him who abides in Him, nor are they different who are one. Grasp the unity while their nature is not separated! Again comprehend the mystery of the undivided nature, while the one is, as is were, the image of the one! He is an image in such a manner that the brightness does not proceed from the reflected image of an external nature, but, a living nature is identical with a living nature, since it is the whole from the whole, and since, while it is the only-begotten nature, it possesses the Father in itself and abides in the Father while it is God.

(70)   Hence, since it is impossible for the heretics to deny these things that the Lord taught in order to reveal the mystery of the birth, they attempt to evade His words by referring them to a harmony of will, and, therefore, in God the Father and God the Son there is not the unity of the

---

89 Cf. 1 Cor. 2.10-12.

Godhead but the unity of the will, just as if the vocabulary of the divine doctrine were limited and either the Lord could not say: 'I and the Father will to be one,' or expressed the same idea by: 'I and the Father are one,' or as if He were awkward in speech and did not declare: 'He who has seen my will has seen the will of my Father also,' and meant to convey this very meaning by the words: 'He who has seen me has seen also the Father,' or as if it were contrary to God's manner of preaching to state: 'The will of my Father is in me, and my will is in my Father,' but that the words, 'I in the Father and the Father in me,' are equivalent to this assertion.

Although all these expressions are loathsome, ridiculous and godless, and our human power of reasoning does not fall a victim to this foolish belief, so that the Lord could not speak about what He willed to do, or that He spoke in a way different from that He intended—for, if we also find Him making use of parables and allegories, it is one thing to confirm what has been said by means of examples, either to render justice to the dignity of the subject matter by the introduction of proverbs or to adapt His words to the occasion—nevertheless, this same passage concerning the unity, the subject that we are at present discussing, does not permit us to draw any other conclusion from His statement than what His words signify. If they are one, therefore, because they will to be one, natures that are separable cannot will to be one, since by reason of their difference in genus and nature they are necessarily in disagreement and will different things. How can they whose knowledge is not one will the same thing, since knowledge and ignorance are opposed to the unity of one will? Consequently, since ignorance is contrary to knowledge, things that are mutually contradictory cannot will the one thing.

(71) But perhaps the words of the Son, which the Father alone knows, may be an approval of the belief, that the Son does not know, who says that He does not know. Unless He had clearly stated that the Father alone knows, He would have left behind Him a matter of the utmost peril for our understanding, so that we might perhaps imagine that He Himself did not know. In His case, since the fact that He does not know is the dispensation of the hidden knowledge rather than an ignorance proceeding from His nature, we must therefore believe that even in the present instance He was not ignorant of what the Father alone knows, for, as we have pointed out above, with God knowledge does not mean learning about that which He had not known, but only the revealing of it. And from the fact that the Father alone knows we do not argue that the Son does not know, for the Son says that He does not know, therefore, in order that others may not know, and His reason for asserting that the Father alone knows is to prove that He Himself also knows. If it is said that God then knew that He was loved by Abraham, when He no longer concealed this knowledge from Abraham, it must also follow that the Father is said to know the day in the sense that He did not conceal it from the Son, for God does not derive His knowledge from a sudden revelation, but expresses it at the opportune moment. If, therefore, in accordance with the mystery the Son is ignorant of the day in order that He may be silent about it, on the other hand we must therefore prove that the Father alone knows the day, because He is not silent about it.

(72) Far be it from us, however, to imagine that there are new bodily changes in the Father and the Son, so that at times the Father either speaks to the Son or is silent. We are aware that occasionally a voice has been sent from heaven in order that the mystery of the Son in our midst might be

ratified by the Father's own testimony, as the Lord says: 'Not for me did this voice come from heaven, but for you.'[90] Besides, the nature of God does not require the combination of actions that are necessary for human functions, as the movement of the tongue, the formation of the mouth, the emission of breath, or the vibration of the air. God is simple. We must comprehend Him with reverence and proclaim Him with piety. We must not, however, strive to apprehend Him by reasoning, but we must adore Him, for a nature that is limited and weak does not perceive the mystery of an infinite and omnipotent nature by its own power of comprehension.

Hence, He is not changeable as if the Godhead were made up of parts, so that in Him the will comes after inaction, speech after silence, work after rest; nor are we to imagine that He only wills something when an incentive for the will is present or that He cannot say anything unless the words are spoken after silence; nor are we to look upon Him as doing nothing unless He proceeds to work. He from whom every nature has derived its laws is not subject to the laws of nature, nor is He who transcends every measure of power limited in anything, either by weakness or by a change in His actions according to the Lord's words: 'Father, all things are possible to thee,'[91] so that the human mind cannot grasp as much as lies within His power. Similarly, He has not deprived Himself of the strength of His own omnipotence, as He states: 'For everything that the Father does, the Son also does the same in like manner.'[92] No labor is required where there is no weakness, for a power that is unable to produce is inferior to a power for which there is no difficulty. The nature of what is done with difficulty is the result of the weakness of its

90 Cf. John 12.30.
91 Mark 14.36.
92 Cf. John 5.19.

power, since a power that requires no labor is unlimited in its strength and is not held captive by the law of weakness.

(73) Accordingly, we have emphasized this fact in order that no one might believe either that God spoke to the Son after being silent or that the Son acquired His knowledge after being ignorant, but that our intellect might be taught by expressions suitable to our nature, which does not perceive how anything can be made known except through one who speaks, and which does not understand how ignorance of anything can be removed in any other way than by knowledge.[93] Consequently, the Son does not know the day, because He maintains silence about it, and, therefore, He says that the Father alone knows about it, because He alone reveals it only to Him.

But, as I have stated, He does not prepare Himself for these difficulties of nature, so that He knows at the moment when He has ceased to be ignorant, and that He hears at the moment when the Father has begun to speak. He, the Only-begotten, taught in no ambiguous fashion His unity with Him when He said: 'All things that the Father has are mine.' He does not speak now of what He is to obtain, since it is one thing for things that exist outside of Him to be His own and something else for things in Him to be His own and, indeed, His very self. The former means to possess the heavens, the earth, and the entire universe, and the latter means that He Himself is in these things that are His own, but His own in such a way, not as if external things are added to Him, but that He Himself subsists by these things that are His own. Consequently, since everything that belongs to the Father is now His own, He indicates thereby the nature of the Godhead, not the sharing of goods that have come into His possession. In regard to that which, as He stated, the Holy Spirit would

---

93 That is, by learning just as a man acquires knowledge of the unknown by means of the known.

receive from Him, He says: 'All things that the Father has are mine. That is why I have said that he will receive of what is mine' in order to make us realize that, while He received from Him, He was likewise receiving from the Father, or that, when He received from the Father, we should bear in mind that He was also receiving from Him. The Holy Spirit, who is the Spirit of God, did not receive anything from creatures, and this makes it clear that He received from those things which are wholly proper to God. Not everything, therefore, that belongs to the Father is His own, so that we are to believe that what He takes from the Son He does not also take from the Father,[94] since we realize that everything that the Father has the Son also has.

(74) This nature, therefore, did not require a change, a questioning, or an oral communication, so that it acquires knowledge after ignorance, asks questions after silence, and hears after the questioning, but, while it remained perfect in the mystery of the unity, as it had its birth from God, so it also had everything from Him. But, since it has everything, it likewise holds fast to whatever is included in everything, that is, the knowledge or the will, so that the Son would not know what the Father knew by questioning Him, or that the Son would not will what the Father wills by a communication from Him. Since everything that the Father has is His, the true essence of the nature belonged to Him, so that He could not will or know anything else except what the Father willed or knew. But He usually reveals the birth by designating the person, since it is said: 'For I have come not to do my own will, but the will of him who sent me.' He does the Father's will, not His own, while He also designates the Father by 'the will of him who sent him.' He makes known in no uncertain terms that He wills the very same thing when He

94 The Father has not given over everything to the Son in the sense that He has retained nothing for Himself.

says: 'Father, I will that where I am, they also whom thou hast given me may be with me.' Hence, since the Father wills that we be with Christ in whom, according to the Apostle, He chose us before the foundation of the world, the Son also wills the very same thing, namely, that we be with Him. Their will is the same in the nature, while He distinguishes the will from the will for the sake of indicating the birth.

(75) Accordingly, the Son is not lacking in the knowledge of anything that the Father knows, and the Son is not ignorant, because the Father alone knows, since the Father and the Son remain in the unity of the nature. What the Son, in whom all the treasures of wisdom and knowledge are hidden, does not know is in harmony with the divine plan for maintaining silence. The Lord bore testimony to this when He replied to the Apostles who had questioned Him about the times: 'It is not for you to know the times or dates which the Father has fixed by his own authority.'[95]

The knowledge is denied to them; not only is it denied, but they are forbidden to be anxious about the knowledge, since it is not for them to know these times. Naturally, after the resurrection, they now interrogate Him about the times, since they had been informed previously when they broached the question, that not even the Son knows, and they could not believe that the Son did not know in the literal meaning of the term, because they again question Him as one who does know. Since they are aware that the mystery of not knowing is according to the divine plan for maintaining silence, they conclude that now, after the resurrection, the time for speaking has at length arrived and they bring forth their questions.

And the Son does not tell them that He does not know, but that it is not for them to know, because the Father has

---

95 Acts. 1.7.

settled this matter by His own authority. Consequently, if the Apostles realize that this statement, that the Son does not know, is in keeping with the plan of salvation and is not a weakness, shall we assert that the Son, therefore, does not know the day because He is not God? God the Father has determined it by His own authority, therefore, in order that it may not come to the knowledge of our human comprehension, and the Son, when previously interrogated, had said that He did not know and now He does not make the same reply that He does not know, but that it is not for them to know, and that the Father, however, has decided upon these times not in His knowledge but in His authority. Since the day and moment are included in the idea of time, it is impossible to believe that the day and moment for restoring the kingdom of Israel is unknown to Him who is to restore it. But, to lead us to the knowledge of His birth through the Father's unique power, He answered that it was known to Him and, while revealing that the right to acquire this knowledge had not been conferred upon them, He declared that this knowledge itself is dependent upon the mystery of the Father's authority.

We[96] are not to imagine, therefore, that the Son does not know because He says that He does not know the day and moment, just as we are not to believe that God is subject to tears, fears, or sleep, when in His human nature He either weeps, or sleeps, or is sad. But, while we keep intact the true nature of the Only-begotten in Him amid the weakness of the flesh—the tears, sleep, hunger, thirst, weariness, and fear—in a similar manner we must understand that, when He declares that He does not know the day and the hour, He is referring to His human nature.

---

96 The authenticity of this last paragraph is doubted because it is not found in many of the original manuscripts of *De Trinitate,* and also the reason it assigns for Christ's lack of knowledge does not seem to be in accord with the rest of St. Hilary's teaching of this subject.

BOOK TEN

THERE IS NO DOUBT that every utterance of human speech has always been exposed to the danger of contradiction. For, when the sentiments of the will do not agree, the ideas in the mind are also lacking in agreement, since in its passionate attachment to contradiction it wages war and raises objections to these statements which it opposes. Even though every statement perfectly conforms to the standard of truth, as long as some look upon it and agree with it in one sense and others take the opposite view, the word of truth is liable to contradiction by its adversaries, because the error of a foolish and sinful will struggles against the truth which it either does not understand or with which it is not satisfied. The stubbornness of a will that has formed its own decisions never knows any limits, and the eagerness for contradiction continues unrelentingly on its course when the will is not subject to reason and there is no eagerness for learning, when we seek to justify these things that we will and adapt the doctrine to these things for which we are striving. The doctrine which emerges will now be founded on the name rather than on the nature, and the theory will no longer be in conformity with what is true but with what pleases us, and the theory is one which the will has employed in defense of its own prejudices rather than one which will arouse the instinct of the will by its grasp of the logical truth.

399

From the defects of the will that is prejudiced, therefore, arises the conflict of opposing ideas and there is a stubborn struggle going on between the statement of the truth and the defense of prejudice, while the truth maintains its position and the will draws up its own defense. Furthermore, if the will did not precede reason but were moved to will what is true by its grasp of the truth, we would never seek for a doctrine that is based on the will, but the consideration of the doctrine would stir up the entire will, and the word of truth would never meet with opposition, since no one would defend as true that which he willed, but would begin to will that which is true.

(2) The Apostle, therefore, was cognizant of these sinful tendencies of the will, and besides his numerous admonitions to defend the faith and to preach the word, he said in his Epistle to Timothy: 'There will come a time when they will not endure the sound doctrine; but having itching ears, will heap up to themselves teachers according to their lusts, and they will turn away their hearing from the truth and turn aside rather to fables.'[1] When they will no longer endure sound doctrine in their eagerness for godlessness, they will gather teachers together for these things which they desire, that is to say, they will compile a doctrine that fits in with their desires, since they are no longer eager to be taught, but to bring together teachers for that which they desire in order that this large number of teachers whom they have sought and assembled may satisfy the doctrines of their own passionate desires. Finally, if they are unaware of the spirit by which this so great fury of foolish impiety will not endure sound doctrine, but will desire what is debased, let them learn about it from the words which the same Apostle writes to the same Timothy: 'Now the Spirit expressly says that in after times some will depart from the faith, giving heed to

---

1 2 Tim. 4.3,4.

seducing spirits and doctrines of devils, speaking lies hypo-
critically.'[2]

And what gain is there in a doctrine that seeks after what
is pleasing rather than what is to be taught? Or what holiness
is there in a doctrine where they do not desire what is to be
taught but to assemble doctrines for that which they desire.
But these things offer inducements to seducing spirits and
confirm the errors of the pretended worship of God. Lying
hypocrisy follows upon the apostasy from the faith, so that
the godliness, which has disappeared from their consciousness,
is at least preserved in their words. Indeed, they cause even
this pretended worship of God to become impious by employing lying words of every description, while they distort the
holiness of the faith through the precepts of their false teachings, since the doctrine which they build up rests upon their
desires and whims rather than upon the faith of the Gospels.
Since their itching ears are tickled when in their uncontrolled
yearning for hearing they are touched by a new doctrine in
accordance with their fancies, they themselves are completely
estranged from the truth and devote their whole attention to
fables, in order to acquire the outward appearance of truth
for these things which they teach, while they are unable to
speak of or hear the things that are true.

(3)   We have arrived, without doubt, at this most troublesome time mentioned in the apostolic prophecy. Since teachers
are now being sought who will proclaim the creature rather
than God, and they are more concerned with human desires
than with the teaching of sound faith, and the itching of
their ears has so aroused them to hear what they desire, that
in the meantime among the teachers whom they have
assembled this doctrine alone prevails at the present time,
according to which the only-begotten God is alienated from
the power and the true nature of God the Father, or He is a

2 Cf. 1 Tim. 4.1.

God of a different substance in our faith, or He is not God. Thus, from both sides, they proclaim a fatal doctrine, since they speak either of two gods differing in their divinity or they assert that He is certainly not a God who possesses the nature from God through His birth. This is pleasing to those whose ears have been set against hearing the truth and have been turned to fables. They no longer endure the hearing of this sound doctrine, and it is banished outright, together with all of its teachers.

(4) Although sound doctrine has been driven into exile by many who have brought together teachers according to their own desires, the true doctrine will not be banished by any of the saints. Although in exile, we shall speak through these books, and the word of God which cannot be bound will circulate in freedom, and while it brings to our mind this same time mentioned in the prophecy of the Apostle, so that when we discover that they cannot endure hearing the truth and find out that they have assembled teachers according to human desires, there will no longer be any doubt about the time, but they will realize that the truth shares the exile together with the teachers of the sound doctrine who have been banished. And we will not complain about the times, but will even rejoice, because iniquity has revealed its true colors during this period of our exile, in which it no longer endures sound doctrine and drives out its teachers so that it may press into service teachers according to their desires. We glory in our exile and rejoice in the Lord that the fullness of the Apostle's prophecy has been manifested in us.

(5) In the preceding Books we have held fast, I believe, to the confession of the pure and spotless truth. Although, according to the usage of human nature, there is no statement that is not liable to contradiction, I think that we have followed such a plan in our complete response that no one can find fault with it except by proclaiming an impious

doctrine. We have so explained the truth of those passages, which the heretics have presumptuously claimed for themselves in accordance with their manner of lying, that we can no longer excuse their opposition on the plea of ignorance, but must consider it as godless. In the present instance, according to the gift of the Holy Spirit, we have also arranged the explanation of the complete faith so that they cannot even invent any accusation against us. They are so accustomed to fill the ears of the unlearned about us that they charge us with denying the birth when we preach the unity of the Godhead, and declare that we are referring to a solitary God by these words: 'I and the Father are one,' so that the unborn God who descends upon the Virgin is born as man, who in alluding to the dispensation of the flesh thus begins with the word 'I,' but then, pointing out His divinity, went on to add 'and the Father,' just as if He were the Father of Himself as man, but, since He is made up of two parts, namely, man and God, He said of Himself: 'we are one.'

(6) We, who acknowledge the birth which subsists without time, have taught that God the Son is not a God of a different nature from God the Father; nor is He co-equal with the unborn one by being Himself unborn, but the Only-begotten is not unequal to Him by birth; nor are they one by the twofold name of a union,[3] but by the birth of a nature; nor are there two gods in our faith by reason of a distinction in their nature; nor, again, is there a singular God, but the Son is indicated in the Father and is in Him, while the nature and the name[4] are in Him, but the Father is recognized and is in the Son, while He cannot be called nor be the Son except from the Father. He is also the living

---

3 That is, the Father and Son are not merely two names for the same person.
4 Because the Son has the same nature as the Father, He rightfully enjoys the 'name'. i. e., God.

image of the living nature, and the form of God in God has been impressed upon Him by nature to such an extent that they are indistinguishable both in power and substance, so that in Him neither the work, nor the speech, nor the appearance differ from those of the Father, but, since the image naturally possesses in itself the nature of its author, the author also worked, spoke, and was seen through His natural image.

(7) And while we indeed proclaim this timeless and ineffable birth of the Only-begotten, that transcends the capacity of all human understanding, we also taught the mystery of the God who was born as man by His birth from the Virgin while at the same time we pointed out the dispensation of the flesh that was assumed, since, when He then emptied Himself of the form of God and received the form of a slave, His weakness in the outward appearance of man did not impair the nature of God, but, while the strength of the Godhead was preserved in the man, the power of God was acquired for the man. Since God was born into man, He was not born, therefore, in order that He might not remain as God, but that the man might be born into God while He remains as God. Emmanuel, that is, God with us, is also His name, so that there is not a lowering of God into the man, but the elevation of the man into God. When He prays to be glorified, this does not, of course, lead to any gain for the nature of God, but for the lowly form that He assumed. He prays for this glory that He had with God before the foundation of the world.

(8) While we were replying to their most absurd statements we also arrived at the explanation of the unknown hour, and, even if according to them the Son were unaware of it, this did not imply any insult to the only-begotten Godhead, since the nature would not allow Him to be brought back to the existence of one who is unborn and has no beginning, for it is to reveal His own unborn origin that the

Father reserves the determination of the still indefinite day to His own authority.[5] Nor may we regard the nature which is in Him as weak, since by reason of the birth there is just as much of the nature in Him as a perfect birth could bestow, nor should we ascribe His ignorance of the day and hour to a distinction in the Godhead, since the reason for claiming this exclusive prerogative of the unborn power in Him is to prove against the Sabellian heretics that the Father's power is without any birth or beginning. But, since we have taught that this avowal of the unborn power is not due to the weakness of ignorance but, rather, to the mysterious plan for maintaining silence, we must now also remove every pretext for the godless teaching and discuss all the doctrines of the heretical blasphemy, in order that the truth of the Gospel may clearly appear from those very texts by which it seems to be obscured.

(9) Most of them do not wish Him to possess the nature of an impassible God, because of His fear during the passion and His weakness in suffering, so that He who feared and was sad did not have either the assurance of a power which is not afraid or that integrity of spirit which does not feel sorrow, but, because His nature was inferior to that of God the Father, He trembled through His fear of suffering and groaned at the brutality of the corporal punishment. And they base these assertions of their godlessness upon the words that were written: 'My soul is sad, even unto death,' and again: 'Father, if it is possible, let this cup pass away from me,' but also: 'My God, my God, why hast thou forsaken me?'[6] and they likewise add these words: 'Father, into thy hands I commend my spirit.'[7] For they seize upon all these

---

5 According to Coustant, Hilary refers here to the claim of the Arians that Christ did not know the hour because this is an exclusive privilege of Him who is unborn.
6 Matt. 26.38,39; 27.46.
7 Luke 23.46.

assertions of our pious faith in order to use them in defense of their impiety as if He feared who was sad and who prayed that the cup might be taken away from Him, as if He felt pain who complained that He was abandoned by God in the passion, and as if He was also weak who commended His spirit to the Father. Nor is anxiety compatible with the likeness of a nature that has become equal to God's in the birth of the Only-begotten, for His prayer in regard to the cup, His complaint about the desolation, and the acknowledgment of His commending confirm His weakness and diversity.

(10) First of all, before we prove from these very texts that He was not subject to any weakness of being fearful in regard to His own person or of feeling pain, we must ascertain what it is that apparently could have inspired Him with fear, so that the dread of an intolerable pain came over Him. I believe that no other reason for fear is alleged except that of His passion and death. And I ask those who argue thus about this matter whether it is reasonable to suppose that He was afraid to die who did away with all fear of death on the part of His Apostles and exhorted them to the glory of martyrdom when He said: 'He who does not take up His cross and follow me is not worthy of me. And he who finds his life will lose it, and he who loses it for my sake, will find it.'[8] Since it is life for Him to die, how are we to believe that He experienced pain in the mystery of His death who restores life to those who die for Him? And since He warns us that we are not to fear those who kill the body, could even death itself have frightened Him through fear of bodily pain?

(11) Besides, what pain of death did He feel who is to die by a deliberate act of His own power? Among the members of the human race the end of life is hastened by an

---

8 Matt. 10.38,39.

external force, such as a fever, wound, accident, or fall, which attack the body, or else the very nature of our body is overcome by old age and falls a victim to that death itself. But the only-begotten God, who possessed the power of laying down His life as well as of taking it up again, in order to complete the mystery of the death in Himself testified that He had accomplished the work of His human sufferings when He drank the vinegar, and, having bowed His head, gave up the spirit. If this right remains to the nature of man that it breathes forth its spirit by itself and finds rest in death, and when the body is dissolved the soul is not weakened and takes its departure, or when the members are broken, pierced, or crushed the soul does not break forth and escape, as if its residence had been violated, then the fear of death may have come upon the Lord of life if, when He gave up the spirit and died, He did not make use of the power of His own free will in order to die. And if He died of His own will and gave up the spirit through His own will, then there is no dread of death where death is within His own power.

(12) Perhaps through the fearfulness of human ignorance He feared this very power of dying which was in Him, so that, although He died of His own will, He feared this thing itself because He was to die. If there are some who think thus, let them decide whether they believe that death was terrible to the spirit or to the body. If to the body, are they unaware that His holy one will not see corruption, and that He will raise up the temple of His body in three days? If death is terrible to the spirit, did Christ fear the infernal abyss while Lazarus rejoiced in the bosom of Abraham? These opinions are foolish and ridiculous, as if He was afraid to die who had the power of laying down His life and taking it up again, and who was about to die for the mystery of human life by a free act of His own will. There is no fear of death in Him who dies freely and who will not remain for a long

time in the power of death, for the willingness to die and the power to come to life again have nothing in common with the nature of fear, since death cannot be feared where there is the readiness to die and the power to live.[9]

(13) Perhaps the pains of the body while hanging on the cross, the cruel fetters of the cords that bound Him, and the bloody wounds caused by the nails that pierced Him are a source of fear. Let us see what body the man Christ had, so that the pain should remain in the flesh that was suspended, bound, and pierced.

(14) It is the nature of bodies that by their association with the soul they are animated with the preception, so to speak, of a sentient soul and are not a dull, lifeless mass. But they feel when struck, experience pain when pierced, freeze when cold, rejoice when warmed, pine away from hunger, and grow fat from food. By a sort of infiltration on the part of the soul which possesses and permeates them, they experience either pleasure or pain in accordance with the circumstances in which they find themselves. Hence, when the pierced or torn bodies experience pain, the sensation of pain is made possible through the sensation of the soul that has been poured into them. Finally, a wound of the body experiences pain up to the bones, and the fingers feel nothing when the nails protruding from the flesh are cut off. If as a result of a defect any part ever becomes decayed, it loses the sensation of living flesh, and when it is cut off or burned, even though otherwise the pain would have been as acute as possible, it will not feel anything, since the association with the soul no longer remains in it. When a pressing necessity arises for cutting the body, the power of the soul is rendered insensible through the drinking of medicine, and the mind, filled with more potent drugs, undergoes a deathlike

---

9 Hilary does not state absolutely that Christ did not fear death, but only that His fear of death did not proceed from human ignorance.

oblivion of its own power of sensation. Then the members are cut off without feeling pain, and the sensation of the flesh, being, as is were, dead, does not feel the blow of the deep wound because the sensation of the soul within it is dormant. Hence, an animated body causes pain to its weak power of comprehension through its union with a weak soul.

(15) If, therefore, the man Jesus Christ lived in the body with the beginnings of our body and soul, and if He were not God, the ruler of His body and soul, when He was formed in the likeness of man, when He was found in the form of man and was born, He may have felt the pain of our body, since He was animated in the body through the conception as well as through the beginning of our soul and body. But, if He assumed the flesh of the Virgin through Himself and He has prepared for Himself and from Himself a soul that was suitable to the body that was conceived through Himself, then the nature of His suffering must be in accordance with the nature of His soul and body. When He emptied Himself of the form of God and received the form of a slave, and when the Son of God was also born as the Son of Man, then God the Word, without sacrificing anything of Himself and His own power, assumed the living man.[10] For, how will the Son of God be born as the Son of Man, or while He remained in the form of God how did He receive the form of a slave, unless (since the Word of God is able by Himself to assume flesh within the Virgin and confer a soul upon the body) the man Jesus Christ was born perfect for the redemption of our soul and body, and assumed our body in such a way that what was conceived by the Virgin became the form of a slave. What the Virgin begot she begot only by His Holy Spirit. Although in the birth of the flesh

10 By his teaching that Christ had a human body and soul, Hilary refutes Apollinaris, who claimed that the divine Word supplied the place of the soul.

she communicated as much of herself as women do when they receive the seeds of the bodies that are to be born, Jesus Christ was not formed through the nature of a human conception. The whole birth, which was brought about by the Spirit, held fast on the one hand to that which is proper to the mother in the birth of the Man, while on the other hand it preserved that which is God's in the power of the origin.

(16) Hence, the Lord expressed that most profound and most noble mystery of the assumption of man in the words: 'No one has ascended into heaven except him who has descended from heaven: the Son of Man who is in heaven.'[11] That He has descended from heaven is the cause of the origin which has been conceived by the Spirit. Mary did not give the body its origin, although she contributed to the growth and birth of the body everything that belongs by nature to her sex. But, in so far as He is the Son of Man, there is the birth of the flesh that was assumed in the Virgin. On the other hand, what is in heaven is the power of the ever-abiding nature, which, after it had originated and created the flesh, did not confine itself in the power of its infinity within the limits of a fixed body. While it remains by the strength of the Spirit and by the power of the Word of God in the form of a slave, the Lord of heaven and the world was present in every circle within and without heaven and the world.

In this way, therefore, He descends from heaven, He is the Son of Man, and is in heaven, because the Word made flesh did not cease to be that which the Word is. While He is the Word He is also in heaven, while He is the flesh He is also the Son of Man, and while the Word was made flesh He is from heaven. He is the Son of Man and is in heaven because the power of the Word does not remain in a corporeal manner; it is not lacking that from which it has descended,

---

11 John 3.13.

and the flesh did not receive its origin from anywhere else than from the Word, and the Word made flesh, while it was flesh, was nevertheless also the Word.

(17) The blessed Apostle, however, clearly referred to the mystery of the ineffable birth when he said: 'The first man from the slime of the earth; the second man from heaven.'[12] By using the word 'man' he taught the birth from the Virgin who in fulfilling her function as a mother acted in accordance with the nature of her sex in the conception and birth of the man. And when he asserted that the second man was from heaven he testified that His origin was from the arrival of the Holy Spirit who came upon the Virgin. Thus, while He was man, He was also from heaven; the birth of this man was from the Virgin and the conception from the Spirit. The Apostle has truly spoken of these things.

(18) When the Lord Himself revealed the mystery of the birth, He spoke as follows: 'I am the living bread that has come down from heaven. If anyone eat of my bread he shall live forever,' calling Himself bread, for He Himself was the origin of His own body. And lest anyone might imagine that while in the flesh the power and nature of the Word had departed from Him, He again declared that He was His bread to make us realize from this fact, His coming down from heaven, that His origin was not from a human conception, while it is revealed that He had a heavenly body. That He was His bread is an acknowledgment of the body assumed by the Word, for He added: 'Unless you eat the flesh of the Son of Man, and drink his blood, you shall not have life in you,'[13] in order to make known the assumption of the flesh, that was conceived by the Holy Spirit and born of the Virgin, through His bread which came down from heaven and through the flesh and blood of the Son of Man, because that

12 Cf. 1 Cor. 15.47.
13 Cf. John 6.51,52,54.

which is the Son of Man is also He Himself as the bread that came down from heaven.

(19)   Hence, the man of this body, Jesus Christ, is the Son of God and the Son of Man, and when He emptied Himself of the form of God He received the form of a slave. There is no other Son of Man than He who is the Son of God, nor is there another in the form of God than He who in the form of a slave was born as the perfect man, so that just as in the nature conferred upon us by God, the source of our origin, a man of the body and soul is born, in like manner Jesus Christ by His power was a man of the flesh and soul as well as God, since He possesses in Himself wholly and truly that which man is, and also possesses wholly and truly that which God is.

(20)   Although many, in accordance with the method whereby they strengthen their heresy, are so accustomed to insult the ears of the unlearned that, because the body and soul of Adam were tainted with sin, the Lord also received the flesh and soul of Adam from the Virgin, nor did the Virgin conceive the whole man by the Holy Spirit. Did these men but understand the mystery of the flesh that was assumed, they would also understand the mystery of the Son of Man who is at the same time the Son of God, just as if He who had received so much from the Virgin also received His soul from her, since every soul is the work of God, but the birth of flesh is always from the flesh.

(21)   For, they do not wish the only-begotten God, who was God the Word and in the beginning with God, to be a substantial God, but merely the utterance of a voice, so that what words are to those who speak so the Son is to God the Father. In their slyness they wish to smuggle in the teaching that the subsisting Word of God who remains in the form of God was not born as Christ the man, so that, since the cause of a human origin rather that the mystery of a spiritual

conception animated that man, it was not God the Word who made Himself man by the birth from the Virgin, but, just as the Spirit of prophecy was in the Prophets, so the Word of God was in Jesus. And they are wont to censure us for saying Christ was not born as a man of our body and soul, since we declare that the Word was made flesh, and that Christ emptying Himself of the form of God, and assuming the form of a slave was born as a perfect man in accordance with the manner of our human formation and likeness, so that He who is truly the Son of God is the true Son of Man, and while a man was born from God He does not therefore cease to be God because a man was born from God.

(22) But, just as He assumed a man from the Virgin through Himself, so He assumed a soul by Himself and the soul is certainly never bestowed by man upon the origin of those who are born. If the Virgin did not conceive the flesh except from God, it is far more necessary that the soul of the body be from nowhere else than from God. And since that Son of Man Himself is at the same time the Son of God, because the entire Son of Man is the entire Son of God, in what ridiculous manner shall we proclaim that, besides the Son of God who is the Word made flesh, there is still another (I know not whom) who has been inspired like a prophet by the Word of God, since the Lord Jesus Christ is the Son of Man and the Son of God? But, because His soul is sorrowful even unto death, and because He has the power of laying down His life and taking it up again, they wish to attribute the soul to something extrinsic and not to the Holy Spirit, as they also do the body which was conceived by Him, since God the Word was born as man while He remained in the mystery of His own nature.

He was born, however, not that He might be first one and then another, but that the God before the man, since He assumed a human nature, might be recognized as both man and God. For, how was Jesus Christ, the Son of God, born from Mary except by the Word becoming flesh; that is to say, the Son of God, since He was in the form of man, received the form of a slave? But that He who was in the form of God should receive the form of a slave is bringing contradictories together,[14] so that there is just as much truth in Him being in the form of God as there is in Him receiving the form of a slave. We are forced to use a common word[15] in order to grasp the true meaning of the nature. He is in the form of a slave who is also in the form of God. While the the latter belongs to the nature and the former to the dispensation, yet because He is both, the same truth is proper to Him, so that He is just as true in the form of God as in the form of man. But, as the assuming of the form of a slave is nothing else than being born as man, so being in the form of God is nothing else than being God. We profess that He is one and the same, not by losing anything that belongs to God, but by the assumption of a human nature, and that He is in the form of God by the divine nature, and was found in the form of a slave by the conception of the Holy Spirit according to the appearance of man. Therefore, since Jesus Christ was born, suffered, died and was buried, He also rose again. In these different mysteries He cannot be divided from Himself in such a manner that He is not Christ, since there is no other Christ than He who in the form of God received the form of a slave, nor is He who died another one from Him who was born, nor is He who rose again another one from Him who died, nor is He who is heaven another one from Him who rose again, but He is not another one in heaven from Him who had previously descended from heaven.

(23)   Hence, the man Jesus Christ, the only-begotten

---

14 His meaning is that it is not natural for a human and divine nature
   to be in one person.
15 That is, the word 'form'.

God, who through the flesh and the Word is the Son of Man
as well as the Son of God, has assumed a true manhood
according to the likeness of our manhood without sacrificing
His divinity. Although a blow struck Him, or a wound pierced
Him, or ropes bound Him, or a suspension raised Him, the
things indeed wrought the vehemence of the passion, but
did not bring Him the pain of the passion, just as any weapon
that passes through water, penetrates fire, or wounds the air
inflicts, it is true, all these pains which are proper to its nature
so that it penetrates, it pierces, it wounds, but the pains that
are directed against these objects do not linger in their nature,
since it is contrary to nature for water to be penetrated, for
fire to be pierced, or for the air to be wounded, although it
is characteristic of the nature of a weapon to wound, to
penetrate, and to pierce.

Our Lord Jesus Christ truly suffers when He is struck,
suspended, crucified, and dies. The suffering which rushes
upon the body of the Lord was a suffering, but it does not
manifest the nature of suffering, while on the one hand it
rages with the function of pain, and on the other hand the
divinity of the body[16] receives the force of the pain rushing
against it, but without feeling pain. That body of the Lord
may indeed have had the nature of our pain, if our body
were of such a nature that it treads upon the waves, walks
upon the waters and does not sink by its movement, and if
the waters do not give way before the footsteps set upon it,
and if it penetrates even solid matters, and if it is not hindered
by the barriers of a closed house. But if that is only characteristic of the Lord's body that by His own soul He is
borne over the water, stands upon the waves, and passes
through walls, why do we, who have been conceived by the
nature of a human body, pass judgment upon the flesh that
has been conceived by the Spirit? That flesh, that bread, is

16 *virtus corporis,* which refers very probably to the divine Word.

from heaven, and that man is from God. He certainly possessed a body to suffer and did suffer, but He does not possess a nature that could feel pain. That body had a nature peculiar and proper to it,[17] that was transfigured on the mountain, drives away fevers by its touch, and restores eyes by its spittle.

(24)   Perhaps He who experienced the pain of weeping, thirst, and hunger must have also had within Himself the nature of other human sufferings. He who is ignorant of the mystery of the tears, the thirst, and the hunger, let him know that He who weeps also brings back to life and rejoices rather than weeps over the death of Lazarus, that He who thirsts bestows the rivers of living water from Himself, that He who is parched with thirst can give drink to the thirsty, that He who is hungry condemns that tree which does not offer its fruit to the hungry, and that that nature is not overcome by hunger which changes the nature of greenness by the command to become barren. If, apart from the mystery of the weeping, thirst, and hunger, the assumed flesh, that is, the entire man, exposed Himself to the natures of sufferings, these things did not come about in such a manner that He was prostrated by the injuries of the sufferings, but that He who weeps does not weep for Himself, that He who thirsts banishes thirst without having to drink, and that He who is hungry does not satisfy Himself through the enjoyment of any kind of nourishment. When He was hungry, thirsty, or wept, we do not see the Lord weeping, eating, or grieving; He assumed the custom of our body in order to reveal the reality of the body so that the custom of our nature satisfied

---

17 Christ's human nature was 'peculiar and proper' to Him because it was not conceived according to the ordinary laws of human generation, was free from human defects, and was intimately united with a divine nature. But He possessed the defects that are common to mankind, as the capability of suffering, dying, etc.

the custom of the body. When He received drink and food, He acceded not to the body's necessity, but to its custom.[18]

(25) He had a body, but a unique one which was of His own origin; He did not come into existence through the imperfections of a human conception, but subsisted in the form of our body by the power of His own divinity, for He truly represents us through the form of a slave, but He is free from the sins and the defects of a human body, so that we are indeed in Him by the birth from the Virgin, but our defects are not in Him because of the power of the origin that has proceeded from Him, while He who was born as man was not born through the imperfections of a human conception. The Apostle clung to the mystery of this birth that was to be revealed when he said: 'But he humbled himself, taking the nature of a slave, being made in the likeness of man, and in habit found as a man,'[19] so that by His assumption of the form of a slave we are to understand that He was born in the form of man, but, while He was made in the likeness of man and found in the habit as man, the outward appearance and the true nature of the body bear testimony to the man, but He who was found in the habit as man does not have the defects of nature.

The birth is in the likeness of our nature, not in the appropriation of our defects. Because the nature of the birth seems to be indicated by the fact that He received the form of a slave, He added that He was made in the likeness of man and found in the habit as man in order that we might not imagine that a nature that has been weakened by defects

---

18 St. Thomas Aquinas, *Summa Theologica* III, Q. 15, art. 5 (London 1913, p. 214) says that Hilary 'uses the word necessity in reference to the first cause of these defects which is sin . . . so that Christ's flesh is said not to have lain under the necessity of these defects, in the sense that there was no sin in it.'
19 Cf. Phil. 2.7.

is essential for a true birth, since a true birth is in the form of
a slave and the likeness of nature is in Him who was found
in the habit as man. He Himself was truly born as man by
Himself from the Virgin, and was found in the likeness of
sinful flesh. And the Apostle bore witness to this fact when
He said in his Epistle to the Romans: 'For what was impossible to the Law, in that it was weak because of the flesh,
God has sent his own Son in the likeness of sinful flesh, and
of sin he has condemned sin.'[20] His eternal appearance was
not as if it were that of a man, but as that of a man,[21] nor
is that flesh the flesh of sin but the likeness of the flesh of
sin, while the external appearance of flesh comes from the
true nature of the birth, and the likeness of the flesh of sin is
free from the imperfections of human suffering. Thus, the
man Christ Jesus also possesses the true nature of the birth
while He is man, and sin is not proper to Him while He is
Christ, because He who is man could not but be man since
He was born, and He who is Christ could not have lost that
which Christ is because He is Christ. Thus, while Christ
Jesus is man, He who is man also possesses the birth of man,
and He who is Christ is not subject to the sinful weakness of
man.

(26) Although the apostolic faith, therefore, which has
testified that the man Christ Jesus was found in the form of
man and was sent in the likeness of sinful flesh, teaches us
the knowledge of this mystery, so that while He is in the
form of man He is in the form of a slave and does not have
the defects of our nature, and since He is in the likeness of
sinful flesh, the Word is truly flesh, still, it is rather the likeness
of sinful flesh than the flesh of sin itself. And since Christ
Jesus is man, He is truly a man, but in the man there cannot

---

20 Cf. Rom. 8.3.
21 According to Coustant, *tamquam hominis* indicates that external appearance, while *ut hominis* refers to the true nature.

be anything else than that which Christ is; thus, the man was born from the birth of the body and He who does not belong to our origin does not have our human defects, because the Word made flesh could not but be flesh, since it was made. And although the Word was made flesh, it has not lost that which the Word is, and, while the Word made flesh cannot lack the nature of its own origin, it can only remain in the origin of its own nature what the Word is, and we must understand that the Word is truly flesh, since it was made, but in such a manner that that flesh is not the Word because it dwelt amongst us but it is the flesh of the Word that dwells in the flesh. While all this is true, let us see whether we are allowed to hold that there was the weakness of bodily pain during all those sufferings that He endured. While we postpone for a little while our explanation of those words from which heresy attributes fear to the Lord, let us look at the events themselves, just as they took place. It is not possible that His words indicate fear when His deeds reveal such self-assurance.

(27) O heretic, in your opinion does the Lord of glory seem to have been afraid of suffering? Peter became for Him 'Satan' and a 'scandal' because he erred through his ignorance of this fact. And he, who raised his voice in protest against the mystery of the passion because of his love for Christ, who had been revealed to him not by flesh and blood but by the Father in heaven, was strengthened in the faith by such a stern rebuke. To what hope will you cling, if you deny that Christ is God and ascribe the fear of suffering to Him? Was He afraid who went forth to meet the armed men in order to allow Himself to be seized? Was there weakness in His body when consternation seized the crowd of persecutors, who upon encountering Him fell helpless to the ground, since they could not endure the majesty of Him who offered Himself to the chains? Accordingly, to what kind of weak-

ness do you believe that this body was subject, when its nature is in possession of such great power?

(28)   Perhaps He feared the pain of the wounds? Did He, I ask, who by His mere touch restored the flesh of the ear that had been cut off dread the nail that pierced the flesh? You who proclaim the Lord's weakness, explain to us this work of the weakened flesh in the very moment of the passion! For when Peter drew forth and wielded the sword, the servant of the priest stood there with his ear cut off. How did the touch of Christ restore the flesh of the ear to the wound of the ear that had been cut off? Amid the flowing blood, the fresh traces of the cutting sword and the body that was disfigured by the mutilation, whence did that come that was not there? How does that follow which does not exist? And how is that restored which is wanting? Does the hand, therefore, that produces these effects feel pain because of the nail? And does He Himself feel the wound who does not allow someone else to experience the pain of the wound? Is He sad through fear of the flesh that is to be pierced whose touch is capable of bestowing flesh after it has been cut off? If this power is in the body of Christ, with what assurance, I ask, do you defend the theory that He is weak by nature, since it belongs to His nature to keep in check every nature of human infirmities?

(29)   Perhaps in their ridiculous and godless perversity they will conclude that His nature is weak because His soul was sorrowful unto death. O heretic, I do not yet blame you for misunderstanding the meaning of this text. But, in the meantime, I ask why do you not recall what He said when Judas departed in order to betray Him: 'Now is the Son of Man glorified'?[22] If the passion was to glorify Him, how did the fear of the passion render Him so sorrowful? Unless,

---

22 John 13.31.

perhaps, He was so unreasonable as to be afraid of suffering that which would glorify Him who suffers?

(30)   Perhaps it will be believed that fear gripped Him to such an extent that He begged for the cup to be taken from Him when He said: 'Abba, Father, all things are possible to thee. Remove this cup from me.'[23] In order that I may not be bothered with other arguments, should you not have been able to condemn your own godless stupidity even from the very text that you had read: 'Put up thy sword into the scabbard. Shall I not drink the cup that the Father has given me'?[24] How could the fear of suffering have caused Him to pray for that to be taken from Him which He was hastening to fulfill in His zeal for completing the divine plan. It is a contradiction to say that He who willed to suffer did not will to suffer. And since you were aware of His readiness to suffer, it would have been more reverential on your part to admit your ignorance of these words than to allow yourself to be so carried away by the rage of your godless folly as to assert that He, of whose willingness to suffer you were aware, prayed that He might not suffer.

(31)   I believe that in defending your godlessness you will also arm yourself with the Lord's words: 'God, my God, why hast thou forsaken me?' Perhaps it is your opinion that, after the humiliation of the cross, the Father withdrew His help from Him, whence arose the complaint about the loneliness of His weakness. If the contempt, the weakness, and the cross of Christ therefore are a disgrace in your eyes, you should not be unmindful of this saying: 'Nevertheless, I say to you, hereafter you shall see the Son of Man sitting at the right hand of the Power and coming with the clouds of heaven.'[25]

(32)   Where, I ask, is there fear in the passion? Where is

---

23 Mark 14.36.
24 John 18.11.
25 Cf. Matt. 26.64.

there weakness? Where is there pain? Where is there disgrace? The godless men say that He is afraid. But He Himself declares that He wills to suffers. They contend that He is weak. But He shows that He is powerful, while His persecutors do not dare to meet Him and are stricken with consternation. They charge Him with feeling pain from the wounds of the flesh. But, while He restores the flesh of the ear out of the wound, although He Himself is flesh, we discover that He is outside the carnal nature of suffering from the wound, for, while He touches the mutilated ear with His hand, that hand is from the body, and, while the hand produces the ear out of the wound, it is self-evident that that hand does not belong to a weak body.

(33)   They say that the cross is dishonorable for Him. Yet, because of this, we are to see the Son of Man sitting at the right hand of the power, and He who was born as man by His birth from the Virgin will return in His majesty with the clouds of heaven. O blasphemer, you do not grasp the causes of natural things and, while you are filled with the spirit of godlessness and error, you do not understand the mystery of faith; in your heretical stupidity you also wander from the truth in your understanding of wordly wisdom. Everything that is feared must be avoided while it is feared, and what is weak derives its sense of dread from the realization of its weakness, and what endures pain has in it an unchangeable nature for suffering, and what is dishonorable is always without honor. But by what process of reasoning do you conclude that our Lord Jesus Christ is afraid of that to which He is hastening, that He who fills strong men with terror trembles because of His weakness, and that He who does not allow wounds to cause pain Himself feels pain when wounded, and that He is disgraced by the humiliation of the cross for whom the cross is the sitting together with God and the return to the kingdom?

(34)   Perhaps you judge that this godless pretext is still left to you, that He was afraid of the descent into hell and the necessity of death itself, since He seems to give evidence of this very fact by these words: 'Father, into thy hands I commend my spirit.' If you read this statement and do not understand it, you should either maintain a reverent silence or pray that you may comprehend it with a pious mind; then you would no longer wander about with your reckless statements that proceed from a rage that is absurd and incapable of grasping the truth. In your opinion, are we to believe that He was afraid of the infernal darkness, the roaring flames, and the entire abyss of avenging punishments who says to the thief on the cross: 'Amen I say to thee, this day thou shalt be with me in paradise'?[26] The power of this nature cannot be restricted, I do not say by fear, but even by the region of this infernal world, since it is not absent from paradise when it descends into hell (just as the Son of Man remains in heaven while He speaks on earth), for He promised paradise to His witness and assures him of the joys of perfect blessedness.

Bodily fear does not affect Him who certainly penetrated into hell, but who is present everywhere by the power of His nature. Through the terror which death inspires, the infernal abyss does not have any claims of its own upon this nature, which is the ruler of the world, which is immeasurable by the liberty of its spiritual power, and in which the delights of paradise cannot be wanting. The Lord who will be in hell will also be in paradise. Cut off a part of the inseparable nature that it may have the fear of punishment, and place a part of Christ in hell that it may experience pain, and leave the rest in paradise that it may reign! The robber asks that He remember him in His kingdom. And I believe that the sigh which he heard when the nail pierced His hands

---

26 Luke 23.43.

inspired him to this faith of a blessed confession, and he learned about the kingdom of Christ through the sorrow of the weakened body of Christ. He prays that he may be worthy of being remembered in His kingdom, and you attribute the death on the cross to fear! The Lord promises that he will soon be united with Him in paradise, and you cast Christ into hell and ascribe the fear of its penalties to Him! This faith guarantees a different hope. The thief merited paradise beneath the cross and acknowledged the kingdom of Christ who was hanging on it, but, since you impute the sorrow that comes from pain and the fear of death to Christ, it necessarily follows that you will fail to obtain paradise and the kingdom.

(35) If we compare the meaning of the words and the deeds, therefore, it is clearly seen that the weakness of a corporeal nature is not in the nature of His body to whom it belongs by the power of nature to drive out every bodily weakness, and, although that passion was directed against the body, it did not bring the nature of pain into the body. Although the form of our body was in the Lord, nevertheless, our sinful weakness was not in the body of Him who does not share our origin, since the Virgin brought Him forth by the conception of the Holy Spirit, and, even if she gives birth according to the function of her sex, she did not receive Him from the elements of an earthly conception. She begot a body from herself,[27] but one that was conceived by the Spirit, and He has indeed the true nature of His own body in Himself, but not the weakness of nature, while that body has the true nature of a body because it has been begotten by the Virgin, and it is outside the weakness of our own body because it had its beginning from a spiritual conception.

(36) The heretics believe, however, that they are able to

---

27 While Hilary carefully differentiates the conception of Christ from that of an ordinary man, he always defends the true motherhood of Mary.

defend themselves against the revelation of the apostolic faith
by these words: 'My soul is sad, even unto death,' so that the
confession of Him who says that He is sad bears witness to
the weakness of His nature and the consciousness of this fact
causes Him to be sad. First of all, I appeal to the judgment
of our human reasoning about the significance of to be 'sad
even unto death.' To be sad 'on account of death' does mean
the same as to be 'sad even unto death,' for where the sadness
is on account of death there the death itself is the cause of
the sadness, but where the sadness is unto death there death
is no longer the cause, but the end, of the sadness. If He is
sad, therefore, not on account of death but unto death, we
must inquire into the reason why He is sad. He is sad not for
an uncertain period nor one which our human ignorance
cannot determine, but unto death. So little was the sadness
which He assumed the result of death that it was removed
by death!

(37)   That we may be able to understand the cause of
the sadness, let us see what has preceded and what follows
this declaration of sadness. The Lord completed the mystery
of the entire passion and faith at the supper during the
Passover. Afterwards, He said that all would be scandalized,
but promised to go before them into Galilee. Peter gave Him
the firm assurance that, even though the others would be
scandalized, he would not be scandalized. But the Lord,
aware by the nature of God of what must be done, replied
that he would deny Him three times, in order that we might be
able to judge how the others were scandalized, since the
latter lapsed into so grave a peril to his faith by his threefold
denial.

Then, after He had taken Peter, James, and John—two of
whom were chosen for martyrdom, while John was to be
strengthened for the preaching of the Gospel—He declared
that He was sad unto death. Next, He went ahead and prayed

as follows: 'My Father, if it is possible, let this cup pass away from me; yet not as I will, but as thou willest.' He begs that the cup may pass from Him. At the moment, it was assuredly present before Him and was then being shed in the blood of the New Testament for the sins of many. He does not ask that it may not be with Him, but that it may pass away from Him. Next, He prays that His will may not be done, and He does not will that the very thing which He wills to be done should be granted to Him. He said: 'Yet not as I will, but as thou willest,' so that, while His will in praying for the cup to pass away makes us realize that He had a share in human anxiety, it does lead to any distinction between Himself and the decree of the will that was united with Himself, and which He possessed in common with the Father. But, that it might be understood that He was not praying for Himself and that it might be clearly evident just what He meant when He expressed His will and prayed that it might not be granted to Him, He began the whole prayer in this manner: 'My Father, if it is possible.' Is there something, therefore, about which He is uncertain whether the Father can do it? If nothing is impossible to the Father, we must see to what He is referring when He expresses this condition, 'if it is possible.' These words follow after the request contained in this prayer: 'And he came to his disciples and found them sleeping. And he said to Peter, "Could you not watch one hour with me? Watch and pray, that you may not enter into temptation. The spirit indeed is willing, but the flesh is weak." '[28] Are the reason for the sadness and the prayer for the removal of the cup still obscure? He commands them to watch and pray with Him that they may not enter into temptation, since the spirit indeed is willing but the flesh is weak. They who had promised in the determination derived from their consciousness of the faith that

---

28 Cf. Matt. 26.40,41.

they would not be scandalized were to be scandalized because of the weakness of the flesh. Hence, He is not sad on His own account nor does He pray for Himself, but He warns them to be vigilant in prayer in order that the cup of the passion may not overwhelm them, and He prays that it may pass away from Him so that it may not remain with them.

(38) He prayed, therefore, that, if it were possible, it might be taken away from Him. Although nothing is impossible to God, as He Himself declared: 'Father, all things are possible to thee,' it is impossible for man not to be overcome by the dread of suffering, nor can the faith be known unless it has been put to the test. Hence, as a man speaking for men He wills that the cup pass away, and as the God from God His will is united with that which the Father wills to be done. He clearly taught the meaning of 'if it is possible' in the words He spoke to Peter: 'Behold, Satan has desired to sift you as wheat. But I have prayed for thee, that thy faith should not fail.'[29] For, all were to be tried by this cup of the Lord's passion. And He prays to the Father that his faith may not fail, so that at least the sorrow of repentance may accompany the frailty of his denial, whose faith did not waver because of the remorse that He felt.

(39) The sadness of the Lord, therefore, is unto death, because at His death the earthquake, the darkness in the daytime, the rending of the veil, the opening of the graves, and the resurrection of the dead now strengthened the faith of the Apostles that had been shaken by the terror of the imprisonment during the night, by the insults endured in the scourging, in the blows, in the spittle, in the crown of thorns, in the burden of the cross, throughout the passion, and, lastly, in the condemnation to the cross that was accursed. Hence, since the Lord knew that all these things would come to an end with His passion, He is therefore sorrowful unto death,

---

29 Cf. Luke 22.31,32.

and He realizes that this cup cannot pass away unless He drinks it, since He says: 'My Father, this cup cannot pass away unless I drink it. Thy will be done.'[30] That is to say, when the passion has been completed in Him, then the fear of the cup will pass away, and this cannot pass away unless He drinks it. And the end of its terror will follow only after He has endured the full terror of the passion in Himself, for, after His death, the scandal of the Apostles' weakness will be driven away by the glory of the miraculous events.

(40)   Although by His words, 'Thy will be done,' He placed His Apostles at the disposal of the Father's will in the scandal of the cup, that is, of the passion, He also used these words when He repeated this prayer for the third time. Afterwards, He said: 'Sleep on now, and take your rest.'[31] He who previously reproached the Apostles for sleeping and now commanded them to sleep and to rest did not act thus without being conscious of some inner reason for His action. We believe that Luke has given us the explanation of this exhortation. After declaring that Satan had desired to sift the Apostles as wheat and that the Lord had prayed for the faith of Peter that it might not fail, he added that after the earnest prayer of the Lord there appeared an angel who strengthened Him, and aided by him He began to pray more earnestly, so that the sweat of His body oozed forth in drops of blood. After an angel had been sent for the protection of the Apostles, and after the Lord had been strengthened by him in order that He might not be sad on their account, He now spoke without fear of sadness: 'Sleep on now, and take your rest.' Matthew and Mark, it is true, have said nothing about the angel and the desire of the devil, but, after the sadness of soul, after the reproach of those who were sleeping, and after the prayer for the transfer of

30 Cf. Matt. 26.43.
31 Matt. 26.45.

the cup, there followed the exhortation to those who were sleeping, and this was not done without a good reason, unless you mean to say that since He who had been strengthened by the help of an angel that had been granted to Him and who would be away from them permitted them to sleep because they were to be watched over by a safe guard!

(41) We must not, of course, overlook the fact that we find nothing in writing about the coming of the angel and the bloody sweat in very many of the Latin and Greek manuscripts. Since a doubt arises, therefore, whether these incidents are wanting in the various books or are extraneous additions (the variation in the books leaves us in uncertainty about this question), then, if heresy seeks to derive some advantage from this fact, in order to claim that He is feeble who requires the help of an angel to strengthen Him, let it bear in mind that the creator of the angels does not need to be defended by His own creature, and, furthermore, that He must be strengthened in the same manner in which He is sad. If He is sad for us, that is, for our sake, then He must be strengthened for our sake and for us, because He who is sad because of us and has been strengthened because of us, has been strengthened in that state in which He was sad. No one will dare to attribute the sweat to weakness, for to sweat blood is even contrary to nature. Nor is it a weakness that the Power does not act in accordance with the custom of our nature, nor can we regard the bloody sweat as favoring the heresy of weakness, since it brings out the reality of the body and is a refutation of the heresy that falsely asserts that He had only a phantom body.[32] Consequently, since the sadness is on our account and the prayer is for us, it can only be assumed that all His actions were for our sake, since all His prayers were for us about whom He was afraid.

(42) The Gospels mutually complement one another,

---

32 A reference to the heresy of the Docetists.

since some are understood through others because they all are the teaching of the one Spirit. John, who was pre-eminently a teacher of spiritual ideals, acquaints us with this petition of the Lord that all the others pass over in silence, when he says that the Lord prayed as follows: 'Holy Father, keep them in thy name. While I was with them I kept them in thy name. Those whom thou hast given me I guarded.'[33] Hence, that prayer was not for Himself but for the Apostles, nor is He sad on His own account who warns them to pray that they may not be tempted, nor is the angel sent to Him who, if He wished, could bring down twelve thousand legions from heaven, nor is He who is troubled unto death afraid because of death, nor does He pray that the cup may pass over Him; He prays that the cup may pass away from Him, but it cannot pass away unless He drinks it. To pass away does not mean to depart from its place, but not to exist at all. And this is indeed the very meaning that the statements in the Gospels and from the Apostles point out when they declare: 'Heaven and earth will pass away, but my words will not pass away.'[34] The Apostle also says: 'Behold the former things have passed away and have been made new,'[35] as He likewise does in the words: 'And the figure of this world will pass away.'[36]

Hence, the cup for which He prays to the Father that it may pass away cannot pass away unless He drinks it, and that for which the Lord prays He assuredly prays for these men whom He Himself has saved as long as He remained with them, and whom He has also entrusted to the Father that they may be saved. But now, since He is about to accomplish the mystery of the death, He prays that the Father may be their protector. Supposing, indeed, that the incident

33 John 17.11,12.
34 Mark 13.31.
35 Cf. 2 Cor. 5.17.
36 Cf. 1 Cor. 7.31.

is true,[37] the presence of the angel who has been sent to Him is not open to question, and the assurance that His prayer has been granted is unmistakable, since at the conclusion of the prayer He exhorts them to sleep. The Evangelist now makes known the result of the prayer that was heard, as well as the confidence with which He exhorted them to sleep in the work of the passion itself, when He says to the Apostles who would escape from the hands of His persecutors: 'That the word which he had said might be fulfilled, "Of those whom thou hast given I have not lost one." '[38] The request in the prayer is fulfilled by Himself, and all are saved. He begs the Father to save in His own name those whom He has saved. And so surely did He save them that, even though the faith of Peter was filled with terror, it did not fail, because of the repentance that immediately followed.

(43) Hence, the prayer of the Lord which John made known, the desire of the Devil which Luke mentioned, and the facts cited by Matthew and Luke—the sadness unto death, the reproach on account of the sleeping, and, again, the exhortation to sleep—leave no room for ambiguity, since by the prayer in John in which He entrusts the Apostles to the Father He fully explains the cause of the sorrow and the request for the removal of the cup. The Lord does not pray that suffering be taken away from Him, but begs the Father to protect the Apostles, since He is about to suffer, and the prayer against the Devil which Luke revealed now breathes confidence, and He permits them to do what He had previously forbidden, to sleep in peace.

(44) Hence, the anxiety of human fear is not found in that nature which is above man, and a body that does not trace its origin back to the elements of the earth is not

---

37 That is, if the words about the angel in Gethsemane are not an interpolation.
38 Cf. John 18.9.

subject to the misfortunes of an earthly body, even though the Holy Spirit brought about the origin of the Son of Man by the mystery of the conception. That is to say, the power of the Most High was also mingled with the power of the body which the Virgin begot from the conception of the Holy Spirit. Since the sensation of an animated body derives its life from its association with the soul that is infused into the body, and the soul that is joined to the body vivifies the body itself to feel the pain that afflicts it, so, where the soul in the blessed ardor of its earthly hope and faith has despised the beginnings of an earthly origin in its body, a body is also formed which has its own proper sensation and life in its sufferings, so that it ceases to feel the pain which it endures. What need is there to say anything more about the nature of the Lord's body and the Son of Man who comes down from heaven? At times, even earthly bodies are unaware of fear and pain where there should be pain and fear.

(45)   I ask whether the Jewish boys were afraid of the flames of the Babylonian furnace that was fed with highly combustible material, and whether the fear of so great a fire seized upon that body of our conception? I also raise the question whether they experienced any pain when they were surrounded by the flames? Perhaps they did not feel any pain, therefore, because they were not burnt, and we are to believe that the fire was deprived of its nature of burning at that moment? Of course, the nature of the body was such that it feared to be burnt and could be burnt. If through the spirit of faith it is possible for earthly bodies, that is, those which derive their origin from the elements of ordinary causes, to be neither burnt nor afraid, then what is contrary to nature in the case of man because of his faith in God is not to be looked upon as something natural in the case of God, if the origin of the nature traces its beginning back to the power of the Spirit. The boys are bound and are in the

midst of the fire and do not fear the fire as they walk up in
it. They do not feel the flame while they are in prayer and
they cannot be burnt while they are in the fire. In their case,
the bodies and the fire lose their proper nature, for the
former are not burnt and the latter does not burn. Yet, in
regard to others, the fire and the body retain their proper
nature, for the bystanders are burnt and those who inflict
the penalty are themselves punished.

O godless heretic, you wish Christ to suffer pain from the
nail that penetrates His hands and for that wound to cause
Him the pain that follows from a piercing instrument. I ask
why the boys did not fear the fire, and why they did not
experience any pain, and what kind of a nature was in their
bodies that it should gain victory over the nature of fire? If
those boys in the ardor of their faith and in the glory of a
blessed martyrdom do not know how to fear things that are
to be feared, should Christ have been sad through His fear
of the cross? Even if He had been conceived according to
the origin of our defects, still, on the cross He was to remain
God, He was to judge the world, and was to be the king of
the eternal ages. And would He have been unmindful of
such great rewards and have trembled with the anxiety of a
shameful fear?

(46) Daniel, who was to be nourished with the food of
the Prophet, does not fear the lions' den. The Apostles rejoice
when they are scourged and suffer for the name of Christ.
For Paul his own sacrifice is the crown of justice. With hymns
the martyrs offer their necks to be cut off by the executioners,
and with canticles they mount the burning fire that has been
prepared for them. When the fear of a natural weakness
has been removed from their bodies, the consciousness of
faith changes their very bodies to such a point that they are
no longer aware of feeling pain, so that the determination of
the soul gives strength to the body and the animated body

feels only that to which it is aroused by the eagerness of the soul, so that the body, invigorated by the soul, does not feel the suffering which the soul despises in its yearning for glory. If these things are natural in men through the intense longing of an ardent soul for glory so that they are unaware of sufferings, are not conscious of their wounds, and do not feel death, shall we then ascribe to Jesus Christ, the Lord of glory (in the hem of whose garment there is power, in the nature of whose body there is spittle and speech, while the man with the withered arm is no longer withered and receives the command to stretch forth his arm, and the man born blind does not suffer from the defects of his birth, while the man with a mangled ear is not mangled), that weakness of a body that has been pierced and is in pain, in which the spirit of their faith has not left these noble and blessed men?

(47) Hence, the only-begotten God endured all the weaknesses of our sufferings that pressed upon Him, but He endured them by the power of His own nature, just as He was also born by the power of His own nature, for, although He was born, He clung to the nature of His own omnipotence in His birth. While He was born in accordance with human law, He was not conceived in accordance with human law, and while He possesses in Himself the nature of a human creature in His birth, He Himself is not included in the nature of a human creature in His beginning. Hence, He endured the weakness of our body in His own body in such a way as to take upon Himself the sufferings of our body by the power of His own body.[39] Prophetic utterance also bears witness to this faith of ours when it declares: 'He bears our sins and suffers for us. And we looked upon him in his sorrows, in his blows, and in his torture. But he was wounded

---

39 That is, by the power of the divine Word dwelling within Him.

on account of our iniquities, and he was made weak on account of our sins.'[40]

The judgment of human reasoning is therefore deceived if it concludes that He experiences pain because He suffers. Although He bears our sins, that is, while He assumes the body of our sin, He Himself does not sin. He was sent in the likeness of our sinful flesh; while He indeed bears sins in the flesh, they are our sins. And He endures pain for us, but He does not endure pain with the feeling of our pain, because He who was also found in the appearance as man, while He has in Himself a body subject to pain, does not have a nature that feels pain, while His appearance is that of a man and His origin is not that of a man, for He was born by the conception of the Holy Spirit. From these facts, therefore, we conclude that He endured pain, was struck, and was tortured. He received the form of slave and was born as man from the Virgin and He has led us to believe that in the passion pain belongs to Him by nature. 'But He was wounded,' yet it was 'on account of our iniquities.' Although He was wounded, the wound was not caused by His own sin, and whatever He suffers He does not suffer for Himself. He was not born as man for Himself, nor is He a sinner by His own conduct. The Apostle testifies to the reason for this dispensation when he says: 'Praying to be reconciled to God through Christ. For our sake he made him to be sin who knew nothing of sin.'[41] He will condemn sin in the flesh through sin; although He is exempt from sin, He Himself was made sin, that is, through the flesh He condemns sin in the flesh who indeed does not know the flesh but was made flesh for us, and therefore was wounded because of our iniquities.

(48) Furthermore, the Apostle knows nothing about the

---

40 Cf. Isa. 53.4,5.
41 Cf. 2 Cor. 5.20,21.

fear of pain in Christ. When he was about to speak of the dispensation of the passion he proclaimed it in the mystery of the Godhead, saying: 'Forgiving you all sins, cancelling the handwriting that was against us in the decree, that was hostile to us, taking it completely away, nailing it to the cross, stripping himself of the flesh he courageously led the Principalities and Powers away, triumphing over them in himself.'[42] Do you believe, therefore, that this Power yielded to the wound of the nail, that it was terrified by the blow of the piercing nail, and was changed into a nature capable of experiencing pain? Yet, the Apostle who speaks while Christ spoke in Him, and who reminds us of the work of our salvation through the Lord, expressed the death of Christ in this manner: He stripped Himself of the flesh, courageously put the Powers to shame, and triumphed over them in Himself.

If His passion is compulsory and not the gift of your salvation, if on the cross there is the pain of the transfixion and not the nailing of the decree in which the sentence of death was written against you, if in death there is the power of death and not the stripping off of the flesh through the power of God, if finally, that death is something else than a disgrace for the Powers, an act of confidence and a triumph, then attribute the weakness to Him if there is something compulsory and a nature, if you wish, to find there force, diffidence, and disgrace. If, on the contrary, these things are proclaimed when referring to the mystery of the passion, what rage is it, I ask, to repudiate the faith of the apostolic teaching, to change the meaning of the true doctrine, and to distort all these facts and to allege against Him the disgraceful accusation of a weak nature, which is the will as well as the mystery, which is the power, the confidence, and the triumph? It is unquestionably a triumph when they seek to crucify Him and do not endure His presence when He offers Himself,

---

42 Cf. Col. 2.13-15.

to be under sentence of death but from it to be seated one day at the right hand of the Power, to be pierced with nails but to pray for the persecutors, to drink the vinegar but to complete the mystery, to be reckoned among the wicked but to bestow paradise, to be raised upon the wood while the earth quakes, to hang on the cross while the sun and the day take to flight, to go forth from the body but to call back souls into the bodies, to buried as one dead but to rise as God, as man to endure all these weaknesses for our sake but as God to triumph in all these things.

(49) But, as the heretics believe, an important and weighty statement still faces us in which there is an admission of weakness, especially since it has come from the mouth of the Lord Himself, when He said: 'God, my God, why hast thou forsaken me?' Is not such a statement the highest form of complaint to lament the fact that He has been abandoned and exposed to weakness? But, how opposed this impetuous deduction of a godless understanding is to the whole tenor of the Lord's utterances, so that He who hastens to death, who will be glorified by it, who will be seated after it at the right hand of the Power, was afraid to die in the midst of these many reasons for happiness, and, accordingly, complains that His own God has abandoned Him to the necessity of dying, since He will abide in the midst of all these blessed ones by undergoing death!

(50) Yes, the heretical spirits even press forward along the road of this blasphemous belief as if it had been prepared for them. They will say that either God the Word was completely absorbed into the soul of the body, so that Jesus Christ, the Son of Man, was not the same as He who was also the Son of God, and that God the Word failed to be Himself while He performed the function of the soul in vivifying the body, or that the man who was born was not Christ at all, because the Word of God dwelt in Him as the Spirit had

dwelt in the Prophets. The error of this absurd heresy reaches greater heights of godless audacity so that Jesus Christ is not Christ before He was born from Mary, while He who exists was not born, but first began to be at that time when He was born. To it they also add this distortion, that God the Word, as if He were some part of the power of God, extends Himself by a sort of unbroken continuity, and dwells in that man who began to exist from Mary, and instructed Him in the powers of the divine activity, yet He lives through the movement and nature of His own soul.

(51)   Hence, through this subtle and pernicious doctrine they are led into the error either that God the Word exists as the soul of the body through a change in His nature that weakens Him and the Word ceases to be God, or, again, by means of an external and separated nature, that man was animated only by the life of the soul that moves Him in whom there dwelt the Word of God, that is, a certain power, as it were, of an extended voice. Thus, the road to the most godless knowledge is completely open, so that either God the Word ceased to be Himself in the soul and did not remain God the Word, or else that Christ did not exist at all before the birth from Mary, because Jesus Christ as a man with merely an ordinary soul and body had no other origin for Himself except this one in which He began to be man. The power of this extended voice from without strengthened Him for the power of His activities, and, when the Word of God again withdrew this extension, He who is now left alone cries out: 'God, my God, why hast thou forsaken me?' Or, certainly, at that time when He was changed into the soul of the body by the nature of the Word of God, He enjoyed the help of the Father in everything, but now, when He is in need and is exposed to death, He complains of His loneliness and reproaches Him who deserts Him. Thus, in every way a deadly menace awaits the faith that has allowed itself to be

deceived, if we believe that a weakness of nature in the Word of God is indicated by His complaint, or that He was not God the Word at all, while the only beginning for Christ Jesus was through His birth from Mary.

(52) Amid these godless and untenable theories the faith of the Church, that has been inspired by the apostolic doctrines, knows the birth in Christ, but is unaware of a beginning. It knows the dispensation, but is ignorant of a division. It does not separate Christ Jesus so that Jesus Himself is not Christ, nor does it differentiate the Son of Man from the Son of God, lest, perhaps, the Son of God may not be also recognized as the Son of Man. Nor does it sever Christ by a threefold faith, whose garment woven from the top in one piece was not torn, so that it divides Jesus Christ into the Word, the soul, and the body. And, again, it does not absorb God the Word into the soul and the body. In Him is the whole God the Word, and in Him is the whole man Christ, while it holds fast to this one thing in the mystery of its confession: not to believe that Christ is anything else than Jesus and not to proclaim that Jesus is anything else than Christ.

(53) I am not unaware of the extent to which the sublimity of the heavenly mystery prepares difficulties for the weakness of our human understanding, so that it is impossible to discuss these questions readily, to distinguish them in our mind, or even to grasp them in our understanding. Since the Apostle, however, realizes that this is an arduous and very troublesome task for our human nature, to comprehend in our judgment the manner in which divine deeds are done, just as if, the more powerful God is in accomplishing them, so much the more acute is the judgment in grasping them,[43] he writes as follows to his lawful son according to the faith,

---

43 This is probably a reference to Arian leader, Eunomius, who boasted that he knew everything about divine matters.

who had received the sacred Scriptures from his childhood:
'Just as when I went to Macedonia, I exhorted thee to stay
on at Ephesus that thou mightest charge some not to teach
otherwise, and not to study fables and endless genealogies,
which beget controversies rather than godly edification, which
is in the faith.'[44]

He forbids him to treat the question of genealogies and to
speak of fables, which give rise to endless controversies. But
he teaches that godly edification is in the faith, in order that
he may define the limits of human reverence in its faithful
worship of God's omnipotence, and that our weakness may
not try to comprehend those subjects which weaken the nature
of our perception. If they are dazed who strain their power
of sight by looking into the brightness of the sun, so that the
nature of their eyes is brought to a point where even their
sense of vision is extinguished if in their curiosity they seek
more eagerly for the source of the blinding light, and as a
result, in their endeavor to see more, they do not see at all,
what are we to expect in the things of God and in the sun
of justice? Will not they who wish to be too wise lapse into
folly? Will not the dullness of a senseless stupidity take the
place even of the keen light of knowledge? A lower nature
will not grasp the principle of a higher nature, nor does
heaven's plan of action come within the range of human
comprehension. Everything that is consciously subject to weakness will be kept within the limits of its weakness.

Hence, the power of God surpasses the human mind, and,
should weakness strive to attain it, it will be made weaker,
while at the same time it will lose this very thing that it
possesses. Being more vigorous, the nature of heavenly things
will exhaust it, because it itself is superior to its power of
comprehension and wears it down in spite of all its stubbornness in trying to reach it. Hence, just as we must gaze upon

---

44 Cf. 1 Tim. 1.3,4.

the sun in such a way as to be able to see it, and admit just
as much of its light as we must receive, in order that we may
not obtain even less than we can if we hope to obtain more,
so we must grasp the heavenly plan in so far as it permits
itself to be understood, and should look for it in so far as it
has offered itself to be comprehended in order that we may
not lose that which has been granted to us, if we are dis-
satisfied with the moderate amount that has been granted.
Accordingly, in God there is something that we can perceive.
It is indeed there if you only direct your desires to that which
is possible. Just as there is something in the sun that you
can see if you only wish to see what you can, but you lose
what you can see when you strive for that which you cannot
see, so in the things of God you also possess something that
you can understand if you will only understand what you
can understand. But, if you aspire beyond that which is
possible for you, that which would have been possible for
you also becomes impossible.

(54)   I shall not yet touch upon the mystery of that timeless birth. This treatise belongs in its proper place.[45] In the
meantime, I shall speak of the mystery of the flesh that was
assumed. At this point I consult the investigators of the
heavenly secrets, so that they may express the mystery of
Christ who was born according to His nature from the Virgin.
Whence do they explain the conception of the Virgin?
Whence the birth from the Virgin? What kind of a reason
will they give here for the beginnings of His birth? How was
He formed in the secret recesses of the mother's womb?
Whence the body? Whence the man? And now, last of all,
what is meant by the Son of Man who remains in heaven
and has come down from heaven? For, in accordance with
the laws pertaining to bodies, to descend is not the same as
to remain. The one is a change in going down; the other is an

---

45 Cf. Book 12.

immobility in remaining. The infant weeps, but is in heaven; the child grows, but remains as God in His fullness. Now, how will the perception of our human understanding comprehend Him when He ascends to where He was before, and when He descends who remains? The Lord said: 'What if you shall see the Son of Man ascending where he was before?'[46] The Son of Man ascends to heaven where He was before and what power of reasoning will grasp this fact? The Son of Man who is in heaven descends from heaven and what power of reasoning will attain to this? 'The Word was made flesh.' What words will express this? The Word is made flesh, that is, God is made man and He who is man descends without descending. He is who was, and He was not what He is. We run through these events and we fail to give an explanation; we see the explanation and we do not understand the events. But we shall know Christ Jesus if we understand Him in this manner, and we shall not know Him if we imagine that we know more about Him.

(55) Now, how great is that mystery of the words and the deeds! Christ weeps, and in His anguish of mind tears flow from His eyes. Whence came these defects into His soul that the grief of sadness draws forth tears from His body? And what bitter event, what intolerable pain, caused the Son of Man, who descends from heaven, to lapse into tears? Furthermore, what was it that wept in Him? Was it God the Word or the soul of His body? Although tears are a bodily function, a certain sorrow of the soul uses the body as its servant and brings them forth as if they were sweat. What, then, is the reason that prompts Him to weep? Does He pay a merited honor by His tears to the impious and parricidal Jerusalem upon whom nothing could befall that would be a fitting punishment for its murder of such great Prophets and Apostles and for the death of its own Lord

---

46 Cf. John 6.63.

Himself? Does the misfortune of this lost and hopeless race also cause Him pain as people bewail the calamities of earthly deaths? What, I ask, is this mystery of the weeping? The soul which is sad weeps. Was it this that sent the Prophets? Was it this that so often wished to gather its chickens together and cover them with the shadow of its wings? But, God the Word is not subject to pain, nor the Spirit to tears. Neither is it fitting for the soul to do anything before the body.[47] Yet, there is no doubt that Jesus Christ really wept!

(56) He also shed tears for Lazarus that were equally genuine. First of all, I ask what prompted Him to weep in the case of Lazarus? Certainly it was not because of his death, which was not unto death but for the glory of God, for the Lord said: 'This sickness is not unto death, but for the glory of God, that through it the Son of God may be glorified.' Hence, the death, which is the reason for glorifying God, did not result in the sadness of weeping. The necessity for weeping did not even exist, since He was absent when Lazarus died. He Himself says clearly: 'Lazarus is dead; and I rejoice on your account that I was not there, that you may believe.'[48] Hence, His absence does not explain His reason for weeping, since it aided the faith of the Apostles, for through His conscious possession of the divine knowledge He, though absent, had made known his death. Consequently, there was nothing that compelled Him to weep, yet He wept. Nevertheless, I want to know to whom will that weeping be ascribed? To God? To the soul? Or to the body? The body by itself alone has no tears, since it sheds them in the sorrow of its grieving soul. There was far less reason, however, for

---

47 We cannot ascribe any activity to the soul before its union with the body; hence, it did not send the Prophets of the Old Law, since it did not then exist.

48 John 11.4,14,15.

God to weep, since He was to be glorified in Lazarus. It is not logical that the soul should call back Lazarus from the grave,[49] and that by the command and power of the soul, which is closely bound up with the body, the soul should be called back to its dead body from which it was already separated. Does He grieve who is to be glorified? Does He weep who is to give life? It is not characteristic of Him who is to give life to weep, and of Him who is to be glorified to feel pain, yet He gives life who wept and who felt pain.

(57)   We are mentioning a few things about many subjects, not because our lack of knowledge makes it necessary for us to do so, or because we are not familiar with what has been said, but in order that a concise presentation of our arguments may obtain a favorable hearing for our complete explanation. The Lord accomplishes and performs actions that are not known in spite of the knowledge of them, actions of which we are aware and which we do not understand, while the actions are real and the power to do them is a mystery,[50] as we shall clearly prove from these statements which He makes: 'For this reason the Father loves me, because I lay down my life that I may take it up again. No one takes it from me, but I lay it down of myself. I have the power to lay it down, and I have the power to take it up again. Such is the command I have received from my Father.'[51]

He lays down His soul of Himself, and I ask who lays it down? We do not doubt that Christ is God the Word, and again we realize that the Son of Man is composed of a soul and a body, since the angel confirms this fact in his words to Joseph: 'Arise, and take the child and his mother, and go

---

49 It is not the human soul of Christ, but the divine omnipotence, that calls Lazarus back to life.

50 The miracles of Christ are known, but the power by which He performs them is unknown.

51 John 10.17,18. From Hilary's explanation of this text in the words that follow it is evident that *anima* can be translated either as 'life' or in its literal meaning as 'soul.'

into the land of Israel, for those who sought the child's life are dead.'[52] Accordingly, I ask to whom does this soul belong? To the body or to God? If to the body, what power does the body have into which life is infused by the movement of the soul? Furthermore, has the body, which is immovable and lifeless without the soul, received any command? If anyone believes that God the Word lays down His soul in order to take it up again, let him prove that the Word of God died, that is, that He was without sensation and life, like a dead body, because He had assumed His soul again in order to live, and would again be vivified by it.

(58) But, no one who shares the gift of reason will assign a soul to God, although it is often written that the soul of God hates the sabbaths and the new moons, and also finds His delights with certain persons.[53] This phrase is generally used in the same sense in which hands, eyes, fingers, arm and heart are attributed to an incorporeal God. Members, that are composed of corporeal parts, are incongruous for the durability of Him who is and who does not change, since a spirit according to the words of the Lord does not have flesh and bones, but this simple and blessed nature endures as one complete whole which includes everything. Hence, God is not infused with life in a corporeal manner through the activity of an interior soul, but He Himself lives a life unto Himself.

(59) How does He lay down His soul or take it up again after it has been laid down? Or what is the meaning of this command? God does not lay it down to death, therefore, nor does He take it up again to life. The body is not commanded to take it up again, because it does not take it up again by itself. It was said about the temple of His body: 'Destroy

52 Matt. 2.20.
53 Cf. Isa. 1.14; 42.1.

this temple, and after three days I will raise it up.'[54] Hence, God raises up the temple of His own body. And who lays down His soul in order to take it up again? The body does not take it up by itself, but it is raised up by God. That which is dead is raised up, and that which lives does not lay down its soul. God, therefore, did not die nor was He buried, yet He declared: 'For in pouring this ointment on my body, she has done it for my burial.'[55] What was poured on His body was done for His burial, and what He is is not the same as what is His, and to be done for His burial is not one and the same as for His body to be anointed, nor is 'His body was buried' synonymous with 'He was buried.'

(60) The understanding of the divine mystery consists in this, to recognize as God Him whom you recognize as man, and to recognize Him as man whom you recognize as God; not to divide Jesus Christ because the Word was made flesh, not to believe that He was buried of whom you know that He rose from the dead, not to doubt that He whose burial you do not dare to deny rose from the dead. Jesus Christ was buried, because He also died. He died who exclaimed when He was at the point of death: 'God, my God, why hast thou forsaken me?' He spoke these words who also said: 'Amen I say to thee, this day thou shalt be with me in paradise.' And He who also promised paradise declared with a loud voice: 'Father, into thy hands I commend my spirit. And having said this, he expired.'[56]

(61) You who now divide Christ into three parts—the Word, the soul, and the body—or who reduce the whole Christ, God the Word, into a mere man of an ordinary nature, make known to us this mystery of great piety which was manifested in the flesh! What spirit did Christ give up?

54 Cf. John 2.19.
55 Matt. 26.12.
56 Luke 23.46.

And who commended His spirit into the hands of the Father? And who was on that same day in paradise? And who complained that He was abandoned by God? The complaint about the abandonment is a weakness in the dying man, but the promise of paradise is the kingdom of the living God. The commending of the spirit is an act of confidence on the part of the one who commends; the giving up of the spirit is the departure of one who is dying. Hence, I ask: Who dies? Assuredly, it is He who gives up the spirit. Who, then, gives up the spirit? Certainly, He who commended His spirit to the Father. If He who commended is the same one as He who died when He gave up the spirit, then I raise the question: Did the body commend the soul or did God commend the soul of this body? It is clear that the spirit often means the soul, as it is even evident from this very fact that Jesus gave up the spirit when He was about to die. If anyone will imagine, therefore, that we are to consider the soul as being commended by the body, namely, that which lives by that which must be dissolved, the eternal by that which is to see corruption, that which remains by that which is to be raised from the dead, then there is no doubt that the same one commended the spirit to the Father who was also with the thief in paradise on that same day. And I ask whether He who was received into the grave remained in paradise, or whether He who remained in paradise complained that He was abandoned by God?

(62) It is the one and the same Lord Jesus Christ, the Word made flesh, who is referring to Himself in all these instances, who is man while He indicates that He is abandoned to death, but, while He is man, He reigns as God in paradise. Then, while He reigns in paradise, as the Son of God He commends His spirit to the Father, but as the Son of Man He surrenders His spirit to death that He had commended to the Father. Why do we now heap insults upon

the mystery? You hear Him complain that He is forsaken in death because He is man; you hear Him who dies confess that He reigns in paradise because He is God. Why do we cling to these words which He uttered in order to let us know about His death merely for the sake of encouraging impiety? And why do we keep silent about that which the same One asserted in order to prove His immortality? If this voice and these words are from the same One who complains that He is abandoned and who declares that He reigns, by what kind of unbelief do we divide our faith so that the same One who also reigns did not die at the same time, since it is the self-same One who has testified in both instances about Himself, both when He commends the spirit as well as when He expires? And if the same One commends and gives up His spirit, and He who reigns dies, and He who is dead reigns, then in the mystery of the Son of Man and the Son of God we find that He who reigns dies and He who dies reigns.

(63) Accordingly, let all godless impiety that is incapable of grasping the divine revelation cease its activity, which does not know that Christ weeps not for Himself but for us, so that the very emotions of our human custom which He also took upon Himself bear witness to the reality of the manhood which He assumed, which does not realize that Christ does not die for Himself, but for our life, in order that the life of mortal men may be renewed through the death of the immortal God, which does not understand the complaint of Him who is abandoned and the assurance of Him who reigns, so that both the dead man as well as the God who reigns are discernible by our mind, because God reigns and because He complains that He dies. He who dies is not another person from Him who reigns, nor is He who commends His spirit another person from Him who expires, nor is He who was buried another person from Him who

rises again, nor is He who descends not one and the same person as he who ascends.

(64) In reference to this subject, listen to the faith of the apostolic doctrine that was taught, not by the knowledge of the flesh, but the gift of the Spirit, since he says to the Greeks who seek for wisdom and to the Jews who ask for signs: 'But we, for our part, preach a crucified Christ—to the Jews indeed a stumbling block and to the Gentiles foolishness, but to those who are called, both Jews and Greeks, Christ, the power of God and the wisdom of God.'[57] Is Christ divided so that Jesus who was crucified is one person and Christ as the power and the wisdom of God is another person? This is a stumbling block to the Jews and foolishness to the Gentiles. To us, however, Christ Jesus is the power of God and the wisdom of God, but a wisdom unknown to the world and not grasped by the prudent ones of the world. And learn from the same blessed Apostle how little it is understood when he says: 'But we speak the wisdom of God, which is hidden in the mystery, which God foreordained before the world unto our glory, a wisdom which none of the rulers of this world has known; for had they known it they would never have crucified the Lord of glory.'[58] Is the Apostle ignorant of the fact that this wisdom is hidden in the mystery and is unknown to the rulers of the world? Does he divide Christ so that the Lord of majesty is one person and Jesus crucified is another person? He contradicts this most absurd and most blasphemous opinion by saying: 'For I determined not to know anything among you, except Christ Jesus and him crucified.'[59]

(65) The Apostle does not know anything else and is determined not to know anything else. But we, by our weak

---

57 1 Cor. 1.23,24.
58 Cf. 1 Cor. 2.7,8.
59 Cf. 1 Cor. 2.2.

understanding and still weaker faith, as judges of the mysteries and detractors of the hidden revelation, sever Christ Jesus, divide Him, and separate Him into two parts. To us, Christ crucified is one person and the wisdom of God is another person. He who was buried is one person and He who descends is another person. The Son of Man is one person and the Son of God is another person. We teach what we do not understand and we who are ignorant find fault. We who are men improve the words of God! We disdain to believe with the Apostle, who writes as follows: 'Who shall make accusation against the elect of God? It is God who justifies. Who shall condemn? It is Christ who died; yes, and rose again, he who is at the right hand of God, who also intercedes for us.'[60]

Is there someone else who intercedes for us than He who is at the right hand of God? Or is He who is at the right hand of God not the very One who rose again? Or is not He who rose again the same as He who died? Or is not He who died the same as He who condemns? Or is not He who condemns the same God who justifies? If it is possible, therefore, let us separate Christ who condemns from the God who justifies, the dead Christ from the Christ who condemns, the Christ sitting at the right hand and interceding for us from the dead Christ. If, therefore, the one Christ is all these things, and there is not one Christ who dies and another who is buried, and one who descends into hell and another who ascends into heaven, according to those words of the Apostle: 'Now this "he ascended," what does it mean but that he also first descended into the lower parts of the earth? He who descends, he it is who ascends also above all the heaven, that he may fill all things.'[61] Do we, then, proceed so far in our godless ignorance and foolish talk as to assert that we are

60 Cf. Rom. 8.33,34.
61 Cf. Eph. 4.9,10.

able to explain whatever is hidden in the mystery of God?
'He who descends, he it is who ascends.' Is there any doubt
that Jesus Christ rises as man from the dead, ascends above
all the heaven, and is at the right hand of God? Will it be
said that the body which lay in the tomb descended into
hell? If, therefore, He who descends is the same one as He
who ascends, and we do not believe that His body descended
into hell, and there is no doubt that the body which rose
from the dead ascended into heaven, what faith is left for us
here except that of the mystery which is hidden and unknown
to the world and to the rulers of the world, so that, since He
who descends and ascends is one and the same person, He
is also for us the one Jesus Christ, the Son of God, the Son of
Man, God the Word, and the Man in the flesh who
suffered, died, was buried, rose again, was received into
heaven, and sits at the right hand of God, and as a consequence of the nature and the dispensation He possesses in
Himself, in one and the same person, both in the form of
God as well as in the form of man, the attributes that belong
to man without any separation from Himself as well as the
attributes that belong to God without any division in Himself.

(66)   Hence, while instructing the faith of our reckless
and ignorant judgment, the Apostle expressed the mystery of
this doctrine as follows: 'For though he was crucified through
weakness, yet he lives through the power of God.'[62] While
proclaiming that the Son of God was the Son of Man who,
although man, according to the divine plan yet remained
God by His nature, he declared that the same One, who lives
by the power of God, was crucified through weakness, so
that, since the weakness was from the form of a slave and
the nature from the form of God, there would be no
uncertainity about the mystery in which He suffered and
lived who had assumed the form of a slave although He was

---

62 2 Cor. 13.4.

in the form of God, and since in the same person there would be the weakness in the suffering and the power of God in the life, then He who suffered as well as lived would not be a different person and one separated from Himself.

(67) The only-begotten God truly endured what men can suffer. Let us have recourse to the faith and words of the Apostle: 'For I delivered unto you first of all, that Christ died for our sins according to the Scriptures, and that he was buried, and that he rose again the third day according to the Scriptures.'[63] He did not use mere explanatory words that might afford a pretext for error, but reminded us that we are to confess the manner of the death and resurrection not so much by the names of the things as by the expressions of the Scriptures, so that our understanding of His death might be in accord with that which the Scriptures pointed out. While He did not disregard our feeble thoughts and the slanders against the faith that might perplex us, he only added this conclusion, 'according to the Scriptures,' to his teaching about the death and the resurrection, in order that we might not become helpless because we were tossed about by the wind of useless disputes or hampered by the absurd subtleties of unsound opinions. The untarnished faith would always be called back to this harbor of its own true religion so that it would believe and confess the death of Jesus Christ, the Son of God and the Son of Man, 'according to the Scriptures.' Thus, a God-fearing assurance was placed at our disposal in the struggle against a degrading doctrine, since we are to believe that Christ Jesus died and rose again just as it is written about Him.

The faith is not exposed to danger and every pious belief is secure in the hidden mystery of God. Christ was born from the Virgin, but, 'according to the Scriptures,' He was conceived by the Holy Spirit. Christ wept, but in such a way,

63 Cf. 1 Cor. 15.3,4.

'according to the Scriptures,' that He rejoiced while He wept. And Christ was hungry, but, 'according to the Scriptures,' when He was without food He displayed His activity as God against the tree that bore no fruit. Christ suffered, but, 'according to the Scriptures,' at that moment He received His confessor with Him in the kingdom of paradise. He died, but, 'according to the Scriptures,' the Lord rose again and sits at the right hand of the Lord. Hence, in the faith of this mystery there is life; such a profession resists every false interpretation.

(68) Assuredly, the Apostle does not allow anything that could cause us to doubt or to say: 'Christ was born, suffered, died, and rose again. But how? By what power? Through what sort of a division? With what parts? Who is he who weeps? Who rejoices? Who complains? Who descends? Who ascends?' In this instance, while revealing that the merit of faith comes only by confessing the true worship of God without hesitation, he declared: 'But the justice from the faith thus says, "Do not say in thy heart: Who ascends into heaven?" (that is, to bring down Christ); "or, Who descends into the abyss?" (that is, to bring up Christ from the dead). But what does Scripture say? "The word is near thee, in thy mouth and in thy heart" (that is, the word of faith, which we preach). For if thou shalt confess with thy mouth that Jesus is the Lord, and shall believe in thy heart that God has raised him from the dead, thou shalt be saved.'[64]

Faith perfects the just man, as it is said: 'Abraham believed God and it was credited to him as justice.'[65] Did Abraham raise any objections to God when He promised him the inheritance of the Gentiles and that the number of his offspring would be as numerous as the stars and the sand? Since the God-fearing faith does not tolerate any uncertainity

64 Cf. Rom. 10.6-9.
65 Cf. Gen. 15.6; Rom. 4.3.

about the omnipotence of God, it is not restrained by the natures of human weakness, but, while it despises all that is perishable and earthly within it, it receives the faith of the divine promise in a measure exceeding the bounds of our human nature. Human law can in no way restrict the powers of God, because God has revealed just as much in the fulfillment as He manifested His good will in the promise. Hence, there is nothing more just than faith. Although in earthly matters impartiality and moderation are to be approved, nothing is more just than for man to believe in the omnipotence of God by realizing that His power is without limitation.

(69) Accordingly, while waiting for this justice in us which is from faith, the Apostle did away with the godlessness of an uncertain and unbelieving vagueness and forbade the misgivings of anxious thought to gain an entrance into our heart by appealing to the authority of a prophetic utterance. He declared: 'Do not say in thy heart: Who ascends into heaven?' He accompanied these words, which the Prophet expressed in this manner, with an explanation in the next sentence when he said: 'That is, to bring down Christ.' The human mind cannot attain to heavenly knowledge by its own power of reasoning, nor does religious faith regard the words of God as uncertain. Christ did not need the help of a human power in order to be brought from the abode of His blessedness into a body through the assistance of someone who has ascended into heaven. No exterior power brought Him to the earth.

We are to hold that He has come in the precise manner in which He has come, and it is genuine piety to confess that Christ was not brought down, but descended. It is the mystery both in time as well as in the work. We are not to believe that He was brought down by someone else because He has recently come, nor are we to assume that His coming in time made Him subject to the power of someone who has brought Him down. He does not even allow infidelity to entertain any doubts about someone else. The prophetic words immediately follow: 'Or, Who descends into the abyss?' And he at once gives the interpretation: 'That is, to bring up Christ from the dead.' The liberty of returning to heaven proceeds from the liberty of descending to earth. But the vacillation of indecision has been removed. The knowledge is in the faith; the foundation is in the power; the effect is in the deeds; the cause is in the omnipotence.

(70) In this matter we must have an unwavering conviction. When explaining the whole mystery of the Scriptures, the Apostle says: 'The word is near thee, in thy mouth and in thy heart.' Our confession of faith must not be slow or expressed in words that leave much to be desired, nor should there be any interval between the heart and the mouth in order that the testimony, which we must render to the true faith, may not be regarded as proceeding from an unbelieving uncertainty. It must be also near us and in us in order that there may be no hesitation between the heart and the mouth and perhaps our faith may not be exactly the same in our mind as in our words, but in order that through the close connection between the mouth and the heart it may bring about an unquestioning acceptance of the true faith in our thinking as well as in our speaking. As in other instances, the Apostle has indeed added an explanation of these words: 'That is, the word of faith, which we preach. For if thou shalt confess with thy mouth that Jesus is the Lord, and shall believe in thy heart that God raised him from the dead, thou shalt be saved.'

It is piety not to doubt; it is justice to believe; and it is salvation to confess. Salvation consists in not being lost amid uncertainties, in not being aroused to foolish talk, in not engaging in any kind of debate about the attributes of God, in not fixing limits for His power, in not searching anew for the causes of the inscrutable mysteries, in confessing the Lord Jesus, and in believing that God raised Him from the dead. What folly it is to pass disparaging remarks about Jesus, who He is and what is His nature, since salvation consists in knowing only this, that He is the Lord! Furthermore, what a blunder it is for our human vanity to stir up controversies about His resurrection, since it is sufficient for life to believe that God has raised Him up! Hence, faith is in simplicity, justice is in faith, and piety is in the confession. God does not call us to the blessed life by means of difficult questions, nor does He lure us on by the various categories of oratorical eloquence. Eternal happiness is obtained completely and easily by believing that God raised Jesus from the dead by confessing that He Himself is the Lord. Let no one, therefore, misuse what we have discussed in our ignorance as a vindication of impiety. We must understand that Jesus Christ died in order that we might live in Him.

(71)   If to make us aware of His death He therefore said: 'God, my God, why hast thou forsaken me?' and 'Father, into thy hands I commend my spirit,' did He not have in mind our confession of faith when He declared that He was weak, rather than leave us in uncertainty? When He was about to raise Lazarus, He prays to His Father. Did He stand in need of prayers who said: 'Father, I give thee thanks that thou hast heard me. And I know that thou always hearest me; but because of the people I spoke, that they may believe that thou hast sent me?'[66] Consequently, He prayed for our sake in order that we might recognize Him as the Son, and, although the words of the petition did not bring Him any personal gain, He spoke for the benefit of our faith. Hence, He does not need help at that moment, but we need to be instructed. He also prays that He may be glorified, and immediately they heard the voice of God the Father from heaven,

---

66 Cf. John 11.41,42.

glorifying Him. And He said to those who were startled at the voice which they had heard: 'Not for me did this voice come, but for you.'[67]

He prays to the Father for us; the Father speaks to us; and all this was done for the sake of our profession of faith. Since the response about the glorification was granted not because of His request for the glorification, but because of the ignorance of His hearers, why do we not realize that His complaint about suffering, amid the greatest joy in suffering, was spoken for the instruction of our faith? Christ prays for His persecutors because they do not know what they are doing. From the cross Christ promises paradise because God reigns. When He drinks the vinegar on the cross Christ rejoices that everything is consummated because He who was about to die has fulfilled the prophecy. He was born for us, suffered for us, died for us, and rose for us. Since this alone is essential for our salvation, to acknowledge the Son of God among the dead, why, I ask, do we die in this godless belief, so that this very fact is the principal argument for the denial of His Godhead, that the Son of God asserted that He was the Son of Man and died, since Christ, while retaining the confidence in His own divinity, revealed that He died by His reference to the assumed man who dies in such peace of mind?

---

67 John 12.30.

BOOK ELEVEN

HILE DISCUSSING the whole and entire mystery of the evangelical faith in its various aspects, the Apostle expressed himself as follows in his Epistle to the Ephesians in the midst of his other teachings about the divine knowledge: 'Even as you were called in one hope of your calling; one Lord, one faith, one baptism, one God and Father of all, who is throughout all, and in us all.'[1] He did not abandon us to the vague and misleading speculations of an undefined doctrine, or expose the minds of men to uncertain theories, but limited the freedom of our intellect and will through the barriers he himself had constructed and set up against them, so that he did not allow us to be wise except in those things that he had preached, since it is forbidden to believe in any other way than in accordance with the clearcut definitions of the unchangeable faith.

Hence, when he preaches to us about the one God he mentions the one faith. Then, after his reference to the one faith in the one Lord, he also reveals the one baptism, so that, since there is the one faith in the one Lord, therefore in this one faith in the one Lord there would also be the one baptism. And because the entire mystery of the baptism and faith is found in the one Lord and also in the one God, he sums up the fulfillment of our hope in the confession of the one

---

1 Cf. Eph. 4.4-6.

459

God, so that, just as the one baptism and the one faith are found in the one Lord, so they are also found in the one God. Both are one, not by a union, but by their own proper attributes, since it is proper for each one to be one, whether to the Father to be what a father is, or to the Son to be what a son is, and the fact that both are one, while retaining their own proper attributes, is the mystery of the unity for both. The one Lord Christ cannot take away from the Father that He is the Lord, nor do we perceive the one God the Father denying to the one Lord Christ that which God is. If, therefore, because there is the one God, it does not seem proper for Christ also to be God, then we have to conclude that, because Christ is the one Lord, God also has no just claim to be the Lord, if the fact that He is one is taken to mean not the mystery but the exclusive limitation of oneness. Hence, just as in the one Lord, so, too, in the one God the Father there is the one baptism and the one faith.

(2) It is no longer the one faith if, in expressing its convictions, it will not hold fast to the one Lord and to the one God the Father. But, how does a faith that is not one confess the one Lord and the one God the Father? Amid so great a variety of doctrines it will no longer be one if some believe that the Lord Jesus Christ groaned with the pain of our weakness when the nail pierced His hands, and that He was deprived of the power of His own nature and strength and trembled in terror at the imminent approach of death, and if, what is the principal matter, they also deny that He was born and, rather, proclaim Him as a creature, if they will call Him God rather than conceive Him as such, because it is a sign of piety to speak of gods,[2] and an awareness of the divine nature to comprehend God as being one.

---

2 The term 'gods' is applied by Scriptures to holy persons, and therefore is unobjectionable. But it would be wrong to refer to Christ as God only in this sense.

Hence, there is no longer the one Lord Christ if, according to some, He as God does not feel pain, and, according to others, He is afraid just as anyone is who is weak; if, according to some, He is God by nature and, according to others, He is God by name; if, according to some, He is the Son by birth and, according to others, He has been given this title. Therefore, there is not one God the Father in the faith if some believe that He is the Father by His power and others that He is the Father by His generation, because God is also the Father of all. Furthermore, does anyone doubt any longer that whatever is excluded from the one faith is no faith at all? In the one faith there is the one Lord Christ and the one God the Father. The one Lord Christ is the one Son, not according to the name, but according to the faith—but only if He is God, if He is unchangeable, if He has never ceased to be either God or the Son. Hence, whoever will preach Christ in any other way than as He is, namely, that He is not the Son or that He is not God, will preach another Christ. He does not belong to the one faith of the one baptism, because, according to the teaching of the Apostle, there is the one faith of His one baptism in which the one Lord is Christ, the Son of God as well as God.

(3) We can no longer deny that Christ is Christ, nor can we bring it about that He is unknown to the world. The books of the Prophets point to Him, the fullness of time that increases daily bears witness to Him, the tombs of the Apostles and the martyrs speak of Him through the miracles that are performed, the power of His name corroborates Him, the unclean spirits confess Him, and the howls of the afflicted demons re-echo His name. But, in all these things there is the bestowal of His power. Besides, in our faith we are to proclaim Him just as He is, so that we have the one Lord in the one faith of the one baptism, not in name, but in our

belief, because, just as there is the one Lord Christ, so there is the one God the Father.

(4)   These new preachers of Christ, by denying everything that belongs to Christ, proclaim another Lord Christ as well as another God the Father, because the latter did not beget but created, and the former was not born but created; hence, Christ is not truly God, since it does not belong to Him by reason of the birth to be God, and the faith does not know of God the Father, since there is no generation by which He is the Father. Thus, they truly praise God the Father in a worthy manner, as it is indeed proper to do, namely, that His nature is unattainable, invisible, inviolable, indescribable, infinite, omniscient, omnipotent, gracious, movable, permeating all things, being inside and outside them, and feeling everything in everything. When they add to this supereminent praise that He alone is good, alone omnipotent, alone immortal, who does not perceive that this reverential eulogy aims at excluding Jesus Christ from this blessedness which honors God by limiting it to Him exclusively, and He Himself is mortal, weak, and evil, while the Father alone has all these attributes? Therefore, they deny His natural birth from God the Father in order that the blessedness which belongs to God the Father by nature may not be in Him by the birth, because the birth bestows the power of that nature which begot it.

(5)   Since they have not been taught by the doctrines either of the Apostles or of the Gospels, in order to justify the unlawful seizure of their own godless confession, they extol the grandeur of God, not with the faith of piety, but with the craftiness of impiety, so that, by stressing all the incomparable attributes of His nature and eliminating any comparison with Him, they may assert that the only-begotten God has a spurious and weak nature, the God (I say) who is the living image of the living God, the most complete form

of the blessed nature, and the only-begotten birth of the unborn substance. If this[3] does not possess the perfect glory of the Father's blessedness and does not reproduce the complete form of the whole nature, it does not have the true nature of an image. But, if the only-begotten God is the image of the unborn God, then the divinity of the perfect and complete nature is in Him through which He becomes the image of the true nature.

The Father is mighty, but, if the Son is weak, He is no longer the image of one who is mighty. The Father is good, but, if the Son belongs to a Godhead of a different kind, then the nature of evil does not reflect the image of goodness. The Father is incorporeal, but, if the Son is enclosed within a body according to the Spirit, then the Incarnate One is no longer the form of one who is incorporeal. The Father is ineffable, but, if speech defines the Son, we do not find the image of a nature that cannot be described in one that can be described. The Father is the true God, but, if the Son is a misrepresentation of God, then He who is false is not the image of Him who is true. The Apostle does not teach that He is partly the image and partly the portion of the form of God, but refers to Him as the image of the invisible God and the form of God. The Apostle could not teach the nature of the Godhead in the Son more explicitly than by the invisibility of God, so that Christ is the image of the invisible God, and certainly He whose substance is visible would not reproduce the image of an invisible nature.

(6) But, as I have explained in the preceding Books, they misrepresent the divine plan in regard to the body that He assumed in order to heap insults upon His divinity and extort reasons for their impious teaching from the mystery of our salvation. If they only held fast to the apostolic faith, they would realize that He who was in the form of God took

---

3 The only-begotten birth.

upon Himself the form of a slave, nor would they make use of the form of a slave in order to degrade the form of God, since the form of God contains the fullness of God within it, and they would treat in a reverential manner whatever pertains to the times and to the mystery, so that no insult would be offered to the Godhead and the divine plan of salvation would lead to any error. But, as I believe, after discussing all these subjects in a most thorough manner, and after making known the power of the divine nature in the birth of the body which He assumed, there is no longer any reason to doubt that the only-begotten God and man did all these things through the powers of God, and as a true man performed all these things in the powers of God, for in His deeds He possesses the nature of the omnipotent God in Himself since He was born from God, and He also has the whole being of a perfect man since He was born from the Virgin, and He subsists with a true body in the nature of God and remains with the nature of God in a true body.

(7) Hence, although the complete explanation which we made in our response brought us down to the glory of the death itself, and we refuted each assertion of the godless confession by the doctrines of the Gospels and the Apostles, still, because these impious men had dared to allege certain statements in order to prove that He had the weakness of a spurious nature after the resurrection, we must give our answer to these accusations. And so, as we have done in other cases, the meaning of their very words will be drawn from these words themselves, so that the truth may be found where it is denied. Words that were spoken simply and through the mouth of God for the enlightenment of our faith must have spoken in this manner so that we would not have to appeal to other words or words drawn from other places to ascertain the reason for which they were spoken.

(8) Among their other godless teachings the heretics are

wont to cite this saying of the Lord: 'I ascend to my Father and your Father, to my God and your God,'[4] so that He does not possess the nature of God, therefore, because His Father is their Father and His God their God. When He admits that God is the Father for others as well as for Himself, then the privilege whereby He was born as God and as the Son ceases through the common participation in the nature and the birth. Let them also cling to those words of the Apostle: 'But when he shall say all things are subject to him undoubtedly he is excepted who has subjected all things to him. And when all things are made subject to him, then he himself will also be made subject to him who subjected all things to him, that God may be all in all,'[5] so that, because that subjection will be looked upon as evidence of a weak nature, He does not possess the power of the Father's nature whose natural weakness has subjected Him to the power of a stronger nature. Let them take this as the best fortified and the most impregnable defense of their entire godless teaching in order to do away with the true nature of the birth, so that, because He is not God by reason of His subjection, and belongs to the order of creatures because of the God and Father who is common to Him and to us, He Himself is rather a creature of God than a birth from God, for creation receives its existence from nothing, but generation possesses the natural author of its birth.

(9) All sophistry is certainly unprincipled, because, when decency has been cast aside, then falsehood opposes truth; meanwhile, it conceals its design to some extent under the veil of an ambiguous justification in order that it may defend its arrogant belief in an unassuming manner. In the present instance, where they have distorted these words in order to weaken the divinity of our Lord, no opportunity for an

---

4 John 20.17.
5 Cf. 1 Cor. 15.26-28.

unassuming defense or a false justification is afforded them, since the plea of ignorance is no longer valid when we discover only the deliberate choice of an irreligious mind. In order to postpone my explanation of the words of the Gospel itself for a few moments, was this teaching of the Apostle unknown, who said: 'And indeed according to the confession of all, great is the mystery of godliness: which was manifested in the flesh, was justified in the spirit, appeared to angels, was preached to Gentiles, believed in the world, taken up in glory'?[6] Is there still anyone so dull of wit as to regard the dispensation of the flesh which the Lord assumed as anything else than the mystery of piety?

First of all, he no longer belongs to the faith of God who no longer holds fast to this teaching. The Apostle does not doubt that all must confess that the mystery of our salvation is not a degradation of the Godhead, but the mystery of great piety. And the mysterious doctrine is no longer shrouded in secrecy, but has been made known in the flesh. It is no longer weak through the nature of the flesh, but has been justified in the spirit, so that through the justification in the spirit the weakness of the flesh is not found in our faith, and the mystery has not been concealed through the manifestation of the flesh, and, because the cause of the mystery is unknown, our confession mentions only the mystery of great godliness.

Thus, the Apostle maintained the order of the entire faith, so that while it is godliness it is a mystery, while it is a mystery it is the knowledge in the flesh, while it is the knowledge in the flesh it is the justification in the spirit, because the mystery of godliness, which is manifested in the flesh, is made known by the justification in the spirit, in order that it may be truly a mystery. And in order that we might realize the nature of the justification in the spirit that was revealed in the flesh, the mystery that was made known in the flesh and

---

6 Cf. 1 Tim. 3.16.

justified in the spirit was seen by the angels, preached to the Gentiles, was believed in the world, and it itself was assumed in glory so that it might be the mystery of great godliness in everything while it is revealed in the flesh, justified in the spirit, seen by the angels, preached to the Gentiles, believed in this world, and assumed in glory. The glory perfects everything, because the mystery of great piety is the assumption of glory and through this faith in the dispensation we are prepared to be raised up and to be made conformable to the Lord in glory. The assumption of the flesh, therefore, is the mystery of great piety, because by the assumption of the flesh there is the manifestation of the mystery in the flesh. We must confess the manifestation in the flesh as nothing else than the mystery of great piety, because His manifestation in the flesh is both His justification in the spirit and His assumption in glory. Finally, by what hope is the mystery of the dispensation in our faith a weakness for the Godhead, since the mystery of great piety must be confessed through the assumption in glory? And because it is no longer a weakness but a mystery, not a compulsion but piety, we must seek for the solution of the words of the Gospel in order that the mystery of our salvation and glory may not afford any pretext for the teaching of impiety.

(10) O heretic, you regard it as an important testimony and as an irrefutable statement about Himself in which the Lord says: 'I ascend to my Father, to my God and your God,' so that, because the one Father is the Father and the one God is God for us and for Him, He is subject to the same weakness as we ourselves, while we are made equal as sons through the same Father and are placed in the same category as slaves through the same God. Since we are a creation by our origin and slaves by our nature, yet, while there is a common Father and God between us, there is also between us a common creation and servitude in regard to the nature.

And this rage of the godless teaching also appeals to this saying of the Prophet: 'God, thy God, hath anointed thee,'[7] so that He does not possess the power of nature that God has, while God, who anoints Him to be His God, has been preferred before Him.

(11) He does not know the God Christ who does not know the God who was born. But, for God to be born is nothing else than to possess that nature that God has. If to be born reveals the cause of the birth, it does not become different in kind from the nature of the author. But a birth that does not become different in kind from the nature is certainly indebted to its author as the cause of its birth, yet it has not renounced the nature of the author within itself, because the birth of God is from nowhere else nor is it anything else. If it is from anywhere else it is not a birth; if it is something else it is not God. But, if God is from God, then God is also the Father of God the Son, the God of His birth, and the Father of His nature, because the birth of God is from God and belongs to that kind of nature which God possesses.

(12) Accordingly, the Lord arranged the plan of this pious and worthy profession of faith in everything that He said in such a manner that the confession of the birth would not offer any insult to His divinity and the God-fearing obedience would not be incompatible with the nature of majesty, but that the birth, which owes its existence to its author, would acknowledge the honor due to Him, and the natural confidence would reveal the consciousness of the nature which came into existence by His birth into God. These words refer to this fact: 'He who has seen me has seen also the Father,' and 'The words that I speak I speak not on my own authority.'[8] Since He does not speak on His own authority,

---

7 Ps. 44.8.
8 Cf. John 14.9,10.

He must be indebted to His author for what He speaks, but if, when He is seen, the Father is seen, then we are made aware of the fact that the nature, which exists as a proof of God in Him, is not estranged from God by being born into God. Or those words: 'What the Father has given me is greater than all.' And again: 'I and the Father are one.'[9] The gift of the Father is an acknowledgment of the birth that has been received, and the fact that they are one is an attribute which proceeds from the birth of the nature. Or those words: 'But all judgment he has given to the Son, that all men may honor the Son even as they honor the Father.'[10] While judgment is given, the birth is not passed over in silence, but, while equal honor is accorded them, the nature is preserved. Or those words: 'I in the Father and the Father in me,' and again: 'The Father is greater than I.'[11] From the fact that they are in each other, recognize the divinity of God from God, but from the fact that the Father is greater, understand the acknowledgment of the Father's authority!

Thus it is also with those words: 'The Son can do nothing of himself, but only what he sees the Father doing. For whatever he does the Son also does the same in like manner.'[12] While He does not act by His own authority, in that which He does in accordance with the birth the Father is His author, yet, since whatever the Father does the Son also does the same in like manner, He subsists as nothing else than as God, while in carrying out everything that God the Father does the nature of the Father's omnipotence subsists in Him. Hence, these things have been made known according to the unity of the Spirit and the property of the nature which is suitable to the Spirit in such a manner that the birth would

---

9 Cf. John 10.29,30.
10 John 5.22,23.
11 John 14.11,28.
12 Cf. John 5.19.

confess the God of His own substance, and the God of His own substance would not be silent about the consciousness of His nature, while God the Son acknowledges God as His Father, since He is born from Him. Furthermore, from the fact that He was born He possesses the complete nature that God has.

(13) Hence, through the dispensation of the great and pious mystery the Father of the divine birth has become, in addition, the Lord of the human nature that He has assumed, while He who was in the form of God was found in the form of a slave. The Son of God was not a slave, since He was God according to the Spirit. And, according to the common estimation, where there is no slave neither is there a lord. He is indeed God and the Father of the birth of the only-begotten God, but, in so far as He is a slave, we can then only consider Him as the Lord when He is a slave. If previously He was not a slave by His nature, and later on began to be according to His nature that which He was not, we cannot assume that there was any other reason for the Lordship except that it was for the slavery, since He then had a Lord through the dispensation of the nature when He offered Himself as a slave by assuming our human nature.

(14) While He who was previously in the form of God remained in the form of a slave, the man Christ Jesus, declared: 'I ascend to my Father and your Father, to my God and your God.' If, therefore, a slave said these words and said them to slaves, by what reasoning is that assertion not that of a slave and applied rather to that nature which does not belong to the nature of a slave, since He who assumed the form of a slave while remaining in the form of God can only be associated as a slave with slaves because He is a slave? The Father, therefore, is the Father for Him just as He is for men, and God is God for Him as well as for the slaves. And since Jesus Christ, as a man in the form of a

slave, spoke these words to men as slaves, there can be no
doubt that He is a Father for Him as for others in His
character as man, and He is God for Him as well as for
everyone in that nature by which He is a slave.

(15) Finally, He prefaced this same discourse with an
introduction in the following words: 'But go to my brethren
and say to them, 'I ascend to my Father and your Father, to
my God and your God.' And I now ask whether we are to
understand that He has brethren in the form of God or in
the form of a slave, and whether our flesh has any partnership with Him in the fullness of the Godhead dwelling in
Him, so that we may be considered His brethren in so far as
He is God? The prophetic Spirit realizes in what respect we
are brethren to the only-begotten God, for He spoke these
words not so much as a man but rather as a worm: 'I will
declare thy name to my brethren.'[13] And a worm, that either
does not come into life through the conception of ordinary
origins, or that comes forth alive from the depths of the
earth, spoke these words in reference to the flesh which had
been assumed and vivified by Him even from hell, and since
He foretold the mystery of the passion in the whole of this
psalm through the prophetic Spirit, He must have brethren
according to that dispensation in which He suffered. The
Apostle also knew the mystery of the brethren and taught that,
as He is the first-born of the dead, so He is the first-born
among many brethren. In so far, therefore, as He is the
first-born among brethren is He the first-born of the dead,
and, since the mystery of the death takes place in the body,
so the mystery of the brotherhood also takes place in the
flesh. Hence, God has brethren according to the flesh, because
the Word was made flesh and dwelt amongst us. Moreover,
the only-begotten God, through His exclusive right as the
Only-begotten, is without brethren.

---

13 Ps. 21.23. Cf. 21.7 for the words: 'I am a worm, and no man.'

(16)   He Himself, who contains the nature of us all in Himself through the assumption of the flesh, was what we are, nor did He cease to be what He had been, since He then had God as His Father by reason of His nature, and now has God as His Father by reason of His earthly state. Now, according to His earthly state, because all things are from God the Father. God is the Father of all, since all things are from Him and in Him. He is not only the Father to the only-begotten God, therefore, because the Word was made flesh, for He is the Father in this sense, that God the Word was in the beginning with God. When the Word was made flesh, He still remains what a Father is, both in the birth of the Word of God as well as in His incarnate state. The Father is the God of all flesh, but not in the sense that He is the Father to God the Word. God the Word did not cease to be the Word, nor was He not flesh. The Word that was made flesh and dwelt amongst us is truly the Word while He dwelt, just as God is truly man while the Word is flesh. To dwell must be characteristic of Him who remains, and to be made flesh must be understood as characteristic of Him who is born. And that He dwelt amongst us is the assumption of our flesh. By reason of the fact that the Word made flesh dwells amongst us God truly possesses our body. Hence, if Christ Jesus, the man according to the flesh, takes away the nature of God the Word, or if the man Christ Jesus, is not God the Word according to the mystery of piety, then it may be an insult to the nature that the Father is the Father and God is God both for Him as well as for us. But, if God the Word, the man Christ Jesus, does not cease to be God the Word, then we and He share together our relationship to the Father and God only according to that nature by which He is our brother, because the message: 'I ascend to my Father and your Father, to my God and your God,' was announced

to the brethren not because the Word is the only-begotten God, but because the Word was made flesh.

(17) In his statement the Apostle did not speak in an imprudent or vague language in order to afford a pretext for godlessness. Thus, in the present instance, the Evangelist introduced the words of the Lord by mentioning the brethren and explained that the whole passage referred to our sharing of that nature in which He is our brother. His words were directed to the brethren, in order that what He taught about the mystery of godliness might not be looked upon as an insult to the Godhead, since our union with Him, whereby the Father is the Father for us as well as for Him and God is God for us as well as for Him, was in harmony with the dispensation of the flesh according to which we were to be regarded as His brethren through the birth of His body. Hence, no one doubts that God the Father is also the God of our Lord Jesus Christ, but this pious belief of ours does not afford any pretext for impiety. He is His God, but not in such a manner, therefore, that He is a God of a different nature from His. But, because He was born as God from the Father, and is a slave according to the dispensation, He also possesses a Father while He is God from Him, and He possesses His God while He is flesh from the Virgin. The Apostle points this out in a short and precise passage when he says: 'Making mention of you in my prayers, that the God of our Lord Jesus Christ, the Father of glory, may grant you the spirit of wisdom and revelation.'[14] For, where Jesus Christ is, there is His God, but where the glory is there is the Father. Hence, He who is the Father of Christ according to the glory is the God of Christ in reference to Jesus. The angel gives the name Jesus to Christ the Lord whom Mary brought forth. In addition, the prophecy speaks of Christ the Lord as a Spirit.

---

14 Eph. 1.16,17.

To very many, these words appear somewhat obscure in Latin, because Latin does not use pronouns, which the Greek language always uses both for elegance as well as for necessity. For it is thus written: *ho Theòs toû kurióu ēmôn Iēsoû Xristoû ho patèr tês dóxēs.* If in our language we were to use pronouns, this sentence would sound as follows: *'Ille Deus illius Domini nostri Jesu Christi, ille pater illius claritatis.'* These words, 'that Lord of ours, Jesus Christ,' and 'that Father of that glory,' express the proper meaning of the idea in accordance with the capacity of our power of comprehension, so that, where the glory of Christ is, there God is His Father, but, where Christ Jesus is, there the Father is His God, while He has God in the dispensation, since He is a slave, and the Father in the glory, since He is God.

(18)   The times or the ages do not cause a difference in the Spirit, so that there is not the same Christ Himself in the body who dwelt in the Prophets by the Spirit. When He declares through the mouth of the patriarch David: 'God, thy God, hath anointed thee with the oil of gladness above thy fellows,'[15] He did not say anything different according to the mystery than He said according to the dispensation of the body which He assumed. He who now confides to His brethren that their Father is His Father and their God His God, then declared that He was also anointed by His God above His fellows, so that, while there is no fellowship with the only-begotten Christ the Word of God, we realize that there is a fellowship with Him by that assumption in which He is flesh. That anointing did not procure any advantage for that blessed and incorrupt birth that abides in the nature of God, but for the mystery of the body and for the sanctification of the manhood which He took upon Himself, as the Apostle Peter testifies when he said: 'For of a truth there assembled together in this city against thy holy Son Jesus,

15 Ps. 44.8.

whom thou hast anointed.'[16] And again: 'You know what
took place throughout Judea; for he began in Galilee after
the baptism preached by John: how God anointed Jesus of
Nazareth with the Holy Spirit and with power.'[17] Jesus,
therefore, is anointed in the mystery of the flesh that was
born again. And there is no difficulty in regard to the manner
in which He was anointed by the Spirit and by the power of
God, since at that moment when He comes up from Jordan
the voice of God the Father is heard: 'Thou art my Son,
this day have I begotten thee,'[18] in order that the anointing of
the spiritual power might be recognized through this testimony of the flesh that was sanctified in Him.

(19)   Moreover, since God the Word was in the beginning
with God, the anointing rejects any cause for or any description of His nature,[19] about which nothing else is made
known than that it was in the beginning. And certainly it
was not necessary for God, who is the Spirit and the power
of God, to be anointed by the Spirit and power of God.
Hence, God is anointed by His God above His fellows. And
if many were anointed according to the Law before the
bestowal of the flesh, then Christ, who is now anointed above
His fellows, is later in time, although He is preferred before
all of His companions who were anointed. Finally, that
prophetic utterance revealed this later anointing when it
declared: 'Thou hast loved justice and hated iniquity:
therefore God, thy God, hath anointed thee with the oil of
gladness above thy fellows.'

A consequent and later cause is never made retroactive so
that it becomes first, for to merit anything follows upon the
existence of Him who is capable of meriting. To merit

---

16 Cf. Acts. 4.27.
17 Acts 10.37,38.
18 Ps. 2.7.
19 This anointing does not mention any pre-existing cause for the divine
   nature of the Word, nor does it give a description of the mysterious
   birth of the Son from the Father.

belongs to Him who is the cause of acquiring merit for Himself. If, therefore, we attribute the anointing to the birth of the only-begotten God, and this anointing has been granted in recognition of His love for justice and His hatred of iniquity, then it is to be understood that the only-begotten God was not born, but was brought forth by the anointing, and now He will be made perfect as God through an increase and gain, since He was not born as God but was anointed into God because of His merits, and now He will be the God Christ as the result of a cause and the cause of all things will not be through the God Christ. What, then, is the meaning of the Apostle's words: 'All things through him and unto him, and he is before all, and in him all things hold together'?[20] God the Lord Jesus Christ is not God because of some things or through some things, but was born as God. And He who is God by birth did not develop into God after His birth through some other cause, but because He was born He is nothing else by His birth than what God is. If He is anointed as the result of a cause, then the benefit of the anointing does not refer to that which does not need to grow but to that which needs the benefit of the anointing through an increase of the mystery, that is to say, through the anointing our man Christ appears as one sanctified. If in the present instance, therefore, the dispensation of the slave is also pointed out by the Prophet because of which He is anointed by His God above His fellows, and accordingly He is anointed because He loved justice and hated iniquity, why will not the Prophet's words refer to that nature of Christ which we share with Him by His assumption of the flesh, since the Spirit of prophecy has exercised particular care in this way, that, while God is anointed by His God, He is His God in the dispensation of the anointing and He is God in the nature? Consequently, God is anointed, but I ask the

20 Cf. Col. 1.16,17.

question whether the Word that was in the beginning with God was anointed? By no means! The anointing is later than God. Since that birth of the Word was not anointed, because it was in the beginning with God, then that must have been anointed in God which comes afterwards in the dispensation, in so far as He is God. And since God is anointed by His God, then everything pertaining to a slave that He received in the mystery of the flesh is anointed.

(20) Let no one, therefore, desecrate the mystery of godliness, that was made known in the flesh, by a godless interpretation, and let no one place himself on an equality with the Only-begotten in the substance of the Godhead. Let Him be a brother to and sharer with us in so far as the Word made flesh dwelt among us, and in so far as the man Jesus Christ is the mediator of God and man. Let us as slaves have a common Father and a common God, and let Him be anointed above His fellows in that nature in which His fellows were anointed, even though He was anointed with a special privilege. In the mystery of the mediator let Him be a true man as well as the true God, the God Himself from God, who has a common Father and God with us in that fellowship by which He is our brother.

(21) Perhaps that subjection, the handing over of the kingdom, and, finally, the end are to be regarded as the abolition of the nature, or the withdrawal of the power, or the weakness of the Godhead. A great many conceive it in this manner: that He is subject to God, since all things are subject to Him, and by His state of subjection He is not God, or, while He transfers the kingdom, He does not possess the kingdom, and, while the end comes upon Him, His dissolution follows upon the end.

(22) Hence, the proper procedure is to have a thorough discussion about the meaning of the Apostle's words, in order that, after we have explained and pointed out the significance

of each and every phrase, we may be capable of understanding the complete mystery by our grasp of the entire passage. He says therefore: 'For since by a man came death, by a man also comes resurrection of the dead. For as in Adam all die, so in Christ all will be made to live. But each in his own turn, Christ as first-fruits, then they who are Christ's, who have believed, at his coming. Then comes the end, when he delivers the kingdom to God the Father, when he does away with all sovereignty and all power. For he must reign, until "he has put all his enemies under his feet." The last enemy, death, has been conquered by him. But when he shall say all things are subject, he is excepted, who subjected all things to him. But when all things are made subject to him, then he himself will be made subject to him who subjected all things to him, that God may be all in all.'[21]

(23)   The Apostle, chosen as the teacher of the Gentiles not by men or through a man but by Jesus Christ, reveals the secrets of the heavenly dispensation in language that is as precise as possible. And he who was raised to the third heaven and heard the ineffable things has made known to the comprehension of the human mind only what our human nature was capable of grasping. He was not unaware that certain doctrines could not be understood immediately upon our hearing of them, for only later on would our weakness formulate in our mind a correct and definite conclusion about what had been poured into our ears. Since a longer period of delay is afforded our mind rather than our hearing—for the hearing is associated with the spoken word, but the understanding with our reasoning—God reveals the knowledge to those who are eager to understand. In his Epistle to Timothy, who had been instructed in the Scriptures from his childhood by the glorious faith of his grandmother and mother, among other things he added the following: 'Take

---

21 Cf. 1 Cor. 15.21-28.

in what I tell thee, for God will give thee understanding in all things.'[22] The exhortation to understand arises from the difficulty in understanding. But the bestowal of understanding by God is the gift of faith whereby the weakness of our reasoning merits the grace of revelation. If, therefore, Timothy, the man of God according to the Apostle's testimony and the lawful son of Paul in the faith, is exhorted to understand because the Lord will give him understanding in all things, we should bear in mind that the Apostle also urges us to understand, since we know that the Lord will bestow the understanding of all things upon us.

(24) And if, perhaps, through a defect of our human nature we shall be held fast in some preconceived idea, let us not reject the gain for our understanding that comes from the grace of revelation, lest what we have once comprehended by our reasoning become so deeply rooted that we are ashamed to arrive at a more correct belief by changing it. Therefore, in order to offer us a prudent and safe guide in these matters, the same blessed Apostle writes to the Philippians: 'Let us then, as many as are perfect, be of this mind; and if in any point you are minded otherwise, this also God will reveal to you. But wherein we have hastened, in the same let us walk.'[23]

Our preconceived ideas do not anticipate the revelation of God. The Apostle has reminded us in what the wisdom of those who are perfectly wise consists, and he awaits the revelation of God for those who are wise in a different way, in order that they may be wise in that which is perfect. If some, therefore, have understood this profound dispensation of the hidden knowledge differently, and we bring forward something that is correct and worthy of credence, let them not be ashamed, as the Apostle says, to become perfectly

---

22 Cf. 2 Tim. 2.7.
23 Cf. Phil. 3.15,16.

wise. Nor should they prefer to remain in ignorance of the truth more than to detest remaining in falsehood. He exhorts those who are wise in a different way and to whom God will reveal it to hasten along the road upon which they have entered, in order that, after they have abandoned the understanding of their first ignorance, they may obtain the revelation of perfect understanding in accordance with the progress of their haste upon the road that they have entered. Let us walk along the road toward which we have hastened. Although the wandering about on a wrong road delays our haste, we shall, through the revelation of God, walk on the road toward which we have hastened and shall not make any changes in the journey of our haste. We have hastened to Christ Jesus, the Lord of glory and the King of the eternal ages, in whom all things have been restored in heaven and on earth, through whom all things are held together, in whom and with whom we shall always abide. Hence, when we walk along this road we are perfectly wise, and if we are wise in a different way God will make known to us that which is perfectly wise. Let us, therefore, again discuss the mystery of the present words in accordance with the apostolic faith and do so in the same manner in which we have previously treated all of these subjects, in order that we may expose the entire reasoning of the godless will, which appeals to the sayings of the Apostles, through the truth itself of the apostolic faith.

(25) Consequently, according to the order of the statements, three things are called into question: first, the end; then, the delivering; and, finally the subjection—so that as a result of them, Christ either ceases to be at the end, or by delivering the kingdom He no longer possesses it, or by being subject to God He finds Himself outside the nature of God.

(26) First of all, it must be noted that this is not the order of the apostolic doctrine. For, in the first place is the

delivery of the kingdom; then, the subjection; and lastly, the end. But, all particular causes have their own particular kinds of causes upon which they are dependent, so that, while the particular things come to an end in other things, the preceding cause always has a cause upon which it depends. There will be an end, but when He has delivered the kingdom to God. He will deliver the kingdom when He has destroyed every Principality and Power. He will destroy every Principality and Power because He must reign. He will reign until He places all His enemies under His feet. He will place all His enemies under His feet because God has subjected all things under His feet. God has subjected them to Him in such a manner that death, the last enemy, is conquered. When all have been subjected to Him, with the exception of Him who subjected them to Him, then He Himself will be made subject to Him who subjected all things to Him. The cause of the subjection is nothing else than that God may be all in all. Hence, the end is for God to be all in all.

(27)   Before everything else, we must now ascertain whether the end is a destruction, the delivery a loss, and the subjection a weakness. If these statements will not go together, because they are contrary to one another, then that true sense in which they were spoken will have to be made known by the words themselves.

(28)   The end of the law, therefore, is Christ. And I ask whether Christ is the destruction or the perfection of the Law? If the Law is not done away with, but fulfilled by, Christ, who is its end, as He says: 'I have not come to destroy the law, but to fulfill,'[24] then the end is not its destruction, but its complete perfection. Everything tends to its end, not in order that it may not be, but that it may remain in that toward which it tends. Everything is for the sake of its end; furthermore, the end does not concern itself with anything

---

24 Cf. Matt. 5.17.

else. But, since the end is everything, it remains completely for itself. And since it does not reach out beyond itself and since it brings gain for itself rather than for any other time or thing, the object of all its hope is ever directed toward the end itself. For this reason the Lord thus exhorts us to a steadfastness in the devout faith that continues to the end: 'Blessed is he who shall persevere to the end,'[25] and certainly not as if dissolution were a blessing and non-existence a gain, and as if the reward of faith were to be found in the destruction of everyone, because the end is the unequaled measure of the blessedness that has been offered to us, and thus they are blessed who persevere to the end of the perfect happiness, since the expectation of faithful hope does not extend beyond this.

The end, therefore, is the unchangeable state of continuing toward the goal for which we are striving. Finally, the Apostle warns us beforehand about the end of godlessness, in order to inspire us with fear of the consequences: 'Whose end is ruin . . . but our expectation is in heaven.'[26] If, therefore, there is an end for the blessed and the godless and the end is conceived as destruction, then the end places the true worship and impiety on an equal level, because both of them, by reason of the end that has been determined, have this in common—that they do not exist. And now is our expectation in heaven, if as a result of the end we cease to exist as the godless do? If the end of the blessed is said to be an expectation, but that of the godless is said to be what is due to them, even in this case we do not believe that the end is their total destruction. For, what kind of a penalty will it be for their impiety if they are wholly incapable of experiencing the avenging punishments, since through the destruction of their being nothing is found that can feel pain? Consequently,

25 Cf. Matt. 10.22.
26 Cf Phil. 3.19,20.

the end is the perpetual perfection of an unchanging state that is reserved for blessedness and prepared for impiety.

(29) Now, therefore, because it can no longer be considered doubtful that we must consider the end not as a destruction but as a state of life whose boundaries we shall not transgress, although we are still keeping certain points in reserve for our more complete explanation of these very words, yet, since we have emphasized these facts merely to clarify our meaning, let us see whether the delivery of the kingdom is to be understood as a loss of ownership in the sense that what the Son delivers to the Father He no longer possesses by this transference. If anyone, carried away by the rage of an absurd impiety, will make such an assertion, he will have to confess that, when the Father handed over all things to the Son, He lost them by handing them over, if to deliver means to be without that which has been delivered. For, the Lord said: 'All things have been delivered to me by my Father.'[27] And again: 'All power in heaven and on earth has been given to me.'[28] Hence, if to deliver means to be without that which has been delivered, then the Father, too, did not have what He had delivered. But, if the Father was not without them, while He delivered them, then we cannot even assume that the Son did not have what He had delivered. If He has delivered all things, and we do not see Him in want of these very things that He has delivered, nothing else remains but to recognize that the explanation of the delivery is to be found in the dispensation, and this is the reason why the Father does not lose anything when He delivers them, and why the Son does not need anything when He bestows them.

(30) There are some other facts, however, which come to the aid of our faith, so that nothing unbecoming may be attributed to the Son because of the subjection, but this

27 Luke 10.22.
28 Matt. 28.18.

very passage in particular comes forward in its own defense. First of all, I appeal to the common estimation whether we believe that in the present case subjection is to be understood in the sense that, just as we subordinate servitude to domination, weakness to strength, and dishonor to honor as qualities that are mutually contrary, in like manner the Son is subject to God the Father because of a diversity arising from a dissimilar nature. If it should be looked upon in this light, then the cautious wording of the Apostle's statement will put an end to this erroneous conclusion of our human judgment. When all things have become subject to Him, then, he says, He must be made subject to Him who subjects all things to Himself, and, by these words, that He will then be made subject, he was referring to the temporal dispensation. If we will conceive the subjection as something different, even though He will become subject at some future date, at the moment He is certainly not subject, and we shall cause Him to be hostile, insolent and impious whom the pressure of time will subdue into a belated subservience after it has, as it were, crushed and suppressed the conceit of His tyrannical impiety.

And what, then, will be the meaning of: 'For I have come not to do my own will, but the will of him who sent me,'[29] and again: 'Therefore the Father loves me, because I do all the things that are pleasing to him,'[30] and: 'Father, thy will be done,'[31] or this saying of the Apostle: 'He humbled himself, becoming obedient unto death.'[32] He who humbles Himself has this quality in His nature that He is not lowly, and He who becomes obedient determines to obey of His own free will, while He becomes obedient by reason of the fact that

---

29 Cf. John 6.38.
30 Cf. John 8.29.
31 Cf. Matt. 26.39.
32 Phil. 2.8.

He humbles Himself. In what manner are we to suppose that the only-begotten God, who humbles Himself and is obedient to the Father until death, will Himself be then made subject to the Father, when all things have been made subject to Him, unless this subjection does not refer to a new obedience but to the dispensation of the mystery, because the obedience is already in existence and the subjection is to take place in time? Hence, in the present instance, the meaning of the subjection is nothing else than the revelation of the mystery.

(31)   We are to understand what it is in harmony with this same hope of our faith. For it cannot be unknown to us that the Lord Jesus Christ, who rose from the dead, sits at the right hand of God, since even the Apostle bears witness to this when he says: 'According to the working of his mighty power, which he has wrought in Jesus when he raised him from the dead, and placed him at his right hand in heaven above every Principality and Power and Virtue and Domination, and above every name that is named, not only in this world, but also in that which is to come. And all things he made subject under his feet.'[33] The statement of the Apostle emphasizes the fact that in accordance with the power of God future events have already taken place. Those things that are to be accomplished in the fullness of time already exist in Christ, in whom there is all the fullness, and in these events that take place in the future there is, rather, the order of the dispensation than something new. God has placed all things under His feet, although they are still to be made subject, so that, in so far as they have been made subject, we perceive the unchangeable power of Christ, but, in so far as they will be made subject, we perceive the progress of the ages that follow one another until the end in accordance with the fullness of time.

---

33 Cf. Eph. 1.20-22.

(32)   It is clearly evident that every hostile power is to be destroyed and this ruler of the air and the power of spiritual wickedness is to be delivered to eternal ruin, according to those words: 'Depart from me, accursed ones, into the everlasting fire which my Father has prepared for the devil and his angels.'[34] But, destruction is not the same as subjection. To destroy a hostile power means to do away with the right of this power so that it no longer remains, and the annihilation of the power means to abolish the government of the kingdom. The Lord also gave testimony about this when He said: 'My kingdom is not of this world,'[35] while He had previously asserted that the ruler of the kingdom is the same as the mighty prince of this world, whose power will come to an end when the government of his kingdom has been abolished. But a subjection which proceeds from obedience and faith is at the same time a proof either of compliance or of change.

(33)   When the Authorities, therefore, have been destroyed, His enemies will be made subject. They will be made subject in the sense that He Himself subjects them to Himself. He will subject them to Himself in the sense that God subjects them to Him. Did not the Apostle realize the force of the words in the Gospel where it is said: 'No one comes to me unless my Father draws him to me,'[36] since, notwithstanding them, it had been written: 'No one goes to the Father but through me'?[37] As He now subjects His enemies to Himself, yet God has subjected them to Him, He bears witness to the fact that in all of His works the work of God is in Him. And since we are to go to the Father only through Him, we do not come to Him unless the Father has drawn us.

---

34 Cf. Matt. 25.41.
35 John 18.36.
36 Cf. John 6.44.
37 Cf. John 14.6.

As long as we recognize Him as the Son of God, we learn the truth of the Father's nature in Him. Thus, when we know the Son, God the Father calls us, and when we believe the Son, the Father receives us, because the manifestation of and knowledge about the Father in the Son come about through the manifestation of God the Father in Him, since the worship of the Father draws us as devout men to Him.

In this manner, therefore, God the Father draws us to Him, while at the same time—and this is the principal issue at stake—we believe in Him as the Father. But, no one goes to the Father except through the Son, for the Father is unknown when the belief in the Son dies within us, since we will not draw near the worship of the Father unless we have already started with the worship of the Son. Thus, when we know the Son, the Father draws us and receives us into eternal life, and both results are due to the Son, while by the revelation of the Father through Him the Father leads us to Him, and He Himself leads us to the Father. Consequently, the mention of this mystery was necessary in order to have a more complete knowledge of the text before us, so that it would be through the Son that the Father draws us and receives us, and we would thereby perceive just how far God has made subject to Him what He Himself had made subject to Himself. That is to say, the nature of God remains in Him by the birth and performs that which He Himself performs, while He performs it in such a way that God performs it, yet He Himself performs what God performs, but in such a way that, in so far as He Himself performs it, the Son of God is understood to perform it, but, in so far as God performs it, the essence of the Father's nature is known to be in Him as in a Son.

(34) Accordingly, when the Authorities and the Powers have been destroyed, His enemies will be brought into subjection under His feet. The Apostle has taught us what

enemies are to be understood when he said: 'In view of the gospel, they are enemies for your sake; but in view of the divine choice, they are beloved for the sake of the fathers.'[38] Hence, we know that these men are enemies of the cross of Christ, but, because they are loved for the sake of the fathers, we are aware that they are destined to be made subject, according to the words that were spoken: 'For I would not, brethren, have you ignorant of this mystery, lest you should be wise in your own conceits, that a partial stupidity has befallen Israel, until the full number of the Gentiles should enter, and thus all Israel should be saved, as it is written, "And there will come out of Sion the deliverer and He will turn away impieties from Jacob; And this is my covenant with them, when I shall take away their sins." '[39] The enemies, therefore, will be brought into subjection under His feet.

(35) We must grasp what follows after that subjection, namely: 'The last enemy, death, has been conquered by him.' The victory over death, however, is nothing else than the resurrection from the dead. When the corruption of death ceases, the eternity of a living and heavenly nature is formed, as it has been said: 'But this corruptible must put on incorruption, and this mortal must put on immortality. But when this mortal puts on immortality then shall come to pass the word that is written, "Death is swallowed up in strife. O death, where is thy sting? O death, where is thy strife?" '[40] Consequently, in the subjection of the enemies death is conquered, and upon the conquest of death a life of immortality follows. The same Apostle testified about how perfect that nature of the subjection is after the subjection of faith, when he said: 'Who will transfigure the body of our lowliness into the likeness of the body of his glory, according

---

38 Cf. Rom. 11.28.
39 Cf. Rom. 11.25-27.
40 Cf. 1 Cor. 15.53-55.

to the works of his power by which he is able to subject all things to himself.'[41] There is also that subjection which is a transition from one nature into another nature, while it ceases to exist by itself in its own nature and is made subject to that one into whose form it passes. It does not cease in order that it may not be, but that it may go forward, and by passing over into the image of the other nature which it has received it becomes subordinate as a result of this change.

(36) Last of all, after death has been finally conquered, in order that his explanation of this mystery might be complete, he then said: 'But when he shall say all things are subject, he is excepted who subjected all things to him; then he himself will be made subject to him who subjected all things to him, that God may be all in all.' Hence, the first step in the mystery is that all things have been made subject to Him, and then He Himself becomes subject to Him who subjects all things to Himself in order that, just as we subject ourselves to the glory of His reigning body, the ruler Himself in the same mystery may again subject Himself in the glory of the body to Him who subjects all things to Himself. We are made subject to the glory of His body in order that we may possess that glory with which He reigns in the body, because we shall be conformable to His body.

(37) The Gospels assuredly are not silent about the glory of His body that is now gloriously reigning. For so it is written, while the Lord says: 'Amen I say to you, there are some of those standing who will not taste death, till they have seen the Son of Man coming in his kingdom. And it came to pass after six days, Jesus took Peter, James and his brother John, and led them up a high mountain by themselves, and Jesus was transfigured before them. And his face shone as the sun, but his garments became as snow.'[42] Consequently, the glory

41 Cf. Phil. 3.21
42 Cf. Matt. 16.28; 17.1,2.

of the body that comes into the kingdom has been revealed
to the Apostles. For, the Lord appeared in the character of
His glorious transformation while He made known the glory
of His reigning body.

(38)   And while He promised His Apostles that they
would indeed have a share in this glory of His, He said:
'The Son of Man will send forth his angels, and they will
gather out of his kingdom all scandals and those who work
iniquity, and cast them into the furnace of fire, where there
will be the weeping, and the gnashing of teeth. Then the just
will shine forth like the sun in the kingdom of their Father. He
who has ears to hear, let him hear.'[43] Were the natural and
bodily ears of all closed to the hearing of words, so that an
admonition of the Lord was necessary in order to hear? But,
while the Lord imparted the knowledge of the mystery, He
demanded a hearing for the doctrine of faith. At the
consummation of the world, therefore, the scandals will be
taken away from His kingdom. Hence we have the Lord who
reigns in the glory of the body until the scandals are removed.
Again, we find ourselves in conformity with the glory of His
body in the kingdom of His Father, resplendent, as it were,
with the brightness of the sun in which He revealed the
nature of His kingdom to His Apostles when He was transformed on the mountain.

(39)   Accordingly, He will deliver the kingdom to God
the Father, but not in such a way as if He were renouncing
His power by delivering it, but because we will become the
kingdom of God by being made conformable to the glory of
His body. He did not say: 'He will deliver His kingdom,'
but 'He will deliver the kingdom,' and He will deliver us to
God after we have become His kingdom through the
glorification of His body. He will deliver us, therefore, to the
kingdom according to this saying of the Gospels: 'Come,

---

43 Matt. 13.41-43.

blessed of my Father, take possession of the kingdom prepared for you from the foundation of the world.'[44] Hence, the just will shine as the sun in the kingdom of their Father. The Lord will deliver as a kingdom to God those whom He has called into the kingdom and to whom He has also promised the blessedness of this mystery when He said: 'Blessed are the pure of heart, for they shall see God.'[45]

He who reigns, therefore, will remove the scandals and then the just will shine as the sun in the kingdom of the Father. He will deliver the kingdom to God the Father, and then they whom He has delivered as a kingdom to God will see God. And He Himself testified what the kingdom is when He said to His Apostles: 'For the kingdom of God is within you.'[46] He who reigns, therefore, will deliver the kingdom. And should anyone ask who is this who delivers the kingdom, he will hear: 'Christ has risen from the dead, the first-fruits of those who have fallen asleep. For since by a man came death, by a man also comes resurrection of the dead.'[47] For this complete statement about the question now before us refers to the mystery of the body, because Christ is the first-fruits of the dead. But, let us learn under what mystery Christ rose from the dead from the Apostle, who says: 'Remember that Christ rose from the dead, of the seed of David.'[48] Hence, he teaches that the death and resurrection belong only to that dispensation in which He is flesh.

(40) He now reigns in this same glorious body until, after the destruction of the Powers and the victory over death, He makes His enemies subject to Him. The Apostle invariably adheres to this order, so that He attributes destruction to the Authorities and the Powers but subjection to the enemies.

---

44 Matt. 25.34.
45 Matt. 5.8.
46 Luke 17.21.
47 1 Cor. 15.20,21.
48 Cf. 2 Tim. 2.8.

When the latter have been made subject, then He, that is, the Lord, will be made subject to Him who subjects everything to Him in order 'that God may be all in all,' when the nature of the Father's divinity has been united with the nature of our flesh that He assumed.[49] In this way God will be all in all, because, in accordance with the divine economy of salvation, He who is from God and man is the mediator between men and God, and as a result of this dispensation He has Himself that which belongs to the flesh, and by reason of the subjection He will receive everything that belongs to God, in order that He may not be God only in part, but God wholly and entirely. Hence, there is no other reason for the subjection than that God may be all in all, since no part of the nature of an earthly body remains in Him, so that He who previously had two natures is now only God, not by casting the body aside but by transforming it through the subjection, not by its destruction through death but by its change through the glorification, while He gains our human nature for God rather than loses God as a result of our human nature. He becomes subject, therefore, not in order that He may not be, but that God may be all in all, since it belongs to Him in the mystery of the subjection to be and to remain that which He is not, while in His death He does not cease to be Himself in such a manner that He no longer exists.

(41)   Although the authority of the Apostle provides us with an adequate and holy certitude for this belief that Jesus Christ, the first-fruits of those who sleep, must be made subject in time and through the dispensation in order that God may be all in all, and from this there results not a weakness in the Godhead but a gain for the nature that He assumed, while He who is man and God is now wholly God, nevertheless, lest

---

49 By *'natura'* is meant the attributes of the Father's nature, such as immortality, incorruption which will be bestowed upon the glorified body.

someone may perhaps conclude that our teaching is not also derived from the Gospels, because we believe that He was glorified in the body while He reigns in it, and afterwards must be made subject that God may be all in all, we must rest the evidence for our faith not only on the words of the Apostle but also on those of the Lord, so that what Christ spoke through the preaching of Paul Christ Himself had already preached before Paul.

(42) Therefore, when He had revealed the bestowal of this glory to His Apostles in no unmistakable terms, He said: 'Now is the Son of Man glorified, and God is glorified in him. If God is glorified in him, God has also glorified him in himself, and has glorified him at once.'[50] We have, first of all, the glory of the Son of Man, and then the glory of God in the Son of Man, by the words that were said: 'Now is the Son of Man glorified, and God is glorified in him.' This refers, first of all, to the glory of the body which borrows its glory from its association with the divine nature. Next comes the advancement to a more complete glory, which is to be secured by an increase of the glory that has already been granted to the body. 'If God is glorified in him, God has glorified him in himself, and has glorified him at once.' God has, therefore, glorified Him in Himself because God has already been glorified in Him. The words, 'God has been glorified in him,' pertain to the glory of the body, in which the glory of God has been recognized in the body, since the glory of God is to be recognized through the glory of the Son of Man. If, therefore, because God has been glorified in Him, God has also glorified Him in Himself, so, by an increase of the glorified God in Him, God has glorified Him in Himself, in order that He may then pass over into the glory of God, since He already reigns in the glory which is derived from the glory of God. God has glorified Him 'in himself,' that is, in

50 Cf. John 13.31,32.

the nature whereby God is what He is, in order 'that God may be all in all,' while He will henceforth continue to be wholly God as a result of that dispensation in which He is man. Certainly He has not kept silent about the time, since he said: 'And God has glorified him in himself, and God has glorified him at once.' He pointed out that the glory which He would acquire after the passion from the coming resurrection was actually present at the moment when Judas went forth to the betrayal, in order that He might reserve for the future the glory with which God would glorify Him in Himself. Although the glory of God was revealed in Him through the power of the resurrection, He Himself will remain in the glory of God, that is to say, after the conferring of the subjection He will abide as God, the all in all.

(43) And how great, indeed, is the folly of the heretics' rage in this instance, when they deny to God that which encourages their own human desires, so that God is helpless in doing for Himself what He is able to do in man! Neither the language nor the judgment of reason declares that God is bound, as it were, by the necessity of His nature to provide for us, but cannot bestow any blessedness upon Himself, not that He whose nature and power are unshaken is in need of any increase, but, because He who is God and is man through the dispensation and the mystery of great piety is lacking in the power to bestow the fullness of that which God is upon Himself, since there is no doubt that He will also permit us to be that which we are not. The end of human life and death is the resurrection, and the most certain recompense of our warfare is an everlasting eternity, which continues not for the perpetuation of the punishment but in order that we may enjoy the reward and happiness of an unending glory. Since our bodies, earthly in origin, are therefore raised to the state of a more excellent nature and are similar to the glory of the Lord's body, will not the God who was found in the form of a

slave, although He had already been glorified in the body in
so far as He is a slave, be nevertheless made conformable to
God, so that He who will grant us the form of His own
glorified body will Himself be unable to bestow anything
more upon His own body over and above that which is
common to us and to Him? From the words, 'Then he will
be made subject to him who subjected all things to him,
that God may be all in all,' most of the heretics, therefore,
conclude that the Son subjects Himself to God the Father in
order that the Father may be God, the all in all, through the
subjection of the Son, just as if God were still wanting in
some perfection which He would receive through the subjection of the Son; consequently, we are to understand that
the complete and blessed divinity is wanting to Him if God
will become all in all through the progress of time.

(44) As a matter of fact, it seems no less sacrilegious for
me, whose only knowledge of God consists in my worship of
Him, to refute these objections as it is to defend them, and
to feel confident that I can express myself in words, which
are even more limited than my thoughts, about the nature
that surpasses the understanding of the human mind, and
first of all, to doubt whether something is wanting to God, or
whether He Himself is full, or whether He who is already
full can possibly be more full. If God is capable of progress,
of whom it is characteristic that He does not receive the
attribute of being always God from anywhere else, so that at
any time He is more, still, He can never reach that point
where nothing is wanting to Him, because a nature that is
capable of progress is never known to have made such progress
that the possibility of some increase is no longer present,
since a nature that tends toward progress, even though it is
constantly making progress, always finds the road to progress
open before it. There is nothing left whereby that which
abides in perfect fullness and is always such can become more

full, because perfect fullness is incapable of an increase to greater fullness. Assuredly, this is the attitude of pious mind: to think about God in such a way that nothing is wanting to Him and that He is full.

(45) Besides, the Apostle knew in what way our voice should render testimony to God when he said: 'Oh, the depth of the riches of the wisdom and of the knowledge of God! How incomprehensible are his judgments and how unsearchable his ways! For "Who has known the mind of the Lord, or who has been his counsellor? Or who has first given, that recompense should be made him?" For from him and through him and unto him are all things. To him be the glory forever.'[51] An earthly intellect cannot fix any limits for God, nor can the faculties of a probing mind sound this depth of His wisdom, nor do the skillful investigators grasp the judgment of His decrees, nor do the unsearchable ways of His knowledge yield to the endeavors of those who pursue them. His whole being is immersed in an incomprehensible depth, and nothing about His attributes will be discovered and nothing will be attained. No one has known His mind, and He has not stood in need of counsel from someone outside of Himself. This whole passage now refers to us and not to Him, through whom are all things, who is the angel of the great council, and who has declared: 'No one knows the Son except the Father; nor does anyone know the Father except the Son, and him to whom the Son chooses to reveal him.'[52] To counteract our feeble intellects, which plunge into the depths of the divine nature in order to define and to limit it, we must make use of the confession of faith which is contained in the testimony of the Apostle, lest a reckless belief seize upon some teachings about God that are different from those that are taught.

---

51 Cf. Rom. 11.33-36.
52 Matt. 11.27.

(46) This is the ordinary way in which we acquire the knowledge of natural causes, that nothing is perceived unless it comes within the range of our perception, as, for instance, something that lies before our eyes, or any work whatsoever that is done after we ourselves have received the power to reason and understand. The former of these, which is either tangible or visible, submits to the judgment of our comprehension and can be determined by our very touch and sight. But the second, which takes place in time, and is, as it were, begotten or brought into being by what we may call a more recent beginning than our own because it does not precede our faculty of reasoning, is also subject to the judgment of our understanding. Our sight, which perceives only things that are seen, does not pass sentence upon invisible things, nor will our mind reach out for the period in which it did not exist and investigate matters that are older than its own origin, since it can decide merely those wherein it is prior in time. And since it is necessarily hesitant about these subjects on account of its natural weakness, its knowledge of the causes is usually incomplete, not to speak of the things that are before it in the eternal plan when its mind would go beyond the time of its birth!

(47) Consequently, since nothing else would ever be known except what was subsequent to our faculty of reasoning, after mentioning the depth of the wisdom of God, the infinity of the inscrutable judgments, the mystery of the unsearchable ways, his ignorance about the unknown mind, and his lack of information about the uncommunicated counsel, the Apostle added: 'For who has first given that recompense should be made him! For from him and through him and unto him are all things. To him be the glory forever.' God who always is is not measurable, nor does any activity of our mind or understanding begin to function before Him. Therefore, He Himself in His totality is an incomprehensible

and unsearchable depth, but His totality is such that we do not limit Him thereby to any measurement, but conceive Him as being boundless, for He did not take what He is from anyone, nor did anyone prior in time give to Him so that He is obliged to repay him who has given it. 'For from him and through him and unto him are all things.'

He does not need those things that are from Him, through Him, and unto Him, neither He who is the origin, nor He who is the designer, nor He who embraces all things; He is outside of the things that are within; He is the Creator of those that have been made; and He Himself is never in want of His own possessions. Nothing is before Him, nothing is from anywhere else, nothing is outside of Him. What growth in fullness is therefore wanting to Him that God may yet be all in all in the course of time? Or whence shall He procure it outside of whom there is nothing, but nothing in the sense that He always is? And by what kind of an increase is He Himself to be made complete who always exists and outside of whom there is nothing? Or by what kind of a growth is He to be changed who says: 'I am and I change not,'[53] since there is no opportunity for a change, nor any cause that will enable Him to make progress, nor is there anything prior to eternity, nor anything else besides God in His relationship with God. Hence, God will not be all in all through the subjection of the Son, nor will any cause make Him perfect from whom, through whom, and in whom every cause exists. He remains, therefore, as He is, always God, and He does not stand in need of improvement who is always that which He is from Himself and unto Himself.[54]

(48) The only-begotten God is not even obliged to undergo any change in His nature. He is God, and this is the name of a complete and perfect divinity. For, as we have

---

53 Mal. 3.6.
54 That is, God is the principle or cause of His own being.

taught above, the meaning of the glory that is again desired, as well as the purpose of the subjection, is that God may be all in all, but it is a mystery not a necessity for God to be all in all. While He continued in the form of God, He assumed the form of a slave, not by any change, but, while He emptied Himself, He also remained hidden within Himself and within His own power even after He had been made empty, while He humbled Himself to the form of our human state so that the weakness of the abasement which He assumed might sustain His powerful and unlimited nature, but His boundless power restrained itself to such an extent as to submit even to endure the body to which it was joined. The fact that He was enclosed within His own power, even though He had emptied Himself did not lead to any loss of His power, since, even when He emptied Himself in the midst of this abasement, He still exercised the strength of the entire power that had been emptied within Him.

(49) It will therefore be a gain for our assumption[55] that God will be all in all. We must again confess that He who was found in the form of a slave when He was in the form of God is in the glory of God the Father in order that it may be clearly understood that He possesses His form in whose glory He shares. Hence, it is only a dispensation, not a change, for He possesses that which He had possessed. But, since that which had a beginning is in the middle,[56] that is to say, the born man, so everything is acquired for that nature which previously was not God, since God is revealed as being all in all after the mystery of the dispensation. Accordingly, these things are for our benefit and our advancement, that is, we are to be made conformable to the glory of the body of God.

---

55 This refers to the assumption of our nature by the Son of God.
56 'In the middle' refers to the earthly life of the Son of God, because it comes between His divine life before the Incarnation and His life of glory after the Resurrection.

Furthermore, although the only-begotten God was also born as man, He is nothing else than God, the all in all. That subjection of the body whereby what is carnal in Him vanishes into the nature of the spirit will bring it about that He who, besides being God, is also man will be God, the all in all, but that man[57] of ours advances toward it.

Moreover, we shall press forward to a glory similar to that of our man, and we who have been renewed unto the knowledge of God shall be again formed into the image of the Creator, according to the words of the Apostle: 'Having stripped off the old man with his deeds and put on the new, one that is being renewed unto the knowledge of God, according to the image of him who created him.'[58] Hence, man is made perfect as the image of God. When he has been made conformable to the glory of God's body he will be raised to the image of his Creator, according to the exemplar of the first man that has been placed before him. And after the sin and the old man, the new man who has been made unto the knowledge of God receives the perfection of his nature, while he recognizes his God and thereby becomes His image, and while he advances toward eternity through the true worship of God he will remain throughout eternity the image of his Creator.

---

57 That is, our human nature that the Son of God assumed.
58 Cf. Col. 3.9,10.

BOOK TWELVE

UNDER THE GUIDANCE of the Holy Spirit we are finally approaching the safe and peaceful harbor of the impregnable faith. And, just as it customarily happens very often in the case of those who have been tossed about by violent seas and storms, that when they are sometimes delayed near the coasts of the harbors by the formidable and mighty waves, the very surging of the mighty and frightening billows at length drives them forward to a familiar and secure anchoring place, so here in Book 12, as I hope, the same thing may happen to us who have been struggling against the tempest of heresy, that, when we shall expose this well-built ship to the waves of the most extreme godlessness, these waves themselves may carry us into the peaceful shelter that we desire. While we are driven about by the uncertain wind of doctrine, we find fear here, danger there, and often, too, there is shipwreck, because on the authority of the Prophet they claim that the only-begotten God is a creature, and that in Him there is no birth, but a creation, since the Person of Wisdom declared: 'The Lord created me as the beginning of his ways.'[1] This is the most powerful wave of their storm; this is the dreadful billow of their swirling tempest; and, when we have met it and come forth unharmed because of our careful navigation, it will bring us to the well-protected harbor itself on the shore for which we yearn.

---

1 Cf. Prov. 8.22.

(2)   We do not place our trust in vague and futile aspirations as do sailors who are abandoned or driven off their course by the variable and unreliable winds, since at times they pilot their vessel more in accordance with their desires than with assurance. Furthermore, the inseparable Spirit of faith is at our side, since He remains with us through the gift of the only-begotten God and leads us to the peaceful waters along an unchangeable course. We do not recognize the Lord Christ as a creature, because He Himself is not such; nor as a being that has been made, because He is the Lord of everything that has been made; but as God, the God who is the unique generation of God the Father. All of us, indeed, have been called and raised to be the sons of God through His gracious condescension, but He is the one true Son of God the Father, and the true and perfect birth, which remains exclusively in the knowledge of both of them. This alone is our true faith: to confess the Son not as adopted but as born, not as one chosen but as one begotten. We do not preach that He either was made or was unborn, because we do not place creatures on an equality with the Creator, nor do we falsely testify to a birth without a begetting. He does not exist by Himself who exists by the birth. Nor is He unborn who is the Son. Nor can He who is the Son be what a son is in any other way than by being born.

(3)   No one doubts that the principles of godlessness are always contrary and opposed to the principles of the true religion, nor can we conceive something in a pious manner when we are aware that is has been conceived in an impious manner, so that either these new reformers of the apostolic faith now divide the Spirit of the Gospels from the Spirit of the Prophets by placing them in contradiction to each other, and allow their quarrels to bring about a separation, or the former have prophesied in one way and the latter have preached in a different way, because Solomon calls us to

the worship of a creature, but Paul blames those who serve creatures. According to the viewpoint of godlessness, these statements certainly do not agree, so that the Apostle, who was taught by the Law and separated by the divine appointment and who speaks through Christ who speaks in him, either did not know this prophecy or disregarded what he knew and was ignorant of the fact that Christ, whom he called the Creator, was a creature, and he who warned us to serve the Creator alone forbade the worship of a creature when he said: 'Those who exchanged the truth of God for a lie, and worshipped the creature disregarding the Creator who is blessed forever.'[2]

(4) Is the Christ God who spoke in Paul too mild in censuring this impious falsehood? Is He too little concerned about condemning the lie that has changed places with the truth? All things have been created by the Lord Christ and, therefore, the proper name for Him is that He is a Creator. The nature and title of what He Himself produced is unsuitable for Him. Our witness is Melchisedech, who proclaims God as the Creator of heaven and earth in the following words: 'Blessed be Abraham by the Most High God, who created heaven and earth.'[3] Osee the Prophet is also a witness when he says: 'I am the Lord thy God who strengthened the heavens and created the earth, whose hands created all the hosts of heaven.'[4] Peter also is a witness, who writes as follows: 'Commending your souls as to a faithful Creator.'[5] Why do we attribute the name of the work to the maker? Why do we give God the same name as our own? He is our Creator, the Creator of the whole heavenly army.

(5) Since all of these texts refer to the Son, through

---

2 Cf. Rom. 1.25.
3 Cf. Gen. 14.19.
4 Cf. Osee 13.4.
5 Cf. 1 Peter 4.19.

whom everything has been made and are to be understood in accordance with the apostolic and evangelical faith, how shall He be made equal to these very creatures whom He has made and be given a name common to all of them? First of all, the reasoning of the human mind rejects this assertion that the Creator is a creature, because creation comes about through a Creator. If He is a creature, He is liable to corruption, is at the mercy of expectation, and is subject to slavery. The same blessed Apostle Paul says: 'For the long expectation of the creature awaits the revelation of the sons of God. For creation was made subject to vanity—not by its own will but by reason of him who made it subject—in hope, because creation itself will also be delivered from its slavery to corruption into the freedom of the glory of the sons of God.'[6]

Hence, if Christ is a creature, He must remain in uncertainty during the long period of hopeful expectation, and His long expectation rather than ours is waiting, and while He is waiting He must be subject to vanity, and He is not subject freely who is subject through necessity. But, since He is not subject of His own free will, He must also be a slave, but, since He is a slave, He must also be exposed to the corruption of nature. The Apostle teaches that all these things are proper to a creature, and when he has been freed from them through the long expectation he will be resplendent in human glory. Oh what a ridiculous and blasphemous description of God, to expose Him to these insults by falsely accusing Him of being a creature, so that He hopes, serves, is subject to necessity and corruption,[7] and is to be delivered into our state and not His own, since we are advancing toward something by means of His gifts!

---

6 Cf. Rom. 8.19-22.
7 Coustant's conjecture is that *corruptus,* both according to the manuscripts and sense, is better than *cognitus.*

(6) With the tremendous growth of unbelief our impiety marches ahead to this reckless and unauthorized assertion: that the Father, too, does not differ from a creature, because the Son is a creature. Christ, who was in the form of God, took the form of a slave, and if He who is in the form of God is a creature, then God will have something in common with a creature, because a creature is in the form of God. To be in the form of God does not mean anything else than to be in the nature of God, and God, therefore, is also a creature, because a creature possesses His nature. He who was in the form of God was not guilty of robbery in making Himself equal to God, because He passed from equality with God, that is, from His form into the form of a slave. He could not pass from God to man unless God emptied Himself of the form of God. He who emptied Himself did not destroy Himself so that He no longer existed, since He was something else than He had been. Nor did He who emptied Himself in Himself cease to be Himself, since the power of the strength also remained in the power to empty Himself,[8] and His passing into the form of a slave is not the loss of the nature of God, since the emptying of the form of God is nothing else than the power of the divine might.

(7) To be in the form of God to such an extent is nothing else than to be equal to God, so that equality of honor is due to the Lord Jesus Christ, who is in the form of God, since He Himself declares: 'That all men may honor the Son even as they honor the Father. He who does not honor the Son, does not honor the Father who sent him.'[9] There is never a diversity in things unless there is also a diversity in honor. The same worship is due to the same things, because either the highest honor will be conferred undeservedly upon those who are inferior or inferiors will be accorded equal

8 Cf. above, 11.48.
9 John 5.23.

honor with their superiors to the humiliation of the latter.
If the Son, as a creation rather than as a birth, will be made
equal to the Father in our worship, then there is no obligation
to honor the Father, since we are bound to show as much
homage as is due to a creature. Because He is equal to God
the Father, in so far as He has been born as God from Him,
He is also equal in honor. He is a Son, not a creature.

(8)   And these are the sublime words of God in reference
to Him: 'From the womb before the day star I begot thee.'[10]
But, as we have often mentioned on previous occasions, the
weakness of our understanding does not draw any derogatory
conclusion about God as if He were composed of internal
and external parts, joined together by members, as is the
case with the beginnings of earthly causes, because He said
that He begot Him 'from the womb,' for He who is free and
perfect and is not included in the cause of natural necessities
and remains the master of His whole nature points out the
attribute of the birth of His Only-begotten through the power
of His unchangeable nature. For Him who is born as the Spirit
from the Spirit, although He is born from the nature of the
Spirit whereby He is Spirit, there is no other cause of that
which is born except it come from the causes that are perfect
and unchangeable, and although He is born from a perfect
and unchangeable cause, He must be born from the cause
with the true nature of the cause itself. The true nature of
the things required for human birth is contained in the causes
that operate within the womb. But God, who is not made up
of parts, but who is unchangeable by reason of the Spirit,
for God is Spirit, is not subject to the natural necessity of
internal causes. Because He taught us the birth of the Spirit
from the Spirit, He enlightened our understanding by citing
our own causes as an illustration, not in order to show how
the birth took place, but to inform us of the generation, so

10 Ps. 109.3.

that that illustration does not lead to anything necessary, but is an aid to our understanding. If the only-begotten God is a creature, what is the meaning of an idea that reveals the idea of a divine birth through the ordinary process of a human birth?

(9) As a rule, God has taught us by employing terms that are commonly understood, since He informs us of the method of His own operation by means of these members of our bodies, when He said: 'Whose hands created all the hosts of heaven,'[11] or again: 'The eyes of the Lord are upon the just,'[12] or again: 'I have found David, the son of Jesse, a man after my heart.'[13] Since the will is signified by the 'heart' through which David was found pleasing because of the uprightness of his morals, and the knowledge of everything is made known by the word 'eyes,' whereby nothing is outside the comprehension of God, and the creative energy of His works is understood by the name 'hands,' since there is nothing that is not from God, consequently, since we are to regard the God who wills, foresees, and does everything as one who performs the actions of a body without the use of a body, why should we not look upon these words, also, 'He begot him from the womb,' in the sense that a spiritual birth is brought to our attention through a bodily cause of human origin, since, where the other names of members are mentioned, the results produced by the other works of God are also known to us?

(10) Hence, since the heart represents the will, the eyes what is seen, and the hands what is accomplished, nevertheless, since God wills, foresees, and accomplishes in a far higher sense than this defective comparison of parts brings out, and since this same comparison is expressed by the heart,

11 Cf. Isa. 45.12.
12 Ps. 33.16.
13 Acts 13.22.

the eyes, and the hands, why is the revelation of a true birth not contained in the phrase, 'He begot him from the womb,' not that He begot Him from the womb, just as He does not act through hands, see through eyes, or will through a heart, but because He uses these expressions to indicate that He accomplishes, sees, and wills all things? So, by employing the word 'womb,' He points out that He truly begot from Himself Him whom He begot, not by making use of the womb as an agent, but to make known the true birth, just as He does not will, or see, or accomplish things through the instrumentality of bodies, but employs these names of parts in order that the power to produce incorporeal results might be understood through the functioning of those that are corporeal.

(11) Consequently, the nature of human custom does not permit, nor do the words of the Lord's doctrine allow, the disciple to precede his master or the slave to command his lord, because the one is subject to the other because of his ignorance, as an illiterate person to one who knows, and is weak because of his state in life, as servitude to lordship. And if such be the case, in accordance with the common estimation of men, by whose example shall we rashly assert and believe that God is a creature and that the Son has been made, since the Master and Lord has nowhere spoken in this manner about Himself to us, His slaves and disciples, nor has He ever taught that His birth was a creation or something made? But, has the Father, too, ever testified that He is anything else but the Son, and has the Son ever asserted anything else about God except that He is His own Father? He declares in unmistakable terms that He was not made or created, as when He says: 'Everyone who loves the Father, loves also the Son who was born from him.'[14]

(12) On the other hand, the works of creation, but not

---

14 Cf. 1 John 5.1.

the birth through generation, have been made. The heavens are not a son, or the earth a son, or the world a birth. It has been said about them: 'All things were made through him.'[15] And the Prophet has declared: 'The heavens are the works of thy hands.'[16] And the same one has also stated: 'Do not neglect the work of thy hands.'[17] Is He not a Son as the painting is to the artist, as the sword to the smith, and as the house to the architect? These are the works of those who make them, but for the Father He alone is the Son who is born from Him.

(13) We are indeed the sons of God, but sons through selection. At one time we were the sons of wrath, but we have been made the sons of God through the Spirit of adoption, and we are given this name because of our merit rather than because of our birth. Because everything that is made was not before it is made, since we were not sons we are made that which we are. Previously we were not sons, but now we are, after we have shown ourselves worthy of this title. We were not born, however, but were made; we were not begotten, but were acquired. The Lord purchased a people for Himself and in this way has begotten them. We know that God has begotten sons, but He does not indicate at any time that this is their true nature. He does not say: 'I have begotten my sons and exalted them,' but: 'I have begotten sons and exalted them.'[18]

(14) Unless, perhaps, from what He said: 'My firstborn son, Israel,'[19] someone will understand this word 'firstborn' in such a way as to deprive the Son of being born in the strict sense of the term, so that, because He referred to Israel as 'my,' then the birth in the true sense may be applied to

---

15 John 1.3.
16 Ps. 101.26.
17 Cf. Ps. 137.8.
18 Cf. Isa. 1.2.
19 Cf. Exod. 4.22.

the adoption of the sons who have been made. Consequently, it is not peculiar to the birth of God, because it was said of Him: 'This is my beloved Son,'[20] since 'my' is also spoken of as proper to those persons who obviously have not been born. But, even that text wherein it is said: 'To a people that shall be born, which the Lord hath made,'[21] proves that they have not been born, although they are said to be born.

(15)   Hence, the people of Israel is born in such a manner that it is made, and because it is said to be born it does not follow that it has not also been made. It is a son by adoption, not by generation, nor is this its proper nature, but a title. For, although the words 'my firstborn' are written about it, 'my beloved Son' differs widely from 'my firstborn son.' Where there is a birth, there is 'my beloved Son'; but where there is a selection from among the nations and an adoption through the will, there is 'my firstborn son.' In the latter case, what is His refers to the first-born; in the former case, what is His refers to the Son. In the birth He is first the Son and therefore beloved, and in the selection He is first the first-born son and then afterwards His son, so that, since Israel was adopted as a son from among all the nations, it was proper for it to be the first-born, but it is evidently proper only to Him who is born as God to be the Son. Hence, there is not a true and perfect birth where it is imputed rather than begotten for it is clear that that people which was born to be a son was also made. Since that which had not been is made, and because it has been made it is said to be born, there is, as a consequence, no true birth, for previously it had been something else before it had been born. Therefore, it was not before it was born, that is to say, before it was made, because he who is a son from among the nations is a nation before being a son, and, consequently, he is not truly a

son because he was not always a son. But, there was never a time when the only-begotten God was not the Son, nor was He anything before the Son, nor was He Himself anything else except the Son. Thus, He who is always the Son has not allowed us to think of Himself as one who at one time had not been.

(16) It is indeed characteristic of human births that there was a time when they were not, in the first place, because all are born from all those who previously had not been. For, although everyone who is born has his origin from him who has been, the latter himself, from whom he is born, was not before he was born. Then, he himself who was born was born after he had not been, while time existed before he was born. He who is born today was not in that time which was yesterday, and he began to be that which is from that which had not been, and it is within the range of our understanding that what is born today did not exist yesterday. Thus his birth, by which he is, takes place after that period when he had not been, for today must first come after yesterday in order that it may belong to that time when it did not yet exist.

In the origin of human things it is indeed universally true that all receive their own beginning, since previously they did not exist, and assuredly first of all in time, as we have explained, and secondly in their cause. And in regard to time there is certainly no doubt that those things which have now had a beginning formerly did not exist, but the same is also true in regard to their cause, because it is certain that these things do not come into being through a cause.[22] Consider all the causes of beginnings and direct your thoughts to the things which have gone before you! You will discover that nothing had its beginning through a cause, while all

22 The meaning here is that everything human is not the cause of its own origin, but comes from nothing.

are created by the power of God to be that which they are, and likewise they are not born from something else. Consequently, by heredity itself it is also natural for every class of beings not to have been and to have had a beginning, while, on the one hand, it is in time after time, and, on the other hand, since all things are always after time, they also derive their cause from things that formerly did not exist, while they are born from these things which previously had not been. Adam, the first parent of the human race, was himself formed from the earth, which is nothing, and after time, that is, after the heavens, the earth, the day, the sun, the moon, and the stars, and he did not have his origin in a birth and had a beginning since he had not been.

(17)   But, it is not possible to maintain that the only-begotten God, for whom there is no antecedent time, had not been at one time. The phrase 'at one time' is itself already prior to Him, and, secondly, the words 'had not been' already indicate a period of time, and time will not begin after Him, but He Himself, who had not been in that time before He was born, will be after time, and that time itself, when He had not been, will take precedence over Him. Furthermore, He who has been born from Him who is is not to be regarded as being born from that which had not been, because in His case He who is is the cause of Him being what He is, and, that which is not is not at the same time the cause of His birth. Hence, He does not belong in time, so that at one time He had not been, nor does He belong in the Father, that is, in His author so that He has received His being from nothing, nor has He afforded us any pretext for saying about Himself that He has been born from nothing, or that He has not been before He was born.

(18)   I realize that a great many of those whose minds have become dull through their godlessness do not grasp the mystery of God, or of those whose rage inclines them to insult

God under the appearance of piety, because they are dominated by an evil spirit, are accustomed to assert before the
ears of the unlearned that, since we say that He has always
been the Son, and has never been anything else except what
He has been, we thereby declare that He has not been born,
because He has always been, for, in accordance with the
common judgment, that which always is is incompatible
with birth. 'The purpose of birth, however, is to bring that
which was not into being; but, according to the common
understanding, to bring that which was not into being means
nothing else than to be born.' Let them also add these
arguments, which are quite penetrating and pleasing to the
hearing. 'If,' they say, 'He was born, then He had a beginning,
and since He had a beginning He was not, and since He was
not we may not assume that He was.' And let them contend,
therefore, that this is the language of a reverent mind: 'He
was not before He was born. For, in order that He might be,
He who was not was born, not He who was.' Nor was He,
who was, in need of a birth, since He, who was not, was born
in order that He might be.

(19)   First of all, men who pretend to have a God-fearing
knowledge of divine things, in which the truth of the
evangelical and apostolic doctrine led the way, should have
rejected the intricate questions of an insidious philosophy and,
instead, should have clung to the faith which is in God. The
sophistry of the syllogistic questioning easily robs a weak
understanding of the defense of its faith, since a captious
allegation by the way it is asked will ultimately deprive a
simple answer and one adapted to question of what it
really intended, so that it no longer retains in its consciousness what it has already lost by its assertion. What will
so certainly lend support to such an inquiry than when
we are asked: 'Is there anything before it is born?' to
reply: 'In our profession of faith that which has not been is

born. It is neither natural nor necessary for that which is to
be born, since something must be born only in order that it
may be and not because it was'? When we have conceded
this, because it is right to make such an admission, then by
our yielding we have been robbed of the consciousness of the
faith and have become ensnared in their godless and injurious
schemes.

(20)   As we have frequently shown, since the blessed
Apostle Paul foresaw this, he warned us to be vigilant in
these words: 'See to it that no one robs you by philosophy
and vain deceit, according to human traditions, according to
the elements of the world, and not according to Christ in
whom dwells all the fullness of the Godhead bodily.'[23] We
must, therefore, be on our guard against philosophy; the
speculations of human traditions are not so much to be
avoided as they are to be refuted. We must not make such
concessions to them in these matters as if they are conquering
rather than deceiving us, for, since we proclaim Christ as the
power of God and the wisdom of God, it is fitting for us not
so much to flee from human doctrines as to reject them, and
to restrain and to instruct the more illiterate in order that
they may not be robbed by these men. Since God can do all
things and can do all these very things wisely in It,[24] and
reason is not wanting to His strength or strength to His
reason, those who preach Christ to the world must oppose the
irreligious and imperfect doctrines of the world by the knowledge of the wise omnipotence, in accordance with that saying
of the blessed Apostle: 'For our weapons are not carnal, but
powerful before God to the demolishing of strongholds, the
destroying of reasoning, and of every lofty thing that exalts
itself against the knowledge of God.'[25]

The Apostle did not leave our faith bare and without the

---

23 Cf. Col. 2.8,9.
24 That is, in Christ, the Wisdom of God.
25 Cf. 2 Cor. 10.4,5.

aid of reason. Although it is a most powerful help to salvation, still, unless it is supported by learning, it will offer, it is true, a safe place of refuge in the time of adversity, but it will not continue at the same time as a strong center of resistance. It will be what castles are for the weak after flight, but not as castles that also inspire those who possess them with an intrepid courage. Hence, we must put an end to the insolent controversies that are directed against God; we must destroy the defenses of their fallacious reasoning, and we must tear down the ingenious arguments which they have erected in defense of godlessness, not by carnal but by spiritual weapons, not by earthly learning but by heavenly wisdom, so that, just as great as is the distinction between divine and human things, so heavenly reason will surpass worldly speculations to an equal degree.

(21) Consequently, let the anxiety of unbelief come to an end, and let it not imagine, because it itself does not understand, that we are denying what we alone comprehend and believe correctly. We teach that He was born by the very sound of the words; we do not teach that He was unborn. To be unborn is not the same as to be born; the latter comes from another, while the former comes from no one. It is one thing to be always eternal without an author, and it is another thing to be co-eternal with the Father, that is, with the author. Where the Father is the author, there is also the eternity of birth; just as the birth is from the author, so an eternal birth is from an eternal author.

Everything that always is is always eternal, but everything eternal is not also unborn. What is born from the eternal possesses the attribute that what has been born is eternal, but what is unborn is unborn with eternity. That which has been born from the eternal, if it has not been born as something eternal, then the Father also will no longer be its eternal author. But, if anything of eternity has been wanting to Him who has been born from an eternal Father, then it is evident that the same thing has been wanting to His author, as what is infinite for the begetter is also infinite for the one begotten. Neither our reason nor our understanding allows anything to be between the birth of the Son of God and the generation of God the Father, because the birth is in the generation and the generation is in the birth. Thus, each takes place without any interval between them, because neither one takes place without the other. Hence, that which is composed only of both continues in everything only as both, because the second does not remain behind in anything, since the second thing itself cannot be in anything without the first.

(22)   Someone incapable of this divine mystery will say: 'Everything that was born has not been, because it was born for this purpose that it might be.'

(23)   And who will doubt, therefore, that what was born in human things has not been at one time? But, it is one thing to be born from him who has not been, and it is another thing to be born from Him who always is. Every infancy had its beginning in time, since previously it had not been. And while it again grew into boyhood it also developed after adolescence into a father. And he is not always a father who has previously advanced into adolescence through boyhood and into boyhood through the beginning of infancy. Hence, he who is not always a father has not always begotten. But, where there is always a father, so, too, there is always a son. Hence, if in your thinking and reasoning you discover that the God to whom it is proper in the mystery of His knowledge to be a father has not always been the Father of the Son whom He has begotten, then you also discover in your understanding and knowledge that He who was begotten has not always been the Son. If it is always proper for the Father to be always the Father, it must always be proper for

the Son to be always the Son. And how will it harmonize with our teaching and understanding if we assert that He has not been before His birth to whom it is proper to be always that which He was born?

(24) Since the only-begotten God contains in Himself the form and the image of the invisible God, He is made equal to Him in all these attributes that are proper to God the Father, through the fullness of the Godhead in Himself. As we have pointed out in the preceding Books, in regard to power and worship He is deserving of being honored and is powerful just as the Father is. Thus, because the Father is always, so, too, because He is His Son, He possesses the quality in common with Him of being always the Son. The evident meaning of the words that were spoken to Moses: 'He who is, hath sent me to you,'[26] is that it is proper for God to be that which is, because that which is cannot be conceived or referred to as that which is not. To be and not to be are contradictory to each other, nor do these two irreconcilable meanings become united in one and the same object, since as long as the one remains the other is not present. Hence, where something 'is,' that which is not cannot be joined with it either in our thought or in our language.

When we go back again over our thoughts and are always being brought back further and further in our understanding of Him who is, this one fact about Him who is is always prior to them: that He is. That which is infinite in God is forever drawing away from the contemplation of our infinite perceptions,[27] so that, no matter how much we may exert ourselves in going back over our thoughts, we shall grasp nothing else before that which is proper to God: that He always is. Even if we were to continue indefinitely, we would

26 Exod. 3.14.
27 Cf. above, 1.6.

always come in contact with nothing else in our knowledge of God than that God always is. Hence, we are not allowed to look upon God in any other way than that in which He has been pointed out to us by Moses and the universal understanding of men. The Gospels testify that the very same attribute is proper to the only-begotten God, since the Word was in the beginning, since this was with God, since it was the true light, since the only-begotten God is in the bosom of the Father, and since Jesus Christ is the God over all.

(25)   Hence, He was and is, because He is from Him who always is what He is.[28] To be from Him, that is to say, to be from the Father, is the birth. To be always from Him who always is is eternity—an eternity not from Himself, but from Him who is eternal. From Him who is eternal nothing else comes except what is eternal. If that is not eternal, then neither is the Father eternal who is the author of the generation. Since it is proper for Him to be always the Father and for Him to be always His Son, and since eternity is implied in that which is, so in the case of Him to whom it is also proper to be that which is it is also proper that He be eternal. No one doubts that generation signifies birth and the birth refers to one who is, and does not refer at the same time to one who is not. Furthermore, it cannot be called in question that no one is born who was, for there is no reason why He who is always eternal through Himself should be born.

The only-begotten God, however, who is the Wisdom of God, the Power of God, and the Word, since He was born, bears testimony to the Father as His author. Since He was born from Him who is, He was not born from nothing. Since He was born before the eternal ages, He must necessarily come before every perception, by reason of His birth.

---

28 Hilary explains (above, 1.5.) that the words 'I am who am' are the most complete definition of God.

He has not allowed us to assert that He was not before He was born. If we are able to comprehend Him in the sense that He was not before He was born, then our comprehension and time are already prior to His birth, since everything that has not been is already within our power of comprehension, and the very meaning of the words 'has not been' makes Him subject to time, for what has not been is a part of time. He who is from the eternal one and has always been is neither without birth, nor has He not been, since that which has always been transcends time, and to have been born is the birth.

(26) Hence, we confess that the only-begotten God was born, but born before the eternal ages. Our profession of faith must be kept within the limits that the words of the Apostles and the Prophets have determined, because the human mind does not grasp the idea of a timeless birth and because it is inconsistent with worldly natures to be born before time. But, if such is to be the manner of our teaching, how shall we again comprehend this same idea[29] and say that He has not been before His birth, since according to the Apostle the only-begotten God was born before the eternal ages? If, therefore, the birth before the eternal ages is not the conclusion of human reasoning, but the confession of a believing wisdom, because the birth comes from the author and what is eternal stretches beyond time, and what was born before the eternal ages is beyond the range of an earthly mind, then assuredly in our irreverent self-will we are now exalting the comprehension of the human mind too highly by asserting, in accordance with worldly knowledge, that He was not before He was born, since an eternal birth surpasses human comprehension and worldly knowledge. But, whatever transcends time is eternal.

(27) We comprehend all the periods of time either by our

---

29 That is, the timeless birth of the Son of God.

speculations or by our knowledge. We know that what is now has not also been on the previous day, for that which was on the day before is not now, but what is now is only now and has not also been on the previous day. But, in our speculations we measure the past in such a way that before the founding of a city there was unquestionably a time when the city that was founded had not been. Since the periods of time, therefore, come within the scope of our knowledge or speculations, we pass judgment upon them according to the understanding of human reasoning, so that we believe ourselves justified in saying about anything: 'It has not been before it is born,' because the times that have already passed always come before the origin of everything. Since in the things of God, that is, in the birth of God, everything is before the eternal time, then we cannot say of Him: 'Before He was born.' nor can we say that He to whom the eternal promise was made before the eternal time has the 'hope of life everlasting,'[30] according to the statement of the Apostle, which the God who does not lie has promised to Him before the eternal time, nor can we say that at one time He had not been. We cannot assume that He whom we must confess as being before the eternal time has had His beginning after something.

(28) Hence, it is contrary to our human nature and knowledge for something to be born before the eternal ages, yet in these matters we believe God's testimony about Himself. Since the apostolic faith has declared, in opposition to the knowledge of human understanding, that He has been born, how can the unbelief of our day again declare, in accordance with the knowledge of human understanding, that He has not been before His birth? What has been born before time has always been born, because that which is before the eternal ages always is. That which has always been born

---

30 Cf. Titus 1.2. The Son of God is not inspired by the hope of ever-lasting life, but possesses it in its fullness.

cannot at one time not have been, for not to have been at one time already shows that it has not always been. That which has always been is incompatible with the idea that it has not always been. If the fact that He has always been renders it impossible for Him not to have always been, then we cannot conceive Him as one who has not been before He was born. We perceive that He has always been born who was born before the eternal ages, even though the birth before time does not come within our power of comprehension.[31] If we are to confess, as it is indeed proper, that He was born before every creature, whether invisible or corporeal, before the centuries and the eternal ages, and before every thought, who, while He was born in such a manner, always is, then we may on no account conceive of Him as not having been before He was born, because He who has been born before the eternal ages is before every thought, and in our mind we must never conceive of Him as not having been, since we must confess that He always is.

(29) An objection to this conclusion is presented in a sly manner: 'If,' they say, 'it is beyond our power to conceive that He was not before He was born, then this only remains within our power to conceive that He who was was born.'

(30) To my critic I will reply whether he remembers me saying anything else except that He was born? Or whether to be before the eternal ages does not have the same meaning as that He who was was born? Because there is really no birth when that which was is born, but He changes Himself through the birth. But, to be always born means that the birth comes before the concept of time, and in an inconceivable manner He was never unborn. Hence, to be born before the eternal ages is not the same as to be before the

---

31 Although we cannot comprehend the birth of the Son from God, we can conceive of it, since it has been made known to us by faith.

birth. But to be always born before the eternal ages excludes the possibility that He had not been before the birth.

(31)   Furthermore, we cannot assume that He was before He was born, for He who is beyond comprehension is not subject to comprehension in anything. If to have always been born is beyond our comprehension, it will no longer be possible for us to conceive of Him as one who has not been before His birth after we have received our comprehension. Since we must, therefore, confess the eternal birth as nothing else than the birth, it is not within our power to conceive whether He had been or had not been before His birth, for the only thing that is always prior to our comprehension is that He was born before the eternal ages. He who does not permit us to consider Him or to speak of Him as anything else except that He was born has therefore been born and always is, for, since He is prior to the very time of our thoughts (because eternal time is before our comprehension), He does not allow our thoughts to pass judgment on Himself in regard to the question whether He has been or has not been before His birth, because it is not characteristic of birth to be before it is born, and not to have been is already a part of time. Consequently, the infinity of the eternal ages swallows up whatever pertains to time, namely, that He has not been, and the birth does not allow what does not belong to it, namely, that He was before He was born. If we shall be capable of comprehending whether He has been or has not been, then the birth itself is after time, because He, who is not always, must have had His beginning after something.

(32)   Hence, the conclusion of our faith, language, and thought is that the Lord Jesus has been born and has always been. If our mind turns back upon itself and examines anything about the Son, nothing else will appear before our probing mind except that He was born and always is. Just

as it is proper, therefore, for God the Father to be without birth, so too it must be proper for the Son to be always, on account of the birth. The birth will announce nothing else than the Father, and the Father will announce nothing else than the birth. These names or nature permit nothing else to be between them. Either He is not always the Father if He is not always the Son, or, if He is always the Father, He, too is always the Son. Just as much time as you will deny to the Son so that He may be the Son, so much time is wanting to the Father so that He is not always the Father, so that, while He is always God, He is not always the Father in that infinitude in which He is God.

(33) The confession of godlessness goes even further, so that it does not add the times of birth to the Son, but the generation of the Father, because the process of generation has been placed within the times of the birth.[32]

(34) Do you regard yourself, O heretic, as pious and religious when you confess, it is true, that He is always God but not always the Father. If it is pious for you to think thus, then you must condemn Paul for his unbelief, when he says that the Son is 'before the eternal ages.' You must also find fault with the testimony that Wisdom renders about Itself, namely, that It was established before the ages and was present when He prepared the heavens. In order that you may attribute a beginning to God in which He is the Father, then first of all settle upon the starting point in which the times had their beginning, and, if they had a beginning, then the Apostle, who declared that they are eternal, is a liar. You are wont to number the periods of time from the creation of the sun and the moon, because it was written

---

32 This is a refutation of the Arians, who claimed that the Father was not always the Father of the Son, but became the Father in the course of time.

concerning them: 'And let them be for signs, and seasons, and years.'[33]

But He who is before the heavens, which, according to you, are also before time, is at the same time before the ages. He is not only before the ages, but before the generations of generations which precede the ages. Why do you limit divine and infinite things by those that are perishable, earthly, and narrow? Paul knows nothing in Christ except the eternity of the ages. Wisdom states that It is not after something, but before all things. In your opinion, the periods of time have been determined from the sun and the moon. But, David points out that Christ remains before the sun when he says: 'Before the sun [is] his name.'[34] And, in order that you may not conclude that the things of God had their beginning with the origin of the world, the same one said: 'And before the moon [are] the generations of generations.'[35] Periods of time are here regarded as of no importance by such outstanding men who were worthy of the Spirit of prophecy, and the human mind has not been afforded any opportunity for reaching into the ages before the birth which transcends the eternal years. Let the faith remain within the limits of the God-fearing teaching, so that the Lord Jesus Christ is the only-begotten God and that He has been born in order that we may confess the perfect birth, and let it not forget that He is eternal when venerating His divinity.

(35) We are charged with lying, and the doctrine preached by the Apostles is blamed along with us, which acknowledges the birth, it is true, but teaches the eternity of the birth, so that the birth bears witness to the author and the eternity in the mystery of the divine birth surpasses the understanding of the human mind. The statement of Wisdom

---

33 Cf. Gen. 1.14.
34 Cf. Ps. 71.17.
35 Cf. Ps. 71.5. The preposition *in* is here added before *initium*.

about Itself is alleged against us which has taught that it was created in these words: 'The Lord created me for the beginning of his ways.'[36]

(36)   And you, O unfortunate heretic, who employ against the faith of the ecclesiastical teaching the weapons which were granted to the Church to refute the synagogue, and who seize the most strongly fortified understanding of the salutary teaching in order to oppose the salvation of all mankind, and who argue from these words that Christ is a creature instead of silencing the Jew, who denies the divinity of Christ before the eternal ages and the power of God in all His works and doctrine, by these words of the subsisting Wisdom! In this instance It declared that It had been created in time for the beginning of the ways of God and for His works, lest, perhaps, we might imagine that It did not exist before Mary, and, on the other hand, It did not wish Its birth[37] to be understood as a creation, because It was created for the beginning of the ways and for the works. That no one might make use of the beginning of the ways, which is beyond doubt the beginning of human knowledge about divine things, in order to subordinate the infinite birth to time, It stated that It was established before the ages, so that, since it is one thing to be created for the beginning of the ways and for the works and another thing to be established before the ages, we might realize that the establishment was prior to the creation, and the very fact that It was established for the works before time would reveal the mystery of creation, because the establishment is before time and the creation for the beginning of the ways and for the works is after time.

(37)   That the creation and the establishment might not hinder the belief in the divine birth, these words follow: 'Before he made the earth, before he established the moun-

---

36 Cf. Prov. 8.22.
37 That is, the birth from God.

tains, before all the hills he begot me.'[38] He who was established before time was already begotten, not only before the earth, but also before the mountains and the hills. And because Wisdom is certainly referring to Itself in this passage, It says more than is heard. All these things, which are pointed out in order to bring out the idea of infinity, are to be understood in the sense that they are not later in time than any other thing or class of beings. Moreover, we shall find that temporal things are wholly inadequate to clarify the idea of eternity, for they do not in themselves make known the beginning of infinity, since they come after other things and since they themselves have been assigned a beginning in time. What is remarkable about the fact that God has begotten the Lord Christ before the earth, since we find that the origin of the angels is older than the earth? Or why should He who was said to be begotten before the earth be also revealed to us as one born before the mountains, and not only before the mountains, but also before the hills, since the hills are mentioned after the mountains, but the name of the mountains appears after the earth? Hence, we cannot believe that He spoke these words in order to make us understand that He is before the hills, the mountains, and the earth, since He excels all those things which are before the earth, the mountains, and the hills by His infinite eternity.

(38) The divine word has not left our understanding without an explanation, for it has made known the meaning of the saying by these words which follow: 'God made the regions, both the uninhabitable parts and the heights that are inhabited under the heavens. When he prepared the heavens and when he set apart his dwelling-place I was with him. When in the upper air he made the clouds above the mighty winds, and when he placed certain fountains under the heavens, and when he made the strong foundations of

---

38 Cf. Prov. 8.25,26.

the earth I was with him forming all things.'[39] What part does time play here? Or how far is it permitted for the thoughts of the human mind to penetrate beyond the infinite birth of the only-begotten God? These things, whose creation we conceive in our mind, do not enable us to comprehend the generation of Him who is prior to all of them, so that, although He precedes them in time, He is not infinite if we merely grant that He was born before temporal things. Since those things are subject to time by their nature, although He is prior to all of them, He is not independent of time, for the nature of these things points to the time of His birth who was born previous to them, while this very fact, that He is placed before temporal things, brings Him into relationship with time.

(39) The word of God and the doctrine of true wisdom speak of perfect things and refer to those that are complete, since they teach that It is prior not to temporal but to infinite things. It was present with God when the heavens were prepared. Is the preparation of the heavens a matter of time for God, so that a sudden movement of thought crept into His understanding, as if it had been previously inactive and dull, and in a human way He searched for material and instruments for the building of the world? The Prophet, however, has a different explanation for the operations of God when he says: 'By the word of the Lord the heavens were established; and all the power of them by the spirit of his mouth.'[40] The heavens were in need of a command from God in order to be established, for their splendor and power in this stability of their unshakable nature did not arise from the proper blending and mixture of any material, but by the breath of the divine mouth. What, therefore, is the meaning of God preparing the

39 Cf. Prov. 8.26-30.
40 Ps. 32.6.

heavens, and of Wisdom, which was begotten by Him, being present, since the creation of the heavens did not come about as the result of any preparation, nor is it characteristic of the nature of God to pause for reflection in the preparation of any work? There is nothing whatsoever in things that was not always with God. And, although they had a beginning in so far as their creation is concerned, they did not have a beginning in so far as the knowledge or power of God is concerned. The Prophet is our witness when he says: 'O God, thou who hast made all things that shall be.'[41] The things that shall be, although they are yet to be in so far as they must be created, have already been made in so far as God is concerned, for whom there is nothing new and unexpected in things to be created, since it belongs to the dispensation of time for them to be created, and they have already been created in the activity of the divine power that foresees the future.

Consequently, since Wisdom now teaches that It has been born before the ages, It teaches that It is prior not only to the things that are created but that It is co-eternal with those that are eternal, that is, in the preparation of the heavens and in the setting apart of the dwelling place of God. The dwelling place was not set apart at the time when this was done, for it is one thing for a dwelling place to be set apart and another thing for it to be formed. Nor were the heavens prepared at the time when they were prepared, for It was present with Him when He prepared them and when He set them apart. Later on, It formed all things with Him who prepared them, and It revealed Its eternity when It was present with Him who prepared them and Its function when It formed them with Him who prepared them. Hence, It now declared that It was also begotten before the earth, the mountains, and the hills, because It taught that It had

---

41 Cf. Isa. 45.11.

been present at the preparation of the heavens to prove that, at the time when the heavens were prepared, these things had already been made with God, because there is nothing new with God.

(40) The preparation of things to be created is uninterrupted and eternal. The body of this universe has not been brought into being by thoughts that follow one another, so that the idea of the heavens came first; next, God provided for and busied Himself with the earth and considered it in detail, so that it was, first of all, spread out on an even surface, then, in accordance with a better plan, was elevated by means of mountains, later on, changed by hills, and, after that, made habitable even in the very highest places; and the heavens that had been prepared and the dwelling place of God were set apart, and the breath of the winds was enclosed within the mighty clouds in the air above; subsequently, certain fountains flowed under the heavens; and, finally, the earth was made firmer by its sturdy foundations. Wisdom declares that It is prior to all these things. Since everything which is under heaven was made by God, and Christ was present when the heavens were being formed and He comes before the eternity itself of the heavens that had been prepared, we are not allowed to suppose that there were individual thoughts in God about these minute matters, because the entire preparation for these things is co-eternal with God. Even if, according to Moses, the strengthening of the firmament, the laying bare of the dry land, the gathering of the waters, the arrangement of the stars, and the generation of the water and the earth in sending forth living beings from themselves are done according to their proper order, there is not even a moment of time discernible in the work of creating the heavens, the earth, and the other elements, because their preparation has been brought about as the result of a like infinity of eternity with God.

(41)   Consequently, although Christ was present in God in these infinite and eternal things, He has granted us only the knowledge of His birth,[42] so that the apprehension of the birth would be just as helpful to our faith in God as the understanding of the eternity of the birth would be in encouraging the pious hopes that were received with it. It is incompatible either with reason or with logic to teach that from a Father who is eternal anyone else but an eternal Son can proceed.

(42)   But the name and avowal of a creation disturbs us! Certainly the name of creation should disturb us if we did not teach about the birth before time and the creation for the beginning of the ways of God and for His works. We cannot conceive of the birth as a creation, since the birth precedes a cause, but the creation is the result of a cause. He who was created for the beginning of the ways of God and for His works was before the preparation of the world and was established before time. Or do the words, to be created for the beginning of the ways of God and for His works, mean the same as to be born before everything? The one includes time in its deeds, but the other conveys the idea of something that is timeless.

(43)   Or perhaps you wish that what is created for the works is to be understood in the sense of being created because of the works, that is, that Christ has been created for the sake of the works that are to be performed, so that He Himself has rather been the slave and the builder of the world and has not been born as the Lord of glory, that He has been created for the task of bringing the world into being, and has not always been at the same time the son of predilection and the king of the ages! Although the general understanding of men shatters this most godless belief of yours, for it is one thing to be created for the beginning of

---

42 That is, the eternal birth of the Son from the Father.

the ways of God and for the works and another thing to be
born before time, this same passage contradicts you so that
you may not misrepresent the Lord Christ as being created
for the purpose of making the world, since it shows us God
the Father as the Maker and the Creator of the world, and
truly offers us a certain guarantee, since He Himself was
present with Him who prepared all things and formed them
with Him.

Although all Scripture will speak of the Lord Jesus Christ
as the Creator of the world, still, in order to do away with
any pretext for the teaching of impiety, Wisdom now declared
that God the Father was the builder of the world, and
taught that It was not separated from the builder since It
was also present with Him who prepared it, and since the
Father prepared and Wisdom formed it with Him when He
was preparing it, and was also present with Him who prepared it, we might thereby perceive that It was not created
on account of the works because It was present at the eternal
preparation of the future works, and also that the Scripture
might not be accused of lying because It formed all things
with Him who prepared them.

(44) Last of all, O heretic, through the revelation of
Catholic doctrine learn from the opening words[43] the meaning of Christ being created for the beginning of the ways of
God and for the works, and be taught about the folly of
your own godlessness from the statement of Wisdom itself.
It began as follows: 'If I shall make known to you the
things that are done each day, I shall not forget to enumerate
those that are in time.'[44] Since It had previously declared:
'O ye men, to you I call, and I send forth my voice to the
sons of men. O ye simple ones, understand subtlety, but ye

---

43 Hilary is here referring to the words that precede the text which he is
   considering, Prov. 8.22, and which he now cites.
44 Cf. Prov. 8.21.

unlearned apply your heart,'[45] and again: 'By me kings reign, and the mighty decree justice. By me the rulers are magnified and by me tyrants possess the earth,'[46] and, furthermore: 'I walk in the ways of equity and I move in the midst of the paths of justice that I may distribute my possessions to them that love me, and fill their treasures with good things,'[47] Wisdom does not remain silent about Its daily work.

In the first place, while It calls upon all of them, It warns the simple to understand subtlety and the unlearned to apply their heart, in order that the zealous and attentive reader may evaluate the meanings of words that are distinct and different. It teaches, therefore, that all things are to be done, understood, praised, and grasped according to Its methods and plans. And It reveals that the kingdom of kings, the prudence of the mighty, the glorious deeds of rulers, and the right of tyrants to possess the land are included in It; also, that It is not involved in iniquities, nor found in the midst of injustice; and that all these things are done in order that It may supply an abundance of eternal goods and of incorruptible riches to those who love It through Its participation in all the deeds of equity and of justice. Consequently, while It declares that It will reveal those things that are done every day, It also promises that It will not forget to enumerate those things which are in time. Now, what stupidity of mind it is to believe that those things belong in time which It mentioned as having been done before time! Those things which are in time include every work which is after time; on the other hand, these things which are before time precede the beginning of time, which is later than they are. Wisdom therefore asserted that It would not forget to speak of those things which are in time when It said: 'The Lord created

---

45 Cf. Prov. 8.4,5.
46 Cf. Prov. 8.15,16.
47 Cf. Prov. 8.20,21.

me for the beginning of his ways and for his works.' Hence,
it is a reference to the deeds which have been done in time;
it is not a teaching about the generation which has been
proclaimed before time, but about the dispensation which
had its beginning in time.

(45) We must seek for the reason why He who was born
as God before time has again been created for the beginning
of the ways of God and for His works. Where there is the
birth before time there is the eternity of an infinite generation,
but, where this same birth appears as a creation in time for
the ways of God and His works, it is connected with the
works and the ways as their cause.[48] Since Christ is Wisdom,
we must first of all see whether He Himself is the beginning
of the way for the works of God. There is, I believe, no
doubt about this, for He says: 'I am the way. No one goes
to the Father but through me.'[49] A way is a guide for those
who are going, a course for those who are hastening, a
safeguard for those who are ignorant, and a teacher, as it
were, of things that are unknown and desired. Hence, He is
created as the beginning of the ways for the works of God,
because He is the way and also leads to the Father. We
must ascertain the reason for this creation, which is in time,
for it is the mystery of the final dispensation[50] in which He
was also created in the body and referred to Himself as the
way for the works of God. He was also created in time for
the ways of God when He humbled Himself to the visible
form of a creature and assumed the appearance of something
created.[51]

---

48 That is, the works and the ways of God are given as the cause why
the Son took human flesh.
49 Cf. John 14.6.
50 That is, the Incarnation of the Son of God.
51 This refers to the manifestations of the Son (according to Hilary) in
the Old Testament, as is clear from the following section; these apparitions were discussed in detail in Book 5.

(46)   Hence, let us see for what ways of God and for what works in time the Wisdom that was born before time was created. Adam heard the voice of One walking in paradise. Do you imagine that the step of the One walking was heard in any other way than in the form of an assumed creation, so that He who was heard walking up and down was present in some created form? I do not ask in what manner He spoke to Cain, Abel, and Noe, and how He was present when He also blessed Henoch. The angel speaks to Agar, and certainly the same One is God. Does He not have the same form when He is seen as an angel as He has in that nature by which He is God? The form of an angel is indeed revealed, while later on there is mention of the nature of God. But, why do I speak about the angel. A man comes to Abraham. Is not Christ as man present before him in the appearance of that creation in such a way that God is also present? A man speaks and is present in the body and is nourished by food, yet He is adored as God. Without doubt, He who was previously an angel is also a man in the present instance so that the diversity in this created nature itself that He had assumed would not permit us to suppose that this is the natural form of God. He was before Jacob, also, in human form, even to the extent of seizing him in wrestling. He fights hand to hand, struggles with His limbs, twists on His side, and adopts all of our movements and our manner of walking. Yet, afterwards, the same One is revealed to Moses as a fire in order that you might learn to believe that the created nature pertained to His appearance rather than to the substance of the nature. At that time He possessed the power of burning within Himself, but He was not subject to the natural necessity of burning, because the burning fire appeared without any harm to the bush.

(47)   Run through the periods of time and consider how He appeared either to the Prophet with His own name, Jesus

[Josue] the son of Nun, or to Isaias, who, according to the testimony of the Gospel, also said that he had seen Him, or to Ezechiel, who was admitted even to the knowledge of the eternal kingdom of the ages, and to all the others to whom He revealed Himself in the form of various created beings for the ways of God and for the works of God, that is, to the knowledge of God and to the gaining of our own eternity. Why does this divine plan for man's salvation lead here and now to such godless insults for the eternal birth? That creation is from time; furthermore, the infinite birth is before time. Maintain, of course, that we are doing violence to the words if the Prophets, if the Lord, if the Apostle, or if any pronouncement has associated the name of creation with the birth of the eternal Godhead! God, who is a burning fire, is present as one created in all these instances in such a way that He could lay aside the created form by that power through which He had assumed it; again, He is able to abolish what has only come into being in order that we might gaze upon it.

(48) The Prophet referred to that blessed and true birth of the flesh, that was conceived within the Virgin, as something created and made, because a being of our own created nature was then born. Assuredly, according to him, there is the name of a true human birth when he says: 'But where the fullness of time came, God sent his Son, made of a woman, made under the law that he might redeem those who were under the law, that we might receive the adoption of sons.'[52] Hence, it is His Son who is in man and who has been made from man, and not only has He been made, but He is also a creature, as it said: 'Just as truth is in Jesus that as regards your former manner of life you are to put off the old man, which is being corrupted according to its deceptive lusts. But be renewed in the spirit of your mind,

---

52 Cf. Gal. 4.4,5.

and put on the new man, which has been created according to God.' We must therefore put on the new man who has been created according to God. He who was the Son of God was also born as the Son of Man, because it was not a birth of the Godhead but a creation of flesh; the new man, created according to the God who had been born before the ages, received the title of His race. He made known the reason why the new man was created according to God when he added these words: 'In justice, holiness, and truth.'[53] There was no deceit in Him; He was made for us justice, and holiness, and He Himself is the truth. Hence, we put on this Christ who is created as the new man according to God. [But He is created according to God, because a man ignorant of sin was created in accordance with justice, sanctification, and truth.[54]]

(49) If, therefore, Wisdom, which declares that It is mindful of those things which have been done in time, has said that It was created for the works of God and for the ways of God and created in such a manner that It could teach that It was established before time, in order that it might not appear as if the mystery of the creation which It had often assumed in various forms had effected a change in Its nature, although the stability of Its establishment afforded no opportunity for a disturbance through the overthrow of its present status, nevertheless, in order that the establishment might not seem to reveal anything else than the birth, It declared that It was begotten before all things. But, now, why is creation regarded as a birth, since that which has been begotten before all things is the same as that which has been established before time? That which has been established before time, however, is the very same thing as that which has been created in time for the beginning of the

---

53 Eph. 4.21-24.
54 The sentence in brackets is found in only two manuscripts.

ways of God and for His works so that we realize that creation
in time does not differ from the birth, which is before time
and before all things. At least, it has not allowed impiety to
plead error as an excuse for its impiety!

(50) Even if the feebleness of the mind was a hindrance
to the understanding of the pious teaching so that it was
unable to grasp the true meaning of creation in the present
instance, still, even from the words of the Apostle, who
regarded the true birth as something that had been made,
you should have concluded that creation, although in an
unlearned but not in an irreverent way, must also prove
helpful to the belief in the generation. When the Apostle
wished to proclaim the birth of the one from the one, that is,
of the Lord from the Virgin without the conception resulting
from human passions, he was clearly justified in saying that
He had been 'made of a woman,' although he knew of His
birth and had often referred to it, in order that the birth
might prove the truth of the generation, and the word
'made' might bear testimony to the birth of the one from the
one. The word 'made' would exclude the conception arising
from human intercourse, since we would learn that He was
made from the Virgin of whom there was no longer any
doubt that He had been born.

But, O heretic, behold how godless you are! No teaching
of the Prophets, the Gospels, or the Apostles has asserted
that Jesus Christ was created by God rather than born from
God. You, however, deny the birth; you declare that He is a
creature not in the sense of the Apostle, who says that He
has been made in order that no one may doubt that He had
been born from one, but in accordance with your own godless
interpretation, so that He has not received His being as God
by a natural birth, since He has received it from nothing
just as a creature does. This is the first poison of your
unhappy spirit, not to designate the birth as something

created, but to accomodate the faith to creation instead of to the birth. Although it would be a sign of a feeble intelligence, it would not indicate a very godless one, to say that Christ was created, therefore, to make us aware that His birth from God was impassible as being that of the one from the one.

(51) The unchanging and apostolic faith, however, does not tolerate any of these opinions. It knows in what dispensation of time Christ was created and in what eternity of time He was born. He was born as God from God and in Him there is the unmistakable divinity of the true birth and of the perfect generation. In the things of God we confess nothing else except what is born and eternal. Nevertheless, He was not born after anything but before all things, so that His birth merely testifies to the author and does not imply that there is anything incongruous between Him and His author. According to the universal confession of faith, the birth from the author is indeed second, because it is from God, yet it is not separable from the author. To what extent our mind will attempt to go beyond the understanding of the birth, to that same extent it must also go beyond the understanding of the generation. Hence, this alone is a reverent manner of speaking about God: to know the Father, and together with Him to know Him, too, who is the Son from Him. Certainly we are not taught anything else about God except that He is the Father of the only-begotten God and the Creator. Let not human weakness, therefore, proceed any further, and let it proclaim this alone in which its salvation can only be found: In regard to the Lord Jesus Christ, it is always aware of this fact that He was born before the mystery of the flesh.

(52) O holy Father, omnipotent God, I shall indeed acknowledge You as the eternal God and also as the eternal Father so long as I shall enjoy the life that You have granted

to me. Nor shall I ever express such folly and impiety so that I, as the judge of Your omnipotence and mysteries, shall exalt this feeble understanding of my weakness above the reverential belief in Your infinity and the faith in eternity that You have made known to me, so that I should teach that You were at any time without Your Wisdom, Power, and Word, the only-begotten God, my Lord Jesus Christ. The weak and imperfect words of our nature do not hinder my understanding of You so that my poverty of speech chokes the faith into silence. Although the word, the wisdom, and the power within us proceed from our own inner activity and are our work, with You, on the contrary, there is the complete generation of the perfect God, who is Your Word, Wisdom, and Power, so that He is always inseparable from You whose birth from You is revealed through these names of Your eternal attributes. He has been born in such a manner that He points out no one else but You as His author; at the same time, He does not cast aside the faith in infinity, because we are informed that He was born before the eternal ages.

(53) You have bestowed many things of this kind in human affairs, and although I do not know the cause, the effect is apparent. A devout faith is found where there is also a natural ignorance. When, through my own power of vision, I raised these weak eyes to Your heavens I believed in nothing else but Your heavens.[55] While I saw there these starry circles, the yearly revolutions, the seven stars,[56] and the morning star, to which You have assigned the various functions of their office, I recognized You as God in these things even though I do not comprehend them. But when I beheld the marvelous swellings of Your sea, although I am

---

55 That is, my earthly vision only led me to the knowledge that God created the world, but not to the manner in which He did so.
56 Ursa Major, the Great Bear.

not aware of the source of the waters or even of the movement of this orderly ebb and flow, I hold fast to the faith in some reasonable explanation even if I do not perceive it, and I also recognize You in these things of which I am ignorant. However, when I now directed my thoughts to the earth, which, through the power of its secret energies, causes the decay of all the seeds that it has received, and that which has decayed is restored to life, that which has been restored to life multiplies, and that which has multiplied grows strong, I found nothing in these things which I can grasp with my own powers of reason, but my ignorance helps me to understand You, and, while I know nothing of the nature that is at my service, I recognize You only through the use of that which is to my own advantage. Since I do not even know myself, I am so impressed that I admire You all the more because I am ignorant of myself. Without comprehending it, I perceive either the movement, or the reason, or the life of my mind that passes judgment, and, while I perceive, I am indebted to You for what I perceive, since You grant me something beyond the beginning of the nature, namely, the understanding of the nature that fills me with delight. And since I know You, though ignorant of what pertains to myself, knowing You, I worship You. And I shall not lessen my belief in Your omnipotence because I do not apprehend things pertaining to Yourself, as if my own power of reasoning could grasp the origin of Your Only-begotten, make myself the master of this subject, and there would then be something in me which would enable me to proceed further than my Creator and my God.

(54) His birth is before the eternal ages. If there is anything which precedes eternity, it will certainly be something that transcends the idea of eternity. It is Your thing,[57] it is Your Only-begotten, not a portion, not an extension, not

---

57 The Son as the 'res' of the Father is worthy of note.

some empty name to fit the theory that You have made it, but it is Your Son, the Son who is the true God from You, God the Father, and born from You in the unity of nature. We are to confess Him as being after You as well as with You, because You are the eternal Author of the eternal origin. While He is from You He is second to you,[58] but while He is Yours He is not to be separated from You, because we must not assert that You have ever been without Your Son, in order that no one may accuse You of being imperfect without the generation, or of being useless after the generation. Thus, the birth merely serves the purpose of making You known to us as the eternal Father of the only-begotten Son who was born from You before the eternal ages.

(55) As for me, it is certainly not enough to deny by means of my faith and voice that my Lord and God, your only-begotten Jesus Christ, is a creature. I will not even permit this name to be associated with your Holy Spirit, who has proceeded from You and has been sent through Him, because I will not say that the Holy Spirit was begotten, since I know that You alone are unborn and the Only-begotten was born from you, nor will I ever say that He was created. I fear that the stigma attached to this name,[59] which I share in common with the others whom You have endowed with life, may also be insidiously imputed to You Yourself. According to the Apostle, Your Holy Spirit searches and knows Your profound things, and my intercessor with You talks to You of subjects that I cannot describe. How can I express without at the same time defaming the power of His nature, which is from you through your Only-begotten, by the name 'creation'? Nothing except what is Your own

---

58 *secundus a te est*: the Son is here called 'second' to the Father in the sense that He derives His eternal origin from the Father, but not in the sense that He is later in time than the Father.
59 The word 'creature.'

penetrates You, nor can the intervention of a power, extraneous and alien to Your own, measure the depths of Your infinite majesty. Whatever enters into You is Yours, and nothing is foreign to You that is present within You as a power that searches.

(56) I cannot describe Him whose words to me are beyond my power of description. Just as from the fact that Your Only-begotten was born from You all ambiguity in language and difficulty in understanding are at an end and only one thing remains, that He was born, so, too, in my consciousness I hold fast to the fact that your Holy Spirit is from You, although I do not grasp it with my understanding. I am dull in Your spiritual things, as your Only-begotten declares: 'Do not wonder that I said to thee, "The wind blows where it will, and thou hearest its sound but dost not know where it comes from or where it goes. So is everyone who is born of the Spirit." '[60] I possess the faith of my regeneration without any understanding on my part. There are no boundaries for the Spirit who speaks when He wills, and where He wills. Shall I place His nature among those of creatures, and shall I, who do not know the reason for His coming and going, although aware of His presence, set limits for the beginning of His origin?

Your St. John says that all things were indeed made through the Son, who was God the Word in beginning with You, O God. St. Paul enumerates all the things that were created in Him in heaven and on earth, both the visible and the invisible. After mentioning that all things had been created in Christ and through Christ, he believed that he had designated the Holy Spirit in a satisfactory manner when he referred to Him as Your Spirit. Such will be my thoughts about these questions, in harmony with these men whom You have especially chosen, so that just as I, following in

---

60 Cf. John 3.7,8.

their footsteps, shall say nothing else about Your Only-begotten that is above the comprehension of my understanding save only that He was born, so, too, I shall assert nothing else about the Holy Spirit that is above the judgment of the human mind except that He is Your Spirit. And I pledge myself not to a futile contest of words, but to the persevering profession of an unquestioning faith.

(57) Keep this piety of my faith undefiled, I beseech You, and let this be the utterance of my convictions even to the last breath of my spirit: that I may always hold fast to that which I professed in the creed of my regeneration when I was baptized in the Father, Son, and the Holy Spirit, namely, that I may adore You, our Father, and Your Son together with You, and that I may gain the favor of Your Holy Spirit who is from You through the Only-begotten. He is a suitable witness for my faith who says: 'Father, all things that are mine are thine, and thine are mine,'[61] my Lord Jesus Christ, who always abides as God in You, from You, and with You, who is blessed forever and ever. Amen.

---

61 John 17.10.

INDEX

INDEX

Beck, A., 6 n., 190 n.

Birth, contrast between human and divine, 205, 318, 515-517, 519-520, 522-523; preserves nature of parents, 237-239, 248, 257, 260, 383, 468, 506

Bishop, must be holy and learned, 283-374; obliged to instruct people, 15, 170

Body, growth of human, 325, 516; man ignorant about many things concerning, 44

Boethius, vii

Brisson, J., xii n., 54 n.

Buttel, M., xiv n.

Cayré, F., xiii n.

Christ, as God: called 'Spirit of God,' 292, 294-296, 306, 506; claims to be one with Father, 249, 252, 259, 261; conquers all enemies, even death, 330-333, 488-489; creator of all things, 49, 105-108, 138, 503, 525, 526, 529; equal to Father in glory, 72, 75-76, 78-79, 121, 344, 359, 361, 363; eternal birth from Father, 32, 36, 66, 94, 527; Father gives all judgment to Son, 469; insult to Father if Son is not God, 356, 515-516; miracles indicate divine power of, 195; Son alone knows Father, 41, 195, 197; Son excludes from Kingdom those who do not recog-nize His divinity, 335-337, 345-347, 354; Son gives eternal life, 243-244, 256-257, 309, 338, 352; Son is image of Father, 36, 55, 85, 265, 312, 316, 404, 462-463; Son knows future events and secrets of others, 381, 387-388, 393, 397-398; Son possesses all that Father has, 67; as man: assumes a real body, x, 12, 55-56, 73, 411, 418, 472; body of, differs from ours in some ways by reason of His conception, 417, 434, 441; necessary for Him to become man, 55; not unworthy of Him to become man, 56, 466, 468; renounces glory due to Him, 358-360; saves mankind, 12, 16, 55, 67, 148, 186, 234, 316, 324; Son becomes man freely, 326; is author of His human body, 54, 56, 57, 413, 417-418; Son makes God known on earth as Father, 71; Son remains God while man, 51, 67, 78, 144, 146, 148, 327, 335, 388, 409-410, 434, 464, 504; fear in, 406, 414-416, 426-427, 437-439; free will in, 371-372; passion of, 407, 415, 436; prayer of, 28, 426-427, 430, 456-457; sensation in, 409, 415; soul of, 413, 432, 435-436; tears of, 442, 444; as Wis-dom, 32, 110; as Word, 234-235

Church, cannot be destroyed, 207; conquers all heresies, 52, 227-228, 231-232; foretold in Old Testament, 158-159; mystical body of Christ, 301, 314; unity in, 280-281, 284-285; universality of, 228

Constans I, Emperor, v

Constantius II, Emperor, v, vi

Coustant, Dom, xv, 16 n., 188 n., 405 n., 416 n., 504 n.

David, prophesies about the coming Son of God, 122-123

Devil, author of heresies, 38, 54, 216, 355

Docetists (heretics), 429 n.

Ebion (heretic), also called Photinus, 226-230

Ebionites, errors of, viii, 22, 37, 48, 53; refutation of, 231-232

Elias, 192

Erasmus, xiv

Eucharist, contains true body of Christ, 285-286, 411; unifies the faithful, 284-285

Eunomius (heretic), 439 n.

Eutyches (heretic), 12 n.

Eyes, of body and of faith, comparison between, 440-441

Faith, is unchangeable, 52, 227, 312, 543; must be professed, 134, 179, 207, 455, 503; necessity of, 14, 18, 52, 207; received through Christ and

Holy Spirit, 62, 284, 295; results following loss of, 254, 399; truths of, must be studied with a pious mind, 45

Father (God), always the Father, 516, 523; author of God the Son, 32, 36, 66, 233, 235, 251-252; in what sense greater than Son, 74, 375, 377, 397, 469, 538; innascibility as proper attribute, 37, 41, 66, 68, 98, 121, 515-516, 523, 525, 541; not solitary, 108, 127, 187, 227, 248, 296, 304; Son makes Him known among men as, 71

Fear, in Christ, 406, 414-416, 426-427, 437-439; in human persons, 407-408; in three young men in furnace, 432-433

Fillion, L., 219 n.

Forster, T., xv n.

Free will, in Christ, 371-372; in human persons, 12, 169, 283, 382

Galatia, home of many heresies, 227

Girard, G., v n.

God, always was, 6-8, 39-40, 66, 95, 517; beauty of, 8, 9; does not need man, 69, 70; existence of, known by reason, 88; goodness of, 5, 96, 187, 189, 337-338; incomprehensible, 8, 13, 40, 66, 496, 517-519; must be believed, 10, 20, 103, 195,

549

520; omnipotence of, 6-7, 15, 89, 146, 189, 440, 454, 462, 540; omniscience of, 97, 382, 462; oneness of, 23, 39, 58, 278, 291, 305, 403; present everywhere, 8-9, 40, 60, 66, 97, 293, 462; spiritual nature of, 183-184; title of, given to holy persons, 233, 235, 251, 252, 460; see also Christ, Spirit

Gods, pagan, belief in, 5, 6

Gomorrah, punished by Son of God, 117

Gospels, hidden in Old Testament, 149; mutually complementary, 430

Grace, makes us sons of God, 214-215; need of, 18, 151, 184; offered to all, 63; received from Christ and Holy Spirit, 18, 292, 298, 403, 479, 489

Greek, quotations in De Trinitate, 216, 274

Heaven, eternity of, 4, 14-15, 217, 482, 488, 494; man's hope for, 10, 76, 277, 284, 366; must be merited, 15, 157, 283, 494

Hell, Christ's descent into, 423; punishment of, 482, 486

Heresy, due to Antichrist, 54, 212, 216, 343; to Devil, 38, 54, 216, 355; to human pride, 13, 16, 29, 87, 89, 133, 185, 218; forces Church to discuss ineffable things, 36

Heretics, distort meaning of Scriptures, 25, 36, 102, 156, 174, 185, 229, 279, 349, 412; folly of, 21, 37, 134, 155, 171, 275, 340, 462, 537; ingenuity of, 17, 39, 133, 212, 275, 465; refuted by own words, 280, 291; victims of ignorance, 170

Hieracas (heretic), errors of, viii, 21, 179; refutation of, 180

Hilary, St., birth, v; bishop, v; conversion, v, 3, 5, 6, 10; death, vii; exile, v, vii, 402; importance in theology, xv; language and style, xiii-xiv; role in Church, vi-vii; works: De synodis, ix, 93 n., De Trinitate, vii-ix, 169-170, 189, 223; Tractatus mysteriorum, xii, 54 n.

Homoousion, heretical meanings given to term, 93; why Catholics chose it, 94-95

Ideas, danger of preconceived, 479; formation of, 139, 497

Ignorance, of man, about things in nature, 44, 539-540

Image, future glory of Son as image of God, 499-500; how Son is image of Father, 313-314

Immortality, reason leads to belief in, 4, 10, 482; divine revelation guarantees, 14-15, 488, 494

Impiety, hinders acceptance of divine truth, 148

Incarnation, foreshadowed in creation of man, 106-108; in apparitions of Son of God under form of angels, 112-113, 120-121, 144-145, 534; nature of God the Father not affected by, 357-358; 373-374

Isaias, foretells coming of Son of God, 162, 539

Israel, first-born among nations, 510

Jacob, vision of God in heaven, 118; wrestles with God, 149

Jeremias, foretells coming of Son of God, 129, 168

Jerome, St., xiv

Jews, believed Messias would be Son of God, 219; ignorant of God as the Father, 157; less guilty than heretics, 220; prone to idolatry, 104; why they wanted to kill Christ, 239-241, 250-251

John, St., the Baptist, 34, 196

John, St., the Evangelist, examination of opening words of his Gospel, 46-51

Joseph, St., 56, 444

Judas, 360, 420, 494

Judgment, glory for just, punishment for sinners, 486, 490, 492; readiness for, 389-390

Julian, Emperor, vi

Kenosis, 311 n.

Kinnavey, R., 86 n., 186 n.

Latin, inferior to Greek in expressing divine truths, 474

Law, Christ mediator of, 152-153; does not contradict teaching of New Testament, 104-105, 111, 135, 149, 162; means Old Testament, 134, 142

Lazarus, 217, 344, 443-444

Le Bachelet, X., xi n.

Leo, St., xv

Light, nature of, 179; why the divine birth is a light from light, 180

Magi, coming of fulfills ancient prophecy, 126; offer gifts at Bethlehem, 57

Man, deified in Christ, 325-326, 357-358, 404, 500; natural happiness not sufficient for, 3

Mani (heretic), errors of, 21, 38, 101, 172; refutation of, 177-178

Marcellus, Bishop, 226 n.

Martyrs, courage of, in sufferings, 433-434; miracles at graves of, 461

Mary, Virgin, virginal conception, 37, 55, 56, 80 n., 130, 220, 409-410, 535

Medicines, certain kind cure all diseases, 52

Milan, Council of, vi

Miracles, known but incomprehensible, 218; performed by

Christ, 68, 69, 70, 217-218, 443-444; at His birth, 56-57; at His death, 73-74

Monstrosities, animal, 237-238

Moses, foretells coming of Son of God, 105-108, 111-112, 114-115; 118-119; teaches oneness of God, 104

Nature, worship of, 5

Navigation, among ancients, 501

Nestorius (heretic), 12 n.

Nice, Council of, vi

Original sin, in man, 14, 160, 328, 424, 435; not in Christ, 412, 417, 424

Osee, predicts coming of Son of God, 124

Otten, B., ix n.

Pain, in Christ, 434-437; in man, 408-409

Palmieri, A., 292 n.

Passion, Christ endured, of His free will, 436; reveals His divinity, 407, 415

Paul of Samosata, Bishop, vi

Paul, St., predicted Arian heresy, 400; saw heaven in vision, 161, 162, 188; spoke constantly of divine Sonship, 214-216, 302

Peter, St., acknowledges divinity of Christ, 188, 205-206; seeks to dissuade Christ from His passion, 208-209, 419

Philip, St., asks to see the Father, 212, 263; Christ's answer to him, 264-266, 271

Philosophy, leads to knowledge of God as Creator, 11; useless speculations of, should be avoided, 14, 318, 513-514

Photinus, *see* Ebion

Powers, spiritual enemies of Christ, 330, 487

Prayer, of Christ, 28, 426-427, 430, 456-457; of Hilary, for guidance, 33-34, 188-190; in gratitude, 538-540

Primacy, bestowal of, on St. Peter, 207

Reason, human, limitations of, 86-87, 133, 455-456, 496-497; relationship with faith, 45, 65, 456, 479, 513, 539

Redemption, brings spiritual life, 75; destroys death, 130, 478, 488; destroys sin, 160; mysteriousness of, 213; proof of God's love, 210; through Christ alone, 16, 234

Reinkens, J., v n.

Res, in meaning of nature, 234; Son as *Res Dei,* 540

Sabellius (heretic), Arians regard Catholics as his followers, 21, 134-135, 178; errors of, 16, 53, 101; refutation of, 228, 230, 246, 342, 374

Sara, Son of God appears to, under form of angel, 112-113

Scripture, Holy, divinely inspired, 61, 104, 167, 248, 348, 431, 502; how to be interpreted, 25, 28-29, 36, 103, 324, 327; language of, to be used, 18, 135, 305; led to Hilary's conversion, 6; must be accepted without hesitation, 35, 108-109; no contradition in, 141, 149, 324, 332, 429, 502

Quotations from or references to:

Acts, 24, 97, 279, 294, 298, 397, 475, 507

Baruch, 129, 168

Colossians, 14, 43, 50, 51, 66, 137, 162, 313, 314, 317, 321, 328, 330, 381, 384, 436, 476, 500, 514

1 Corinthians, 24, 30, 46, 58, 62, 63, 71, 87, 104, 127, 214, 279, 297, 299-301, 391, 411, 430, 449, 452, 465, 478, 488, 491

2 Corinthians, 61, 127, 316, 333, 430, 451, 514

Daniel, 97

Deuteronomy, 96, 103, 120, 121, 127, 134, 154, 160, 165, 235

Ephesians, 58, 301, 302, 450, 459, 473, 485, 536

Exodus, 6, 98, 120, 152, 233, 509, 517

Galatians, 58, 281, 535

Genesis, 47, 105, 109, 111-118,

137, 145, 146, 149, 150, 385, 386, 453, 503, 524

Hebrews, 100

Isaias, 7, 44, 71, 96, 97, 112, 123, 125, 126, 128, 154, 156, 160, 162, 165, 191, 435, 445, 507, 509

James, 97

Jeremias, 18, 98, 129

John, 11, 20, 24-29, 42-44, 47, 50, 51, 53, 54, 59-62, 65, 71, 72, 74, 75, 77, 78, 81, 84, 85 96, 98, 100, 105, 116, 118, 126, 129, 138, 150, 152, 163, 170, 193-197, 199-201, 203, 210, 211, 216-218, 220, 228, 229, 233, 235, 236, 238-240, 243, 245, 246, 248, 250, 252, 256, 259, 262, 265, 278, 279, 283, 285-287, 289, 290, 296, 303, 308, 309, 313, 316, 317, 323, 333, 338, 339, 341-344, 349-352, 359, 360, 364-372, 375, 378, 381, 394, 410, 411, 420, 421, 430, 431, 442-444, 446, 456, 457, 465, 468, 469, 484, 486, 493, 505, 509, 542, 543

1 John, 211-213, 216, 508

Luke, 25, 27-29, 33, 56, 94, 145, 206, 219, 293, 405, 423, 427, 446, 483, 491

2 Machabees, 105

Malachy, 97, 256, 498

Mark, 26, 27, 96, 97, 134, 196, 219, 323, 335-337, 345, 347, 394, 421, 430

Matthew, 27, 28, 35, 42, 44,

51, 53, 54, 73, 97, 124, 150, 170, 190, 191, 193-196, 205, 206, 208, 209, 216, 221, 293, 324, 336, 338, 340, 346, 373, 386-389, 405, 406, 421, 426, 428, 445, 446, 481-484, 486, 489-491, 496, 510

Osee, 124, 503

1 Peter, 503

2 Peter, 18

Philemon, 126

Philippians, 311, 329, 363, 417, 479, 482, 484, 488

Proverbs, 32, 100, 110, 501, 525-527, 531, 532

Psalms, 8, 97, 98, 105, 122, 124, 126, 142, 184, 186, 234, 294, 468, 471, 474, 475, 506, 507, 509, 510, 524, 527

Romans, 58, 62, 96, 111, 127, 158, 160, 165, 214, 215, 253, 292, 305, 306, 320, 334, 418, 450, 453, 488, 496, 503, 504

1 Thessalonians, 382

1 Timothy, 96-98, 401, 440, 466

2 Timothy, 274, 400, 479, 491

Titus, 273, 274, 520

Wisdom, 9

Seals, reproduce impressions, 310; why Father placed seal on Son, 311-312

Semi-Arians, 93 n.

Sensation, in Christ, 409, 415; in man, 408

'Silence,' one of the Aeons of Valentinians, 175

Soul, human, in Christ, 413, 432, 435-436; in man, 8, 32, 63, 408, 443

Spirit, often used for soul, 446-447; term applies to each divine Person, 59-60, 94, 234, 293-294

Spirit, Holy, called 'gift,' 35, 58, 59; distributor of graces, 59, 62-63, 289, 293, 298-299, 501-502; divinity of, x, 33, 38, 58-59, 289, 294, 396, 541, 543; proceeds from Father through Son, 59, 289-291, 395-396, 542-543

Subjection, of Christ, brings glory, 499-500; not unworthy of Him, 483-484, 487-488

Sulpicius Severus, vi

Teaching, ancient method of, vi

Tears, of Christ, 442, 444

Tertullian, xiii, 9 n.

Thomas, St., the Apostle, acknowledges divinity of Christ, 81-82, 236-237

Thomas Aquinas, St., xi, xv, 36 n., 58 n., 99 n., 417 n.

Timothy, St., 478

Tradition, about Jewish Scriptures, 6

Trinity, incomprehensible, 39, 66, 519, 522; known only through revelation of God Himself, 151; should be expressed in noble language, 34; unity of nature in, 23, 39, 67, 108, 278, 365, 403, 541

Valentinian (heretic), errors of, viii, 21, 38, 101, 175; refutation of, 175

Wisdom, Christ called, 32, 110; present with God at creation, 110, 526-528; purpose of Its creation, 11, 525

Word, Christ called, 234-235; not utterance of a voice, 47-48, 234; personal existence of, 234-236, 243, 412-413

Worms, generation of, 471

Zachary, St., 56